THE NEW AMERICAN
PHILOSOPHERS

THE NEW AMERICAN
PHILOSOPHERS

An Exploration of Thought Since World War II

ANDREW J. RECK

LOUISIANA STATE UNIVERSITY PRESS *Baton Rouge*

To the memory of Jacob Drell

PREFACE

This book is the sequel to *Recent American Philosophy* (New York, 1964). It concentrates on philosophy in America since World War II, whereas the earlier volume treats philosophy in the period between the two world wars. By virtue of its contents and the method of presentation employed, the present volume stands on its own, although the two volumes together and separately aim to demonstrate the richness, diversity, and originality of American philosophy during the twentieth century.

The new American philosophers are C. I. Lewis, Stephen Pepper, Brand Blanshard, Ernest Nagel, John Herman Randall, Jr., Justus Buchler, Sidney Hook, F. S. C. Northrop, James Kern Feibleman, John Wild, Charles Hartshorne, and Paul Weiss. Nine of the twelve are considered in separate chapters, but three of them—Nagel, Randall, and Buchler—because of the philosophical principles they share and because of their common institutional affiliation, are presented in a single chapter on Columbia University naturalism. Since the philosophers have been allowed, so far as possible, to speak for themselves, the text abounds with quotations from their works. The dozen philosophers have been selected on the basis of the representativeness, comprehensiveness, and originality of their philosophical contributions. Whatever misgivings may be felt over the omission of some philosophers, there can be no doubt that the twelve philosophers here treated deserve inclusion in any book that undertakes to assess American philosophy since World War II.

As an exploration of contemporary American philosophy, this book cannot be considered a thorough survey of the field. Not only is it too soon to complete such a survey, but also the vast majority of American philosophers currently make their contributions to specialized disciplines through scattered journal articles, as yet not ready for synthesis. Nevertheless, much has happened in American philosophy since World War II, and it is helpful to take our bearings. In doing so, I have focused on those thinkers who have presented their thought over a range of philosophical fields in a number of published book-length works. Consequently several prominent American thinkers, though mentioned, have not received extensive consideration—e.g., Richard McKeon because his major work is yet to be published, Willard Van Orman Quine because his philosophical contributions are narrowly restricted to the technical field of modern logic. Other philosophical scholars would, no doubt, have approached my task differently, and I would invite them to do so. Certainly no survey of contemporary American philosophy will ever be possible unless explorations such as this one are attempted.

Acknowledgments are due to many persons and institutions for making this work possible. I wish to thank Professors Pepper, Blanshard, Hook, Northrop, Feibleman, Wild, Hartshorne, and Weiss, and one other who has preferred to remain unnamed, for having read and helpfully commented on early drafts of the chapters devoted to their philosophies, although, of course, I remain responsible for all errors of fact and interpretation. I wish also to thank the George A. and Eliza Gardner Howard Foundation, administered by Brown University, for the award of a fellowship for the academic year 1962–63, which enabled me to begin the volume, and the Tulane University Research Council, which furnished me the leisure in 1967–68 to complete it. Grateful acknowledgment is made to Martinus Nijhoff, The Hague, Netherlands, for permission to reprint with revisions "The Philosophy of Charles Hartshorne" and "The Philosophy of Brand Blanshard," which were originally published in *Tulane Studies in Philosophy*, X (1961), 88–108, and XIII (1964), 111–47 respectively; and to the editors and the publisher for permission to reprint with revisions "The Philosophical

Context of F. S. C. Northrop's Legal Theory," which originally appeared in the *Tulane Law Review*, XXXIV (1960), 505–22. Constant discussion of points in American philosophy with my colleague Dean Robert C. Whittemore has helped keep me on track. I am also grateful to Mrs. Freda Faber for having typed my manuscript and to Miss Kathy Hershey of Louisiana State University Press for her editorial assistance. And I owe a special debt to my wife for having encouraged and advised me through the years I have devoted to the study of American philosophy and the preparation of this book.

A.J.R.

London and New Orleans
February, 1968

CONTENTS

CHARLES HARTSHORNE
Process Philosophy, Panpsychism, and Panentheism

PAUL WEISS
Systematic Metaphysics and Open Thinking

INTRODUCTION

The study of American philosophy, which has lagged behind the study of American literature by at least a half century, came of age at the time of World War II. Herbert W. Schneider's *History of American Philosophy* (1),* first published in 1946, marks the new maturity. Absorbing and superseding the earlier contributions of Woodbridge Riley (2) and Harvey Gates Townsend (3), Schneider's *History*, now in its second edition, and supplemented by the works of W. H. Werkmeister (4) and Joseph L. Blau (5), firmly establishes the study of American philosophy as a significant aspect of American culture. Indeed, Schneider's *History* itself appeared at just the right moment in America's cultural history. World War II had just ended; college enrollments were bursting with veterans curious about their heritage and anxious over their destiny; and the patriotic pride of an America emerging victoriously from war to take first place among the nations of the world found a partial outlet in those intellectual pursuits which inspired the introduction of college and university programs in American studies, on American history, American institutions, American literature, and American thought.

Paradoxically, just as scholars in increasing numbers have begun to devote their attention to American philosophy, there has occurred a sharp disappointment, if not disgust, with what philosophy in America has become. In recent years this feeling has found expression in several widely circulated magazines and in the popular

---

* References are at the end of each chapter.

press (6). More serious still is the neglect of American philosophy in a recent collection of essays by fourteen young American thinkers which ironically bears the title *Philosophy in America* (7). This book, edited by Max Black, illustrates the extent to which British analytic philosophy dominates the minds of the young American academic philosophers. Though not about American philosophy, the book is intended to be a sample of American philosophy today. Strikingly, the contributors seem not to be aware that much in contemporary philosophy has happened anywhere but in England. Whereas John L. Austin is cited six times, A. J. Ayer five, Peter Geach five, H. L. A. Hart twelve, G. E. Moore four, Bertrand Russell seven, Gilbert Ryle more than eight, and Ludwig Wittgenstein more than nineteen, among American thinkers Willard Van Orman Quine is mentioned six times, John Dewey and Charles Peirce each twice, George Santayana once, and Josiah Royce and William James not at all.

Yet, in view of the copious flow of books and articles from American philosophers today, the present condition of American philosophy exhibits exceptional vitality. The negative judgments prevalent in the popular magazines and the neglect on the part of a productive minority within the universities are due, in part, to an insufficient sampling of the evidence—the growing literature of American philosophy. Except in anthologies destined for classroom use, and usually organized to illuminate a special field or problem rather than to represent the authors' philosophies, the course of American philosophy since pragmatism has not received the attention it deserves. To some extent, the historians have abetted this condition of neglect. In the first edition of Schneider's *History*, which is divided into eight parts, the historian of American philosophy brought the reader up to the beginning of the twentieth century, and quit. In the first sentence of his "Preface and Acknowledgments" he confessed: "Part IX of this work is entitled 'New Realism and New Naturalism,' but I shall not live to write it." Fortunately, Schneider did live to write the beginning of Part IX: "Emergence of Naturalistic Realisms," and so the second edition of his *History* presents the incomplete results of his investigations into a period of American philosophy reaching a full generation later than the point at which his first edition terminated.

The result has been to direct our imagination toward a golden age or classic period in American philosophy which culminated about the turn of the century and dissipated sometime before the Great Depression. It is universally acknowledged that during this period America's only indigenous philosophical movement came into being—pragmatism. Further, it is widely believed that the age was graced by six great thinkers—Charles Peirce, William James, Josiah Royce, John Dewey, George Santayana, and Alfred North Whitehead. This view of American philosophy, correct in its high regard for the genuine merits of the six classic thinkers, is wrong in its estimation of temporal perspective. For one thing, only Peirce, James, and Royce belong to the period before World War I; all were gone before America's entry into that war; and even then one of them, Peirce, was known only to a few philosophers until the publication of his writings in the 1930's and thereafter. The other three did their major work after World War I and died after World War II. Santayana left America never to return before the First World War, while Whitehead did not migrate to America until after that war. And over four decades stretch between the deaths of two of America's most famous pragmatists—William James and John Dewey.

In *Recent American Philosophy* (8) an attempt was made to deepen appreciation of the creativity and originality of American thought by focusing on the philosophies of ten men: Ralph Barton Perry, William Ernest Hocking, George Herbert Mead, John Elof Boodin, Wilbur Marshall Urban, DeWitt H. Parker, Roy Wood Sellars, Arthur O. Lovejoy, Elijah Jordan, and Edgar Sheffield Brightman. Many of these men had studied with the classic six, and, at least in the earlier part of their careers, all ten were contemporaries with them. All but one of the ten philosophers in *Recent American Philosophy* are dead, and all made their major contributions in the period between the two wars, although some of them published before World War I and after World War II. They philosophized when it was still possible to classify thinkers, though never with precision, as naturalists, idealists, pragmatists, and realists. These ten thinkers furnished new perspectives on the works of the classic six, and judicious assessment of their contributions has extended the so-called classic period or golden age of American philosophy.

The story of American philosophy did not end with the advent of World War II. A generation has elapsed since then, and although America's achievements in other fields have perhaps been more conspicuous, it is erroneous to suppose that American vitality and creativity and originality are absent from her philosophical activities. In order to portray the range and diversity of American philosophers in the period since World War II, attention is given here to twelve thinkers. The new American philosophers are C. I. Lewis, Brand Blanshard, Stephen Pepper, Ernest Nagel, John Herman Randall, Jr., Justus Buchler, Sidney Hook, F. S. C. Northrop, James Kern Feibleman, John Wild, Charles Hartshorne, and Paul Weiss. Although these thinkers matured before the advent of World War II, their major works have appeared in the postwar years, and their influence is being exerted now and may continue in the future. A philosophy is usually the fruition of long years of study, harvested in old age. The twelve philosophers selected for consideration here, while they produced works prior to World War II, have published their most important books in the past twenty-five years. And all but one of the twelve are living and writing today.

These twelve philosophers are presented with particular attention to the development and the total structure of their thought. Criticism is kept to a minimum. Otherwise what the philosophers say would be obscured either by the piecemeal presentation of their thought or by the intrusions of the critic. To estimate the greatness of a work it is helpful to assume that the work is great, at least great enough to warrant sympathetic study. That assumption has guided the writing of the present volume.

In the Princeton study of American philosophy from 1930 to 1960, sponsored by the Ford Foundation, Richard Schlatter, the general editor, commented that the essays by John Passmore on philosophical scholarship, Manley Thompson on metaphysics, Roderick M. Chisholm on epistemology, William K. Frankena on ethics, and Herbert Feigl on philosophy of science left him "with the impression that we have had in recent years no giants who are philosophers pure and simple rather than scholars and historians" (9, p. x.). However excellent the individual essays may be, there can be no denying that the impression Schlatter received is the one they make. For the contributors to the Princeton study—hostile or indifferent to speculative or systematic philosophy and committed to chopping up the *corpus* of a man's thought into separate disciplines—employ a method which precludes the comprehension of greatness in philosophy, just as a microscope would conceal rather than reveal a huge building. Would Kant, hailing from an isolated, substandard university in a Prussian province, his thought tangled in an obscure and heavy prose, have seemed great in his day had a similar method been used on him? The method of sympathetic, synoptic interpretation and presentation utilized in the present volume offers a perspective on the philosophers which should afford an appreciation of their greatness.

It is illuminating to consider these twelve philosophers in relation to the four philosophical tendencies prevalent in the preceding period. Naturalism, the philosophy which owes much to science, claims the largest number of adherents. Four of the twelve—Nagel, Randall, Buchler, and Hook—are avowed naturalists. Pepper, too, might be called a naturalist, although he has his own terms for the types of philosophy and has been engaged in the elaboration of a new type. Pragmatism, however, is represented not only by the naturalists, especially Hook, but also by Lewis. Although realism has remained a strong current, affecting Northrop, Wild, Feibleman, and Weiss, only Blanshard might be recognized as an idealist. There are, of course, idealist elements in the thought of Hartshorne, but he would prefer to be called a process philosopher. Hartshorne's case is not the only one which points up the inadequacies of the old classification. Even Wild, particularly in his latest phase of development, might be called more correctly an existentialist than a realist. Logical empiricism may be regarded as a distinct movement, including in its compass thinkers as diverse as Lewis and Nagel. Weiss's eclectic speculative system, finally, defies all known classifications.

The classic six American philosophers still influence the works of the twelve philosophers in the present volume. While the influence of Royce has receded, it is evident in the thought of Lewis, Blanshard, and to a lesser extent Weiss. James's influence has dwindled, too, although it is at present manifest in the phenomenological and existentialist directions of Wild. Dewey's influence is strongest on Hook, and after Hook on the Columbia naturalists Buchler and Randall. Santayana almost competes with Dewey for having affected, via Frederick Woodbridge, the thought of men like Randall; Pepper too owes much to Dewey and Santayana, but on him the influence of Perry, rather than of any of the classic six, is stronger still. Santayana has particularly affected the speculative philosophical systems of Feibleman and Weiss. Peirce and Whitehead, however, emerge as the two most influential philosophers. Northrop owes much to Whitehead, and Buchler to Peirce, while Feibleman, Weiss, and Hartshorne all acknowledge their indebtedness to both Whitehead and Peirce.

Consideration of where the philosophers were born, where they studied, where they have taught or teach, serves to illuminate the continued spread of culture across the American continent. All except one were born in the United States, and they hail from every region of the country. New York City looms large in the picture of contemporary American philosophy: four of the twelve were born there, four were educated there, and four teach there. All but one have earned doctorates in philosophy—six from Harvard University, four from Columbia University, and one from the University of Chicago. Because philosophers move more these days than they did in the past, it is not so easy to fix their institutional ties. C. I. Lewis, after a period of teaching at the University of California in Berkeley, began a long tenure at Harvard; he may well serve as the link between the earlier and the later periods of American philosophy. Another, after studying at Harvard, devoted his career to philosophy at Berkeley. Still another, after studying at Chicago and teaching for three decades at Harvard, now teaches at Yale. Indeed, with four of the twelve teaching there, Yale has the largest count, followed by Columbia with three. Columbia by right is regarded as a center of naturalistic philosophy; Yale, encouraging a diversity of viewpoints, has nurtured speculative philosophy and so is often identified with idealism. Harvard's decline from absolute pre-eminence as an institution of philosophical studies is evident from the figures. Dominant at the beginning of the period, Harvard is now rivaled by Columbia and Yale. Meanwhile, philosophy has risen in the South and Southwest: two of the philosophers represented in the present volume teach in institutions in this region.

The twelve philosophers in this volume have made major contributions to the special fields of philosophy. Logic has been significantly advanced by the work of C. I. Lewis; philosophy of science by Northrop and Nagel; theory of knowledge by Lewis, Blanshard, and Northrop; metaphysics by Randall, Buchler, Feibleman, Hartshorne, and Weiss; theory of value by Lewis and Pepper; ethics by Lewis, Blanshard, and Weiss; aesthetics by Pepper, Feibleman, and Weiss; phenomenology by Wild; philosophy of society and law by Hook, Northrop, Feibleman, and Weiss; philosophy of religion by Randall, Hartshorne, Wild, and Weiss; and history of philosophy by Randall. The list could be indefinitely expanded. In brief, all the branches of philosophy and all the higher institutions of culture—art, religion, politics, science—are treated by the twelve philosophers, some by all of them, and all by some of them.

One feature of contemporary American philosophy, little noticed even by the community of academic philosophers themselves, deserves special mention—the revival of speculative metaphysics. No doubt pragmatism and logical positivism at the beginning of the period and linguistic analysis in recent years, despite a growing interest in metaphysics as a field for analysis, have discouraged speculative metaphysics. Nevertheless, in 1947 the *Review of Metaphysics* was founded, in 1950 the Metaphysical Society of America was established, and in 1965 a professed metaphysician became president of the Eastern Division of the American Philosophical Association.

Further, the twelve new American philosophers illustrate in their work the intimate connection between thought and life. This connection holds even when the philosopher is not intentionally a pragmatist. It is most conspicuous in those cases in which the philosopher seems to be compelled to articulate his thought in the presence of a confrontation of powerful forces. The confrontation may be at the level of theory alone—as, for example, the confrontation of speculative metaphysics and of logical positivism in the thought of Feibleman, or the confrontation of classical metaphysics and process philosophy in the thought of Weiss. The confrontation may be mainly theoretical, but it may also involve passionate practical concerns—as, for example, the confrontation of traditional philosophy and existentialism in the thought of Wild. On the other hand, despite the theoretical character of the problems and their formulations, the confrontation may be intensely practical—as, for example, the confrontation of pragmatism and Marxism in the philosophy of Hook, and the confrontation of East and West in the thought of Northrop. All the main currents of contemporary thought and practice flow in the philosophies under discussion in the present volume. Should any man seek from philosophy specific guidance on the burning practical and ideological issues of the present, let him look to the philosophies of Hook or of Northrop. These two thinkers, above all, have formed their theories in relation to the moral, legal, and ideological crises of our times.

The main purpose of the present volume is to demonstrate that great philosophy, or philosophies, are still being created in America. If this fact is not now recognized, it is due not to the new philosophers themselves, but to their interpreters and their public, and also to the inevitable lag between the conception of novel ideas and their popularization or public assimilation. With regard to purely speculative theory or to urgent practical guidance, the twelve American philosophers individually and collectively hold their own in comparison with twelve philosophers drawn from any other period or nation. The golden age of American philosophy did not end with World War I, nor with the Great Depression, nor with World War II; it continues to the present. Classic philosophers are still among us.

NOTES TO INTRODUCTION

1 Herbert W. Schneider, *A History of American Philosophy* (2d ed.; New York: Columbia University Press, 1963).
2 Woodbridge Riley, *American Thought from Puritanism to Pragmatism* (New York: Henry Holt, 1915).
3 Harvey Gates Townsend, *Philosophical Ideas in the United States* (New York: American Book Company, 1934).
4 W. H. Werkmeister, *A History of Philosophical Ideas in America* (New York: Ronald Press, 1949).
5 Joseph L. Blau, *Men and Movements in American Philosophy* (Englewood Cliffs, N.J.: Prentice-Hall, 1952).
6 J. Glenn Gray, "Salvation on the Campus: Why Existentialism Is Capturing the Students," *Harper's*, CCXXX (May, 1965), 53–59; "No Jam in the Traffic of Ideas," *Times Literary Supplement*, November 25, 1965, p. 1082; "What (If Anything) to Expect from Today's Philosophers," *Time*, January 7, 1966, pp. 24–25; and Lewis S. Feuer, "American Philosophy is Dead," New York *Times*, April 24, 1966, Sec. 6, pp. 30–31, 122, 124.
7 Max Black (ed.), *Philosophy in America* (Ithaca, N.Y.: Cornell University Press, 1965).
8 Andrew J. Reck, *Recent American Philosophy* (New York: Pantheon Books, 1964).
9 Roderick M. Chisholm and others, *Philosophy* (Englewood Cliffs, N.J.: Prentice-Hall, 1964).

THE NEW AMERICAN
PHILOSOPHERS

I

C. I. LEWIS

Conceptualistic Pragmatism and Logical Empiricism

LIFE AND WORKS

Clarence Irving Lewis has been the American thinker who has most influenced academic philosophy since World War II. Although he had won some recognition shortly after World War I, it was not until the 1940's and 1950's that thinkers other than symbolic logicians and his immediate students began to reckon seriously with his thought. Time has placed Lewis in the second generation of the "golden age of American philosophy." Born on April 12, 1883, in Stoneham, Massachusetts, he died at his home in Menlo Park, California, on February 3, 1964. More than any other thinker who has become prominent in recent years, Lewis serves as the link between the glory of American philosophy at the beginning of the century and its current vitality. He received his B.A. from Harvard University in 1906 and his Ph.D. in 1910, when Royce, James, George Herbert Palmer, and Santayana graced her faculty. Lewis began his teaching career in 1905 at a high school in Quincy, Massachusetts, and next taught at the University of Colorado. After receiving his Harvard doctorate, he moved on to the University of California at Berkeley. Returning to Harvard as an assistant professor of philosophy in 1920, he became a full professor in 1930 and later Edgar Peirce Professor of Philosophy. After his retirement from Harvard he joined the faculty of Stanford University for several years. On the whole, then, Lewis has been intimately connected with Harvard throughout the first half of the twentieth century, drawing upon and adding to her philosophical fame.

Like other American students who reached maturity in the late nineteenth and early twentieth centuries, Lewis came under the spell of Herbert Spencer's evolutionism. In 1930 he admitted: "Nothing comparable in importance happened after that until I became acquainted with Kant" (1, p. 31). Once acquainted with Kant, however, he abandoned Spencer; indeed, his course on Kant became a classic for students at Harvard. Among the American philosophers under whom he studied, Lewis singled out Royce as his "paradigm as a philosopher" (1, p. 32). Spencer, Kant, Royce— these three may seem to be unlikely sources for Lewis' philosophy, which is identified as a species of pragmatism. Elaborating a theory of knowledge along Kantian lines (2), Lewis has chosen to call his philosophy "conceptualistic pragmatism." At a time when John Dewey, the leading American pragmatist, was calling upon his colleagues to look away from the problems of philosophers and to concentrate on the problems of men, Lewis was engaged in the technical development of epistemology and of mathematical logic. For his contributions to formal logic, in 1950 Lewis was awarded the Butler Medal in Philosophy by Columbia University, Dewey's own institution.

For both the logic and the epistemology Lewis' debt to Royce, which he readily acknowledged, is considerable. It is well known that Royce was the leading exponent of German philosophy at Harvard in his generation, but what is less well known is that Royce, at the instance of Peirce, was the first professor of philosophy at Harvard to investigate symbolic logic and to encourage its development as a field of study (3). Royce stimulated Lewis' early interests in symbolic logic. In 1910–11, when he was Royce's assistant in logic, Royce put into his hands the first copy of Volume I of *Principia Mathematica* to arrive in Cambridge. This work by Whitehead and Russell is the classic treatise from which all subsequent advances in mathematical logic in the twentieth century set out.

Lewis devoted many years to the study of logic. In particular he was disturbed by the conception of implication offered in the extensional logic of *Principia Mathematica*. This relation, known

as material implication, had little in common with the usual relation of implication, since material implication holds between two
propositions if any of the three following conditions is met: 1)
the first proposition is true and the second is true, 2) the first proposition is false and the second is false, and 3) the first proposition
is false and the second is true. From such a definition of implication
all sorts of paradoxes and absurdities result. For example, a false
proposition materially implies any proposition, and a true proposition is materially implied by any. In his endeavor to resolve these
paradoxes Lewis invented an intensional logic of strict implication.
As a young philosopher on the faculty of the University of California at Berkeley, Lewis published in 1918 his first book, *A Survey
of Symbolic Logic* (4), which contains not only the first history
of the subject in English but also, in Chapter V, his intensional
logic of strict implication. This system, corrected and enlarged in
the 1932 text *Symbolic Logic* (5), is an intensional logic which
defines implication in terms of the logical modalities of possibility
and necessity. Thus a relation of strict implication holds between
two propositions if it is impossible for the first proposition to be
true and the second to be false.

Though settling some of the perplexities generated by the extensional logic of material implication, the intensional logic of
strict implication impressed upon Lewis the fact that logic rests
ultimately upon epistemological principles which need clarification
and explanation. Lewis' adherence to a pragmatic conception of
mind as an evolved natural instrument and his appreciation of
Kantian epistemology joined to give birth to his distinctive theory
of "conceptualistic pragmatism." In the Howison Lecture at Berkeley in 1926 Lewis unveiled his theory (6), but it did not receive
its comprehensive presentation until 1929 in a work which is already an acknowledged American classic—*Mind and the World-
Order* (7). Following Kant, Lewis analyzed knowledge and divided
its fundamental features into the formal and the material, the conceptual and the empirical. Unlike Kant, however, he stressed a
pragmatic element at the heart of theoretical knowledge.

On the one hand, there are conceptual meanings which mind

constructs in alternative sets and employs pragmatically. These concepts are ways mind intelligently interprets experience, although in and for themselves they possess a certainty and immutability that goes beyond any specific application. Further, they constitute formal systems, and their relatedness is fixed once the postulates for these systems have been stipulated. They are connected by a kind of necessity which is logical, and to which mind must conform if it is to think at all. That does not mean that there is one single all-embracing set of concepts; it only means that whatever set is employed to meet specific needs must be conformed to. Logic is a tool which lays demands on its user.

On the other hand, there is the given. If the concept is the logical and communicable element in knowledge, the given is the qualitative and ineffable element. The concept is the form, the given the material, of knowledge. The given is that part of knowledge which the mind can neither alter nor create. It is present in the sense imagery that accompanies all concepts; it is the sensuous feel of experience to which all judgments must be true. So insistent is Lewis on the mutual independence of these two elements in knowledge that it is very difficult to grasp how they come together. The given may be totally idiosyncratic from person to person, although it consists of so-called qualia, i.e., qualitative universals, which may be arranged in structural patterns. The concept, on the other hand, is wholly logical and is not reducible to qualia. While initially the mind must have taken its cue from the given in order to arrive at concepts, concepts once obtained comprise another cognitive dimension altogether.

Whereas universal and necessary knowledge has to do with concepts and their interrelations alone, empirical knowledge is quite a different matter. Between the two main factors in knowledge—the concept and the given—comes the interpretation to effectuate their wedding. The intelligent human being applies concepts to interpret what is given. The application of concept to given is interpretation, and it makes up what is called empirical knowledge. The application of specific concepts to the given is determined not only by the nature of the given but also by the purposes of the thinker. Every interpretation reaches beyond what is given at the moment and anticipates the future content of the given. Thus empirical knowledge can never be certain but is merely probable.

The only species of recent pragmatism which does justice to a priori knowledge represented in the formal systems of logic and mathematics, Lewis' conceptualistic pragmatism is a sophisticated species of logical empiricism (8). Perhaps the most pervasive tendency in Anglo-American philosophy from the mid-1930's to the mid-1950's, logical empiricism was, by the end of World War II, the dominant philosophy in the United States. Unlike traditional empiricism, which regards the principles of logic and mathematics as empirical generalizations, logical empiricism has upheld the existence of purely formal truth in logic and mathematics as distinct from and independent of empirical knowledge.

In December, 1945, at the first national assembly of philosophers after America's entry into the Second World War, Lewis delivered the prestigious Carus Lectures before the general meeting of the American Philosophical Association at the University of California at Berkeley. His lectures, published the next year under the title *Analysis of Knowledge and Valuation* (9), became the text from which American philosophizing set out in the immediate postwar years. No other American work in philosophy has stimulated as much discussion and comment in the journals. A technical yet lucid work, *Analysis of Knowledge and Valuation* sums up the thought of a major creative philosopher in logic, epistemology, and value theory. In epistemology Lewis adopts an analytic and critical procedure. Knowledge exists; the task of epistemology is to define the different types of knowledge and to formulate their criteria. Since knowledge is exhibited in statements and judgments, Lewis focuses on these, distinguishing three types: analytic statements, empirical judgments, and value judgments. In each area he offers a closely reasoned theory which reveals his independence of mind and originality of thought. Rejecting the linguistic theories of the a priori, he nevertheless proposes a purely analytic theory, in which meanings rather than words are central. Accepting the verification theory of empirical judgment, he adds to it a validation theory and shifts the discussion of induction from the issues concerning the uniformity of nature to the consideration of the character and function of memory. Having adopted a naturalistic theory of values, he yet defended the objectivity of values, and at a time when most logical empiricists were inclined to consider value statements as emotive expressions, he emphasized the cognitive nature of valuation.

Analysis of Knowledge and Valuation is Lewis' greatest work. Its intrinsic merit and widespread influence have combined to make Lewis the only American philosopher since Dewey and Santayana to be accepted as a subject for the Library of Living Philosophers. This is not to say that Lewis published nothing after his *Analysis.* In 1954 he gave the Woodbridge Lectures at Columbia University, which he published in 1955 under the title *The Ground and Nature of the Right* (10). This thin volume presents fundamental normative considerations relevant to Lewis' ethical theory. In 1956 he gave the Mahlon Powell Lectures at Indiana University and, admittedly taking up "a direction of thinking" derived from his teacher Josiah Royce, Lewis presented his social philosophy, which he published in 1955 as *Our Social Inheritance* (11). At the time of his death Lewis was at work on a manuscript on ethics. He left this manuscript to his son Andrew Lewis, along with the request that Charles A. Baylis and William Frankena, with the assistance of John Lange, prepare it for publication (12). The foundations of all of Lewis' thought, however, are laid in the *Analysis of Knowledge and Valuation,* and upon this work the present chapter will concentrate.

THEORY OF ANALYTIC TRUTH

The developments of symbolic logic and pure mathematics in the twentieth century, accompanied by the increasing employment of such systems in the rapidly advancing empirical sciences, have brought these formal sciences, viewed as sources of a priori knowledge, to the center of philosophical consideration. An adequate account of knowledge must reckon with such a priori knowledge. On this topic Lewis took the standard logical empiricist position—

namely, that all a priori (universal and necessary) knowledge is analytic. Despite the suggestions that either the distinction between the analytic and synthetic cannot be sharply drawn, as Willard Van Orman Quine and Morton White contend (13), or even that there are synthetic a priori truths, as Arthur Pap argued (14), the thesis of the analyticity of all a priori knowledge has been commonly held by the majority of logical empiricists. For Lewis, however, this thesis did not mean the relativity of analytic truth to the language system, as logical positivists such as Rudolf Carnap (15) and Hans Reichenbach (16) had once contended. On the contrary, analytic statements are for Lewis more than linguistic tautologies. His theory of analytic truth, therefore, states the definitive characteristics of analytic truth, the method by which they are ascertained, and, further, the pragmatic element in analytic a priori knowledge.

Definition of Analytic Statements

According to Lewis, analytic statements are statements which we know to be true by reason of what the statements themselves mean. As statements of our own intended meanings, analytic statements can be understood only if the nature of meaning is clarified. It is necessary, then, to grasp the meaning of meaning before the meaning of analytic truths can be understood.

Meaning   The theory of meaning must take account of the kinds of things that have meaning and also of the modes of meaning.

Consider first the kinds of things that have meaning. C. S. Peirce, the father of pragmatism and also of the theory of signs in the United States, defined meaning as a pragmatic relation: some sign *s* comes into relation with some mind *m* so that *m* interprets *s* to mean some object *o*. Organisms take things given in experience as signs preparing them for further things to be given in experience. For Peirce, then, chairs, words, winks, clouds, meter readings, gestures have meanings. Since, however, Lewis' objective is the analysis of knowledge, he restricts his investigation to knowledge so far as it finds verbal expression. Thus, for Lewis, the kinds of things that mean are terms, statements, and syncategorematics.

Terms are linguistic expressions which name or apply to a thing linguistic meaning or with respect to sense meaning. Linguistically considered, "the intension of a term is to be identified with the conjunction of all other terms each of which must be applicable to anything to which the given term would be applicable" (9, p. 39). The term "cat" intends the term "animal" and the term "feline" and the logical product of these two terms. With respect to sense meaning the intension of a term is the criterion in mind governing use of the term in applying it to and interpreting the thing. A statement, too, has intension. Formally considered, the intension of a statement is the class of all statements it logically implies. Analytically, it is the criteria held in mind when the statement is employed.

The Meaning of Analytic Statements   For Lewis analytic statements are not meaningless tautologies; analytic statements have meaning, holophrastically and analytically. They also exhibit meaning in each of its four modes. All the things to which the terms that make up an analytic statement apply are consistently thinkable together only so far as they possess the properties signified by the terms. This is tantamount to saying that it is impossible to deny an analytically true statement, for the denial of an analytically true statement would be self-contradictory, and so not thinkable. For example, no cat that is not feline is conceivable. Thus all analytic statements are true and have universal extension. Yet all that analytic statements tell us about existence is that, for example, if the term "cat" applies to an existent thing, the term "feline" also applies to that thing; it does not tell us whether or not cats exist. Similarly, in the mode of comprehension all analytic statements are universal, because they apply to every possible or consistently thinkable world. There is no possible or consistently thinkable world in which cats would not be feline. Further, because analytic statements have universal comprehension, they have zero intension. The comprehension of any statement is inversely proportional to its intension, so that any statement which applies to all consistently thinkable worlds demands no limiting criteria in mind governing its application. In that sense the intension of an analytic statement is zero.

All analytic statements, since they have universal comprehension and zero intension, have in effect the same meaning. This gives rise to the so-called paradoxes of analytic truth. "The cat is feline" means the same as "2 plus 2 equals 4." Further, the need for the elaboration of formal systems in logic and mathematics seems jeopardized, since the possession of one analytic statement is tantamount in a sense to the possession of all. Lewis met this difficulty frontally, appealing to the distinction between holophrastic and analytic meaning. Holophrastically all analytic statements mean the same; analytically analytic statements may be different. As he said:

The holophrastic or resultant meaning of any analytic statement is simply its zero intension with respect to which it has the same meaning as every other analytic statement, and follows logically from anything and everything. This holophrastic significance indicates simply that the truth of it imposes no limitation on reality, or on any conceivable world; that it requires nothing to be the case for which there is any consistently thinkable alternative. But the *analytic* meaning of an analytic statement, from which this holophrastic zero intension of it is resultant, is the assertion of some specific relationship of intensional meanings, or of a relationship of classes or other entities which is cognitively derivable from such a relationship of intensional meanings. And with respect to this analytic meaning, every analytic statement asserts something different from any other which is not an analytically comparable expression (9, p. 94).

The Foundation of Analytic Truth

Whereas logical positivists have considered the statements of logic, the statements of mathematics, and definitions to be syntactical formulae and calculi validated by the formation and transformation rules of an arbitrarily established language system and devoid of meaning until semantically interpreted, and have held that whether a statement is analytic is relative to the language system which embodies it and so is a matter of convention, Lewis defended a quite different position. The logical positivist theory, he intimated, stems from a failure to distinguish linguistic meaning from sense meaning. This distinction may be understood by a consideration of the three differentiated levels of relationships between verbal expressions and the logical meanings expressed.

First, there is the syntactical symbol. It is devoid of all meaning except that which may be derived from its relations with other syntactical symbols. Within limits prescribed by the postulates and rules of inference governing a linguistic system, the relations of syntactical symbols are arbitrary. The postulates and rules of inference may themselves be matters of convention, giving the linguistic system the status of a very abstruse and esoteric game. Usually, however, as in the case of logical and mathematical systems, the thinker's selection of postulates and rules of inference is prompted by his intention to supply deductively the theorems which solve or clarify leading difficulties. As long as terms are considered abstractly in relation to each other and to nothing else, they afford what Lewis called "linguistic meaning."

Second, there is the correlation of a syntactical symbol with a property in things which makes the term applicable thereto or with a criterion in mind which governs its application. Such correlation is, of course, a matter of convention, but it points to objective properties and mental criteria which are neither arbitrary nor merely linguistic.

Third, there is the relation of properties in things and criteria in mind expressed by terms, and this relation is neither conventional nor linguistic. These relations of objective properties and of mental criteria constitute the fixed basis of all meanings expressed in language. Always accompanied by sense imagery, the mental criteria are what Lewis called "sense meaning."

Thus Lewis maintained that analytic statements—e.g., mathematical propositions, logical formulae, definitions—are true not by reference to linguistic meaning, but by reference to the sense meanings expressed by these statements. Indeed, an examination of linguistic rules and postulates is helpful when dealing with analytic truth, mainly because of the sense meaning which is represented by these rules and postulates, which lies beyond them and which, in the final analysis, supports them. That linguistic meaning is separate from sense meaning is, in fact, a result of abstraction, for colloquial language so closely intertwines the two that the naïve are forever confusing the word with its meaning. The sophisticated abstraction, however, has its own shortcomings. One disastrous error has been to make linguistic meaning central to epistemology. Writing before the British philosophers of ordinary language had made much headway in the United States, Lewis concentrated on the formalists who equated language with artificially constructed symbolic systems. The upshot of their procedure was to generate a new, special, and perhaps insoluble problem for philosophy—to explain how it is possible for abstract formal systems constructed artificially to be applied to experience. In the terminology of Rudolf Carnap, the study of syntactics, which investigates the symbols themselves and their interrelations in formal systems, must be supplemented by the study of semantics, which investigates the relations between symbols and their objects (18). From Lewis' standpoint Carnap's discipline of formal semantics is otiose; the problem with which formal semantics deals is dissolved once attention is paid to sense meaning.

To return to the main topic under consideration, analytic statements are, according to Lewis, validated by the sense meanings which they express. These sense meanings are not to be construed as simple atomic-image presentations. Here Lewis borrowed a concept from Kant—the concept of schema. Sense meanings are schemata; they are certain routine mental activities terminating in an imagined result. Hence sense meanings are emphatically not sense presentations. Logical positivists and operationalists have confused this point. As criteria in mind, sense meanings are logically prior to sense presentations and determine the applicability of terms to these presentations. Sense meanings also furnish the criteria by which to determine whether or not a direct experience of the sense confirms or falsifies a given belief; but this aspect of sense meaning is an aspect of empirical judgments, not of analytic statements.

Every analytic statement is checked by direct reference to its sense meaning. Such reference is almost a matter of direct inspection—of simply knowing what the terms mean and what the meanings include. In this way, both analytic and self-inconsistent statements are known as such without reference to any specific sense presentation or matter of fact. In this fundamental sense all analytic truth is a priori.

An example will illuminate the point. By definition every square is rectangular. But that is because the schema or routine activity which results in the sense-recognizable character to which the term "square" applies includes the schema or routine activity to which the term "rectangle" applies. A simple experiment of the imagination reveals this feature of sense meanings—that in instances of analytic truth they overlap. No appeal to the actual empirical situation is necessary. At the same time the relatedness of these sense-recognizable characters, these sense meanings, can not be explained away as fictions. They are fixed and unalterable; no application of the will, no reliance on practical need, nothing human can change them.

Following Socrates, Lewis conceived philosophy as an activity by which meanings are reflectively explicated, concepts analyzed. Like Socrates, he never supposed that this enterprise meets with easy success. On the contrary, the discovery of analytic truth is an arduous undertaking. And like other processes of knowing, analysis is subject to error, when, for instance, the thinker is confused and fails to see what the meanings are. However, an error in analysis may be corrected simply by taking thought, hard as this may be.

The Pragmatic Factor in Analytic Knowledge

So far it may seem that Lewis' theory of analytic a priori knowledge is not pragmatist in character but rather neo-Kantian. What validates analytic statements is their peculiar kind of sense meaning; an analytic truth applies to all that is consistently thinkable and consequently refers to no specific existent situation. By contrast, pragmatism insists emphatically upon specific existent situations and the development of practical means to cope with them. Although the concern with consistent thinkability seems to be a sign of a theoretic impulse to comprehend a transcendent reality of infinite possibility, Lewis was unequivocally opposed to a non-pragmatic interpretation of the a priori.

According to Lewis, analytic truth is rooted in practical interests, its development attributed to two features of practical human life. First, we do not always know, in practical situations, what does not exist. At best all we can do is attempt to determine what may exist. The attempt will succeed to the extent that we know what exists and can think of what is compatible with what exists. We are then, and only then, able to judge the practical significance of a given situation. Secondly, we are forever contemplating alternatives of practical action, for we intend to decide the best course of action. Whenever this occurs we are considering at least one possible world, the world compatible with our choice, and perhaps even a second possible world, one compatible with the rejected alternative, which never will be actual. Further, we must be able to think through the logical implications of each course of action. Logic is thus an important practical instrument partly because it has application beyond the existent world.

The pragmatic factor in knowledge is further manifest in the selection of particular sense meanings. True, there is a paradox in Lewis' theory. On the one hand, analytic statements are statements of our own intended meanings. On the other hand, sense meanings are fixed and unalterable, so that no human desire can alter analytic statements which represent them. While the first proposition seems to make pragmatic decision central to analytic truth, the second seems to place analytic truth beyond the pale of pragmatist considerations. Lewis, however, found both propositions compatible, because they reflect two different but complementary kinds of questions.

First, what classifications of the consistently thinkable shall be made? What meanings, in other words, shall be entertained? What criteria shall determine the classifications? The answers here always rest with pragmatic decision. Those classifications are made which appear to be most practical in terms of our specific needs and purposes. Those meanings are entertained which are most useful. Classifications are determined in accord with sense-recognizable criteria on purely pragmatic grounds, and no classification determined in accord with one criterion precludes other possible classifications in accord with different criteria. In this sense, analytic statements are statements of our own intended meanings.

Second, what is the status of the relations which sense meanings have to each other? What also is the status of the properties sense meanings signify? Here the answers differ from the pragmatic ones supplied above. Whether or not a given entity falls within the comprehension of a certain classification is independent of human choice; it depends on whether or not the entity has the property or properties signified by the term for the classification. And further, the relations that hold between sense meanings are as they are and cannot be made otherwise; no pragmatic decision can affect them.

<h3 style="text-align:center">THEORY OF EMPIRICAL KNOWLEDGE</h3>

A priori analytic statements are, according to Lewis, validated by reference to the sense meanings which they express. Although these sense meanings are psychologically derived from the directly given data of senses, their origin by no means vitiates their a priori status. Logically sense meanings govern the interpretation of the directly given data of the senses. But the data of sense present problems different from those of direct analysis, and here Lewis proceeded to an examination of empirical knowledge. Whereas analytic statements, which hold of all consistently thinkable worlds, have universal comprehension and zero intension, empirical judgments do not have universal comprehension, and their intension is between universal and zero. Based on the data of the senses, empirical judgments may quite well be false and so not even hold of this world. To prove them true, then, demands wholly different procedures from those of direct inspection and the rigorous analysis of meanings. But before attending to the way empirical judgments are established, Lewis first distinguished the types of empirical judgments.

Types of Empirical Judgments

Lewis differentiated three types of empirical judgments: expressive statements, terminating judgments, and objective beliefs.

Expressive Statements   The basis of all empirical knowledge is the immediately given data of the senses. These data are qualitatively specific and form the cues on which we act. They are what we get by direct inspection. The logical positivists insisted that all empirical knowledge is ultimately verified by reference to these data, and they called the final empirical judgments reporting such data "protocol statements." Unfortunately they disagreed over whether such protocol statements should consist of terms describing the psychological data of experience or of terms referring to the macroscopic physical objects of the ordinary world. Carnap suggested that the decision to use a phenomenalistic or a physicalistic language for protocol statements was a matter of convention, but some positivists or empiricists dissented. Lewis, however, held that the basic judgments with which empirical knowledge begins deal with immediate data of sense, not with physical objects. Yet he acknowledged that language is hard pressed to report these data, since language is shot through with concepts, and the empirical data, to be the bedrock of knowledge, must be wholly devoid of concepts. But where the logical positivists were inclined to maintain that protocol statements were indispensable to all empirical knowledge and had to be elucidated in order to guarantee the basic unity of the sciences, Lewis believed that these statements, which he termed "expressive statements," are necessary only for the purposes of epistemological analysis and need not be too exacting, provided simply that what is being indicated is understood. For expressive statements are formed to indicate the qualitatively specific, direct, and indubitable content of experience—the immediate apprehension of the senses. As statements, of course, they may be true or false, but only liars can make false expressive statements. For what one experiences, this complex of sensory qualities, is indubitable and certain.

Terminating Judgments   Immediate apprehensions of data of sensation are infallible. Expressive statements refer directly to these data but may be true or false. Taking the sense data as cues, the organism engages in action, anticipating experiences of further data therefrom. Terminating judgments bridge the stages of the organism's reception of the initial data, of the organism's motor responses to these data, and of the organism's reception of the final data upon completion of the action. These final data either measure up to or fail to measure up to anticipations. Terminating judgments always find their cue in what is given; but they also always state something which is verifiable only by a course of action resulting in sensory immediacy.

Lewis represented terminating judgments by the form: "If *a* then *e*," or rather, "*s* being given, if *a* then *e*." It is important to note that both the antecedent and the consequent of terminating judgments must be phrased in expressive language describing the immediately given. The *s* is always an expressive statement indicating the sensory cue; the *a* is always an expressive statement indicating the sensory feel of the motor and muscular activities required by the hypothesis of action; and the *e* is always an expressive statement of the anticipated sensory result. In the formulation of terminating judgments no reference to objective states of affairs, which are not confined to what is given simply in its sensory immediacy, is allowed. Otherwise the role of terminating judgments in epistemological analysis would fail.

Another point is worthy of mention. The if-then relationship connecting the hypothesis and the consequent of a terminating judgment is a probability connection. It is a natural connection learned through experience. Its acceptance constitutes a rejection of that empiricism which, as expounded by the early Wittgenstein and by Bertrand Russell, posits a metaphysical atomism of discrete and disconnected states of affairs. More will be said on this score later.

Objective Beliefs Objective beliefs comprise what is ordinarily meant by empirical knowledge. They are assertions about objective reality. Examples of objective beliefs are: "There is a sheet of paper before me." "Rima is preparing dinner." "Several Soviet satellites are in orbit." These beliefs, which may be as general as the laws of nature, hold of some states of affairs. They are, moreover, never certain, but merely probable. The validation of objective beliefs is the central problem of knowledge of the empirical type.

Validation of Empirical Judgments

The question of validating empirical judgments is divisible into two subsidiary questions: 1) How do we *verify* empirical judgments?

What constitutes evidence that they are true or false? 2) How do we *justify* empirical statements? What are the grounds on which we can reasonably assert them or believe them?

Verification   All knowledge about existence, all empirical beliefs expressed in the objective statements of the natural and social sciences, all statements in ordinary language about existent things or events, are to be verified solely by the immediate and certain presentations of the senses. Logical positivists (Moritz Schlick, Hans Reichenbach, Rudolf Carnap, A. J. Ayer) and operationalists (P. W. Bridgman in physics, C. C. Pratt in psychology) have emphasized the principle of verifiability as central to meaning and to truth, and although it would be historically rewarding to trace the development of the verification theory in order to appreciate the character of Lewis' version (16, Pt. 1), here it suffices to note two differences between Lewis' theory and the theories of the logical positivists and operationalists.

Operationalists and logical positivists sometimes include in their basic verifying statements (atomic propositions or protocol statements or observation sentences) objective terms which impute existence beyond the sensory immediacy of direct perception. After the performance of a given operation implied by a scientific concept, both the operationalists and the positivists are confronted with phenomena which they describe in objective terms, e.g., meter readings. This procedure commits them to a commonsense epistemological realism which concedes to observation direct acquaintance with physical objects occupying a space-time system, and which transmits to them the traditional difficulties of perceptual error. Lewis emphatically opposed their method. Scientific methodology may rest with commonsense realism, but epistemological analysis cannot. Besides, Lewis' theory departs from the standard versions of logical positivism and operationalism by its emphasis on the meaning of an empirical belief in advance of its verification. For Lewis every empirical belief has a sense meaning prior to the procedures and operations which verify it. There is, in other words, a schema, an imagined pattern of routine activities culminating in specific anticipatable results, which accompanies every empirical belief. It is by virtue of this criterion in mind that mind is able to recognize the sense presentations that verify or confirm the belief.

Every objective belief asserts a meaning up to and beyond an exhaustible series of confirming experiences, and is therefore said to be nonterminating. No objective belief can ever be verified as absolutely certain. In fact, each instance of verification, once obtained, passes over into the justification of the objective belief, increasing its probability of being true. But in no case can it confirm an objective belief once and for all. Nor does an instance of falsification constitute proof of its absolute falsity, although it does increase its improbability. Hence empirical knowledge can not attain theoretical certainty. It can, however, supply a high degree of genuine probability—enough to furnish practical certainty.

The process of verifying an objective belief involves first deducing from it the terminating judgments it strictly implies, then acting in the manner required by the antecedents of the terminating judgments, and finally determining whether the sense presentations expressed by the consequents will hold. An example will be helpful. The objective belief x ("There is a book to my left.") strictly implies y ("Certain conditions holding, and certain sense presentations being given, if I look to my left I shall see a book."). Now translate y into the expressive language of a terminating judgment. The result is something like this: "A sensory *feeling* of looking ahead being given, if there is a sensory *feeling* of turning my head to the left, then probably there will follow a certain sensory immediacy of color, shape, size indicating a book." According to Lewis, this terminating judgment can be found to be absolutely true or absolutely false. It belongs to the class of ultimate sense certainties upon which the whole structure of empirical knowledge rests.

This leads directly to a consideration of the if-then connection. Few topics have incited as much discussion in recent philosophical literature as this relation, especially in its guise as the "contrary to fact condition." For Lewis the if-then connection of a terminating judgment is a crucial concept. Challenging the Humean empiricism and the logical positivism of disconnected and discrete states of affairs, he construed this relation as a probability connection learned from experience. None of the current notions of implication is adequate to express Lewis' conception. Material implication fails because the falsity of the antecedent in material implication allows any consequent to follow, whereas the if-then relation of a terminating judgment specifies that when the antecedent is contrary to fact, certain consequences and not others probably result. In fact, since certain consequences may be expected to follow from the affirmation of an antecedent, the antecedent is often denied. For the same reasons the if-then relation as conceived by Lewis is not a formal implication, since formal implication is but a class of material implications. Nor, finally, is it a matter of strict implication. Strict implication requires that it is impossible or inconceivable for the antecedent to be true and the consequent to be false, whereas the if-then relation of the terminating judgment requires less. Moreover, the meaning of the antecedent does not include the meaning of the consequent, as in the case of strict implication. Nevertheless, the if-then relation of the terminating judgment expresses a connection which is learned from experience and cannot be explained away. Without it there would be no value in taking seriously the power of knowledge to guide action and the power of action to affect human experience—either by affirming some antecedents to contribute to the occurrence of desirable consequences or by negating others to avoid the occurrence of undesirable consequences.

Justification The verification of an empirical statement is a matter of translating it into the specific terminating judgments that express the sensory immediacy of actual experience. If empirical knowledge is to guide action, however, we cannot expect to translate all empirical statements into the actual terminating judgments that confirm them. To warrantably assert, for example, that if I jump out of the window I will injure myself does not require me to jump out of the window. It is largely this kind of consideration which has provoked the criticisms of the verification theory and the discussions of contrary to fact conditions. Further, if empirical knowledge is to guide action, it must be concerned with the future eventualities of human experience. At the moment of judging these future eventualities, we must be content with what is rationally credible. The criteria of rational credibility are the grounds of belief and constitute the nature of justification. What are these criteria? How can we justify one judgment of future eventualities over another?

These questions cannot be dismissed easily with the observation that past experience justifies our beliefs. For then the problem of induction, of the uniformity of nature, comes to the fore. That nature, or experience, has had a certain character and structure in the past is no guarantee that it will have the same in the future. The uniformity of nature—the principle upon which induction traditionally rests—cannot itself receive empirical demonstration, since every proof, if empirical, presupposes the principle and so is fallaciously circular. Lewis' suggested solution is straightforward: "Past experience on the basis of which we say that we generalize is not the ultimate datum for generalization from experience. It is only the memory of such experience which is the actually given datum" (9, p. 264). This statement, unassuming as it appears, has revolutionary implications for empiricist epistemology. Plagued with explaining the uniformity of nature, and finding none, empiricists have nonetheless continued the rule of induction from past to future experience. They have proceeded with practical correctness but without theoretical justification. Lewis offered a new approach to justifying induction. He transformed the question concerning the uniformity of nature into another question altogether—the question of the validity of memory.

Lewis makes two points in his argument for the validity of memory: first, any remembering is prima facie credible; and second, the credibility of the whole sweep of empirical beliefs, all of which are dependent on memory and direct perception, is assured by their congruence. Let us consider each point in turn. First, the prima facie credibility of any remembering simply as remembering is a conclusion arrived at through introspection. When a recalled incident comes into consciousness, it is accepted as credible just as it stands, though of course it may be checked by further experience. But because our memories sometimes do not pass the test of verification, something more reliable than mere prima facie credibility is re-

quired. The second basis for the validity of memory is the congruence of beliefs. As Lewis stated it, "A set of statements, or a set of
supposed facts asserted, will be said to be congruent if and only if
they are so related that the antecedent probability of any one of
them will be increased if the remainder of the set can be assumed
as given premises" (9, p. 338).

Congruence, then, seems to be similar to coherence, but it differs
in two important ways. First, while congruence demands more than
mere consistency, it requires less than the logical entailment of beliefs, which is the professed ideal of the coherence theory. But in
fact, since the whole truth is not contained in any existent system,
the coherence theory too must be satisfied with less than logical entailment. On the other hand, to relax with mere consistency as governing the acceptance of a body of beliefs is to make little headway.
Contingency is a peculiar feature of empirical knowledge, so that
the range of statements with which any empirical statement is
consistent is indefinite, excluding only the contradictory of that
statement and limited only by the power of the imagination. Congruence, therefore, is neither the mutual entailment nor the logical
consistency of empirical beliefs. What it is may be best understood
through a consideration of probability theory, specifically the theory
of conjoint probability. According to this theory, several separate
confirmations of an hypothesis increase its probability more than
any single confirmation alone would and more than the mere sum
of single confirmations would. Consequently, empirical beliefs are
congruent in that the probability of any one of a given set is increased by finding the others in that set to be true. Finding the
other beliefs true by the test of experience is the second difference
between congruence and coherence.

The final test of empirical truth is, for Lewis, no mere relationship of statements to statements. On the contrary, empirical
knowledge is unequivocally what experience confirms. Some of the
statements of the congruent set must refer directly to experience, for
without that reference there can be no empirical knowledge.

As a dimension of the validity of empirical beliefs, justification
can neither be ignored nor treated as inexplicable. An empirical

belief is rationally credible or justified if it is congruent with the set of related beliefs memory supplies at the moment of judgment. Various remembered beliefs become premises, and the relationship of the belief in question to these premises is an a priori determinable relationship. The rules of logic apply here, and once the inference is drawn the belief in question is assured of having genuine probability on the given premises.

Lewis, then, was able to meet head on the crucial question: How do we know that what has held for the past will hold for the future? His answer was straightforward: We do not really know anything about the future certainly, but we do know that some beliefs presently formed are more credible than others, and that their credibility is not a property of what holds for the future but is based on their inferability from a congruent set of remembered beliefs. If we are interested in proving the truth of these beliefs, we then set out to verify them, and once again anything may happen, although experience appears to favor the rationally credible.

Thus Lewis' theory of empirical knowledge not only elucidates the grounds of belief in a strictly special sense, but also shows that empirical knowledge is genuine knowledge. Experience is the proof of its genuineness.

THEORY OF VALUATION

Although Lewis' theory of knowledge is in essential respects a logical empiricist theory, the a priori consisting wholly of analytic statements and empirical knowledge tied to methods of verification, he departs in value theory from the noncognitivist positions of standard logical empiricism. For standard logical empiricism, i.e., logical positivism, maintains that any statement concerning values is cognitively meaningless, since it can neither be validated by formal rules or meanings nor be confirmed by experience. However, the logical positivists have conceded that such cognitively meaningless sentences may be meaningful in another sense—in the sense of emotive meanings. A sentence is emotively meaningful if it expresses the attitude or feelings of its speaker and/or aims to evoke like attitudes or feelings in the hearer. For the logical positivist, statements concerning values are statements which, though noncognitive, are emotively meaningful.

No doubt the emotivist (or noncognitivist) theory of value judgments has suited the times. Advocated in undeveloped form in the decade before World War II, it gained numerous adherents. The clash of ideologies, reflecting fundamental disagreement over values, allowed no hope of rational solution. It seemed that only resort to arms could resolve the conflict by destroying one of the warring sets of ideologies. In 1945 by far the most sophisticated ethical theory yet offered by the emotivists was published by Charles Stevenson. No recent book in ethics has aroused as much discussion as his *Ethics and Language* (19). As Stevenson has said, "My methodological conclusions center less on my conception of meaning than on my conceptions of agreement and disagreement" (20, p. 142). Thus his theory has been especially suited to a period in history divided by rival ideologies, each positing a scheme of values in conflict with the others'. According to Stevenson, there are disagreements of beliefs and of attitudes. Disagreements of belief are settled by direct reference to the facts relevant to the disputed situation, since beliefs are concerned with how matters are truthfully to be described and explained. Disagreements in attitudes, on the other hand, are not so decided, since attitudes have to do with how matters are "to be favored or disfavored, and hence how they are to be shaped by human efforts" (19, p. 4). Ethical disagreements are essentially disagreements of attitudes, as Stevenson attempts to show by translating ethical statements into working models which reveal their content and structure.

According to Stevenson, in the first pattern of analysis, a value assertion such as "X is good" is *approximately* equivalent to the assertion: "I approve X; do so as well" (19, pp. 20 ff.). The first clause, stating that I approve X, is a factual assertion, descriptive of the psychological fact of approval. The second clause, commanding others to do so as well, is an awkward rendering of that feature of ethical statements whereby they aim to arouse the emotions or direct the attitudes of the hearer. Thus any ethical statement is twofold: it describes the emotions or attitudes of the person making the judgment, and it attempts to influence the emotions or attitudes of the hearers. It is the second feature, expressed by the imperative, which is peculiar to value judgments and is the source of ethical conflict. In instances of such conflict the disputants may appeal to beliefs or persuasive methods to convince each other. Although Stevenson's recognition of the role of beliefs as supporting reasons for ethical conclusions sets his theory somewhat apart from the early emotivist theories of Russell, Carnap, Reichenbach, Schlick, and Ayer, he nonetheless emphasizes that the connection between supporting beliefs and ethical conclusions is not logical, but *psychological* (19, pp. 30, 113, 114–15, 130, 133). Thus values do not constitute objective states of affairs, but rather they reflect subjective attitudes toward objective states of affairs. Value terms describe nothing; their purpose is to stimulate attitudes. And the reasons employed to support ethical statements are similarly oriented toward affecting attitudes.

According to Stevenson's second pattern of analysis, the assertion "This is good" means "This has qualities or relations X, Y, Z ..." plus the laudatory emotive meaning. Here, at least, some objective criterion for the ascription of value terms is to be expected, for emotive and descriptive meanings are so intertwined that the latter gives direction to the former. However, the second pattern of analysis adds no new content to ethics beyond what is manifest in the first pattern (19, p. 209), so that the choice of one pattern instead of the other is merely a choice between forms of language (19, p. 242). Thus the second pattern of analysis offers nothing more than a persuasive definition. That is to say, a value term, with its areas of vagueness and vast emotive force, is defined in context as being X or Y or Z, but that X or Y or Z is decided upon is purely a matter of approval, expressible in terms of the direct value-predications that are treated by the first pattern of analysis. Consequently, the fact that a definition of the "good" offered by a philosopher includes certain factors and excludes others is simply an indication of that philosopher's attitudes and feelings as well as of his desire to influence others in the same direction (19, pp. 224 ff.). Hence, for Stevenson, the term "good" remains primarily emotive.

Lewis openly repudiated noncognitivism or emotivism in ethics, despite its high degree of sophistication. He offered an epistemology, not so much as the clarification of the foundations of science, but in order to demonstrate that "valuations represent one type of empirical cognition; hence that their correctness answers to a kind of objective fact, but one which can be learned only from experience and is not determinable *a priori*" (9, p. viii). In this way Lewis sought to prove that "empiricism in epistemology and naturalism in ethics" do not imply a "Protagorean relativism or that moral skepticism which would destroy the normative by reducing it to merely emotive significance" (9, p. viii).

Thought and Action

The cause for the wide divergence between Lewis' theory and the noncognitive value theories of many logical positivists and empiricists is not hard to find: Lewis' theory is an offshoot of the more general philosophy of pragmatic naturalism. Whereas most logical positivists and empiricists start with an analysis of scientific knowledge, pragmatic naturalists usually begin with the natural agent coping with a practical environment and struggling for survival and advance. This setting completely transforms the nature of the problem. Instead of being some abstract set of terms and statements subject to empirical discovery and logical critique by a standard observer, knowledge for the pragmatist is the instrument employed by concrete beings passionately concerned about their own existence and the goods to be enjoyed in that existence. "Knowledge, action, and evaluation are essentially connected. The primary and pervasive significance of knowledge lies in its guidance of action; knowing is for the sake of doing. And action, obviously, is rooted in evaluation" (9, p. 3). Hence the emphasis on action gives to knowledge a utilitarian role. Indeed, knowledge is justified only if it can lead to the realization of values in experience. Cognition itself is invalidated unless it plays an all-important role in valuation.

For Lewis action, which embodies the operation of the cognitive, is distinguished from behavior. "Action is behavior which is deliberate or decided upon; which is subject to critique and could at least be altered on reflection" (9, p. 366). This definition seems to assume that man is a free agent, although Lewis nowhere examines or argues the assumption in detail. He does, however, mention that the determinist conception of man as compelled by external and internal causes is based on "the absurdity of first setting up [an] animistic metaphor and then turning it against that kind of fact which alone gives it any content" (9, p. 484 n).

As deliberated and decided upon, action has an *intent*, i.e. the *expected* result of the action, and a *purpose*, i.e. the *desired* part of the expected result (9, pp. 366–67). The *sensibleness* of an action is judged by whether or not the intent is deemed to be of comparative value. Further, a sensible action may or may not be successful, since the *success* of an action arises from the achievement of its purpose. Often, regardless of how valuable a purpose may be, the action may fail to realize it, or again, realizing the purpose, the agent may discover that the anticipated value of the result is not present when the result is actualized. Sensible, successful action, then, requires first, that the intent of the action have comparative value; second, that the intent be realized through the action; and third, that the actual result be found as valuable as anticipated.

"Success is the desideratum of action" (9, p. 370). But since success is dependent upon so many circumstances beyond the control of the agent, the practical justification of an action is more important than its success. An action is practically justified "if and only if the intent of it is an expectation which is a *warranted empirical belief*" (9, p. 371). While in single instances actions, guided by intentions of comparative value and executed with a competent assessment of instrumental relationships, may still fail to be successful, it is highly unlikely that an agent, always more or less practically justified, can fall short of some measure of success in the whole range of his actions. Hence empirical belief plays a major role in valuation.

Value Judgments

An analysis of valuation logically involves a consideration of the types of empirical judgments of value. These judgments fall into three classes: expressive statements, terminating judgments, and objective beliefs.

Expressive statements do not make assertions of objects, but are limited to expressing that which *seems* or *appears* within a given experience. Expressive statements, as involved in valuation, indicate "a value-quality found in the directly experienced" (9, p. 374). For example, if, while listening to a concert, I say, "This is good," presumably I intend to report a directly experienced character. Such statements are self-verifying and subject to no possible error, except linguistic ones; and although they are true or false, because it is possible to lie about what is experienced, yet they are not judgments, and consequently not knowledge (9, p. 375).

After direct and indubitable apprehension of value characters, amenable to formulation in expressive statements, come terminating judgments. The agent, taking the apprehended data as cues for action, engages in action and anticipates certain experiences of further data. Terminating judgments trace the stage of qualitative immediacy felt by the organism receiving the initial data, then the stage of motor responses, and finally the stage in which the organism receives the final data which measure up to or fail to measure up to anticipations. Terminating judgments always find their cue in what is given; but they state something which is verifiable only by a course of action resulting in another state of qualitative immediacy. They are always conditional. When an organism experiences a given presentation, if it acts in such and such a way, then it may expect so and so. An example will be helpful as regards the clarification of terminating judgments of value: Let us suppose that I see a peach, and, in light of past experience, I know that if I bite into it I shall enjoy the taste. Expressed in the form of a terminating judgment, the statement would be something of this sort: "A fuzzy-surfaced, yellow-green-orange colored, round shaped, peach-*seeming*, being given; if the motor activities of face muscles, jaws, and salivary glands usually associated with 'biting into and eating' be felt, then an enjoyed taste is experienced." This judgment is verified or falsified by whether or not the experience of the enjoyed taste occurs as expected. Consequently it represents a form of knowledge.

Objective beliefs are the statements that make up what we ordinarily mean when we speak of empirical knowledge. They are assertions of objective reality. As a type of value predication, they ascribe the objective property of value to an existent or possible existent. Objective beliefs of value are, like other objective beliefs, confirmable by means of the terminating judgments which can be deduced from them. To assert, "That music is beautiful," is to assert an objective belief that can be confirmed if I put myself in the situation which enables me to hear the music and I find it beautiful.

The Nature of Value

Valuation is a mode of empirical cognition for Lewis. What, then, is its object—value? According to Lewis, "value" is a term "used exclusively in the sense of a value-quality, value-character or value-property of something, or of a *kind* of value-quality, character, or property" (9, p. 393). "Value" is predicable of immediate experience and also of existent objects or possible existent objects. We shall examine first the sense in which "value" is predicable of immediate experience, for this is the primary meaning of the term. In accord with this primary meaning, value is "a quality unmistakably identifiable in the direct apprehension of it when disclosed in experience" (9, p. 400).

Valuation involves, for Lewis, a fundamental act of intuition of value within experience. First, "everybody knows what it [value] is; and if anyone should not, we could hardly tell him" (9, p. 400). Having "no parts or distinct ingredients," standing "in no invariant context," and lacking "stable correlations," value in this sense is "ineffable" and "unanalyzable" (9, p. 400). Secondly, men have described the immediately valuable in so many different ways "as sometimes to arouse suspicion that they are not talking about the same thing" (9, p. 401). Either they were all intending the same thing, about which serious controversy can be raised, or they were merely implicated in a vast verbal confusion having little significance. Only the former alternative does justice to the caliber of the thinkers who engaged in the enterprise of defining value. Thus Lewis undertook to specify the meaning of value.

As he said, "Immediate or directly findable value is not so much one quality as a dimensionlike mode which is pervasive of all experience" (9, p. 401). Moreover, he described "immediately or directly findable" value as a stubborn, irreducible fact of experience, as that in terms of which all value judgments are verified. Further, "value-disvalue is that mode or aspect of the given or contemplated to which desire and aversion are addressed" (9, p. 403). For "the immediately good is what you like and what you want in the way of experience; and the immediately bad is what you dislike and do not want" (9, p. 404).

A crucial term in Lewis' description of immediate value is "dimension" or "dimensionlike mode." While agreeing with G. E. Moore concerning both the irreducible qualitativeness of value and the requirement that it be apprehended intuitively, Lewis differs radically from Moore in that he regards value not as a simple quality or presentation like yellow, but as a *mode* or *dimension* of presentations. Thus values do not adhere solely to presentations. Rather there is a "general level of value-feeling," belonging "to the background rather than to any item which stands out in it" (9, p. 424). Lewis described this background as a "vague remainder of the felt, not definitely localizable," "inchoate," "a euphoric or dysphoric condition . . . likely to be attributed to 'ourselves,' or to 'things in general' " (9, p. 425). Since, therefore, directly findable value-quality "tends to be determined in some part by the relation of that presentation to the context of it" (9, p. 426), Lewis insisted that it cannot be characterized as *given*.

Nevertheless, the value dimension, despite its difference from the presentations of which it is a dimension-like mode, is so intimately connected with them that Lewis advanced the following formula: "Describe the given content adequately in *other* respects than value, and we can make shift to evaluate it from that description" (9, p. 402). Nor should the use of the term "dimension" suggest that value is subject to mathematical measurement, for the value-dimension of one set of presentations may be different in *kind* from the value-dimension of another set of presentations.

Moreover, value-feeling attaches as much to the pervasive mood of the feeler as to the presentations felt. That is to say, the context of a presentation affects the value-quality with which the presentation is given. Such contexts are divided into three groups. First, there is "the influence of a background of organic sensations and conditioning" (9, p. 429). Second, there is "the context represented by anticipatory associations, whether merely habitual or explicitly cognitive" (9, p. 429). The odor of coffee in the morning, for example, is valuable largely because it signifies coffee to be drunk. Third, there is the purely subjective context, "exemplified by the relatively free associations of the day-dream" (9, p. 430). Sentimental reminiscence, for instance, may enhance the value of listening to a piece of music.

Consider Lewis' analysis of the nature of the good life, which he identified with happiness. It is "a temporal Gestalt of experience in the sense of being its included and mutually qualifying parts" (9, p. 503). Hence, in our most primary experience of value, i.e. in the living of life as a whole, value as felt is always mediated by its interrelation with other parts of the whole value experience. In this Gestalt no presentation can be considered solely in itself; it is incorporated in an internally related whole to which it contributes, and from which it derives its own value. Thus presentations touched with the poignant or tragic, in themselves disvaluable, may be so comprehended in the whole of life that they enhance its value-depth and dimension, and consequently are esteemed valuable.

Types of Value

Lewis distinguished different types of value. First there is "intrinsic value," which is the value immediately findable in experience. It is "usually described as that which is good in itself or good for its own sake" (9, p. 382), and it "attaches exclusively to realizations of some possible value quality in experience itself" (9, p. 389).

Besides intrinsic value, there is extrinsic value—i.e. value as ascribed to objects—of which there are two classes: inherent and instrumental (9, p. 392). Inherent value is ascribed to an object whose presentation leads directly to an immediate experience of value. Instrumental value is ascribed to an object if the object leads to other objects which in turn lead to an object of inherent value. An example will serve to illustrate the character of each class. According to Lewis, "esthetic objects belong to the class of those objects the value of which is *peculiarly* inherent" (9, p. 435). A poem, for instance, is valuable not because it is productive of other objects, but because it is the kind of object from which an immediate experience of value is derived upon its presentation. Objects having instrumental value are objects which lead to objects of inherent value. It is on this basis that instrumental value is to be distinguished from utility. The utility of an object is its conduciveness to other objects, whether or not these objects possess inherent value or conduce to objects having inherent value. The instrumental value of an object is its conduciveness to an object of value, either remote or near. For instance, a pen has instrumental value by virtue of its use in the construction of objects, e.g. a poem, which has inherent value.

The reasons for the distinction between intrinsic and extrinsic value are clear enough. According to Lewis' theory, which takes the active agent as primary, the end of action is always some positive value-quality ingredient in human life (9, p. 432). Experiences of intrinsic value may not, however, be ascribable to the object because certain subjective or abnormal conditions affect the context (9, p. 433). But despite such variations in intrinsic values which betray their subjectivity, extrinsic values are objective. This distinction makes specifiable a sense in which value may be described as objective, though rooted in immediate experience.

Objectivity of Value

For Lewis ultimate value is intrinsic value, and extrinsic values are valuable because they conduce to intrinsic value, i.e. to the directly experienced value. As he put the matter, "The goodness of good objects consists in the possibility of their leading to some realization of directly experienced goodness" (9, p. 387). By identifying the value of an object with its possibility for experience, Lewis escaped subjectivism. For a possibility for experience is independent of experience in that it is possible whether or not there is an experience to actualize it. In this fundamental sense Lewis affirmed the objectivity of extrinsic values. When an immediately apprehended value-quality or property is so affected by what is personal or peculiar to the individual that the object conducing to the experienced actuality is not likely to conduce to similar experiences in others, it is deemed subjective (9, pp. 416, 528). When the quality is such that the object is capable of leading to similar experiences in others, then it is objective (9, p. 410).

However, in one important respect objective value-qualities differ from objective physical properties. The physical properties are subject to indirect tests, while value-qualities, though susceptible in certain cases to such tests, are never limited to them. Whereas with respect to "hardness" or "roundness" the unsure corroborations of feeling have been supplanted by objective tests, "with respect to goodness, the mode of feeling remains the head and front of the whole matter, and no more precise test of objective value would be true to our intent. *Apparent* value in the thing—the possibility of some *experience* of value-quality in connection with it—is of the essence" (9, p. 382).

Value attributions, like any other attributions, are attributions of potentiality when referring to objects. Some attributions of potentiality for experience lie within the nature of the object (9, p. 519). Others are attributions of potentiality "as realizable under certain conditions, known or assumed as *actual* or determined to be probable" (9, p. 520). As Lewis said, "When viewed in their relation to experience, all properties of things are potentialities" (9, p. 520). By means of the concept of potentiality Lewis affirmed the objectivity of extrinsic values. So, regardless of the function of feeling in valuation, value judgments prove to be as objective as other empirical beliefs.

ETHICS AND SOCIAL PHILOSOPHY

As a pragmatist Lewis stressed the practical bearing of judgment on action, and so in a fundamental way he acknowledged ethical norm as the broad category which applies to all knowledge and experience. Yet he was aware of the aesthetic values, for he conceded that the immediately valuable, that at which all conduct is aimed, is a quality of experience distinctively aesthetic. Lewis said: "All experience is esthetic in the broad sense of being presentation of some quality-complex in which value or disvalue is directly findable" (9, p. 439). In contrast with the broadly aesthetic quality of experience is the specifically aesthetic, which is associated with the arts and which occurs only when this broadly aesthetic quality of experience "becomes object of the esthetic attitude; only if the experience is marked by absorption in the presented content on its own account" (9, p. 439). On the one hand, then, all evaluations, like all other knowledge, are moral in the sense that they legislate for human conduct. On the other hand, all action aims to terminate in an immediate experience which is broadly aesthetic.

Nowhere is Lewis' theory that ultimate, intrinsic values—the goals of action—are aesthetic more patent than in his conception of the end of moral action, the *summum bonum*. However it be conceived, the *summum bonum*, according to Lewis, "will in any case be projected as some ideal wholeness of self-contained living; some blessedness to be steadily maintained; some perduring experience having its self-justifying quality as esthetic" (9, p. 439). For Lewis, moreover, the *summum bonum* is the good life. This is a point "not to be argued," for the good life "is the universal and rational human end; the end we aim at so far as we approve of our aims and of ourselves in aiming, and do not recognize some perversity or foolishness or weakness of will in our motivations and our doings" (9, p. 483).

Although Lewis depicted the good life, the *summum bonum*, in terms which reflect the broadly aesthetic quality of immediate experience, he never once retreated from his pragmatic emphasis upon the essentially active character of human life. For human life is oriented toward future possibilities, even though these possibilities are not as poignant as what is now immediately felt. Human life, therefore, is subject to concern and to imperatives. Lewis wrote: "Man, being higher than the animals but a little lower than the angels, is permanently liable to a kind of schizophrenia, and can neither be whole-heartedly impulsive nor whole-heartedly rational. The sense of the future moves him, but not sufficiently to make him automatically responsive. He has to 'move himself' in order to come into accord with the dictates of the reasonable. Hence the sense of the imperative" (9, p. 484). In the concept of the imperative Lewis' discussion moves from a treatment of empirical valuation —which touches upon all goods, including the *summum bonum*— to a consideration of "the ground and nature of the right." Thus Lewis concluded his *Analysis* with a sharp distinction between the principles of ethics and questions of valuation (21). "Valuation," he wrote, "is always a matter of empirical knowledge. But what is right and what is just, can never be determined by empirical facts alone" (9, p. 554).

In his small book *The Ground and Nature of the Right*, Lewis elucidated the distinction between the good and the right. He said: "The achievement of the good is desirable but conformity to the right is imperative" (10, p. 59). Whereas good or bad may be predicated of anything, right and wrong apply strictly to some possible human activity. Indeed, right and wrong are predicable only of those human activities which "are corrigible and determinable by decision, and hence are subject to deliberation and to critical assessment" (10, p. 78). The modes of right coincide with the normative, the imperative, of which Lewis distinguishes several types: first, the technical right, which legislates "how to do so and so or how to achieve some particular species of common purposes" (10, p. 13); second, the logically or cognitively right, which regulates mental activities of thinking, believing, or inferring; third, the prudentially right, which has to do with the correctness of acts so far as their results affect the doer; and fourth, the morally right, which pertains to acts so far as they affect others. The technically right lacks universality, inasmuch as one is free to choose or to reject a given mode of occupation and its specific imperatives. But the other types of right are universal, giving rise to two normative philosophical disciplines: logic and ethics. Whereas, in one sense, since the norms of action prevail upon thought, ethics is the most universal discipline, in another sense logic is prior to ethics, since right believing is indispensable to right doing. Indeed, that action may be right or wrong is due to the fact that it is guided by beliefs which are amenable to criticism.

In his endeavor to establish the criteria of right doing, Lewis examined the standard of intention and the standard of consequences and concluded that neither standard alone is adequate. Instead, he found that intentions and consequences are inseparable. "What the intention of an act comprises," he said, "is simply that total body of consequences which the doer expects in taking this commitment" (10, pp. 45–46). Of course, it is easy to deem an act subjectively right if the intention behind it is moral whether or not the anticipated consequences result, and objectively right when its consequences are good, but Lewis emphasized that this position will not do. For the objective rightness of an act also refers to the intention of the doer. "The primary concern of ethics is with the moral integrity of the doer and his final responsibility" (10, p. 51). "An act . . . is objectively right to do just in case, on the evidence available to the doer, it is that alternative of action which affords the (correctly judged) highest probability of good results" (10, p. 56).

The rightness of an act, therefore, depends upon the conformity of the doer to imperatives which, when realized, promise the highest probability of good results. Since these imperatives are principles of right decision, they are, to use Lewis' word, "rational." They bear directly upon thinking, and proximately upon doing, as doing is the issue of thinking. Since thinking aims at objectivity and generality, the rational imperatives pertain to these matters. The root imperative is the Law of Objectivity: "So conduct and determine your activities of thinking and of doing, as to conform any decision of them to the objective actualities, as cognitively signified to you in your representational apprehension of them, and not according to any impulse or solicitation exercised by the affective quality of your present experience as immediate feeling merely" (10, p. 89). This, in substance, is the fundamental demand to be rational.

Further, since man is a social being with a history and a moral evolution based upon the development of his society, his rational imperative must also be imperatively *social* if it is to be adequate to life. Thus the individual doer is obligated "to respect other persons as the realities we representationally recognize them to be— as creatures whose gratifications and griefs have the same poignant factuality as our own; and as creatures who, like ourselves, find it imperative to govern themselves in the light of the cognitive apprehensions vouchsafed to them, by decisions which they themselves reach, and by reference to values discoverable to them" (10, p. 91). This obligation finds expression in two imperatives: the Law of Compassion and the Law of Moral Equality. "The Law of Compassion dictates that we recognize other creatures as being, like ourselves, subject to enjoyment and suffering" (10, p. 91). Its command is: "Recognize, in your action affecting any sentient being, that claim on your compassion which comports with its [the sentient being's] capacity to enjoy and suffer" (10, p. 92). The Law of Moral Equality "is peculiarly relevant to moral dealing with our full peers, and dictates respect for others not only as ends in themselves but as entitled to full self-determination of their individual action, to some privacy of decision, and to freedom from coercion in their decisions taken, so long as they bring no harm to others and accord to others a like freedom" (10, p. 92). Its command is: "Take no decision of action which is member of any class of decisions of doing all members of which you call upon others to avoid" (10. p. 93).

In *Our Social Inheritance*, Lewis followed up "a direction of thinking" imparted by his teacher Josiah Royce. In so doing Lewis carried out the implications of his own theories of knowledge and morality for social philosophy. Of course he carefully stressed the naturalistic elements—the biological constitution of human nature —requisite to social existence. The urgency of Lewis' foray into social philosophy is a result of the crisis perpetrated by the acceleration of social change, giving rise to the "question whether the strain of adjustment so put upon our native equipment of intelligence and emotion, and especially upon our mores, may rise to the point where it becomes of itself an outstanding human problem."

The individual, Lewis continues, "is still born with the same biological equipment as in the dawn of history. But the life he lives moves further and further away from that to which, by this endowment, he is natively prepared to adjust" (11, p. 41). As the title of Lewis' essay in social philosophy indicates, our social heritage particularly is emphasized for making possible the civilized conditions of individual life. For civilization the prime requisite is man's social memory, which "retains not only what has been learned from his individual experience but also what has been inculcated by the experience of generations past and of the race" (11, p. 20). This and man's individual self-consciousness are the basic factors for social evolution.

Among all natural beings man alone has the freedom to achieve self-chosen goals, and this freedom, which he exercises individually and within society, is at one point described by Lewis as "the highest good of all, and essential to all other goods save only those of good fortune" (11, p. 55). When ruled not by impulse but by intelligence and reason, freedom effectively contributes to the cumulation of social and individual goods. Individual freedom, no less than social order, is a critical ingredient in the social evolution of mankind. For moral progress, an offspring of natural evolution, hinges upon a social inheritance enriched by individual experimentation. As Lewis has said: "The social order is the main selecting and preserving agency. But without the freedom of private judgment—often dissident to tradition—there would be no intellectual innovation, and progress would dry up at the source" (11, p. 106).

NOTES TO CHAPTER I

1   C. I. Lewis, "Logic and Pragmatism," in George P. Adams and William Pepperell Montague (eds.), *Contemporary American Philosophy* (New York: Macmillan, 1930; reprinted by Russell and Russell, 1962), II.
2   See Bella K. Milmed, *Kant and Current Philosophical Issues* (New York: New York University Press, 1961), Chs. 4 and 5.
3   See Harold N. Lee, "Royce as Logician," *Tulane Studies in Philosophy*, IV (1955), 61–74.
4   C. I. Lewis, *A Survey of Symbolic Logic* (Berkeley: University of California Press, 1918).

5   C. I. Lewis and Cooper Harold Langford, *Symbolic Logic* (New York and London: Century, 1932).

6   C. I. Lewis, *The Pragmatic Element in Knowledge* (Berkeley: University of California Press, 1926).

7   C. I. Lewis, *Mind and the World-Order* (New York, Chicago, and Boston: Scribner's, 1929).

8   As a sophisticated form of logical empiricism, Lewis' philosophy denies the possibility of synthetic a priori knowledge; but against such forms of logical empiricism as logical positivism, it regards a priori knowledge as knowledge having a content and not as formal tautology, and it upholds the cognitive claim of value judgments. These remarks will be amplified in the ensuing discussion. For a popular statement of logical empiricism construed narrowly and crudely as logical positivism, see Herbert Feigl, "Logical Empiricism," in Dagobert D. Runes (ed.), *Twentieth Century Philosophy* (New York: Philosophical Library, 1943), 373–416.

9   C. I. Lewis, *Analysis of Knowledge and Valuation* (LaSalle, Ill.: Open Court, 1946).

10 C. I. Lewis, *The Ground and Nature of the Right* (New York: Columbia University Press, 1955).

11 C. I. Lewis, *Our Social Inheritance* (Bloomington: Indiana University Press, 1957).

12 Charles A. Baylis, "C. I. Lewis's Theory of Value and Ethics," in "Commemorative Symposium on C. I. Lewis," *Journal of Philosophy*, LXI (1964), 560. In this paper, however, Baylis draws exclusively upon the published writings, especially upon *Analysis of Knowledge and Valuation*.

13 See Morton G. White, "The Analytic and Synthetic: An Untenable Dualism," in Sidney Hook (ed.), *John Dewey: Philosopher of Science and Freedom; A Symposium* (New York: Dial Press, 1950), 316–30; and W. V. O. Quine, "Two Dogmas of Empiricism," in *From a Logical Point of View* (2d ed., rev.; New York and Evanston: Harper and Row, 1963), 20–46.

14 Arthur O. Pap, *Semantics and Necessary Truth* (New Haven: Yale University Press, 1958).

15 Rudolf Carnap, *The Logical Syntax of Language* (London: Kegan, Paul, Trench, Trubner, 1937).

16 Hans Reichenbach, *Experience and Prediction* (Chicago: University of Chicago Press, 1935).

17 Ludwig Wittgenstein, *Tractatus Logico-Philosophicus* (London: Routledge and Kegan Paul, 1922).

18 See the following works by Rudolf Carnap: *Foundations of Logic and Mathematics* (Chicago: University of Chicago Press, 1939); *Introduction to Semantics* (Cambridge: Harvard University Press, 1942); *Formalization of Logic* (Cambridge: Harvard University Press, 1943); and *Meaning and Necessity* (Chicago: University of Chicago Press, 1947).

19 Charles L. Stevenson, *Ethics and Language* (New Haven: Yale University Press, 1945).

20 Charles L. Stevenson, "Meaning: Descriptive and Emotive," in "Symposium on Emotive Meaning," *Philosophical Review*, LVII (1948).

21 This distinction has led William Frankena to argue that Lewis' ethics is ulti-
mately a special brand of noncognitivism, even though Lewis himself did not
see it to be so. See the following articles and discussions by Frankena: "Lewis'
Imperatives of Right," *Philosophical Studies*, XIV (1963), 25–28; "Ethical
Theory," in Roderick M. Chisholm and others, *Philosophy* (Englewood, N.J.:
Prentice-Hall, 1964), 387–91; "C. I. Lewis on the Ground and Nature of the
Right," *Journal of Philosophy*, LXI (1964), 489–96; and "Three Comments on
Lewis's Views on the Right and the Good," in "Commemorative Symposium on
C. I. Lewis," *Journal of Philosophy*, LXI (1964), 567–70.

II

STEPHEN C. PEPPER

Philosophy of Values

Stephen C. Pepper, Mills Professor of Philosophy and Art Emeritus at the University of California at Berkeley, once ascribed the origin of one of his major books "to a consuming personal desire to know the truth" (1, p. vii). Pepper confessed: "As a boy I sought it in what was nearest at hand in the doctrines of a church and struggled with what I later found were the perennial issues of theology. Then for a time I sought it in physics" (1, p. vii). When physics failed him, he "discovered philosophy" (1, p. vii). After he had tried, under the guidance of George Herbert Palmer at Harvard and through a study of the writings of T. H. Green, to commit himself to philosophical idealism, he experienced so severe a revulsion that he "turned into a dogmatic materialist" (1, p. vii). Only pragmatism and Gestalt psychology shook Pepper free from the grip of dogmatic materialism. Just as his intellectual principles underwent crisis after crisis, so his values, caught up in the violent changes that were sweeping the world, faced challenge and disruption. Pepper remarked: "Individualistic democracy, which through the first quarter of the century I naively accepted as the unquestionable social ideal, met with severe jars, and became subject to criticism" (1, pp. vii–viii).

Theory and practice converged to compel Pepper to establish the grounds and evidences of his beliefs. Neither dogmatic idealism nor dogmatic materialism would do. For a time, however, Pepper admitted: "I tried to find an adjustment of the evidences of both of these theories in a third, pragmatism. But I soon came to the conclusion that pragmatism was just one more theory, probably no better nor any worse than the other two" (1, p. viii). But the drive for truth persisted, pressing him "toward the study of evidence and hypothesis—toward a reliable method rather than a reliable creed" (1, p. viii). But at that time, during the 1930's and 1940's, the logical positivists were ascendant, and toward them Pepper's immediate reaction was, in his own words, "suspicious and hostile" (1, p. viii). He amplified:

I felt from their attitude and the tone of their statements, even before critically studying them, that they were not meeting the problem that needed to be met. I doubted if many of them had ever fully felt the problem. This was a question of truth and of the justification of human values. To think that this question could be met in the manner of a puzzle and in terms of correlations, statistics, mathematics, and language struck me as fantastic. Here was a method running away with issues, evidence, and value itself. It was, as Loewenberg once remarked, methodolatry (1, pp. viii–ix).

A "question of truth and of the justification of values"—that is the crucial question to which Pepper has devoted his life. Born in Newark, New Jersey, on April 19, 1891, Stephen Coburn Pepper was the son of a noted portrait painter. He was educated at Harvard University, where he received his B.A. in 1913, his M.A. in 1914, and his Ph.D. in 1916. Pepper heard Santayana lecture and studied under Palmer, but of all his Harvard teachers of philosophy it was Ralph Barton Perry who exerted the major influence upon his intellectual development. After a year as instructor at Wellesley College in 1916–17, he was called to military service in World War I. In 1919 he joined the department of philosophy at the University of California at Berkeley, where he became a full professor in 1930, and eventually chairman of the department of philosophy and also chairman of the department of art. The *University of California Publications in Philosophy*, particularly during the 1920's and the 1930's, reveal that the members of the department of philosophy at Berkeley engaged in a stimulating and enriching exchange of ideas. Certainly Pepper's own thinking has added to and profited from the thinking of such distinguished colleagues as George P. Adams, David Prall, Jacob Loewenberg, Paul Marhenke, D. S. Mackay, Edward W. Strong, and William R. Dennes. As teacher, as academic administrator, and above all as the author of ten books and scores of articles, Stephen Pepper occupies a prominent position in contemporary American philosophy.

While C. I. Lewis had taught that the immediate quality of all experience is aesthetic, it was Pepper who, more than any thinker of his generation, made aesthetics and the philosophy of art the technical fields of study they are today. Other thinkers included in the present volume were later to make significant contributions to the area, particularly Feibleman and Weiss, but none matches Pepper as aesthetician and philosopher of art.

Pepper's interest in the arts, inspired in the first instance by his father, came to fruition early. His first book, *Modern Color*, was written in collaboration with a painter; it describes and recommends a new method of painting colors (2). In 1949, a generation later, Pepper published his *Principles of Art Appreciation*, a textbook designed to introduce undergraduate students to the fine arts (3). Pepper's work in aesthetics is, consequently, no abstract essay, but rather the product of a sensitive thinker intimate with the arts. In 1937 his *Aesthetic Quality* appeared, surpassing John Dewey's *Art as Experience* (1934) in precision and purity, and marking the definition of a new type of aesthetics—a pragmatic, or contextualistic, aesthetics (4). *The Basis of Criticism in the Arts*, which grew out of lectures delivered at Harvard and California, and which was published in 1945, states a new kind of aesthetic criticism; it proposes to estimate the value of a work of art by considering the judgments made from the standpoints of the four major alternative aesthetic theories (5). Pepper's Mahlon Powell Lectures at Indiana University, published in 1955 as *The Work of Art*, seek to elucidate what precisely the work of art is (6).

In value theory Pepper's contribution ranks alongside the works of Wilbur Marshall Urban (7, pp. 157–66), Ralph Barton Perry (7, pp. 19–34), DeWitt H. Parker (7, pp. 183–94) and C. I. Lewis.

In 1947 Pepper presented his value theory in compact form in *A Digest of Purposive Values* (8). Eleven years later he offered his comprehensive theory under the title *The Sources of Value*. Setting out from a detailed and technical consideration of the purposive act as described by Edward Tolman, Pepper in *The Sources of Value* detects in the concept of the selective system the unifying principle of the general theory of value (9). Compressing the discussions of *The Sources of Value* with the intent of reaching an undergraduate audience, Pepper formulates, in his 1960 textbook *Ethics*, a social-adjustment theory of ethics (10).

Early in his career Pepper exhibited a deep concern for metaphysics. At first this concern was manifest as a preoccupation with the method and types of metaphysics. In several articles (11) as well as in *World Hypotheses* (1), now in paperback, Pepper expounded an original and influential theory of philosophy. Regarding metaphysical theories as world hypotheses, Pepper traced their origin to root metaphors in ordinary experience, and, until very recently, he concluded that there were only four adequate world hypotheses, but that they were *equally* adequate. Now Pepper has pressed farther, and in his Carus Lectures, delivered before the Pacific Division of the American Philosophical Association in 1961, and published under the title *Concept and Quality*, he has projected a new world hypothesis based upon the purposive act as a root metaphor (12).

THEORY OF METAPHYSICS

World Hypotheses presents a theory of metaphysics, not a metaphysics. A metaphysics is a specific kind of belief which attempts to embrace all facts and to organize them within a coherent system. A metaphysics is, in Pepper's phrase, "a world hypothesis." A world hypothesis, moreover, is an unrestricted hypothesis, as distinct from the restricted hypotheses characteristic of the special sciences. For Pepper there is no basic difference between an empirical scientific hypothesis and an empirical world hypothesis—only a difference of scope. *World Hypotheses* is, according to its subtitle, "a study in evidence." An essay on philosophical method, it examines the source, the nature, and the grounds of metaphysics.

The Nature of Beliefs

Before examining world hypotheses, Pepper discusses the nature of beliefs in general. Because beliefs are accessible to observation, classification, and analysis, he treats them as empirical objects in the world. Because they are vehicles of truth or falsity, he analyzes them with the intent of discovering the criteria of their reliability. Knowledge, he holds, consists of reliable beliefs, and beliefs are reliable when supported by evidence.

Pepper accepts neither utter skepticism nor dogmatism as knowledge. Dogmatism fails because the kinds of evidence to which it necessarily appeals—infallible authorities, self-evident principles, or indubitable facts—are nowhere to be found. Pepper is emphatic on this point: there is no certain evidence of any kind; or, if there is, it is not known. Paradoxically, this is the germ of the failure of utter skepticism. Lacking evidence to support its claim that on every topic the evidence *pro* and *con* is equally divided, utter skepticism is found to rest upon the dogmatic claim that "the world is certainly doubtful" (1, p. 9).

Common sense also fails to be knowledge. Despite its "security"—evident in the persistence of its concepts and judgments in contrast with constant revisions of more scientific ones—common sense is not as definitely cognized or cognizable as criticized knowledge, and, further, it is "cognitively irritable," tossed about by confusions and internal contradictions (1, pp. 42–43). Yet common sense is an item of evidence which, as the starting point, plays an indispensable role in the cognitive process, although it is "an item of evidence that ought to be doubted"—a dubitandum (1, p. 47).

Knowledge, consisting of beliefs supported by criticized evidence, is the work of corroboration. Pepper distinguishes two types of corroboration: multiplicative and structural. Multiplicative corroboration is the "corroboration of man with man"; structural corroboration is the "corroboration of fact with fact" (1, p. 47). To illustrate the distinction, Pepper considers the problem of determining the strength of a chair to support the weight of a man (1, pp. 48–49). Multiplicative corroboration occurs when several persons sit in the chair and report its strength. Structural corroboration occurs when from an examination of the parts—nails, glue, wood—of the chair, it is inferred that the chair is strong enough. Pepper terms the products of multiplicative corroboration "data" and the products of structural corroboration "danda" (1, p. 48).

The concept of danda, unlike the concept of data, is an unfamiliar one. Data are the elements of invariant evidence discovered by the instruments of the empirical sciences and by the formal rules of logic and mathematics; danda inevitably involve hypotheses. To illustrate the characteristics of danda Pepper effectively cites two passages—one from H. H. Price, the other from John Dewey—in which each thinker, convinced that he is describing the ultimately given in the perception of an object, e.g. a red tomato, provides an account quite different from that of the other, since each has imported into his descriptions the danda of the theory to which he is committed. Hence danda intrude into even the most critical cognitions of perceptual experience, and, unlike data, they appear as facts corroborated structurally rather than multiplicatively. As Pepper elucidates: "Danda are the facts that seem to be given as we note the extended corroboration of fact by fact. Or, better, danda are facts that *ought* to be given if the hypothesis which describes an extended mass of structural corroboration were true" (1, p. 70). He adds elsewhere: "A dandum is what ought to be the precise determination of the evidence presented if it has the structural relationships with the other items of evidence which confirm it; or, abstractly stated, if the theory of the structure of the evidence is true" (1, p. 324).

The issue between positivism and metaphysics Pepper pins to the rejection or acceptance of danda. Positivism is defined as that type of philosophy which restrictively identifies knowledge with beliefs founded on data (1, p. 60). Permissible as a method which rightly stresses the role of data in science, positivism is condemned when it becomes dictatorial and dismisses danda and the beliefs dependent upon danda. As Pepper insists, positivism then inconsistently requires the very sort of evidence and beliefs it denies (1, p. 64).

Assured of the possibility of structural corroboration and of beliefs supported by danda, Pepper takes seriously the metaphysical enterprise of constructing world hypotheses which reach beyond the limits of science.

Root Metaphor Theory

A world hypothesis "is one that all the facts will corroborate, a hypothesis of unlimited scope" (1, p. 77). By "unlimited scope" is meant the capacity of the hypothesis to explain every fact, permitting no isolated fact to fall outside it. Besides unlimited scope, a world hypothesis claims to be precise, to fit exactly, to conform to, to apply to, to describe or refer to the facts under consideration (1, p. 76). The adequacy of a world hypothesis depends upon its scope and precision, and world hypotheses are evaluated according to their adequacy.

World hypotheses are objects in the world, comprising a class of objects whose peculiarity is that its members "cannot reject anything as irrelevant" (1, p. 1). Thus Pepper wishes "to study world hypotheses as objects existing in the world, to examine them empirically as a zoologist studies species of animals, a psychologist varieties of perception, a mathematician geometrical systems" (1, p. 2). To explain the origin of world hypotheses and by consequence to illuminate the systematic character and interrelatedness of their categories, Pepper has framed an hypothesis concerning world hypotheses—the root metaphor theory. According to this theory, the key to the construction of a world hypothesis is some area of commonsense fact in terms of which all other areas of fact are interpreted. This original area of experience becomes, therefore, the "basic analogy or root metaphor" of the world hypothesis (1, p. 91). By means of the root metaphor theory Pepper classifies and describes the principal types of world hypotheses.

Principal World Hypotheses

According to Pepper, there are four principal world hypotheses: formism, mechanism, organicism, and contextualism. These four, along with the inadequate world hypotheses of generating-substance, animism, and mysticism, encompass the entire history of Western philosophy. Pepper's four principal world hypotheses match those which Ralph Barton Perry believed to be the present philosophical tendencies: organicism is idealism, mechanism is naturalism, contextualism is pragmatism, and formism is realism (7, pp. 8–10). But where Perry stressed epistemology and method, Pepper emphasizes the structure of the categories and their source in common experience. At any rate, for Pepper, each world hypothesis stems from a root metaphor which generates its set of categories, and each, while preserving its categorial integrity, embraces tolerantly a variety of philosophical representations.

Formism Commonly called "realism," formism is the world hypothesis associated with Plato, Aristotle, the medieval scholastics, and their contemporary heirs (1, p. 141). "The root metaphor of formism is similarity"; it is embodied in two types of commonsense experience, which give rise to two species of formism (1, p. 151): immanent formism (1, p. 152), and transcendent formism (1, p. 162). Immanent formism springs from the observation of the common characters of particular things; its categories, consequently, are characters, particulars, and participation (1, p. 154). These categories pertain to things as these things are. Transcendent formism originates in the commonsense experience of the artisan working to produce some object according to a plan or in the observation of organisms developing as if according to a plan (1, p. 162); its categories are norms, matter, and the principles for the exemplification of norms in matter (1, p. 163). These categories pertain to things as these things may be or ought to be. Amalgamation of the two species of formism, though never quite complete, has been attempted, with a resultant merger of their categories (1, p. 170).

As regards scope, formism is an excellent hypothesis, firmly grounded in the pervasive experience of similarity and ample enough to include all facts. However, it suffers from imprecision. A dispersive theory, formism permits multiple and even inconsistent interpretations of the facts (1, p. 142).

Mechanism Commonly called "naturalism" or "materialism," mechanism is associated with Democritus, Lucretius, Descartes,

Hobbes, Locke, Berkeley (14), and Hume (1, p. 141). "The root metaphor of mechanism is a machine. It may be a machine like a watch or a machine like a dynamo" (1, p. 186). The difference in type of machine is fundamental, signaling a shift from a mechanical theory of matter, which takes the physical atom or atomic particle for the ultimate unit of reality in the universe, to an electrical theory of matter, which points to the electromagnetic field as the basic reality. Mechanism, then, is either discrete or consolidated (1, p. 187).

The categories of mechanism are of two sorts: primary and secondary. The primary categories are field of location (space), primary qualities, and laws expressing the relatedness of primary qualities in the field; the secondary categories are secondary qualities, laws connecting secondary qualities to primary categories, and laws expressing the relatedness of secondary qualities (1, pp. 193–94).

As an integrative theory, mechanism capably explains facts precisely in a tightly systematic manner, but it achieves its precision at the expense of scope. While the strength of mechanism flows from its ties with natural science, its weakness resides in the gap between its primary categories, which it handles so effectively, and its secondary categories, which have to do with qualities and values (1, p. 121).

Organicism   Commonly called "absolute idealism," organicism is associated with Schelling, Hegel, T. H. Green, F. H. Bradley, Bernard Bosanquet, and Josiah Royce (1, pp. 141–42). Its root metaphor is often confused with "organism," but because of the heavily loaded biological connotation of that term, it is more accurately identified with the historic event, provided stress is placed upon the integration of the event rather than upon the duration of its process (1, pp. 280–81).

Because every historic event is an organic process involving both structure of integration and temporal process, the categories of organicism are twofold: progressive and ideal. The progressive categories, noting "the steps involved in the organic process" (1, p. 281), are: first, fragments of experience; second, relations and implications of these fragments; third, contradictions and oppositions; and fourth, the organic whole (1, p. 283). The organic whole, coming at the end of a temporal process, is the last of the progressive and the first of the ideal categories. "Noting the principal features in the organic structure ultimately achieved or realized" (1, p. 281), the ideal categories include: fifth, the implicitness of the organic whole in the fragments; sixth, its transcendence of the contradictions, etc.; and seventh, its economy and salvational function (1, p. 283).

Like mechanism, organicism is an integrative theory; its strength is vigorously displayed in the systematic manner in which it deals with its facts, but its concomitant defect, manifest in its usage of the concepts of appearance and reality, is its incapacity to treat facts on an equal footing. The achievement of organicism resides in its description of mind in the creative pursuit of truth; its crucial failure lies in the contradiction between its progressive and its ideal categories. "Organicism . . . requires the progressive categories to give it scope, yet the progressive categories involve time and change and finitude; yet time and change and finitude cannot be true, since only the absolute is true and in the absolute is no time, nor change, nor finitude" (1, p. 314).

Contextualism Commonly called "pragmatism," contextualism is associated with Peirce, James, Bergson, Dewey, and Mead (1, p. 141). Pepper's presentation of pragmatism as a metaphysics, one of the most original parts of *World Hypotheses*, establishes it on a footing equal to that accorded more ancient philosophies. For its root metaphor contextualism, like organicism, has the historic event. Pepper writes: "The real historic event, the event in its actuality, is when it is going on *now*, the dynamic dramatic active event. We may call it an 'act,' if we like, and if we take care of our use of the term. But it is not an act conceived as alone or cut off that we mean; it is an act in and with its setting, an act in its context" (1, p. 232).

The major categories of contextualism are change, novelty, quality, and texture (1, p. 235). Pepper has elaborated contextualism in aesthetics in his book *Aesthetic Quality*, and more discussion of these categories will follow later. At present it is worth noting that since contextualism, unlike organicism, has no ideal categories, it emphasizes the process, its novelties and vivid qualities. The consequence is that contextualism is dispersive, explaining facts in alternative ways, that it is tentative in all its conjectures about the structure of the world, and that it is ready to ascribe to the cosmos ineradicable indeterminateness and chance. Thus Pepper confronts the contextualist with a dilemma: "Either you must confine yourself to believing only in the facts of direct verification, in which case your theory lacks scope; or if you admit the validity of indirect verification and acquire scope, you must admit that nature has a determinate structure and so fall into the contradiction of both affirming and denying this structure of nature" (1, p. 279). To which the contextualist is granted the swift reply: "How can you be so sure that nature is not intrinsically changing and full of novelties?" (1, p. 279).

Eclecticism

These four principal world hypotheses are equally adequate, although none is absolutely free of weaknesses. Equal adequacy portends tolerance. No world hypothesis can be established merely by exposing the difficulties of its rivals. Indeed, no world hypothesis may disparage the factual interpretations of the rival world hypotheses. It is tempting to suppose that it would be simple to arrive at a superior world hypothesis through eclecticism, but such a supposition would be entirely mistaken. "Each world hypothesis is autonomous" (1, p. 98). And the autonomy of each assures its freedom from refutation. This same autonomy precludes the mixture of one world hypothesis with another. Bluntly Pepper lays down the maxim: "Eclecticism is confusing" (1, p. 104).

No doubt the avoidance of eclecticism sharpens the clarity of Pepper's exposition of each world hypothesis. Yet Pepper does not absolutely exclude eclecticism from all contexts, since, in his own italicized words, he stands for *"rational clarity in theory and reasonable eclecticism in practice"* (1, p. 330). In practice much is gained in the investigation of a subject when the judgments of the subject from the standpoints of all four world hypotheses are considered. Pepper defines "reasonable" or "postrational" eclecticism as "simply the recognition of the equal or nearly equal adequacy of a number of world theories and a recommendation that we do not fall into the dogmatism of neglecting any one of them" (1, p. 342).

Pepper's contributions to aesthetics conform to his rule against eclecticism in theory and his approval of postrational eclecticism in practice. *Aesthetic Quality* is a pure contextualistic theory, perhaps the only pure one ever to be expounded. *Principles of Art Appreciation*, where philosophical speculations are kept to a minimum, stresses "the value of pleasure in art" because it is "the easiest approach for our times, the least controversial" (3, p. iii), and so is explicitly based upon a naturalistic or mechanistic theory. Yet *The Basis of Criticism in the Arts* affords an outstanding application of reasonable eclecticism in practice. And without disparaging the claims of any of the major theories, *The Work of Art* attempts to define precisely what a work of art is.

A Contextualistic Aesthetics

Aesthetic Quality is, as its subtitle proclaims, *A Contextualistic Theory of Beauty*. Having outlined an aesthetic theory on pragmatic principles as early as 1932, Pepper was shocked by the appearance in 1934 of John Dewey's *Art as Experience*, for Dewey's book contained, besides the anticipated pragmatist elements, wholly unexpected organistic elements. Needless to reiterate, for Pepper eclecticism in aesthetics, as in metaphysics, is confusing. Thus in *Aesthetic Quality* Pepper presents a pure contextualistic theory. He affirms that "there is very little stated in *Aesthetic Quality* that is not also better stated in *Art as Experience*." The point, he continues, "is merely that many things are *not* stated in *Aesthetic Quality* which are said in *Art as Experience*, and which I believe should not be said by a pragmatist" (15, p. 372). Pepper's exposition of a contextualistic point of view in aesthetics, however, is avowedly undogmatic, since it is recognized to be "only one of several equally good points of view" (4, p. 7).

A single sentence sums up Pepper's contextualistic aesthetics:

"Quality is the life of art, organization the body" (4, p. 114). "A great work of art is an organization of intense qualities" (4, p. 116). Since Pepper's comprehensive treatment of organization in art leads into the technical details of art, its elements and composition (4, Ch. v–viii), and so bears on topics beyond our present concern, we shall bypass it and proceed to his theory of quality. Above all, quality distinctively defines the aesthetic field. As Pepper writes: "The aesthetic field is that of the quality of events. Great beauty is great enhancement of quality" (4, p. 19).

Although quality, as "an ultimate notion or category in contextualism," is indefinable (4, p. 21), it is not closed to theoretical understanding. It may be understood by means of the description and analysis of qualitative occurrences and their relations to other categories. Pepper proceeds by elucidating an event characterized by quality. The event selected for this purpose is, of course, an aesthetic event: a spectator sees a painting.

To understand quality, then, it is necessary to understand event, the root metaphor of contextualism. Stressing process and change, Pepper defines an event as "a section of continuous duration or temporal flow." He adds that "events in all their details and in themselves are processes" (4, p. 32). Isolate a single process in the event, and you have what Pepper calls a "strand." Detect a connected pattern of strands, and you have what he calls a "texture" (4, p. 32). According to this analysis, the complex aesthetic event of spectator-perceiving-painting consists of the personal texture of the organism and the impersonal texture of the painting, so that it is a personal-impersonal texture.

Quality is a character of every event and changes along with the event. This type of quality is what Pepper calls "event quality" (4, p. 40). While analysis enables us to grasp the structure of the event and its relationship to other events, it is helpless when we seek event quality, since this quality consists in the feeling of the event as a totality (4, p. 21). Here Pepper joins with such thinkers as Benedetto Croce and Henri Bergson in recommending that we engage in intuition until "all details vanish and a rich quality takes full possession of the event" (4, p. 27). With Pepper, however, pure intuition plays a significant cognitive role. Effectuating the grasp of immediacy, which Pepper describes as "the beginning and end of all knowledge" (4, p. 30), intuition is "the most illuminating of activities." He writes: "It gives us direct insight into the nature of the world. It shows us what is real there, it realizes events. To feel the quality of an event is to feel the actual working of a part of the world process. It is to stop swimming and rest upon a wave, and to feel the cosmic currents, and the movement of the world swell. Art is thus fully as cognitive, fully as knowing as science" (4, p. 31).

Besides "event quality," which is apprehended only through intuition, there is another kind of quality called "relationship quality," which is cognized through the method of intuited analysis (4, p. 40) and of which there are two kinds: similarity and individuality. Pepper writes: "Similarity, on analysis, consists in two or more textures having strands which converge, or tend to converge, upon another texture or upon a strand of another texture, which is said to be common to the first two textures. Thus all the chairs in this room are similar because I can sit in any one of them. They all have strands leading into the texture of my intention to sit down" (4, pp. 40–41). Although the quality of similarity, attained through analytic understanding, is indispensable to practical usage and to science, it is not basic to aesthetics, since it is a "thin quality." However, the relationship quality of individuality is basic; in Pepper's terms, it is "the central principle of massive aesthetic experience" (4, p. 42).

Interwoven with the continuous flow of events, the quality of individuality "involves the sense that cables of strands carry over from one event into another and another, and even when spread apart can be reassembled and spun again" (4, p. 42). Thus the quality of individuality is the result of fusion and funding. After acknowledging his indebtedness to John Dewey for having pointed out how the aesthetic value of beauty consists in the fusion of qualities into a single whole, Pepper has sought, especially in later work, to provide a deeper and more probing clarification of this conception (6, pp. 151 ff.). Fusion is the flowing together of qualities into a sensuously immediate whole, and funding is a specific type of fusion involving memory (6, p. 153). "Funding is the fusion of meanings from past experiences into a present experience" (6, p. 21). Pepper goes so far as to suggest that there are no absolutely simple qualities; he holds that "the concept of fusion is coextensive with that of quality and enters into every event that quality does" (6, p. 171).

As Dewey has taught that the purpose of art is the enhancement of direct experience, Pepper conceives the job of the artist to be the heightening of quality. Whereas intellectual analytical activity, practical activity, and the regular activity of habit or monotony deaden quality, the artist strives to intensify quality through novelty and conflict, and to do this he must stimulate emotion. First of all, emotion is "the very essence of quality." It is, in fact, "the very quality of the event itself when this event is voluminous, intense, and highly fused" (4, p. 89). Moreover, since emotion arises from the blockage of a vital pattern of action, it follows that "conflict is the source of emotion" (4, p. 94). At any rate, the artist deals in emotions because his task is to intensify quality through novelty and conflict (3, Ch. 6).

What, then, is novelty? Pepper distinguishes three senses of the concept (4, p. 61). First, there is the novelty of *uniqueness*. Every event differs from every other event merely by its occurrence; each exhibits the novelty of uniqueness, being this here-now and no other. Pepper does not regard the novelty of uniqueness as special to the field of aesthetics. Second, there is *naïve* novelty. It consists in the intrinsic vividness of quality of an event. As Pepper puts it, "there is first the fresh event intrinsically glowing with quality" (4, p. 71). The original condition of every event, naïve quality is unfortunately too soon eroded by the deadening processes of intellectual, practical, and regular activities. The rescue of novelty from the dullness of analytic understanding, habit, and monotony involves the third kind —*intrusive* novelty. Although art does try to get back to naïve quality, its usual course—since habit is a pervasive feature of life—is to follow the method of intrusive novelty, to seek "not the avoidance of habit but a vivifying of the structure of the aesthetically troublesome habit itself" (4, p. 65). This method, moreover, involves "the intrusion of one habit into the fringe of another making the event glow by a suppressed and hardly noticeable conflict" (4, p. 71).

"Conflict is an extreme case of intrusive novelty" (4, p. 72). Conflict enhances quality, it promotes intrusive novelty, by ranging habit against habit or against some other obstacle. Pepper cites dramatic conflict, which pits purpose against purpose, as the most effective form of conflict in art. He says: "The ideal aesthetic material . . . seems to be a rich, resourceful, and strong personality stirred by a powerful drive to some end, in the way of the attainment of which resistant and stinging obstacles are placed" (4, pp. 74–75).

A Theory of Criticism

While *Aesthetic Quality* is occupied solely with the presentation of a purely contextualistic aesthetics, *The Basis of Criticism in the Arts*—which Pepper has designated a "prolongation" of the conclusions of *World Hypotheses* into the field of aesthetic criticism —advances mechanism, formism, and organicism, along with contextualism, as affording equally adequate bases for criticism. In the last analysis, Pepper in this work adopts a reasonable eclecticism in practice whereby all four theories are employed in estimating the value of a work of art. At the outset it should be made clear that, despite the objections (16), his theory of criticism is not a mere deduction from his metaphysics. A brief examination of his philosophical career, as is evident from his writings, reveals that Pepper's experience with the arts and his concomitant concern with aesthetics developed at the same time as, if not prior to, his concern with metaphysics. Indeed, his conception of the root metaphor as the ground of metaphysics has the ring of the literary art, and the very manner in which he depicts the world hypotheses—particularly organicism and contextualism—triggers associations with musical and pictorial compositions. Further, Pepper is quite clear in pointing out that his approach to the theory of criticism is determined by the evidence and by the best means of handling this evidence. The facts upon which aesthetic theory rests are, of course, values. Much more will be said about Pepper's theory of value below. Here it suffices to note that, for Pepper, an aesthetic theory descriptively defines the aesthetic field with attention fixed on aesthetic facts (values), and that from the aesthetic field are derived standards of criticism, quantitative measures for determining the amounts of aesthetic value. Although aesthetic criticism is bound up with metaphysics, it yet remains empirical. "The problem of criticism is ultimately the problem of the evidence for the legitimacy of the criteria of criticism" (5, pp. 3–4). Since there are four equally adequate world hypotheses capable of handling all evidence, there are four critical theories, linked with these hypotheses, capable of handling all aesthetic evidence.

The novelty of Pepper's position in criticism, therefore, consists in "the thesis that there are at present a number of equally adequate criteria, which need to be kept in mind and adjusted to one another for the full understanding of the aesthetic value either of a single work, or of an artist's total achievement" (5, p. 16). Let us briefly look at each of these four theories. Mechanism in aesthetics, best represented by Walter Pater, George Santayana, and David Prall, defines "the field of aesthetic values" to be "things liked or disliked for themselves"; it locates values in "the feelings of pleasure and displeasure" (5, p. 44). The critical standards of mechanistic aesthetics are "the intrinsic dimensions of pleasure and displeasure, namely, the number, duration, and intensity of them" (5, p. 45). Contextualism is aesthetics, represented by John Dewey and Irwin Edman, defines the aesthetic field as "voluntary vivid intuitions of quality" (5, p. 56); and the contextualistic standard is: "The more vivid the experience and the more extensive and rich its quality, the greater its aesthetic value" (5, p. 57). Organicism in aesthetics, represented by Schelling, Coleridge, Hegel, and Bosanquet, identifies value with integration, aesthetic value with the "integration of feelings" (5, p. 74). The organicist standard consists in "the degree of integration and the amount of material integrated" (5, p. 79). Formism in aesthetics, represented by Plato, Aristotle, the medieval scholastics, John Ruskin, and Hippolyte Taine, describes aesthetic value broadly as "conformity to natural norms" (5, p. 105), and more strictly as the field of "perceptions satisfying in themselves to the normal man" (5, p. 107). Stressing conformity to a norm, formistic aesthetics centers on the normal man as a biological, psychological, and social entity and makes of him "a sort of governor over the whole aesthetic field. It holds art to the healthy golden mean, to what is sane and sound" (5, p.111).

Each theory justifies a particular set of objective critical judgments of the work of art. Since the four theories are equally adequate, it follows that four equally valid sets of objective judgments can be made upon every work of art. Thus in practical criticism Pepper recommends the method of reasonable eclecticism. To illustrate this method Pepper selects a sonnet by Shakespeare and one by Gerard Manley Hopkins and evaluates each from the standpoints of all four theories (5, Ch. 6). This new type of criticism, esteeming Shakespeare's sonnet beautiful according to all four theories and Hopkins' beautiful only according to one, is significant not because of what it discloses about the respective merits of the two works of literary art, but rather because of its broad implications for critical theory and practice. The method is meaningful and original in that it calls, on the one hand, for tolerance among equally adequate aesthetic theories and, on the other hand, for the fullest possible appreciation of the art object allowable on the basis of all four theories.

The Art Object

As early as 1937, Pepper recognized, in a discussion of the individuality of the art object, that the work of art has two distinct aspects—physical and aesthetic (17, p. 83). Then, in an article published in 1943, Pepper sought to define, after a consideration of the types of aesthetic judgments, what an aesthetic object is (18). He noted that there are three types of aesthetic judgments: the judgment of the aesthetic value of immediate experience, the judgment of the aesthetic value of a work of art or thing of nature, and the judgment of aesthetic taste; and he concluded that each type of judgment reveals a different facet of the aesthetic object. Even in *The Basis of Criticism in the Arts,* where he was primarily occupied with the theories and practice of criticism, he came to perceive, at least toward the end, the need for a clarification of *that about which* the theories and the critical judgments are made. To meet this need he tacked on a supplementary essay treating the nature of the aesthetic object. This essay provoked pointed discussion in the journals, pressing Pepper to reply that what he had written was both ambiguous and incomplete (19). In 1953 he seized the opportunity

afforded by his Mahlon Powell Lectures at Indiana University, published as *The Work of Art*, to advance an unambiguous theory of
the art object. Marking off three facets of the work of art—the control object, the perceptions of aesthetic immediacy, and the object
of criticism—these lectures shift focus from judgment and its criteria to the *object* of judgment. By consequence, the work of art
emerges into sharply sketched objectivity, each of its three distinct
facets at last clearly described.

The control object, or aesthetic vehicle, whether a physical work
of art or a natural object of beauty, is "that continuously existing
object, generally physical in nature, which carries the aesthetic values, preserves them and controls them for perception" (6, p. 16).
Its two essential properties are its permanence, or continuous existence, and its capacity as a stimulus or a set of stimuli. As a con-
figuration of physical properties, the control object in such arts as
painting or sculpture is the actual thing which is subject to barter
or exposition, although in other arts, such as poetry, it is indeed
quite a thin physical object. But since on the one hand it is composed of continuously existing physical elements, and on the other
hand it stimulates a human nature also constituted of constant patterns and in conformance with social traditions, the control object
is a stable factor in the aesthetic experience.

The perception of aesthetic immediacy is "the experience a spectator has at any one time when stimulated by the vehicle. This
is the object we see and feel and fill with meaning" (6, p. 17).
Here within the area of experience the aesthetic object appears
as a consummatory satisfaction, as a value directly enjoyed for
itself. But unlike the enduring control object, the perception of
aesthetic immediacy is fugitive, lasting only a few seconds at most.
Indeed, its transiency serves to heighten the need for fusion to facilitate a cumulation of fleeting perceptions. For fusion, according
to Pepper, shows how "a present perception can enfold and have
telescoped into it a great quantity of previous perceptions of the
same object" (6, p. 26). Such fusion, however, leads directly beyond
the mere perception of aesthetic immediacy to the object of criticism.

At one time termed "the aesthetic work of art" to distinguish it from "the physical work of art" or the control object, the object of criticism is "some sort of synthesis or evaluative goal of the sequence of perceptual immediacies" (6, p. 30). While Pepper describes it as the "object perceived by a person who has become a competent spectator," he notes that "it is not the taste of the competent spectator that defines the object but his capacity to respond to the relevant materials" (6, p. 38). Here the emphasis is put upon the relevant materials, for, above all, the object of criticism is an object, so complex an object, in fact, that Pepper approaches it by means of all four equally adequate critical theories in order to avoid neglecting or missing any part of its value. Like the control object, the object of criticism has an enduring existence; yet, like the perception of aesthetic immediacy, it is, when in the presence of a competent spectator, available to immediate experience. Pepper explains this dual character by means of the concept of dispositional properties. A dispositional property, he says repeatedly, is a potentiality; it has a seat and a character. The seat of a dispositional property is the actual physical thing in which it exists. Its character is what it is realized to be when the conditions necessary for its realization are met. Strictly speaking, the object of criticism is a dispositional property or a set of dispositional properties. Its seat is the control object; its character is the optimum consummatory area or the optimum area of appreciation of the relevant characters stimulated by the control object (6, p. 55). Thus the object of criticism is, literally, "a potentiality or dispositional property of the vehicle" (6, p. 31).

THEORY OF VALUES

Pepper's theory of values, influenced by the interest theory of Ralph Barton Perry and the purposive behaviorism of Edward Tolman, is empirical and naturalistic. Pepper's original plan for his major work in value theory, *The Sources of Value*, was like that for *The Basis of Criticism in the Arts*—to begin with a mechanistic theory of value, and, when that vein appeared exhausted, to shift to a formistic theory, and so on. But the discovery of the concept of "selective system" altered this and became the element of linkage for all the empirical phases of value. Thus *The Sources of Value* proposes "a comprehensive hypothesis of the main lines of relationship among the facts bearing on human decisions" (9, p. 1). Instead of assuming, as Perry did, that there is a common character of value running through all values (9, p. 10), Pepper adopts a field-oriented approach. Since the problem of human decision-making obviously exists, and since decisions may be good or bad, there is, Pepper explicitly presumes, a field of facts relevant to this problem, and this field of facts is nothing less than the field of values (9, p. 14).

This field of values, moreover, is amenable to empirical investigation, and, like any field of facts, it is subject to descriptive definition. Pepper writes: "A descriptive definition stipulates that a symbol shall be defined by a set of symbols which truly describe a field of facts. The symbol is defined by a true description of facts. The expression is a definition because it consists in a stipulation regarding the meaning of a symbol. But it is also stipulated that what is meant by the symbol shall be a description true to fact. Such a definition by stipulation is characterized by truth to fact" (9, pp. 280–81). Descriptive definitions of values signal the qualitative criteria that differentiate values from other kinds of facts (9, pp. 283 ff.). Consequently, they serve also as the criteria of evaluative judgment. Descriptive definitions of values contain concepts which may be employed quantitatively, in ethics as in aesthetics, to ascertain the amount or degree of value possessed by the facts to which they are applied (9, pp. 288 ff.). According to Pepper, therefore, cognitively objective, empirically verifiable judgments are as possible in the field of values as they are in the field of physical facts. And because of the seriousness of human decision-making, they are certainly no less urgent.

Now Pepper's advocacy of an empirical, naturalistic value theory, like Lewis', comes at a time when linguistic ethics, almost dominant in recent discussions of values in Great Britain and the United States, denies that value judgment is a cognitively true or false estimation of empirically testable facts. Pepper distinguishes two schools of linguistic ethics—the intuitionists and the value (or emotive) judgment schools (9, p. 19)—and he rejects both. The intuitionists, led by G. E. Moore, analyze value terms such as "good" and conclude that these terms denote indefinable, intuitable qualities, while the value judgment theorists—emotivists such as A. J. Ayer and Charles Stevenson, or prescriptivists such as R. M. Hare—analyze value judgments and conclude that they are not cognitively meaningful statements which are either true or false but rather emotive or prescriptive statements capable of influencing human action. Against the intuitionists Pepper argues that the reports of their allegedly cognitive intuitions are often incompatible, that such intuitions, even if real, have no directive influence on human behavior, and that whatever content they possess proves, upon analysis, to be borrowed from one or more of the empirical theories they deny (10, pp. 271–74). Against the emotivists and the prescriptivists Pepper raises several objections, many of which are explicit in the discussions of C. I. Lewis and Brand Blanshard contained in this volume.

But Pepper's most trenchant and original line of criticism, in which he shares with the emotivists and prescriptivists the desire to preserve the traditional role of value judgments as directive of human behavior, culminates in a dilemma. Thus Pepper asks of the emotivist or prescriptivist:

Is he defining the field of ethics as that of linguistic imperatives (and the like) or the dynamic emotive behavior that frequently manifests itself in imperative (and other) linguistic forms? If the former, he turns ethics into a branch of linguistics: namely, the study of those forms of sentences which are neither true or false. But in doing this [he] would lose contact with the usage of the term "ethics" and its traditional concern with dynamic human conduct. If, however, he accepts the other alternative and defines the subject matter of ethics as types of emotive behavior often expressed in imperative gestures and words, he becomes an ethical empiricist capable of giving descriptions of these facts—declarative sentences, true or false. But then he abandons the characteristic tenet of his school which is that value judgments are neither true nor false (10, p. 285).

The Purposive Act

To find "the best available answers to man's most engrossing problem—how to obtain well-grounded decisions for action"—Pepper enters "the study of the commonsense field of value by way of purposive behavior, and thence work[s], area by area, over the whole field" (9, p. 34). He therefore sets out to expound a psychological theory of the purposive act. Adhering to a behavioristic method modified sufficiently to permit introspection to operate within an objective framework (9, pp. 35–37), Pepper concentrates on the purposive act because, like Ralph Barton Perry, he expects to find therein the basis for a general theory of value. Like Perry, too, he defines purposive activity as "docile adaptive behavior," for purposive acts are "acts which prepare against a future contingency, not automatically but in a *novel* manner specifically suited to the contingency. The organism *invents* the means of meeting the situation. He learns how to handle it. He exhibits *intelligent* behavior" (9, p. 39).

Positive purposive activity is appetition. A superordinate act, the appetitive purposive act exhibits a structure which consists of three principal features: the governing propensity, subordinate acts, and the goal (9, p. 45).

The governing propensity consists of two main parts: the drive and the anticipatory set (9, p. 47). "The drive supplies the energy for purposive activity" (9, p. 49). Furthermore, it is characterized by three features: an impulsive pattern, which is either a bodily need or a neuromuscular tension, and which supplies the dynamics of the drive; conditions of quiescence, which determine the goal of the impulse; and innate readinesses, which are links along the path of the drive and help it to its goal. Besides considering the nature of the drive, Pepper inquires into the number. Are drives reducible to one, or are they irreducibly many? His answer is a modified multiple drive theory, designating as drives such instinctive appetites as hunger, thirst, sex, elimination, etc.

If the drive is the dynamic engine of the purposive act, the blind instinctive impulse supplying all the energy, the anticipatory set is its cognitive directing eye (9, p. 49). "The function of this set is to specify a goal for the selective guidance of the organism toward the quiescence of the drive. It is to show the organism an object that will satisfy the drive or serve as a means to its attainment" (9, p. 63). The anticipatory set is a cognitive act and is susceptible to error as well as truth; Pepper describes it as a kind of hypothesis subject to verification (9, p. 67). "Anticipatory sets come into being by a process of learning" (9, p. 88). Hence Pepper examines a learning theory and finds in trial-and-error activity, based upon conditioned reflex learning with some additions, the basis of inventive learning characteristic of the highest intelligence (9, Ch. 5). Along with other factors, anticipatory sets and their development through learning are influential in the effectuation of value mutations, i.e. changes in the goals from which the purposive organism anticipates the quiescence of his impulse patterns.

The subordinate acts constitute the second feature of the structure of the purposive act. They serve "to fill the gap between the drive and its quiescence pattern" (9, p. 115). Although the subordinate act possesses a structure similar to that of the superordinate act, its function differs. A subordinate act is a means to an end, the end being the satisfaction of the drive. Explicitly rejecting Dewey's means-end continuum, Pepper declares that satisfaction is terminal (9, pp. 118 ff.). Sometimes the subordinate acts fail to reach the goal set by the anticipatory set, and the purposive activity is blocked. When blockage occurs, the original impulse may be diverted to another goal, or a new impulse may occur either to strengthen the original one or to seek a different goal. In any case a value mutation occurs. At this juncture, Pepper adds to the theory of drives as instinctive impulses a theory of injectives. An injective is "an innate drive." But Pepper continues: "It is not an instinctive appetition since its goal is always (except in the special conditions when it acts independently) a subordinate goal within some other purposive activity. . . . It functions in an instrumental role, backing up another impulse" (9, p. 161). Fright, aggression, initiative are injectives (9, p. 166). Pepper pauses to remark that moralists have wrongly indicted man's appetitions and ignored his injectives as the sources of moral and social disorders (9, pp. 162–63).

The goal of the appetitive purposive act is the third feature of its structure. It consists of two factors: the goal object and the quiescence pattern. The goal object is "the object of reference of the anticipatory set," and the quiescence pattern is "the reciprocal of the impulse pattern of the drive and the actualization of the conditions of the quiescence" (9, p. 167). Devoting almost an entire chapter to criticisms of Perry's alleged neglect of the quiescence pattern and exclusive emphasis on the goal object (9, Ch. 9), Pepper insists that the terminus of the appetitive purposive act is not the goal object, which is simply the condition for the terminus, but rather the quiescence pattern construed as the reduction of tension. This quiescence pattern he equates with pleasure (9, pp. 196–98).

Not all purposive activity is positive in the manner of appetition. Some is negative, and negative purposive activity is aversion. Pepper tackles the task of constructing a theory of aversion. He describes the basic structure of simple aversion to consist of a riddance pattern, an injective, a quiescence of riddance pattern, and a quiescence of injective (9, p. 201). A riddance pattern occurs when some unpleasant or painful event hurts the organism sufficiently for it actively to seek escape from the disturbing source of stimulation (9, p. 200). The riddance pattern triggers an injective, such as fright or aggression, to supply energy for the organism to act. The mollification of the riddance pattern, its quiescence, is followed by the quiescence of the injective. This simple structure of aversion, of course, may be further complicated by the addition of other elements, such as apprehensive sets. Indeed, throughout this very compressed, skeletal survey of purposive acts, important elements and complexities have been omitted which are included in the fuller sketch—along with numerous diagrams of purposive activity and its variations—which Pepper provides in his voluminous *Sources of Value*.

Now the question may arise: What has all this psychology of purposive acts to do with values? Only by turning to Pepper's concept of the selective system is the answer supplied. For the study of purposive activity is preliminary to the consideration of the concept of the selective system—the central concept in Pepper's investigation of values.

The Selective System

The concept of the selective system is "the guiding concept linking the successive levels of value"; it is regarded "as the defining concept for the term 'value' " (9, p. 3). Near the conclusion of the study, a selective system is defined as "a structural process by which a unitary dynamic agency is channeled in such a way that it generates particular acts, dispositions or objects (to be called 'trials'), and also activates a specific selective agency (to be called 'the norm') by which some of the trials are rejected and others are incorporated into the dynamic operation of the system" (9, pp. 667–68).

Whenever there is a relationship among facts such that some facts are selected and others are rejected in accord with criteria established by the relationship itself, there is a selective system, and this relationship is tantamount to a natural norm. For "a natural norm consists of a dynamic agency operating through a selective system which selects against some value facts and for others" (9, p. 286). Further, Pepper describes the dynamics of the selective system as a "split dynamics." He says:

The same dynamic agency which charges the norm in terms of which the selection is made likewise charges the trials which are pro and con. . . . The dynamics charging the norm and that charging the trials selected pro and con by the norm is the same. This is what makes the trials relevant to the norm, and also the selection of them pro and con. So to speak, the trials are compelled to recognize the authority of the norm to correct them, because their energy, their very life, has all its source in the energy of the norm. If the norm ceases to energize the trials, the trials receive no more energy; their life goes out; they cease to exist, and no more selections are made among these trials by the norm (9, p. 664).

In accord with this conception of the split dynamics of a selective system Pepper regards obligation as an empirical relation. He writes: "The relation of the trial act to the corrective agency is a relation of obligation. The trial act *ought* to conform to the requirements of the corrective agency. This 'ought' is sanctioned by the dynamics of the system, because, if the trial act fails to conform, not only will it be rejected by the normative agency in the system but also it will lose all the dynamics it contained, since the only motivation it had was that split off from the normative agency" (9, p. 366).

As an empirical relation, of course, obligation may be described in statements subject to verification (9, p. 367).

According to Pepper, there are seven principal selective systems: first, the structure of the purposive act; second, the consummatory field; third, the personal situation; fourth, the personality structure; fifth, the social situation; sixth, the cultural pattern; and seventh, natural selection (9, p. 663). Let us consider each in turn.

First, analysis of the psychological structure of the purposive act led Pepper to discover the centrality of selective systems in the field of values. "The stratified relationship of subordinate to superordinate acts in purposive behavior is one such system. It is only through this system that the superordinate act legislates selectively over the subordinate acts" (9, p. 286). In purposive behavior, besides the opposition of appetition to aversion, Pepper distinguishes three selective systems, each with its appropriate values. "They are *conative value*, colloquially known as desire (favor or liking versus disfavor or disliking), *achievement value* (success versus frustration), and *affective value* (pleasure versus pain or unpleasantness)" (9, pp. 304–305). The selective system of affective value is also the basis for the principal selective system of the consummatory field, to be considered below.

Pepper defines conative value as "the charge of a drive on an impulse pattern, a riddance pattern, or a cognitive set" (9, p. 320). This charge may be positive or negative, depending upon an organism's wanting or not-wanting (9, p. 313), and it may be measured according to intrinsic standards of intensity, duration, and number (9, p. 321). Achievement value also is either positive or negative. Pepper defines positive achievement value as success and negative achievement value as frustration, the former consisting in "the attainment either of the object or else of the quiescence of a set of conative references charged by a drive," the latter consisting in "the delay or failure of such attainment" (9, p. 331). It, too, may be measured by such standards as intensity and extensity as well as by those pertaining to speed and correctness, standards conspicuously linked with those of conative value (9, pp. 331–37). Pepper is persuaded that conation and achievement converge as phases of a single selective system (9, p. 327). The norm of the purposive act, of which the conative-achievement selective structure is the leading exemplification, is "the reduction of the drive" (9, p. 665). Finally, the values the purposive act yields are conative-achievement values (9, p. 668).

The second principal selective system is the one operating through and upon affection. Distinguishable from the conative-achievement structure, this system is the consummatory field of the organism (9, p. 340). Affective value is either positive or negative, identified with pleasure or pain. The norm of the consummatory area is "that of maximizing the gratuitous satisfactions available in the field" (9, p. 666). The values yielded by the consummatory field are affective values (9, p. 669).

Third, Pepper analyzes the personal situation as a selective system by way of Kurt Lewin's concept of an organism's life-space (9, Ch. 16). Lewin's concept, which describes "actual relations holding among anticipated sequences of acts, and . . . the degrees of freedom or of obstruction for these acts" (9, p. 412), is easily amalgamated with Pepper's conception of the purposive act with its drive component, anticipatory set, subordinate acts, and goal. The amalgamation, however, preserves the fundamental difference between purposive structure and life-space as distinctive selective systems: "one [the purposive structure] is primarily explanatory of choices of means for the satisfaction of a single drive; the other, primarily explanatory of choices between competing drives or the terminal potential objects of such drives" (9, p. 422). Further, the dynamics of life-space is derivative; it is "the dynamics of the component drives that enter into it," so that its "selective activity . . . is of the resultant type" (9, p. 451). Since the values in life-space—though the same as those in purposive acts—converge, conflict, cooperate, and interrelate in numerous ways, it is necessary to channel them so as to render them consistent with the reality of the situation. Hence prudence is the special virtue of the personal situation (9, pp. 432 ff.), inasmuch as the norm of this system is "that of the maximum of achievement and of gratuitous satisfaction available from the contributory drives in view of the reality of the situation"

(9, p. 666). The personal situation as a selective system yields prudential values (9, p. 670).

The fourth selective system, that of personality structure, marks a shift from the values of acts to the value of the agent (9, p. 455). Analyzing personality structure not merely as "a selective system determining what drives are released into life-space and what satisfactions will be demanded of a situation," but also, and more importantly, as an "integrative process" whose "distinctive trait is that it operates not on acts but on dispositions to act—that is, on drives and their interrelationships" (9, p. 456)—Pepper defines "personality as a system of dispositions for purposive behavior having its seat in a biological organism" (9, p. 463). In a lucid chapter with profound metaphysical overtones (9, Ch. 17) which draws upon insights gathered from Freudian individual psychology, Mead's social psychology, and the ethics of self-realization from its beginnings in Greek philosophy, Pepper delineates two types of norms of personality structure: "the roles and conscience demanding conformity, and the maximum of integration for the dispositions of the personality" (9, p. 666). The values which personality structure yields are character values (9, p. 670).

The fifth selective system is the social situation, and Pepper credits John Dewey with having called attention to it. (9, p. 519). Like the personal situation in the sphere of individual behavior, the social situation is a selective system instituting a natural norm; but, whereas drives comprise the dynamic elements in the personal situation, individual persons constitute the dynamic components in the social situation (9, p. 520). "The norm for a social situation is that of the maximum reduction of tension or attainment of consummatory satisfactions for all the persons involved so far as the reality of the situation will permit" (9, p. 666). The values yielded by the social situation are social values (9, p. 671).

The sixth selective system is the cultural pattern. "A cultural pattern is to a social situation what a personality structure is to a personal situation" (9, p. 571). Thus Pepper defines a cultural pattern as a set of dispositions whose seat "consists in the physical organisms of the persons interrelated by institutionalized behavior together with the artifacts embedded in these relations" (9, p. 573).

As personality structure imposes norms for conformity and personal integration, so the cultural pattern "institutes two types of norms: institutions, including religion, that demand conformity; and the maximum of cultural integration" (9, p. 667).

The seventh selective system is natural selection. At present, when philosophers tend to ignore the connection of evolution and ethics, Pepper stands out for his appreciation of Darwin's importance for value theory. Rejecting both the tooth-and-claw and the continuous progress concepts of evolution (9, pp. 616–27), Pepper contends that the dynamics of natural selection is provided by "the vital energy of an interbreeding population" (9, p. 627), that its norm is the continuance of the life of this population, and that consequently the values it generates are survival values. Moreover, with the advent of man as a social animal, evolution as selective system moves up from the biological to the cultural level. Then natural selection operates upon cultural patterns.

From a survey of the selective systems it is noticeable that while for the first three—the purposive act, the consummatory field, and the personal situation—the entire dynamics of the systems could be accounted for in terms of the basic drives designated in the examination of the purposive act, the dynamics of the remaining four systems cannot be similarly explained. The crucial turning point arises in the consideration of personality structure as selective system, for by means of the norm of conscience acts are selected which are often contrary to individual values. Not until natural selection is considered, however, does it become sharply evident that the dynamics of selective systems has another source in addition to instinctive purposive drives. Pepper sums up his conclusion this way:

Our enquiry has brought out that there are only two basic instigating dynamic sources for the selective systems listed above: one is the instinctive purposive drives; the other, the vital forces of evolutionary selection. The two dynamic sources overlap in many of the selective systems, and it is pertinent to remember that evolutionary selection underlies purposive selection even though the latter has acquired a sphere of independence among docile organisms. That is to say, purposive behavior with its repertory of drives is a product of natural selection, and will be maintained by natural selection as long as it remains adaptive, but it would surely be eliminated by natural selection if ever it should cease to be adaptive in its life zone (9, pp. 664–65).

The Ethics of Social Adjustment

In *The Sources of Value* aesthetic values drop almost entirely out of sight, so much so that Pepper himself has expressed surprise that he devotes no separate section to the examination of these values (9, p. 693). Of course, as he points out, this is justified, since he has extensively treated aesthetic values elsewhere. Moreover, he makes statements about the nature and status of aesthetic values *pari passu* in contexts dealing with other kinds of values, and he concludes the volume suggesting lines of connection between the treatments of the various selective systems and the different types of aesthetic theories (9, p. 698).

The Sources of Value does not concentrate upon aesthetics, but it obviously does focus on ethics and on the facts and criteria relevant to human decisions. In his *Ethics*, in fact, Pepper has isolated as "the pivot of ethical inquiry . . . human conduct or human purposive action and the criteria growing out of purposive action and determining its correctness or incorrectness," and he has observed that the actual scope of ethics includes "all criteria that have a normative control over the criteria embedded in human purposive action" and also "all acts, dispositions, institutions, and whatever else is subject to human purposive control" (10, p. 10). Each type of selective system delineated becomes the germ of a distinctive ethical theory. And in his *Ethics*, striving to introduce students to his own ethical theory by way of a critical assessment of the alternative theories, Pepper spells out the connection between the selective systems and particular theories and correlates, in some detail, selective systems with ethical theories. These correlations are: the cultural pattern with cultural relativism and cultural absolutism (10, Ch. 4), the purposive act, the consummatory field, and the personal situation with hedonism (10, Ch. 5), the social situation with pragmatic ethics (10, Ch. 7), personality structure with the self-realization theory (10, Ch. 8), and natural selection with the evolutionary theory of ethics (10, Ch. 9).

At first it might seem that, as in the case of the world hypotheses, Pepper would consent to the coexistence of a set of rival theories. However, in the field of values this is not his strategy. Each ethical theory delineated above is valid as far as it indicates a describable selective system determining a type of value; yet each is held inadequate for its failure to account for values lying beyond its range. Further, the problem of human decision-making is too pressing a practical problem to permit additional complication by the acknowledgment of several rival sets of criteria. Of course, a need for the unification of the criteria for human decisions does not guarantee such a unification. Yet throughout the field of values the structure of the selective system with its split dynamics is exemplified, and values are traced to two sources: the impulse patterns of individual organisms and the vital energy of the interbreeding population. Upon these foundations—common structure and sources— a unified theory of the field of values is constructed.

What bearing does this theory of values have upon ethics? Pepper's answer is that it leads to the ethics of social adjustment (10, Ch. 13). The ethics of social adjustment draws its evidence mainly from a consideration of the characteristic behavior of the selective systems, whereby some legislate over others. The interplay between values, involving the legislation of some over others, emerges conspicuously in the selective system of the personality structure, where conscience serves to check the drives of the individual for a self-realization incompatible with the survival of society. A bipolarity of human values exists between the individual values of purposive satisfactions and the survival values of man and his society. This bipolarity, stemming from the two sources of value, asserts its influence on ethical norms. The dynamics of the purposive drives, tending always to decrease social pressure, shapes the cultural pattern into an open society, the social situation into one of freedom, the personality structures of men into characters with initiative, their personal situations into situations of enjoyment, and their purposive structures into consummatory areas of pleasure. On the other hand, the dynamics of the evolutionary process, always increasing social pressure, molds the cultural pattern into that of the functional society, the social situation into one of security, the per-

sonality structures of men into disciplined characters, their personal
situations into situations of achievement, and their purposive structures into conative-achievement structures bent on success (10, p.
328). Moreover, this bipolar dynamics of value assumes sharp, unambiguous form in the competition between the two major types
of social organization: the individualistic democratic society with
its emphasis upon freedom and individual happiness, and the
functional authoritarian society with its emphasis upon security
and order (10, pp. 322–23).

As long as the individual values of purposive satisfactions and
the survival values of the group do not conflict, all is well. When,
however, they oppose each other, "man is confronted with his most
serious type of moral problem." Then, Pepper says, "some adjustment must be made for man's very survival or that of his society,
and this is what leads to the social adjustment theory" (10, p. 320).
What sort of adjustment? No simple formula can be given, since,
after all, the adjustments required will vary with the situations
which generate their need. Nevertheless, Pepper does offer a rule
of procedure: "Find out as well as you can what degree of social
pressure your society is subjected to" (10, p. 330). For, as he says,
"the degree of integration necessary for security, and the degree of
freedom of satisfactions that may be safely permitted, depends on
the social pressure upon a society. The greater the pressure the
greater the degree of social integration required; the less the pressure the greater the amount of freedom for the individual satisfactions safely available" (10, p. 323). This, in sum, is the meaning of
the ethics of social adjustment.

SELECTIVISM, A NEW WORLD HYPOTHESIS

Pepper's contributions to the theory of metaphysics, to aesthetics
and art criticism, to value theory, to ethics, diversified as they are
and developing over the years as they have, nevertheless exhibit a
unity of method and intention. Whether his philosophy will culminate in the kind of comprehensive account of man and the world
which only a world hypothesis can afford is the question which in
recent years Pepper has sought to resolve by proposing a new world

hypothesis (12). It appeared to him that "the most likely prospect for an adequate world hypothesis lay in a direction midway between the paths laid out by the mechanistic and the contextualistic categories" (20, p. 37). Pepper's discovery of the concept of selective system in the investigation of value has, indeed, suggested to him a fertile new root metaphor from which to project a novel world hypothesis. He has termed his new world hypothesis "selectivism" (12, p. 18).

Pepper has approached his new metaphysics by way of a critical examination of Whitehead's philosophy (21), his judgment of which has undergone a remarkable revision since the publication of *World Hypotheses*. Then, having condemned Whitehead for eclecticism, Pepper charged him with the illegitimate fusion of the incompatible positions of mechanism and formism, and with compounding the confusion with elements of contextualism and organicism. At that time Charles Hartshorne took issue with Pepper (22). According to Hartshorne, Whitehead had perceived a new root metaphor quite different from the traditional ones Pepper recognized, and Pepper had failed to take due notice of it. Hartshorne, in keeping with his own philosophical commitments, identified the new root metaphor in Whitehead as social in character, indicating the Whiteheadian conception of reality as a social process in which the societies of actual occasions are major factors.

Today Pepper is ready to concede that, in fact, Whitehead had groped for and successfully suggested a new root metaphor, although Pepper still differs with Hartshorne as to precisely what it is. Pepper sees Whitehead's new root metaphor as the "actual occasion," and this Pepper translates as the "purposive act." Taking the purposive act, then, as the root metaphor of a new metaphysics, Pepper proceeds to describe it.

Such an act, as we watch it going on, is through-and-through qualitative. It has a distinctive unity, drive, and aim. It has a degree of extensiveness both spatially and temporally. It is closely engaged with an environment with which it is in constant contact. It has simpler and more complex forms. It seems to involve in it every qualitative feature we can imagine. If one has come to believe that the actuality of the universe is qualitative throughout, and any appearances to the contrary are abstractions from this qualitative base, a purposive act is as fair a sample of such a whole as we are like to find (21, p. 74).

Of course, Pepper insists that there are numerous serious defects in Whitehead's treatment of the new root metaphor and in his elaboration of the original metaphysics which radiates from it. Of Whitehead Pepper succinctly remarks: "What he has succeeded in doing with a very limited and defective use of this root metaphor is perhaps a token of what might be done with it in a more extended way" (21, p. 88).

Pepper has listed the major sets of categories of the new world hypothesis based on the selective act. There are qualitative categories and conceptual categories (12, pp. 28–30). Qualitative categories include: categories for a single qualitative strand—such as felt quality, duration, intensity, reference to goal, blockage, splitting, selection, and satisfaction; categories of context of qualitative strand—such as simultaneity, articulation, anticipations, fusion, and specious present; and categories of qualitative range—such as the present, the past, the future, and the controlling environment (12, pp. 28–29). The conceptual categories include: categories for unit physical element—such as bodily action, continuity, energy, vector character of bodily energy, interaction with environmental activities, vector changes, selection of response mechanisms, quiescence patterns; categories of physical structure—such as body, articulation of behavior in an integrated act, dynamic dispositions; and categories of physical environment—such as space-time, and configurations of matter (12, pp. 29–30).

In advance of the publication of *Concept and Quality* Pepper had revealed what in brief compass his philosophy could do with the time-worn problem of the mind-body relation (20). According to Pepper's solution, the same occurrence—qualitatively felt mental event—may be expressed by means of the qualitative categories or by means of the conceptual categories, introspectively or behavioristically. As he later put the issue in *Concept and Quality*: "In the description of a purposive action, almost alone in the whole expanse of nature, we have both a highly articulated qualitative description and a highly articulated conceptual description which refer to exactly the same actual process. The bifurcation of nature into conceptual system and qualitative experience meet here at this point. Here is where the crotch of fork is from which the bifurcation extends" (12, p. 27).

Clearly, Pepper's new metaphysics promises to do justice to the reality of quality underlined by his contextualistic aesthetics, while at the same time it would explain the origin, nature, and role of the abstractions from quality—in other words, the concepts indispensable for natural science. Moreover, the basal idea of the new metaphysics—the purposive act—liberated from its original context in human experience and generalized to apply in natural situations throughout the cosmos, coincides with the fundamental concept in Pepper's empirical theory of values. Thus it is, despite its late discovery, the root metaphor of Pepper's entire philosophy as well as of his metaphysics. Hence, bringing to culmination a fruitful lifetime of philosophical explorations, Pepper steps forward with a new world hypothesis. Whatever may be the critical outcome, his bold venture calls to mind words he wrote over a generation ago: "No world hypothesis that we have is fully adequate. All the world hypotheses we have only make claims upon the whole universe, none actually possesses it. That uttermost ideal may even be humanly unattainable, or cosmically impossible. In the hope of knowledge, we cannot very well help but seek it" (23).

NOTES TO CHAPTER II

1 Stephen C. Pepper, World Hypotheses: A Study in Evidence (Berkeley and Los Angeles: University of California Press, 1948).
2 Carl Gordon Cutler and Stephen C. Pepper, Modern Color (Cambridge: Harvard University Press, 1923).
3 Stephen C. Pepper, Principles of Art Appreciation (New York: Harcourt, Brace, 1949).
4 Stephen C. Pepper, Aesthetic Quality: A Contextualistic Theory of Beauty (New York and Boston: Scribner's, 1937).
5 Stephen C. Pepper, The Basis of Criticism in the Arts (Cambridge: Harvard University Press, 1945).
6 Stephen C. Pepper, The Work of Art (Bloomington: Indiana University Press, 1955).
7 Andrew J. Reck, Recent American Philosophy (New York: Pantheon Books, 1964).

8   Stephen C. Pepper, A *Digest of Purposive Values* (Berkeley and Los Angeles: University of California Press, 1947).

9   Stephen C. Pepper, *The Sources of Value* (Berkeley and Los Angeles: University of California Press, 1958).

10 Stephen C. Pepper, *Ethics* (New York: Appleton-Century-Crofts, 1960).

11 Stephen C. Pepper "Truth by Continuity," *University of California Publications in Philosophy*, X (1928), 27–59; "Categories," *ibid.*, XIII (1930), 73–98; "Middle-Sized Facts," *ibid.*, XIV (1931), 3–28; "How to Look for Causality— An Example of Philosophic Method," *ibid.*, XV (1932), 179–203; "A Contextualistic Theory of Possibility," *ibid.*, XVII (1934), 179–97; "Root Metaphor Theory of Metaphysics," *Journal of Philosophy*, XXXII (1935), 365–74; "On the Cognitive Value of World Hypotheses," *ibid.*, XXXIII (1936), 575–77; and "Metaphysical Method," *Philosophical Review*, LII (1943), 252–69.

12 Stephen C. Pepper, *Concept and Quality, A World Hypothesis* (LaSalle, Ill.: Open Court, 1967). A preview of this work appeared as "A Proposal for a World Hypothesis," *Monist*, XLVII (Winter, 1963), 267–86.

13 See Stephen C. Pepper "A Criticism of a Positivistic Theory of Mind," *University of California Publications in Philosophy*, XIX (1936), 211–32.

14 Pepper's equation of Berkeley's subjective idealism with truncated mechanism (*World Hypotheses*, 223 f.) has raised eyebrows. See D. W. Parker's review, *Journal of Philosophy*, XXXIX (1942), 529; and L. Hoekstra, "Pepper's *World Hypotheses*," *ibid.*, XLII (1945), 85–108. See also Pepper's "Reply to Professor Hoekstra," *ibid.*, XLII (1945), 107.

15 Stephen C. Pepper, "Some Questions on Dewey's Esthetics," in Paul Arthur Schilpp (ed.), *The Philosophy of John Dewey* (Evanston and Chicago: Northwestern University Press, 1939).

16 See, for example, D. W. Parker's review of *The Basis of Criticism in the Arts*, in *Philosophical Review*, LVI (1947), 90–95.

17 Stephen C. Pepper, "Individuality of a Work of Art," *University of California Publications in Philosophy*, XX (1937).

18 Stephen C. Pepper, "Esthetic Object," *Journal of Philosophy*, XL (1943), 477–82.

19 See N. Berall, "Note on Professor Pepper's Aesthetic Object," *ibid.*, XLVIII (1951), 750–54. Stephen Pepper, "Further Consideration of the Aesthetic Work of Art," *ibid.*, XLIX (1952), 274–79. James L. Jarrett, "More on Professor Pepper's Theory of the Aesthetic Object," *ibid.*, XLIX (1952), 475–78. Pepper, "On Professor Jarrett's Questions about the Aesthetic Object," *ibid.*, XLIX (1952), 633–41.

20 Stephen C. Pepper, "A Neural-Identity Theory of Mind," in Sidney Hook (ed.), *Dimensions of Mind*, (New York: New York University Press, 1960), 37–56.

21 Stephen C. Pepper, "Whitehead's 'Actual Occasion,'" *Tulane Studies in Philosophy*, X (1961), 71–88.

22 See Charles Hartshorne's review of *World Hypotheses* in *Ethics*, LIII (1942), 73–74.

23 Stephen C. Pepper, "Middle-Sized Facts," *University of California Publications in Philosophy*, XIV (1931), 15.

III

BRAND BLANSHARD

Idealism and Rationalism

LIFE AND WORKS

Brand Blanshard, Sterling Professor of Philosophy Emeritus at Yale University, is the leading rationalist in contemporary American philosophy. An "austerely intellectual business" is Blanshard's phrase for philosophy (1, p. 6). "Its business," he has said, "is to analyze fundamental concepts, such as self, matter, mind, good, truth; to examine fundamental assumptions, such as that all events have causes; and to fit the conclusions together into a coherent view of nature and man's place in it" (1, p. 6). To be sure, it is the business of philosophy to "take account of values," so that it "has much to say of beauty and deformity, of good and evil, of the issues of religious belief" (1, p. 6). However, "it is pledged to discuss these issues with scientific detachment and dispassionateness" (1, p. 6). According to Blanshard, since the plain man is concerned with the problems which the philosopher treats, the philosopher is required, when he writes, to express his thoughts clearly, cogently, and with feeling. Among contemporary American philosophers Blanshard is unique in the importance he attaches to philosophical style. Lamenting the abuses of style by leading philosophers of recent times, Blanshard endorses Whitehead's striking assertion: "Style is the ultimate morality of mind" (1, p. 67).

Blanshard's conception of philosophical style is suited to his philosophical rationalism. His judgment of Santayana is pertinent. Santayana, he readily concedes, is "the most distinguished recent exemplar of imaginative prose in philosophy" (1, p. 49). Philosophy, however, is "an attempt to establish something by argument, and the reader who reads for philosophy will be impatient to know just what thesis is being urged, and what precisely is the evidence for it" (1, p. 49). Hence Santayana's style "is not, as philosophic style should be, so transparent a medium that one looks straight through it at the object, forgetting that it is there; it is too much like a window of stained glass which, because of its very richness, diverts attention to itself" (1, p. 50). As a philosophical stylist Blanshard succeeds where Santayana failed.

As a writer Blanshard has few equals in lucidity and cogency. His style embodies the acuteness and clarity of his thought. Of immeasurable aid to students, careful analytical tables of contents delineate the well-planned movement of the argument in each of his books. A distinction is sometimes drawn between the kind of philosophical activity that spreads speculatively over a wide region of reality or experience, and the kind of philosophical activity which concentrates analytically upon a minute area of argument. Blanshard's work incorporates both kinds of philosophical activity, the speculative and the analytical, in such a manner that each enhances the other.

Brand Blanshard was born in Fredericksburg, Ohio, on August 27, 1892. His twin brother—Paul—is the prominent journalist and social critic. Orphaned at an early age, the Blanshard brothers had the initiative, the intelligence, and the industry to complete their education. Brand Blanshard later expressed his and his brother's high regard for education when he succinctly stated its two goals to be "a disciplined sense of values and a disciplined power to think" (2, p. xii). In 1913, Brand Blanshard graduated from the University of Michigan, where DeWitt Parker and Roy Wood Sellars then represented idealism and realism respectively (3). As a Rhodes scholar Blanshard studied at Oxford from 1913 to 1915 and, after military service during World War I, again from 1919 to 1920. Under the tutelage of H. H. Joachim, Blanshard was immersed in British neo-Hegelian idealism, an immersion which was to guide and color his entire philosophical career. At Columbia University in 1919 he earned his M.A., with John Dewey as his major professor. At Harvard in 1921 he was awarded the doctorate in philosophy, with C. I. Lewis as his dissertation director. After teaching at Michigan for four years and at Swarthmore for twenty, Blanshard was called to Yale University in 1945 to head the department of philosophy, a department which he has described as "a stronghold of metaphysics" (4, p. 429). This wide and deep experience with the main currents of Anglo-American philosophy during the twentieth century ably prepared Blanshard for the prominent role he has played in imparting to rational idealism the most persuasive and effective formulation it has ever received.

Blanshard's two-volume work *The Nature of Thought* (5) has been acclaimed the most impressive contribution to idealist epistemology and metaphysics to appear in its time (6). Published in 1939 on the eve of World War II, the work came slowly to gain the attention and study it deserved (7). The tumult of the times distracted minds from metaphysical meditations, and, in addition, a general recession of Blanshard's type of philosophizing had set in several decades earlier. Bosanquet and Bradley had been replaced by Moore and Russell. The neo-Hegelian philosophical logic upon which rational idealism depends had been abandoned for the new mathematical logic. Realism, pragmatism, logical positivism, and linguistic analysis had first challenged idealism, and then, with victory assured by the number of adherents, simply ignored it. Wherever idealism still breathed, its life seemed restricted to religion and values. But Blanshard, a sharp critic of the new modes of philosophizing, did not join in the retreat of idealism. A skillful polemicist, he has engaged in a consummate constructive effort for idealism within the fields of logic and epistemology. It is impossible to predict whether idealism will gain numerous adherents in the future, but if it does, the revival—at least in the Anglo-American philosophical community—will germinate from Blanshard's philosophy.

The emphasis of Blanshard's idealism is squarely placed upon reason. He is today the most articulate living spokesman for reason in the world. In the concluding paragraph of *The Nature of Thought*, penned with the Second World War hovering in sight,

Blanshard states that his philosophy is but one variation on the "ancient doctrine of 'the great tradition,' of what Professor Urban has been persuasively urging as *philosophia perpetua* or *perennis*, the doctrine of the autonomy and objectivity of reason, the doctrine that through different minds one intelligible world is in course of construction or reconstruction" (5, II, p. 519), and he expressed the desire that, despite the impending chaos, his "insistent and re-iterated emphasis . . . on the membership of minds in one intelligible order may serve, however minutely, to confirm the belief in a common reason, and the hope and faith that in the end it will prevail" (5, II, p. 520). Blanshard's presidential address to the Eastern Division of the American Philosophical Association—undelivered because no meetings were held during World War II—is a defense of reason against the attacks upon it by behaviorists, psychoanalysts, and logical positivists (8). In his Gifford Lectures at St. Andrews in 1952–53, and in his Carus Lectures before the American Philosophical Association in 1959, Blanshard again elaborated the theme of reason.

At present Blanshard is completing a trilogy on reason, of which two volumes have already appeared. The first, *Reason and Analysis* (9), based on the Carus Lectures, is both critical and constructive. Besides taking logical positivists and linguistic analysts to task for undermining reason, Blanshard projects the ideal of a rational system of necessary knowledge representing the world as an intelligible whole of internally related parts. The second, *Reason and Goodness* (10), based on the second series of the Gifford Lectures, considers the role of reason in morality and is particularly critical of those recent movements in moral philosophy—such as subjectivism and emotivism—which have sought to minimize or deny that role. The third volume, *Reason and Belief*, now being written, takes up topics considered in Blanshard's first series of Gifford Lectures, entitled "The Revolt Against Reason," wherein he sharply criticized the derogation of reason in recent theology of the neo-Thomist, neo-orthodox, and existentialist varieties.

Since the role and defense of reason is central to Blanshard's philosophy, study of the nature of thought takes precedence over other considerations. In *The Nature of Thought* Blanshard seeks, as he says in the Preface, to bridge the gulf between the findings of scientific psychology and the demands of logic and epistemology, and his work progresses from intimate commerce with the facts and concepts of empirical psychology in the opening pages to increasingly speculative and metaphysical considerations toward the end. The dominating metaphysical interest to which the work yields Blanshard ascribes "in part to a certain advance in insight," and he attaches to it "somewhat higher value" than to the earlier, less speculative parts of the book (5, I, p. 14). Thus *The Nature of Thought* reflects the confrontation of empirical psychology, with its attendant philosophical theories, by rational idealistic philosophy, just as *Reason and Analysis* mirrors the confrontation of positivist and analytic philosophy by philosophical rationalism. The result, in both instances, has been the victory of rational idealism, with appropriate assimilation of the positive values of the opposed theories.

There is at present in the United States a revival of interest in philosophy of mind, in philosophical psychology. Stimulated, no doubt, by Ludwig Wittgenstein, Gilbert Ryle, John Wisdom, John L. Austin, and their British followers, American philosophers in increasing numbers are directing their attention to the field. There has been a rash of publications and symposia directed to philosophy of mind and related topics. Moreover, it was the subject selected for the first postdoctoral study program for professional philosophers which was supported by a grant from the Carnegie Corporation, conducted under the auspices of the American Philosophical Association, and held during the summer of 1966 at the University of Colorado. Further, even the American Psychological Association, after its arduous and on the whole successful effort to dissociate itself from its parent, philosophy, has recently established for its annual programs a special section on philosophical psychology.

Brand Blanshard is undoubtedly the greatest living American philosopher of mind. As contributions to philosophical psychology, Blanshard's works belong on the shelves beside those of William James, George Herbert Mead, and John Dewey—a position due them by considerations of geography and of excellence—while their philosophical character earns them a place next to the works of F. H. Bradley and Bernard Bosanquet as well. In truth, Blanshard may be counted a British as well as an American philosopher.

Blanshard's basic tenet concerning the nature of thought is that it is purposive. Mind itself, of which thought is an activity, is defined by its purposiveness. To the question whether there is a universal and essential feature which mind possesses exclusively, Blanshard's answer is clearly affirmative: "Wherever mind is present, there the pursuit of ends is present. Wherever that pursuit is wholly absent, mind is absent. And when mind is present, it is present precisely in the degree to which ends are in control" (11, p. 184). "Mind is purposive to its very roots; it is in its essence a set of wants cropping out into desires and of desires pressing for their fulfilment," (5, I, p. 195).

Because mind is essentially purposive, it is, as Blanshard acknowledges, fundamentally conative. But this in no way signifies that its cognitive role is subordinate to other functions. Mind itself is not the same as consciousness; as it is identified with purposiveness, mind exists where there is no consciousness. "Mind," he declares, "is not a single process, but a set of processes, a quiverful of arrows of desire" (11, p. 192). Among these desires is the theoretic impulse, the desire to think, to reason, to understand. Thought, then, is a distinguishable process or set of processes within the conative activity of mind, a process exhibited in rational consciousness.

Thought, like the mind whose activity it is, is essentially purposive. "Thought is that activity of mind which aims directly at truth" (5, I, p. 51). Furthermore, it is purposive in two senses: "It aims at revealing the outside world; it aims equally at satisfying an inner demand" (5, I, p. 490). The former Blanshard calls the transcendent aim of thought, the latter the immanent end. The immanent end of thought consists in the fact that mind "seeks fulfilment in a special kind of satisfaction, the satisfaction of systematic vision" (5, II, p. 262). The transcendent end consists in the fact that thought "seeks fulfilment in its object" (5, II, p. 262). Now Blanshard argues that, just as various desires constituting mind are unified in an all-embracing goal, similarly the immanent and transcendent ends of thought converge. But the road to this conclusion is a long one, traversing the fields of epistemology and metaphysics.

Thought, according to Blanshard, aims directly at truth. Its simplest form is judgment, since "nothing simpler could yield either truth or falsity" (5, I, p. 51). And the simplest form of judgment is perception, for perception occurs whenever there is "the barest and vaguest apprehension of anything given in sense *as* anything . . ." (5, I, p. 53). Thus the study of thought properly opens with an examination of perception.

Perception

What is perception? Drawing heavily upon the Gestaltists, Blanshard frames the following definition of perception: "Perception is an experience in which, on the warrant of what is given in sensation, we take some object to be before us. It is the sort of experience we have in the apprehension of red as red, or of an orange as an orange. Such experience is an achievement, since in the unbroken continuum with which we start, nothing is grasped *as* what it is" (5, I, p. 76).

The primitive experience into which perception enters as a particular activity of thought, then, is a sort of "unbroken continuum," the perceptual activity being one of responding to something given in sensation and of judging that there is an object. What this primitive experience is cannot be accurately spelled out, but Blanshard is quite clear on one point: "From the very first, universals are present. The growth of perception is a process in which these gradually come to explicitness" (5, I, p. 77). And he is equally clear in stating that perception involves an inferential element. The structure of perception consists in "a relation between what is actually given in sense and what is only thought or judged" (5, I, p. 120).

What is actually given in sense may at first appear to justify the theory that knowledge is anchored in a pure given, unaffected by thought. But without collapsing the distinction between sensation and thought, Blanshard nonetheless concedes that probably "we never in practice succeed in reaching a datum unaffected by thought" (5, I, p. 118). Since any line drawn between the given and its extension proves to be arbitrary and changing, we may as well assume that there is no such line.

It is germane to note that Blanshard distinguishes several senses of "the Given." First, of course, there is the primitive experience into which perception intrudes. Second, there is the given of sense, which is "what is presented, the qualitative character of sensations [which] can only be accepted passively" (5, I, p. 213). Third, there is the given of concepts and categories. What we do with the given of sense is done under "limits rigidly fixed; our construction always proceeds under the charter and constitution laid down by the categories" (5, I, p. 213).

The presence of the given in any or all of these senses, however, does not obstruct the inferential activity in perception. The intrusion by thought into the given in sense is the cue to perception, adding meaning to the total situation. Perception, an active confluence of sense and thought, takes for granted, i.e. unquestioningly believes in, objects which lie beyond what is given in sensation. Thus, for Blanshard, perception is "a movement that may be described as implicit inference, in which neither what is sensed nor what is taken for granted is singled out for express attention" (5, I, p. 120).

As a movement beyond what is given in sense to something that is believed, perception requires a factor of perceptual meaning, although "the ratio of meaning, so to speak, may vary greatly, so that at times the perception is very nearly pure sensation, while at the other extreme it is very nearly pure idea" (5, I, p. 181). What supplies perceptual meaning? According to Blanshard, perceptual meaning originates in psychical dispositions. The mind operates in perception as if there were preformed dispositions, deposits of past experience, which, though not conscious, are brought into play when needed (5, I, p. 182). In its teleological nature, perception, functioning in mind that is economical of consciousness, employs agencies, i.e. draws upon and is served by dispositions, which lie outside the field of consciousness. Though cognizant of the scientific objections to the concept of mental dispositions, Blanshard is unable to find any better theory of perceptual meaning to account for the fact that in perception, as in thought, something not yet actual, a desired end, somehow controls and directs an actual process whereby the end comes to be.

The offices of perceptual meaning are several, both positive and negative. While perceptual meaning may blind us to what is before us or cause wide divergences in the perceptions of various persons, it is still helpful in that it sharpens discrimination, directs observation and widens its range, and maintains attention. Despite these positive advantages, however, "it breeds continual error" (5, I, p. 214). Nevertheless, perceptual meaning has a structure of *depth* and *integration*. The structure of depth is a hierarchy of meanings generated by and dependent upon continuity of interest; that of integration is an organization of meanings initiated and sustained by what Blanshard calls "the reflective interest, that is, the desire to understand" (5, I, p. 222). Whatever perception may afford in accuracy, complexity, and flexibility, it has three major shortcomings: first, "*it is dependent upon the chance offerings of the moment*"; second, it "*cannot abstract*" (5, I, p. 251); and third, it is "*relatively helpless in dealing with what is new*" (5, I, p. 253).

Idea

The advance from perception to ideas "marks our escape from the mind of an animal" (5, I, p. 257). "The escape is very plainly a translation into a larger world" (5, I, p. 251). But the question arises: What is an idea, or, as Blanshard chooses to call it, a free idea? And the answer, briefly, is: "A free idea is an explicit thought which is independent of what is given at the time in sense" (5, I, p. 258). Then the question becomes: What is the nature of this thought? And to answer this question Blanshard examines the leading theories in the field, with the result that his work provides the best critical survey of recent epistemology.

Critique of Alternative Theories   Many of the authors and theories Blanshard discusses will survive for future generations of students through his pages. His critique of the theory of ideas as images is the most extensive and thorough in philosophical literature. His examinations of the views of such diverse thinkers as E. B. Titchener and Bertrand Russell are models of incisive criticism. His withering polemic against behaviorism deserves wider study among professional and academic psychologists than it has so far received. Blanshard condemns behaviorism—which he regards as a species of identity materialism—as "a local cult which is in a minority at home, and has made few converts abroad," and as having gained a hold "upon persons whose acquaintance with the history of thought has supplied no standards with which to evaluate it" (5, I, p. 339).

Pragmatism, too, is subjected to probing criticism. Despite his almost monotonous rejections of the instrumentalism, futurism, empiricism, behaviorism, and humanism contained in pragmatism, Blanshard acknowledges the validity of one of pragmatism's central theses: "Thought *is* a means to an end; it is in its essence instrumental, it may be described not illegitimately as a kind of intention or purpose. Where the pragmatist is wrong is not in his insistence that thought is a means, but in what seems to us his perverse refusal to recognize that thought has an end of its own. Unfortunately this mistake is fundamental" (5, I, p. 393).

Blanshard also probes the varieties of realism in recent philosophy. Realism, associated primarily with G. E. Moore, proposes, according to Blanshard, "to abolish ideas by breaking them up and dividing the spoils between acts and objects" (5, I, p. 414). But this replacement of ideas by mental acts will not do for Blanshard; unable to find introspective evidence for such acts, he rejects them. Critical realism tries to replace ideas with essences. Deeming critical realism to be "the most plausible and convincingly defended of all the theories . . . so far considered," Blanshard applauds it for making "a bold attack on the paradox of knowledge" by "holding to an identity between experienced content and the nature of physical things." But, he continues, "in attempting to square its assertion with the admitted dependence of that content on bodily change, it falters, equivocates, and ends in unintelligibility" (5, I, p. 444).

Theory of Idea   Blanshard's theory of the idea, coming after his critical treatment of other theories, is fundamentally irenic. An idea, he argues, "refers to an object, yet is not the object; . . . calls words and images in aid, yet is itself neither word nor copy; . . . changes with bodily changes, but is more than any bodily change; . . . is always a means to an end, though not always to an end that is practical" (5, I, p. 473). Perhaps this irenicism stems in large measure from Blanshard's heritage, for, although he had worked it out on his own without being aware of following anyone, he came eventually to see "that something very like it was the common property of metaphysicians of the Platonic turn of mind from the father of the great succession down to Bradley, Bosanquet, and Royce" (5, I, p. 518). Of this host Blanshard singles out Royce as the philosopher "whose agreement may be claimed more confidently and in more detail" (5, I, p. 518). What this theory of the idea is Blanshard has stated superbly:

Thought in its essence is an attempt to attain, in the sense of achieving identity with, a special end of its own. The relation between idea and object must be conceived teleologically, as the relation of that which is partially realized to the same thing more fully realized. When we say that an idea is *of* an object, we are saying that the idea is a purpose which the object alone would fulfil, that it is a potentiality which this object alone would actualize, a content informed by an impulse to become this object. Its nature is hence not fully intelligible except in the light of what it seeks to become. Mind, in taking thought, attempts to pass beyond its present experience to what it would be but is not yet, and so far as it has the thought of this end, it already *is* the end *in posse*. The idea is thus both identical with the object and different from it. It is identical in the sense in which anything that truly develops is identical with what it becomes. It is different in the sense in which any purpose partially realized is different from the same purpose realized wholly (5, I, p. 473).

Blanshard offers this concept of the idea as the solution to the paradox of knowledge. Dating back to the days of Plato in the *Meno*, this paradox consists in the relation of true ideas to their objects, with which they are identical and yet from which they are different. Blanshard's solution is to conceive thought as "a half-way house on the road to reality. . . . The idea can then be *both* the same as its object *and* different; the same because it *is* the object *in posse*; different because that object, which is its end, is as yet incompletely realized" (5, I, p. 494).

Two remarks are pertinent here. First, the identity between idea and object is purposive. An object is meant by a particular idea when the idea is directed toward the object, and the object is known when the purposive cognitive impulse crystallizing in the idea is satisfied. Second, this purposive identity is approximative; ideas differ in the degree to which they adequately identify with their objects. "Truth is the approximation of thought to reality" (5, II, p. 264).

Besides solving the paradox of knowledge, Blanshard's theory of the idea confirms his account of the transcendent and the immanent ends of thought. As regards the immanent end of thought, whereby the process of thinking is governed by some ultimate satisfaction it seeks, this theory of the idea analyzes the process as an actualizing of what is at present only potential. As regards the transcendent end of thought, which locates the satisfaction of thought in its object beyond, this theory considers the idea as "a partially realized purpose or . . . the object itself *in posse*" (5, I, p. 519). In this sense Blanshard's theory guarantees that "any fulfilment we may attain of the immanent end is also a partial realization of the transcendent end, and that what satisfied the intellect *was* so far the real" (5, I, p. 519).

Kinds of Ideas   Having advanced his basic theory of the idea, Blanshard next considers the kinds of ideas, although, as he insists, "there are really *no types* of idea at all, but only stages in the development of a single function" (5, I, p. 567). First are the "tied ideas" which are the component parts of perception, implicit but serving thought in significant ways, as the unsensed grounds of perceptual inferences. In human consciousness, ideas, instead of being wholly tied to perception, are free, their development paralleling the evolution of language.

Images, considered by many psychologists to be the final form of the idea, do not, according to Blanshard, exhaust the character of the idea in its fullest expression, although they do play useful roles in thought. The image is essentially the image *of* something and as such it contains a self-transcending meaning. Sometimes, of course, it is the whole content of thought, but such thought is less than fully developed, since "for most thinking, imagery is inadequate, irrelevant, and uneconomical" (5, I, p. 565).

Since ideas are not reducible to images, Blanshard embarks upon an exploration of the idea as concept. As he says, "From the beginning of its traceable history, thought works through identity in difference" (5, I, p. 568). All thought therefore is implicitly directed toward the universal. The universal is the object of the concept. The nature of the concept can be understood only if the nature of the universal is clarified, but discussion of the universal is deferred till later. However, since the idea as tied, as free, as image, as concept is an element in the process of thinking, more light can be thrown upon its nature by an examination of reflective thought.

Reflective Thought   Blanshard's treatment of reflective thought conforms to his ideal of "a modest eirenicon," since it seeks "to supply in outline an account of the reflective process in which the presence and operation of the logical ideal are recognized as clearly as the logicians have a right to demand, while the process is still regarded as a psychological one, consisting of a series of steps" (5, II, pp. 35–36). He defines understanding as "apprehension in a system" (5, II, p. 33) and reflection as "a movement toward self-completion on the part of an imperfect system of ideas" (5, II, p. 98).

Reflection, which is initiated when something outside a system of ideas challenges that system, moves in four stages. First, the problem, which arises from the challenge, is specified. Second, the basis upon which the theory is suggested is broadened by reading, consulting, and observing. Third, there is the advance of theory, what Blanshard terms "the leap of suggestion" (5, II, p. 98). Finally, the movement of reflection concludes with the establishment of coherence between the suggested theory and experience.

Truth

Blanshard's description of reflection leads directly to the theory of coherence as both the test and the nature of truth. A. C. Ewing has acclaimed Blanshard's treatment of the coherence theory of truth, a treatment which owes much to the influence of H. H. Joachim, as the most masterly formulation available (6, p. 81).

Coherence as Test of Truth   Blanshard's case for coherence as the test of truth is advanced by means of a critique of its most formidable rivals: correspondence and self-evidence. The correspondence theory is challenged precisely where it claims to be strongest—in the area of facts. For the so-called facts to which the proponent of correspondence appeals prove, upon scrutiny, to be shot through with concepts. When we attempt to bring theory down to earth, "the facts with which our judgments were to tally seem forever to elude us, and we find ourselves in a region where, on every side, there are only judgments and still more judgments" (5, II, pp. 229–30). Hence correspondence gives way to coherence.

Similarly, self-evidence is attacked in its presumably strongest area—in the area of the so-called axioms of mathematics and laws of thought. Such axioms and laws, Blanshard emphasizes, exhibit their validity not simply in isolation by appeal to self-evidence, but rather within a system of judgments to which they belong. Even the ultimate laws of logic—such as the law of contradiction—are justifiable, if at all, solely by means of coherence, insofar as their denial involves intellectual paralysis. Hence self-evidence yields to coherence.

Coherence as Nature of Truth   For Blanshard coherence is the nature of truth as well as its test. His argument is based upon his conception of the relation of thought to its object. The immanent end of thought, the satisfaction of thinking, comes with understanding, and the aim of understanding "is to achieve systematic vision, so to apprehend what is now unknown to us as to relate it, and relate it necessarily, to what we know already" (5, II, p. 261). At the same time, operating throughout the processes of thinking is its transcendent end—to seek satisfaction in an object. "To think of a thing is to get that thing in some degree within the mind. To think of a colour or an emotion is to have that within us which if it *were developed and completed*, would identify itself with the object" (5, II, pp. 261–62). Blanshard maintains that these two ends are really one, that their unity "is the metaphysical base on which our belief in coherence is founded" (5, II, p. 263). Otherwise the relation be-tween thought and things would be contingent. Knowledge, when it occurs, would be a matter of luck, and there would be no sound reason for pressing on with scientific investigations. The intelligibil-ity of the world, its conformity to the immanent end of thought, or rather the identity of this immanent end with the structure of real-ity, is the necessary postulate upon which science and rational phi-losophy proceed. It is a world "in which intelligence finds an answering intelligibility" (6, p. 361).

What exactly is coherence? Blanshard writes: "Fully coherent knowledge would be knowledge in which every judgment entailed, and was entailed by, the rest of the system" (5, II, p. 264). He cites systems like Euclidean geometry as "the most perfect examples of coherence that have been constructed." Of these he says: "If any proposition were lacking, it could be supplied from the rest; if any were altered, the repercussions would be felt through the length and breadth of the system" (5, II, p. 265). But even these systems, he observes, fall short of the ideal, since they consist of unproved pos-tulates which are not derivative from each other, and since they are so abstract as to have omitted the actual characters of things. In a completely coherent system, he adds, "No proposition would be ar-bitrary, every proposition would be entailed by the others jointly and even singly, no proposition would stand outside the system. The integration would be so complete that no part could be seen for what it was without seeing its relation to the whole, and the whole itself could be understood only through the contribution of every part" (5, II, pp. 265 66).

Of course Blanshard never says that perfectly coherent knowledge is actually attained. That would be tantamount to dogmatism. But he does contend that thought moves toward this ideal as its end. Existing knowledge, warranted by the partial coherence of incom-plete systems, is true to the extent that it approximates this ideal. Thus no enervating skepticism results from the fact that any actual knowledge is always less than the complete truth. After all, the ideal remains as that which is to be sought, and the means of seeking it is to rely upon whatever coherence emerges in existing systems of judgments, with a readiness ever to revise them in the light of new challenges.

Further, Blanshard's theory entails the doctrine of degrees of truth. As he says, "A given judgment is true in the *degree* to which its content could maintain itself in the light of a completed system of knowledge, false in the *degree* to which its appearance there would require its transformation" (5, II, p. 304). But in adopting and expanding the doctrine of degrees of truth, Blanshard carefully avoids the mosaic sense of coherence, according to which coherence consists in "an omnibus affair of component judgments," some true, some false (5, II, p. 305). Rather, drawing once again upon the teleological conception of mind, he advances the approximative sense of degrees of truth: " 'Truth', writes Bosanquet, 'I believe to be the degree in which the character of reality is present within a proposition or set of propositions.' That is our view exactly" (5, II, p. 311).

ETHICS

"The main question of our time in ethics," writes Blanshard in the opening sentence of *Reason and Goodness*, "is whether moral judgment expresses knowledge or feeling" (10, p. 27). Injected into current discussion first by Edward Westermarck in 1906 and later by A. J. Ayer in 1936—each contending that moral judgments are but expressions of feeling—the present issue is a narrowing of the older and larger question of Western ethics: "What are the roles of intelligence and of the non-rational parts of our nature in achieving the good life?" (10, p. 29). Although from a cursory consideration of the Greek ideal of reason and the Christian ideal of love Blanshard concludes that thought and feeling are both indispensable for the achievement of the good life, he is unable to specify the part each contributes. "Thought and feeling," he remarks, "contribute so subtly and variously to the achievement of every form of good that no full account of their interplay is practicable" (10, p. 70). Happily, it is possible to cope with the present narrower form of the issue—namely, the question of the functions of reason and feeling in moral judgment.

The Problems of Moral Judgment

The theoretical specification of the roles of reason and feeling in moral judgment involves a host of problems concerning the objectivity of moral standards, the relativity of the right, the rational or emotive character of ethical disagreements. These problems may be concentrated on the question whether reason or feeling makes the decision when a judgment about goodness or rightness is made.

Blanshard discusses this technical problem within the broad framework of the history of moral philosophy. For the first time on a large scale the issues in contemporary ethical theory, issues which for the most part have lent themselves to presentation in the technical journals, are presented in historical perspective. David Hume, Samuel Clarke, the Third Earl of Shaftesbury, Francis Hutcheson, and Henry Sidgwick pass in parade in a graceful, erudite, lucid study of British ethics. Of this group Sidgwick, though severely criticized for his hedonism, emerges as a major moralist; his *Methods of Ethics* is cited as unequaled for "combined subtleness, thoroughness, lucidity, and fairness" (10, p. 90).

Critique of Contemporary Alternatives   With the foray into history behind him, Blanshard proceeds to examine the major contemporary ethical theories: subjectivism, deontology, instrumentalism, and emotivism.

Upon analysis subjectivism is found to admit of three degrees: first, moderate subjectivism (Hume), which tends to equate the judgment of rightness with the feeling of people in general; second, extreme subjectivism (the emotivists), which identifies the judgment of rightness with the expression of a feeling; and third, a midway position (Westermarck), which views the judgment of rightness as a description of the individual's feeling. The second variety of subjectivism is criticized further below as emotivism. It is upon Westermarck's variety that Blanshard concentrates his critical powers. For Westermarck had arrived at his ethical theory from investigations of the differing customs and moral concepts of various societies, so that he readily surrendered the traditional view of ethics as a normative science and reduced ethics to "an adjunct, though a useful adjunct, of psychology and anthropology" (10, p. 110). No doubt Blanshard's strictures on Westermarck are aimed at the social sciences in general, so far as the social sciences try to resolve normative questions of right and good by merely descriptive methods. There are, for Blanshard, rational moral principles which hold regardless of how men feel individually or socially at a given time.

Deontology (H. A. Prichard, W. D. Ross, E. F. Carritt) holds that judgments of right take precedence over judgments of good, and that such judgments, pertaining to duties and obligations, are prima facie right or self-evident. While Blanshard agrees with the deontologists that reason is capable of apprehending that certain experiences or patterns thereof are intrinsically and necessarily good, and that reason is also capable of inferring the consequences of a suggested action, he does not agree that reason is capable of perceiving that certain actions are right in virtue of and so far as they have a certain character. Here Blanshard thinks the deontologists are mistaken, though not entirely. "The act is seen to be right," he declares, "in virtue of producing goodness, if not in consequences, then through being the kind of act it is. And reason is involved not only in seeing it to be of a certain kind, but also in seeing the filiation of this kind with a way of life as a whole" (10, p. 160).

Instrumentalism (John Dewey), which defines logic as "a 'theory of inquiry,' a study of the process by which doubts are satisfactorily removed," conceives ethics as "the same study with a more restricted subject-matter" (10, p. 164). "Ethics . . . is the study of how to solve problems where values are involved" (10, p. 165). Although Blanshard repudiates this form of naturalistic ethics, arguing that moral reflection need not be prompted by a practical problem, that a moral judgment is not universally a proposal to act, that, indeed, the resolution of practical problems may be devoid of moral value, he nonetheless deems correct Dewey's insistence "that moral choice should be directed not to conformity with rule but to the produc-

tion of good." He also approves Dewey's conception of moral goodness as so intimately bound up with human needs and desires that
"its very meaning is in satisfying them, and so fulfilling human nature" (10, p. 193).

Against emotivism (Ayer and Stevenson), which C. I. Lewis and
Stephen Pepper had already castigated and which is now dubbed
"the Boo-Hurrah theory of ethics" (10, p. 195), Blanshard launches
three main arguments.

First, emotivism dislocates goodness from its proper place of resi-
dence in the objects of experience. Although Blanshard admits that
"the abolition from the world of all forms of consciousness would
abolish value also" (10, p. 199), he nonetheless denies that goodness depends wholly on human attitudes. For Blanshard insists that
goodness is a quality which belongs to experiences in virtue of what
these experiences are, since men ordinarily enjoy experiences of
goodness without adopting attitudes toward them.

His second argument against emotivism is that "in thus denying
that there is any goodness or badness in objects apart from our attitudes toward them, it also denies by implication that an attitude of
favouring is ever more *appropriate* than its opposite; and this again
conflicts with universal convictions" (10, p. 214).

Finally, and most crucial of all from Blanshard's standpoint, emotivism "takes ethics out of the sphere of the rational" (10, p. 216).
This removal of ethics from the field of the cognitively meaningful
is due to the standard logical empiricist classification of all statements into three classes: analytic, empirical, and cognitively meaningless. Ethical statements, unlike empirical statements, do not
describe what is the case and are subject to disagreements for which
there are no cognitive methods of resolution. Unlike analytic statements, they have a bearing on the world, and they affect human action. Hence ethical statements are placed in the class of cognitively
meaningless statements. Blanshard sharply comments that the logical empiricists' "neat and expeditious way of disposing of everything in metaphysics, theology, and ethics, that does not fit into
one particular philosophy of science no longer carries weight with
us" (10, p. 218).

Blanshard deduces eight paradoxical and inadmissible implications of ethical emotivism. First, it "implies that no statement of right or good is ever true" (10, p. 220); consequently, no criteria of appropriateness for judgments of rightness or goodness, or for feelings of approval or disapproval, are available. Secondly, it implies that value terms never have the same sense for different persons or for the same person at different times, since these terms ascribe no objective character, public to different men, but merely express subjective, individualistic feelings. Thirdly, since according to emotivism ethical beliefs are neither true nor false, "no two of us ever agree in ethical belief" (10, p. 222); but then, fourthly and paradoxically, neither can we disagree (10, p. 224). Fifthly, it follows, then, that "no one ever makes a mistake on a moral question" (10, p. 226); and sixthly, by implication, emotivism repudiates the widespread belief "that we can correct, and continue to correct, mistaken notions in morals" (10, p. 227). Seventhly, it implies "that one can never give *relevant* reasons for or against an ethical judgment" (10, p. 228). But this implication does not square with the universal practice of arguing for ethical judgments, often with considerable cogency, and it perversely tends to reduce moral discussion to propaganda. Finally, emotivism "allows no objective court of appeal to which ethical disputes may be carried" (10, p. 234); it establishes propaganda and force as the final arbiters of morality. Thus, for Blanshard, the moral world of emotivism is one in which "the very notion of impartial justice is without meaning. There can be no verdict in accordance with deserts because there are no deserts. There is no real guilt, no real innocence. This seems to me moral anarchy" (10, p. 236).

According to Blanshard, linguistic ethics, through the writings of J. O. Urmson, Stephen Toulmin, and R. M. Hare, is to be credited with loosening "the moorings that tied ethics for a time to emotivism," although this, too, is embroiled in emotivism and logical positivism because of "parochial reverence for the gospel according to Wittgenstein" (10, p. 265). Blanshard is unequivocal in his repudiation of linguistic ethics. He denies that "meta-ethics has no ethical implications and may be discussed in a logical vacuum, antiseptic to moral commitments. This doctrine, however popular," he writes, "is untrue. To adopt certain meanings for 'right' and 'good' as the valid ones is also to elect a way of life" (10, p. 263). He even predicts that the program of the linguistic moralists to reduce all ethical discussion to discussion about language and the usages of ethical terms, each allegedly having its own logic, will in short time pass away, since otherwise "ethics will have become a level plain extending as far as the eye can see and littered, it is to be feared, with dry bones. If that consummation is not reached, it will be because the direction of the movement is discerned, and good sense calls a halt to it" (10, p. 263).

Theory of Moral Judgment   In the foregoing criticisms of the alternative theories of moral judgment, Blanshard's own theory may have been discerned. Two basic theses stand out. First, "the fundamental judgment was the judgment of good, not right" (10, p. 266). This thesis guides Blanshard's rejection of deontology. Second, the judgment of good is "irreducible, in the sense that it could not be resolved away into the expression of an emotion, a command, or any other non-cognitive attitude" (10, p. 266). The corollary of this is that there is an objective goodness of which moral judgment is made. This thesis guides Blanshard's rejection of subjectivism, instrumentalism, and emotivism.

The Nature of Goodness

The primary question for moral philosophy thus becomes: What does moral judgment assert? What sort of character belongs to the subject of which moral judgment asserts good?

Before presenting his own theory, Blanshard examines three contemporary answers to this question. According to one theory, good is a simple quality. According to a second, good is a relation. Since G. E. Moore is "the most influential advocate in recent times of the first position," Blanshard investigates Moore's conception of goodness as "a simple 'non-natural' quality present in everything that is good intrinsically" (10, p. 266). He judges Moore to be "wrong in holding that goodness is a simple unanalysable quality, but right in holding that when we talk about the goodness of someone's pleasure or the badness of someone's pain, we are talking about something objective, in the sense of belonging in the object, and not merely in our attitude toward it" (10, p. 289). Since R. B. Perry's interest theory of value is "the most persuasive" of the relational theories (10, p. 274), Blanshard examines it and finds that Perry is "wrong in holding that value consists in interest, but . . . right in holding that for the person who has no feeling about an object, that object has no value, and hence there is no value in the world except as relative to consciousness" (10, p. 289). Since, finally, A. C. Ewing's theory of goodness as fittingness is a supremely sophisticated endeavor to retain a relational theory of value while overcoming the defects of earlier versions, Blanshard probes it and finds that "Ewing was wrong in reducing goodness to the appropriateness of favour, though he was right in holding that goodness does not vary with attitudes actually taken" (10, p. 289).

Blanshard's criticisms of the extant theories of goodness underline his conception of the goodness of experience as "an objective character of it, not reducible to feeling and not necessarily variable with feeling, and yet in some sense dependent on it" (10, p. 289). But additional clarification of the concept of goodness is demanded. Blanshard explicitly repudiates the so-called internal method, which analyzes meanings by stressing what plain men mean when they use words; he favors the external method, which essays "a study of goodness that places it in its wider human and biological context" (10, p. 291). He asserts that "value is so fundamental in human life that its true character can be seen only against the background of human nature" (10, p. 292). And he adds that the intrinsically good is "that which this nature finds in itself attractive"; consequently, "its attractiveness has something to do with its answering that nature's needs and demand" (10, p. 292).

Eight clearly stated propositions sum up Blanshard's presentation and explanation of a theory of goodness grounded in human nature. First of all, conscious processes, stemming from mind, are goal-seeking (10, p. 293). Second, desire springs from and is limited by the experience of satisfaction (10, p. 295). Third, what is desirable grows out of what is actually desired (10, p. 297). Yet, fourth, that things are desired or that they satisfy does not exhaust what makes them desirable or satisfactory (10, p. 298). This point calls for special attention. The desirable is never equated with the actual experiences of desire. Thus, as Blanshard says, "goodness is satisfactoriness, which consists jointly in the fufilment of impulse-desire by the content it demands and the attendant satisfaction" (10, p. 302). Yet, fifth, human impulse-desires define our major goods. In asserting that goods are demarcated by impulse-desires, Blanshard in effect deems man to be not a fallen nature but an inevitable seeker after great goods; "his whole life is a groping after them" (10, p. 342). In holding that the fulfillment of man's desires and impulses constitutes the very meaning of goodness, Blanshard adopts the view of Stephen Pepper, who, he says, has shown "fine insight" in calling such impulses as aggression and fear "injectives" and in considering them to be "not drives with ends of their own; [for] they are summoned up when other drives are frustrated, and are nature's means of intensifying or safeguarding them" (12, p. 110). Further, in the sixth place, the process of realizing the good is governed by its goal—the good—although, as the purpose governing the process of its attainment, the good is defined only in the process (10, p. 304). Seventh, "the good or desirable always outruns the desired" (10, p. 305).

At last, in the eighth place, Blanshard is able to define the good in the sense of the ethical end. It is, he affirms, *"the most comprehensive possible fulfilment and satisfaction of impulse-desire."* He means by comprehensive fulfillment "one that takes account not only of this or that desire, but of our desires generally, and not only of this or that man's desires, but of all men's" (10, p. 311). Pertinent here is Blanshard's distinction between fulfillment and satisfaction. One must keep in mind that he is elaborating a moderate form of the ethics of self-realization most widely associated with Aristotle, T. H. Green, and Bernard Bosanquet. He is therefore prepared to esteem fulfillment, the realization of the potentialities of the person, as more important than satisfaction, the enjoyment by the individual of his fulfillment. Nevertheless, Blanshard readily concedes that "a fulfilment that is without normal satisfaction is to that extent a defective good" (10, p. 337). In his Howison Lecture, entitled "The Impasse in Ethics and a Way Out," delivered at the University of California at Berkeley in 1954, Blanshard succinctly summed up his position in the following formula: "To say of an experience that it is intrinsically good means, then, two things: first, that it satisfies; second, that it fulfils. Pleasure without fulfilment, as Aristotle saw, is hardly possible. Fulfilment without pleasure, as Mill saw, is valueless. Of two experiences that equally fulfil, the one we enjoy more is the better. Of two experiences that we equally enjoy, the one that fulfils more is the better" (12, p. 110).

After defining the good, Blanshard proceeds to define the concepts of the right and the ought, concepts which denote properties of acts. "A right act," he says, "is one that tends to bring into being at least as much in the way of satisfying and fulfilling experience as would any available alternative" (10, p. 322). Similarly, the meaning of the ought is translated to signify that sense of necessity short of compulsion to act in a certain way if certain ends are to be achieved (10, p. 331).

Now although Blanshard defines goodness in relation to human desires, he does not abandon the determining role of reason in regard to goodness. Following the lead of T. H. Green, he argues that, while thought differs from desire, they are "so intimately bound up together that thought is impossible without desire, and desire without thought" (10, p. 347). As he says, "Our goods . . . lie in the fulfilment not of bare impulses, but of desires into whose nature thought has entered once and for all, with its own demands for consistency, integration, and expansion" (10, p. 347). "What is good is the achievement of the end; in this end the fulfilling content is as important as the satisfaction; and in the determination of that fulfilling content, reason is absolutely essential" (10, p. 348).

METAPHYSICS

Although Blanshard rarely engages in direct metaphysical theorizing, apart from concern with such basic human experiences as knowing and moral conduct, his writings are nonetheless replete with metaphysical concepts, positing a system of idealism unparalleled for its clarity of style and strength of argument. The transcendent aim of thought to realize itself in an object with which it becomes identical implicates a full-scale metaphysical theory of objective reality in line with the great tradition from Plato to Hegel and through Bradley, Bosanquet, and Royce. Correlative to the distinctive phases of thought—in perception, in free ideas, and in reflection culminating in ordered vision—are definable ontological entities. Since Blanshard's psychological and epistemological considerations often obscure the ontological, it is necessary to take care to elicit and define the various types of entities. It is my intention here to demarcate briefly the principal types of these objects and to locate them within the total system of reality which Blanshard's philosophy presents.

Thing

Perception is the most primitive level of thought; its objects are things. While all animal experience and most human experience occur on the level of perceiving things, the perceptual achievement of objective fufillment in things is nevertheless deemed a poor one. As Blanshard says: "Those solid everyday things which seem constructed in a fashion so firm and so inevitable are really thrown together in a most hit-or-miss way, and if thought for a time comes to rest among them, this is only because it has ceased to press its own interest and has surrendered to the competing claims of convenience and practical necessity" (5, I, p. 121).

In his remarkable chapter "The Thing and Its Architecture" in *The Nature of Thought* (5, I, Ch. 3), Blanshard studies the thing so far as possible within the limits of psychology, underscoring the incapacity of the psychology of the unsophisticated to account for things whenever basic metaphysical difficulties crop up. He equates the thing with a combination of qualities and sets out to discover the principles whereby these qualities are combined. Since the categories of substance and quality prove too recondite for the unsophisticated perceiver, Blanshard appeals to more accessible principles to explain how it is that qualities are grouped together to constitute the unity of the thing. He cites five such principles: first, the joint prominence of qualities; second, the movement of qualities; third, their joint change; fourth, their joint utility; and fifth, the Gestaltist "law of *pragnanz*," which normally organizes the perceptual field in the most economical fashion. In large measure, then, the unity of things is the result of the selectivity of the perceiver, as is borne out further when Blanshard turns to explain the unity of the thing through temporal spans. Resemblance and continuity of qualities, which presumably support the temporal unity of the thing, depend mainly upon the purposes of the perceiver and his convenience. The problem of the unity of the thing is additionally complicated when it is considered that the qualities which cluster to make up things are not of the same order but are different. "Convenience is here dictator" (5, I, p. 147).

How is the thing related to the given in perception? According to the experience of the plain man, the answer is simple. "The thing simply stands there, apparently given as a whole, as solid and stolid and secure from private manipulations as a boulder on a plain" (5, I, p. 148). While this is, of course, the naïve view of the relation of things to common perception, disturbing questions arise over the spatial externality, the substantiality, and the independent existence of things. Blanshard regards five facts of common experience sufficient to guarantee the widespread belief in the independent existence of things: first, our expectations are often defeated; second, some qualities do not lend themselves to our control while others do; third, groups of qualities evince a constant rate of change apart from our perception; fourth, our different senses concur in their reports concerning particular things; and fifth, others corroborate our experiences. As regards the spatial externality and substantiality of things, however, Blanshard finds that, while psychology can tell us something about how we think of them, it cannot adequately treat the metaphysical issues entailed. "What the substance-attribute relation really is is a matter often disputed among philosophers, but this much would seem to be clear, that it is too fundamental to our ways of thinking to admit of psychological explanation" (5, I, p. 154).

One point will become clearer in the subsequent discussion.

Blanshard explicitly denies that there is really in the core of each thing a substantial "it" which is inaccessible to perceptual or conceptual grasp. He observes that the notion of the "it" in which qualities inhere has "all but dissolved into thin air" under the advance of philosophic sophistication, and he readily concludes: "To me a thing is a set of characters in relation, and ultimately in necessary relation" (9, p. 485).

Universals

Things are not ultimately real, and consequently they are not the final objects with which thinking rests. The free idea also seeks to realize itself in an object, and this object is the universal. Thus the question arises: Just what sort of entity is the universal? Blanshard examines two theories: the theory of the abstract universal, which he judges false, and his own theory of the concrete universal.

The theory of the abstract universal is favored by traditional formal logic and even by symbolic logic. The abstract universal is a class of objects with one or more attributes in common (5, I, p. 581). The higher in the scale of generality, the less content the universal has; the lower in the scale, the more content. Against the theory of the abstract universal Blanshard levels five arguments. First, universals, e.g. color and figure, cannot always be marked off in thought from their specific differentiations. Second, universals, qua abstract identities, may be embodied in alien contents, since the features which embody the universal through addition to it may be indifferently either essential or accidental. Third, since abstract universals have less content with each stage of higher generality, it follows that the more insight one gains into a class of things, the less actual content is conceived. This, for Blanshard, is nonsense (5, I, p. 587). Closely linked to the third argument, the fourth argument against abstract universals stresses that, while understanding increases with generality, the desired generality consists in "the making explicit and detailed of what was germinally present already, the evolution of the undeveloped," rather than in the omission or enumeration of associated characteristics (5, I, p. 588). Finally, the theory of the abstract universal clashes with the fact that essential characteristics are often lacking in members of the class, though these wanting members continue to be regarded as instances of the universal. Thus Blanshard comes to the positive conclusion that the universal is "not an extract from its species" but "the undeveloped schema of its species" (5, I, p. 590).

According to Blanshard, the plausibility of the theory of abstract universals depends upon the existence in nature of an identical quality which runs through all the members of the species without variation and the possibility of forming an idea of this identical quality which can be used to advantage. On these two points Blanshard is uncompromising: "Such identities *neither* exist, *nor* can be thought" (5, I, p. 600). Universals, such as color or figure or animality, are not movable building blocks out of which species are indifferently constituted; they are rather potentialities realized in their differentiations. And, further, our thought of them exists as the thought of these differentiations.

At this juncture Blanshard passes from the critique of abstract universals to his own constructive theory. For purposes of clarity it is germane to note that Blanshard distinguishes four senses of the term universal: the abstract universal, the generic universal, the qualitative universal, and the specific universal (5, I, p. 624). As regards the abstract universal, the alleged common character of a genus, Blanshard's rejection has already been observed. As for the qualitative universal, such as whiteness or sweetness, it differs, according to Blanshard, only in degree from the generic universal. What remains central to Blanshard's theory are the generic universal and the specific universal, for they are the keys to the concept of the concrete universal.

The critique of the abstract universal contains many suggestions for the positive theory of the generic universal. This theory is based on two fundamental theses: "The first is that the generic universal *is* the partial realization of its more specific forms, second is that it exists only as the *thought* of these" (5, I, p. 609). With Cook Wilson, Blanshard affirms that the generic universal as conceived is indeterminate and that, if it were fully developed, it would be the various individuals it embraces. But, unlike Cook Wilson, Blanshard insists that as a potentiality the generic universal "does not exist in the real world independently of mind; its only being is in thought"

(5, I, p. 620). His reasoning is wholly metaphysical. "The fully real is never indeterminate and never potential. These adjectives belong to thought" (5, I, p. 621).

The thesis that generic universals exist in thought, but not in reality, does not make Blanshard a nominalist. On the contrary, he maintains that there are specific universals which do exist in nature. A specific universal is an entity, such as a completely specific color or odor or taste, "which may be identical with itself in various contexts" (5, I, p. 624). According to Blanshard's theory of the concrete universal, "the individual things in which the generic universal would be realized may themselves be resolved away into specific universals" (5, I, p. 625).

The doctrine of the concrete universal, entailing the conception of the individual thing as a congeries of specific universals, therefore, rules out the existence of particulars. Blanshard discounts the existence of particulars on the ground that the advocacy of particulars rests on false and vague premises. Particulars are not necessary to account for the forcefulness and vividness of qualities. Specific universals may serve, since, instead of being dim, shadowy, and bloodless, they are repeatable yet vivid qualities (5, I, p. 634). Similarly, universals, instead of being the products of reflection, exhibit the compulsory characteristics of forcefulness which allegedly belong only to particulars. Nor will the distinction between perception and conception serve to indicate the existence of two types of objects, particulars and universals, since there is a gradual shading between these two phases of thought. Moreover, since nothing about the thing eludes analysis into universals, the supposition that universals are wholly determinate and exhaustible conceptually, whereas things are indeterminate and inexhaustible because of their particularity, is mistaken. And the definition of things as particular in terms of spatial and temporal relations also fails, since these relations are in principle repeatable and we are still "tarrying within the land of universals" (5, I, p. 639). In treating spatial and temporal relations as repeatable and so as universals, Blanshard of course raises new questions concerning their status. Further, the doctrine of specific universals posits the existence of identities which cut across spatio-temporal loci, giving rise to an extraordinary situation. Identity and spatio-temporal difference both seem indispensable to thought; yet they contradict each other. According to Blanshard, one must be abandoned, and it is the spatio-temporal arrangement which must go. "It is, no doubt, a shock to common sense to hear that spatio-temporal arrangement cannot be real just as it appears, but at least this is not nonsense or inconsistent with itself. On the other hand, a general denial of identity would be both" (5, I, p. 649). And so we remain in the land of universals. If we try to escape from this land of universals by defining the particularity of things in terms of all relations a thing has to all other possible things, we again meet with no success. For, as Blanshard concludes, "all that we commonly call particulars, pots and pans, mountains and rivers, are now seen to be universals. The only true particular is the absolute" (5, I, p. 639).

Hence Blanshard calls for a reconception of particularity. Accordingly, "particularity, properly conceived, is the uniqueness achieved by *exhausting* a thing's relations" (5, I, p. 651). With space and time dismissed, with the thing analyzed into a congeries of universals, Blanshard has at last attained a vision of the world as an intelligible and necessary whole in which thought is fulfilled. In a passage in which he even quotes F. H. Bradley, Blanshard writes:

There is now no particularity in things that is alien to thought and unassimilable by it, nothing that resists inclusion in that intelligible system of universals at which thought aims. To be sure, thought in reaching this aim would pass over into reality and commit suicide *as* thought. Still 'there is nothing foreign that thought wants in desiring to be whole'; its end is a system of universals, not an aggregate of particulars. In short, it is required by the nature of thought, and not interdicted by the nature of things, that thought should go on to bridge the interval between itself and its object, and, by compassing both 'what' and 'that' within one whole, should override their difference (5, I, p. 632).

Cosmic Necessity

The primary characteristic of the intelligible whole which thought seeks is necessity. The conception of coherence as the test and the nature of truth centers on the entailment of every part of the system by every other part. "A proposition is true precisely to the extent to which it is necessary, and necessary to the extent that it is true" (5, II, p. 301). "Perfect coherence would mean the necessitation of each part by each and all of the others" (5, II, p. 429). The goal of thought is, then, an intelligible system of necessarily related parts.

What is necessity? According to Blanshard, there are three theories of necessity: formalism, empiricism, and his own theory of concrete necessity. Formalism, linked with the name of Kant, holds that necessity "plays a genuine and important part in experience, but is confined to certain regions; it is characteristic of certain forms or relations connecting abstract elements" (5, II, p. 335). Blanshard consistently rejects the formalist theory, because the abstract forms and relations with which it identifies necessity are, like the abstract universal, too skeletal and empty of content to hold in experience and reality.

A far more serious challenge to Blanshard's ideal of intelligibility is raised by empiricism, which maintains that "necessity does not exist at all; it can be, and has been, explained away" (5, II, p. 335). In its traditional form empiricism treats necessities in thought as generalizations or habits, and it is indicted by Blanshard for failure to account for logic in deductive and inductive processes. The laws of thought can neither be dismissed as psychological habits nor be reduced to empirical generalizations. In its contemporary form empiricism has sought to account for logical and mathematical necessities by treating them as analytic and tautological. The resultant position is known as logical positivism, or logical atomism. Both in *The Nature of Thought* and in *Reason and Analysis* Blanshard subjects logical atomism to scathing criticism, and in the later work he also scrutinizes and rejects the various forms of linguistic philosophy.

Blanshard ascribes the rise of logical atomism to the convergence of two independent lines of thought upon a single world view. On the one hand, the verifiability theory of meaning has supported the analysis of factual statements into atomic statements describing atomic facts. On the other hand, the new conceptions of mathematics and logic equate them with conventional systems of language which, though asserting nothing about the world, prove useful in the clear and precise organization of such assertions. These lines of thought culminate in Wittgenstein's *Tractatus*, the basic handbook of logical atomism.

No philosophical standpoint is more antithetical to Blanshard's own position than logical atomism, for logical atomism is nothing less than the contradiction of the sort of monism propounded by British neo-Hegelian idealism. Whereas the idealists have contended that "the world is a single individual whose parts are connected with each other by a necessity so intimate and so organic that the nature of the part depended on its place in the Absolute," the logical atomists have maintained the very opposite, "that a full knowledge of the world, instead of revealing it as a complete unity, would pulverize it into atoms" (9, p. 145). The upshot of logical atomism was a radical alteration of the role of reason in philosophy. Reason would no longer have as its task the tracing of necessities between facts and the understanding of the world as a coherent system, for no necessities exist between facts, nor, for that matter, is the world intelligible as a whole. Thus logical atomism demotes reason to "a highly specialized function which could be properly performed only by experts, the function of identifying the logical or linguistic equivalences that appeared in mathematical systems" (9, p. 145).

Fortunately it is not necessary to review all of Blanshard's detailed and penetrating criticisms of logical atomism. The logical atomists themselves had recognized some of the defects in their own theories—e.g., the picture theory of logical form—and had moved on to different theses. Especially noteworthy in Blanshard's discussion, however, is his rejection of the atomic fact as an abstract particular. Ironically he chides the logical atomists, so-called empiricists, for "their baggage of dogmatic metaphysics"—their adherence to the doctrine of characterless logical subjects for atomic statements—and he advises them to "become more genuinely empirical" (9, p. 175). Logical subjects, he insists, are always contents, just as the predicates are contents. "The two contents—subject and predicate—are asserted jointly of a reality that falls beyond either. This reality is not to be known by burrowing under the qualities and relations of things in search of some mysterious 'existence.' So far as it is knowable at all, it must be known by studying the threads of connection within the content asserted, and then between this and the world outside it" (9, p. 175).

Logical atomism fails because it dismisses necessities a priori and consequently is less than empirical. Its theses, as regards both the verifiability theory of meaning and the analytic a priori, prove unstable and untenable, and the cumulative impact of these theses, in all their variety of formulation, is the steady erosion of the role of reason in philosophy. With the breakdown of logical atomism, however, no restoration of reason has occurred. Instead, linguistic analysis has arisen.

Linguistic analysis simply shifts the philosophical enterprise from preoccupation with the meanings of words to concern for the uses of words. But here again Blanshard marshalls impressive reasons for repudiating a way of philosophizing which is dominant at present. First, in looking to the uses of words in ordinary language to answer philosophical questions, the linguistic analyst begs the questions, because he assumes that the desiderated knowledge is already contained in the plain man's use of ordinary language (9, p. 372). In the second place, ordinary language is "a particularly inadequate guide for philosophical thinking" (9, p. 373), since ordinary usage is the product of practical men who make conceptual distinctions only as demanded by their practical purposes. Thirdly, the method of linguistic analysis is far from determinate; the very meaning of the phrase "ordinary usage" is ambiguous, as is evident in the writings of the different analytic philosophers. Fourth, ordinary usage of words themselves is ambiguous, so that either linguistic philosophy must prescribe standards which focus on some uses and neglect others, or it "may study all the ordinary uses, however many of them there are, and however trivial some of them may be; and then it will become a promiscuous and largely pointless enterprise" (9, p. 376). Fifth, linguistic philosophy confuses correctness with truth. "To use an expression correctly, or with propriety," Blanshard remarks, "is to use it in accord with prevailing practice or with philological authority. To use it with truth is to express through it a judgment that accords with fact" (9, p. 377). Finally, "ordinary usage may mislead, distort and deceive" (9, p. 377). Too often, as acute thinkers have long insisted, ordinary usage may obscure scientific facts and logical structures, and it is only by pressing inquiry beyond the limits of ordinary language that errors are overcome and knowledge is advanced.

For Blanshard the negative task of repudiating contemporary analytic philosophy is entwined with the positive program of restoring reason to its dominant position by right in the philosophical enterprise. By reason Blanshard means "the power and function of grasping necessary connections" (9, p. 382). In another place, he says that "the prime office of reason" is "the discovery of necessary connections" (9, p. 422). The kind of necessity Blanshard has in mind is concrete necessity.

According to Blanshard, necessity "holds in degree everywhere; it is the characteristic, not of special forms, but of a whole or system into which everything apparently enters" (5, II, p. 335). This theory of necessity, he continues, "was suggested by Plato, brought to a little more explicitness in the 'scientia intuitiva' of Spinoza, developed with vast power and obscurity by Hegel, stated brilliantly by Bradley and by the Royce of pre-logistical days, and given its most adequate, though hardly its most attractive, expression by Bosanquet" (5, II, p. 335). Now Blanshard nowhere asserts as a dogma that the world is a necessary whole. "Though one cannot without some absurdity say that anyone has ever *proved* the world to be a necessary system, one can still postulate it and then examine how far the actual exercise of reason goes toward justifying the postulate" (9, p. 383).

In seeking necessity everywhere and in different degrees, Blanshard finds that it always consists not absolutely but in relation to a system. Consider the relation of implication between two propositions, and note that, according to Blanshard, this relation does not exist in isolation. "Implication is systematic interdependence. It is a relation between parts of a whole imposed on them by the nature of the whole itself" (5, II, p. 430). From this relativistic conception of implication, according to which it is precisely a function of a "system partially revealed in the terms as related," Blanshard goes on to argue that implication is "various in kind" and "various in degree" (5, II, p. 430).

Now whether the world is an intelligible whole, a necessary system the parts of which imply each other, comes to pivot in part on the theory of causality and in part on the doctrine of relations. "A relation is internal to a term when in its absence the term would be different; it is external when its addition or withdrawal would make *no* difference to the term" (5, II, p. 451). By definition internal relations alone establish the sort of intelligible whole which thought postulates.

Blanshard adduces five arguments to demonstrate the theory of internal relations. First, he employs the argument from the relation of difference: "Everything is related to everything else by the relation of difference at least. If it were not so related, it would clearly not be the thing it is, since then it would not differ from that which is admittedly other than itself. But a relation that could not be theoretically changed without changing the thing itself is precisely what we mean by an internal relation. Whence it follows that everything is related internally to everything else" (5, II, pp. 476–77). Secondly, a relation gives rise to a property, known as a relational property, which belongs to the nature of the term it relates, so that any change in the relation affects the nature of the term. The nature of a term includes all the features of the term, since, despite the claims of traditional logical theory, no distinction can be drawn between essence, property, and accident. Thirdly, the relations individualize the terms, so that any change of relations signifies that the terms are different. The uniqueness of a thing is, indeed, due to its relations. "What makes these stones *these* stones is an infinity of relations, temporal, spatial, and other. Nor are the relations mere *rationes cognoscendi*. They are part of that which individuates; they are part of what goes to make the specific differences of the terms. Two stones that were exactly alike not only in quality, but in these relations as well would not be two stones but one. The qualities of what we call a single stone, if they had two differing sets of relations, would not make one stone, but two"

(5, II, p. 486). Fourthly, this argument that relations render terms unique applies also to universals. Like F. H. Bradley, Blanshard holds that a perfect knowledge of the world would make possible a relational knowledge of all the characters related to a unique situation, and from a perfect knowledge of this situation, in turn, a knowledge of all its other relations could be deduced (5, II, pp. 491–92).

Blanshard's fifth argument for the internality of relations rests upon his extraordinary theory of causality. He argues "(i) that all things are *causally* related, directly or indirectly; (ii) that being causally related involves being *logically* related" (5, II, p. 492). Causality is for Blanshard a cardinal postulate of science and rational investigation, and, although recent physics has cast doubt on the indispensability and validity of this postulate, Blanshard takes pains to allay these doubts by showing that such developments as the Heisenberg principle of indeterminacy are methodological only and do not touch upon the causal relatedness of elements of reality. But more than this, Blanshard strives to equate causal relatedness with logical relatedness. He insists that causality involves an irreducible element of logical necessity, despite the fact that it is perhaps impossible to grasp the logical necessity in most causal relations. He dismisses the regular sequence theory, the only major alternative to his own theory, as ultimately unintelligible. While it is conceivable, it is unreasonable, in that, if true, no conclusion in a line of reasoning is ever necessitated by the evidence (9, Ch. 11). Of course the entire argument for logical necessity in causality falls short of the requirements of absolute demonstration. Yet examination of particular causal relations induces the insight that causality expresses the natures of the terms it relates, the causal term acting the way it does because of its nature, and the effect term being acted upon the way it is because of its nature. Causality itself illustrates the internality of relations. And the postulate of causality is accepted because, in Blanshard's words, "It is the part of reasonableness to accept a conclusion, even when indemonstrable, if it makes sense of things and no alternative does" (9, p. 471).

The world, therefore, is an intelligible whole of internally and necessarily related parts. It is identical with the immanent end thought sets itself when, according to Blanshard's analysis, it seeks satisfaction in the most comprehensive, the most integrated, coherent system of judgments. Hence "the immanent end of thought is no will-of-the-wisp; it is relevant to the experienced nature of things; to the best of our knowledge the immanent and the transcendent ends coincide" (5, II, p. 516).

Blanshard's rationalism, with its view of the world as a necessary whole of internally related parts, has not gone unchallenged. Indeed, it has provoked what may well be the most important controversy in American philosophy today. In his critical essay "Sovereign Reason" (13), Ernest Nagel, a Columbia University naturalist, a Carus Lecturer like Blanshard, and America's most accomplished philosopher of science, has aimed nearly thirty pages of unrelieved polemic against Blanshard's theory. In the conclusion Nagel charges that "the vision he [Blanshard] has called up of the scope and office of human reason is not without grandeur and inspiring power, and its insistence on system and rational order reveals its sources in human aspirations." But, Nagel continues, "like all visions which feed on uncontrolled and exaggerated hopes and fancies, it is a vision that cannot permanently serve to guide the energies of sober men" (13, p. 292). Originating in the naturalistic philosophy which is the topic of the next chapter of this volume, Nagel's gravamen against Blanshard focuses on the doctrine of internal relations; it denies the kind of cosmic necessity which Blanshard's doctrine propounds. After many years of silence Blanshard has replied, briefly in the concluding pages of *Reason and Analysis,* and more recently at greater length and with full dialectical vigor in his contribution to *Philosophical Interrogations* (14). Defending his theory of internal relations, Blanshard undertakes step by step to demolish Nagel's objections. He reaffirms his conception of necessity, not as a mere relation between abstractions, but as a concrete connection holding in the world and operating in thought. As Blanshard presents the conflict between Nagel and himself, what is at stake is nothing less than two conceptions of rationality—to use the language of an earlier period, empirical naturalism versus dialectical idealism. As Blanshard puts the issue: "Nagel's rational man is one whose thinking is at every step determined by what (relatively to logic) is pure contingency; this purely contingent process leads with gratifying frequency to conclusions entailed by premises; and when they turn up, they are embraced with a glad cry. . . . The rational man, as I view him, does not always stumble and grope in darkness till he arrives at conclusions by luck, and then for the first time exhibit his rationality by accepting them. Necessity aids in the process and not only at the end" (14, p. 240).

In advancing a conception of the world as a rational system of logically necessary parts in which thought is satisfied, Blanshard differs from his idealist predecessors in one important respect. He does not contend, as they have done, that this world is also a system of value. On the contrary, breaking with the idealist tradition, Blanshard affirms, first, that "between the rational as the logically necessary and the rational as the morally right, there is an abyss of difference," and, second, that "to pass from 'everything is rational', in the sense of necessity, to 'everything is rational', in the sense of right, is to stultify one's moral perception" (9, p. 491). In Blanshard's philosophy arguments drawn from metaphysics and philosophical logic reinstate the idealist conception of the world as a logical whole of necessary parts, but considerations of the principles of moral philosophy do not so far justify the attribution of supreme value to the world as a whole.

NOTES TO CHAPTER III

1 Brand Blanshard, *On Philosophical Style* (Bloomington: Indiana University Press, 1954).
2 Brand Blanshard, "Introduction," *Education in the Age of Science* (New York: Basic Books, 1959).
3 See Andrew J. Reck, *Recent American Philosophy* (New York: Pantheon Books, 1964), Chs. 6 and 7.
4 Brand Blanshard, "Epilogue," in Arthur Pap, *An Introduction to the Philosophy of Science* (New York: Free Press, 1962).

5 Brand Blanshard, *The Nature of Thought* (2 vols.; London: Allen and Unwin, 1939).

6 T. M. Greene, Review, *Journal of Philosophy*, XXXVII (December 5, 1940), 686; and A. C. Ewing, Review, *Mind*, LIII (January, 1944), 75.

7 Ewing's review, through no fault of his own, appeared nearly five years after the publication of *The Nature of Thought*.

8 See Brand Blanshard, "Current Strictures on Reason," *Philosophical Review*, LIV (July, 1945).

9 Brand Blanshard, *Reason and Analysis* (London and LaSalle: Allen and Unwin and Open Court, 1962).

10 Brand Blanshard, *Reason and Goodness* (London: Allen and Unwin, 1961).

11 Brand Blanshard, "The Nature of Mind," in Sidney Hook (ed.), *American Philosophers at Work* (New York: Criterion Books, 1956).

12 Brand Blanshard, "The Impasse in Ethics and a Way Out," *University of California Publications in Philosophy*, XXVIII (1954).

13 This article appeared in Sidney Hook and Milton R. Konvitz (eds.), *Freedom and Experience* (Ithaca, N.Y.: Cornell University Press, 1947); in Ernest Nagel's own volume, *Sovereign Reason* (Glencoe, Ill.: Free Press, 1954); and in A. C. Ewing (ed.), *The Idealist Tradition: From Berkeley to Blanshard* (Glencoe, Ill.: Free Press, 1957). All references to this essay are to Nagel's *Sovereign Reason*.

14 Sydney and Beatrice Rome (eds.), *Philosophical Interrogations* (New York: Holt, Rinehart and Winston, 1964).

IV

NAGEL, RANDALL, AND BUCHLER

Columbia University Naturalism

NATURALISM AND ITS METROPOLITAN SETTING

In 1944 *Naturalism and the Human Spirit* (1) was published by Columbia University as the eighth volume in a series of studies issued under the auspices of the department of philosophy. This work has done for naturalism in contemporary American thought what *New Realism* (1912) and *Essays in Critical Realism* (1920) did for the realistic movements in the first quarter of the twentieth century (2). That *Naturalism and the Human Spirit* has not gained the attention the earlier works aroused is due mainly to its untimely appearance. In 1944 all Americans, including the philosophically-minded, were too preoccupied with the exigencies of the Second World War to devote themselves wholly to philosophy. Yet, as the realistic volumes did for an earlier generation, *Naturalism and the Human Spirit* amplified a tendency in American thought which was to spread in the postwar years.

John Dewey contributed the opening essay, a polemical piece directed against the so-called "anti-naturalisms," the antiscientific and religious doctrines which arose in the wake of the war. The list of the other contributors and the titles of their essays reveal the nature and range of naturalist concerns in America at mid-century. Sterling P. Lamprecht of Amherst College contributed "Naturalism and Religion"; Sidney Hook of New York University, "Naturalism and Democracy"; Abraham Edel of the City College of New York, "Naturalism and Ethical Study"; Eliseo Vivas, then of Wisconsin University, "A Natural History of the Aesthetic Transaction"; Herbert W. Schneider, then of Columbia University, "The Unnatural"; George Boas of Johns Hopkins University, "The History of Philosophy"; Edward W. Strong of the University of California (Berkeley), "The Materials of Historical Knowledge"; Thelma Z. Lavine of Wells College, "Naturalism and the Sociological Analysis of Knowledge"; Ernest Nagel of Columbia University, "Logic Without Ontology"; Yervant H. Krikorian of the City College of New York, "A Naturalistic View of Mind"; William R. Dennes of the University of California (Berkeley), "The Categories of Naturalism"; Harry Todd Costello of Trinity College (Hartford), "The Naturalism of Frederick Woodbridge"; Harold A. Larrabee of Union College, "Naturalism in America"; and John Herman Randall, Jr., of Columbia University, "Epilogue: The Nature of Naturalism."

In spite of differences of formulation and emphasis, these essays express the central ideas of contemporary naturalism. The dominant trait is a commitment to science, with science understood to signify not so much a definite system of knowledge as a disciplined method of inquiry. In the investigation of its subject matter—nature—science as a method excludes radical dualisms or bifurcations. Hence nature is one, or rather continuous; and man is a wholly natural being: his mind is rooted in nature and is not separate, and his values, instead of subsisting in some realm apart, originate in his natural desires, which have natural consummations. Thus naturalism aggressively repudiates antinaturalisms or supernaturalisms. Whatever science may discover nature to be, nature is all there is. Without supernatural agencies to assist or to hinder him, man is on his own as a natural being. Collectively men form societies to share experience and to work together toward common ends, but the setting for all human endeavor and achievement can never extend beyond nature. Contemporary naturalism, therefore, is essentially humanistic.

In addition to stating the central ideas of the naturalistic movement, *Naturalism and the Human Spirit* discloses a basic geographical fact. While the contributors represent institutions spread across the continent, there is a pronounced cluster in the East—in particular, in New York City. Seven of the fifteen were members of the faculties of institutions in New York City; four were from Columbia University. And the volume is dedicated to Morris Cohen (1880–1947), longtime professor of philosophy at the City College of New York, mentor of many of the contributors, and advocate of what Joseph L. Blau has termed "rationalistic naturalism" (3, pp. 334–43). That John Dewey, the leading exponent of "experimental naturalism" (3, pp. 343–55), heads the list of contributors not only indicates the unity of intent behind the variety of expression among naturalists but also points up the sense in which Columbia University may be regarded as the capital of the movement. For, as Randall has said, Dewey was "the greatest man and thinker ever to have been associated with this University" (4). As a matter of fact, Dewey shared his leadership at Columbia with another philosopher, one whose thought was not neglected in *Naturalism and the Human Spirit*—namely, Frederick J. E. Woodbridge (1867–1940). As a philosopher, as a founder and an editor of the *Journal of Philosophy*, as an administrator who served as Dean of the Columbia University Graduate School, Woodbridge had been one of the most eloquent spokesmen for humanistic naturalism. Indeed, he had succeeded in stating the classic thought of Aristotle in a contemporary idiom (5). Woodbridge's influence, like Dewey's, is still felt in Philosophy Hall on Morningside Heights today; it is perhaps most effective in Randall's thought and teaching.

It would be erroneous, however, to restrict naturalism as a movement to a few thinkers and a limited geographical area. As Larrabee has shown, the history of naturalism in America is a long one, and its geography is continental (1, pp. 319–53). Nevertheless, at present it flourishes not in mountain ranges, verdant fields, and virgin forests but in New York City, a bustling metropolis of steel and concrete. Indeed, it concentrates in the ring of New York colleges and universities among which Columbia is preeminent. Randall has described the "essence of the American spirit" as cosmopolitan, and he has found that spirit at its best in our cosmopolitan cities: San Francisco, Chicago, and New York (6). But Randall has gone beyond the boundaries of his city and his university to name the genius who has most inspired contemporary naturalism —"that cosmopolitan spirit whose influence has been exerted almost wholly on American philosophizing, Santayana" (1, p. 363). The Santayana Randall has in mind is the author of *The Life of Reason*, the thinker who characterized Aristotle with the lines that Woodbridge loved to quote: "Everything ideal has a natural basis, and everything natural an ideal fulfillment" (1, pp. 298, 363).

Santayana, Dewey, Cohen, and Woodbridge—these are the older naturalists, the founding fathers of the movement. Today the naturalists are legion, but among them three, all Columbia University professors, stand out: Ernest Nagel, John Herman Randall, Jr., and Justus Buchler. Each in his own way has advanced the cause of naturalism: Nagel by heightening its scientific character; Randall by adding an historical dimension; and Buchler by deepening and reforming its metaphysics. In addition to their technical contributions, Randall and Buchler have collaborated in writing a paperback college outline presentation of philosophy to propagate their naturalistic outlook (7). Let us now consider the thought of each in turn.

THE SCIENTIFIC NATURALISM OF ERNEST NAGEL

Ernest Nagel was born in Czechoslovakia on November 16, 1901. A naturalized American citizen, he graduated in 1923 from the City College of New York, where he studied under Morris Cohen. He received his M.A. from Columbia University in 1925 and his Ph.D. in 1930. For one year he taught at City College before joining the faculty of Columbia University, where he rose through the ranks, to become John Dewey Professor of Philosophy in 1955. In 1966 he joined the faculty of Rockefeller University, but returned to Columbia the following year. His association with Morris Cohen led to their joint authorship of the highly successful textbook *An Introduction to Logic and Scientific Method* (8). From Cohen, Nagel learned the primacy of the role of reason in science, and this rationalism, allied with realism and naturalism, was reinforced by the instruction at Columbia.

Nagel's career is remarkably similar to that of Cohen. Like Cohen, Nagel is a beloved teacher. Like Cohen, he possesses a rare genius for lucid exposition of the most recondite matters in logic, mathematics, and natural science (9). And, like Cohen, Nagel has directed his talents to the composition of essays and book reviews for professional journals, scientific periodicals, and literary reviews. Two of his books—*Sovereign Reason* (10) and *Logic Without Metaphysics* (11)—are simply collections of previously published material. Not until 1961, with the appearance of *The Structure of Science* (12), did Nagel produce a work which, although it contains some previously published material, yet satisfies the structural requirements of a book.

Contextualistic Analysis

Nagel's collections of studies do not lack unity. Although *Sovereign Reason*, for instance, which consists of sixteen essays, neither constitutes "a systematic discussion of a single philosophic problem," nor exhibits "a consecutive development of a single philosophic theme," it "does deal with a set of related problems," and provides "an evaluation of various proposals by influential writers for resolving many paramount issues in the philosophy of science" (10, p. 9). Nagel breaks down the problems treated by philosophers of science into four main types: the problem of "the relation of theory to gross experience," the problem of the nature and basis of reliable knowledge, the perennial quest for a total view of the universe, and the class of problems dealing with the relations of science to society (10, pp. 10–12). For dealing with each type of problem, Nagel offers specific proposals, proposals which, though not always explicitly, involve a unity of thought and procedure. This unity, which is as flexible as the problems demand, stems from Nagel's commitment to the method of contextualistic analysis.

According to the method of contextualistic analysis, no question should be so general that it can never be answered by evidence drawn from some specific subject matter; no problem should be discussed except in relation to the context that fixes its meaning; no method should be employed which replaces the problem it resolves with a new, insoluble difficulty; and no answer to a problem should be accepted if it assumes a completed body of knowledge (10, p. 13). Thus Nagel claims that "the best work [in the philosophy of science] . . . has been done by men who have sought to understand human reason by examining its operations in controlled inquiry, and who have interpreted the meaning of theoretical constructions in terms of their manifest functions in identifiable contexts" (10, p. 16).

Employing the method of contextualistic analysis, Nagel approaches the four general problems in the philosophy of science and evaluates the contributions of other thinkers. First, he deals with the problem of the relation of theory to gross experience, which has inspired the conception of philosophy as the critique of abstractions. He examines and criticizes, to take one example, Bertrand Russell's efforts to explain the concepts of "instants" and "atoms" in physics; and he condemns Russell for merely replacing one set of abstractions by another set of equally remote constructions (10, pp. 161–89). Secondly, on the problem of reliable knowledge, Nagel concedes that particular errors arise but denies that a problem of error in general exists. He criticizes Reichenbach for assuming that there is a problem of knowledge, and consequently for having to cope with the timeworn question concerning the proof for the existence of the external world (10, pp. 225–65). Thirdly, Nagel treats the quest for a total view, which he considers "an intelligible and worthy ideal," since it may serve, though its goal is unattainable, as the foundation for "general directives for human effort" (10, p. 14). But he rejects the schemes of Peirce, of Whitehead, and of Dewey (10, pp. 60–67, 154–60, 147–49) to furnish "a set of 'ultimate' categories which are compatible with *every possible* order of events, or which ascribe by vague analogy to everything in nature traits that are *known* to characterize only a limited sector of it" as "misleading verbal game[s]" or, in any event, as programs which "have still to prove their worth as alleged instruments either of explanation, criticism, or fruitful classification" (10, p. 14). Finally, on the question of the relation of science to society, Nagel repudiates the derivation of standards of human values from scientific conceptions of reality, but he insists that men should use the scientific method of controlled inquiry to solve social problems. In effect, his naturalistic conception of reason and scientific intelligence is reminiscent of John Dewey's. "The life of reason as embodied in the community of scientific effort," Nagel writes, "is thus a pattern of life that generates an autonomous yet controlling ideal" (10, p. 306).

Logical Empiricism

Nagel was one of the first American thinkers to take sympathetic account of the works of Wittgenstein, Schlick, and Carnap. His historic report "Impressions and Appraisals of Analytic Philosophy in Europe," originally published in the *Journal of Philosophy* in 1936 and reprinted in *Logic Without Metaphysics* in 1956, remains pertinent to current discussions. In this essay Nagel described the analytic movement at Cambridge University in the 1930's under G. E. Moore and Ludwig Wittgenstein, when the latter was already abandoning the theses of the *Tractatus Logico-Philosophicus* (1922) for the techniques of ordinary language analysis. Nagel's article was, after Herbert Feigl's (13), the first essay to introduce American philosophers to the logical positivism of the Vienna circle then led by Moritz Schlick. It related and appraised the thought of Rudolf Carnap, who was at that time at Prague, expounding the views that philosophy is the study of the logical syntax of language and that metaphysics should be dismissed because it rests on mistakes of grammar. It also praised the work of Polish logicians little known in America. Nagel assimilated these external influences without succumbing to the narrow, often negative, programs they gave rise to in so many other students (14).

As Manley Thompson has noted, a rapprochement between American pragmatists and naturalists on the one hand, and European positivists on the other, has never materialized on the scale anticipated in the thirties (15, pp. 131–32). But Nagel's own philosophy has adapted much of the teaching of logical positivism to the more resilient framework of contextualistic naturalism. Imbued by Cohen with a sense of the importance of reason, by Woodbridge with an appreciation of nature full-qualitied and substantial, and by Dewey with a conception of experience as objective and structured, Nagel has shaped logical empiricism into a balanced and tolerant philosophy. Thus it might better be labeled, to use the term he chose for the Carus Lectures he delivered in 1964, a rational empiricism. Indeed, Nagel epitomizes the absorption of the concerns and techniques of analytic philosophy into the broader stream of naturalism, an American naturalism into which the currents of pragmatism and of realism had already flowed.

Naturalism Defined

In 1954, on the occasion of his presidential address before the annual meeting of the Eastern Division of the American Philosophical Association, Nagel articulated the central tenets of his naturalism. Committed to the method of contextualistic analysis, on the ground that philosophers do their best work when they examine and solve specific problems in determinate subject matters, Nagel nonetheless seized the opportunity to sketch a general world view. For, as he conceives it, "naturalism embraces a generalized account of the cosmic scheme and of man's place in it, as well as a logic of inquiry" (11, p. 6).

Two theses are fundamental to naturalism. "The first is the existential and causal primacy of organized matter in the executive order of nature. This is the assumption that the occurrence of events, qualities and processes, and the characteristic behaviors of various individuals, are contingent on the organization of spatio-temporally located bodies, whose internal structures and external relations determine and limit the appearance and disappearance of everything that happens" (11, p. 7). This thesis rules out the agency of supernatural forces in and beyond nature, whether the supernatural power be viewed as a supposed immaterial spirit guiding the course of events or as allegedly immortal souls surviving natural death. "The second major contention of naturalism is that the manifest plurality and variety of things, of their qualities and their functions, are an irreducible feature of the cosmos, not a deceptive appearance cloaking some more homogeneous 'ultimate reality' or transempirical substance, and that the sequential orders in which events occur or the manifold relations of dependence in which things exist are *contingent* connections, not the embodiments of a fixed and unified pattern of logically necessary links" (11, pp. 7–8). Embracing the existence of mental events, of men continuous with nature, of human history and society, and of human values, Nagel's naturalism is clearly not the kind of materialism which reduces all phenomena to mere appearances of organized matter behaving in conformity to mechanical laws. However, it is a materialism in another sense. Whatever occurs, including mental events, Nagel holds, "is contingent upon the occurrence of certain complex physico-chemical-physiological events and structures. . . ." (11, p. 24). Hence naturalism means that "irreducible variety and logical contingency are fundamental traits of the world we actually inhabit" (11, p. 9).

Theory of Logic and Mathematics

Despite an early commitment to Morris Cohen's kind of realism, Nagel has formulated the implications of naturalism for logical theory better than any of his contemporaries. In the preface to the first edition of *An Introduction to Logic and Scientific Method* he and Cohen had described the ideal text as one which "would find a place for the realistic formalism of Aristotle, the scientific penetration of Peirce, the pedagogical soundness of Dewey, and the mathematical rigor of Russell" (8, p. iv). In contrast with Nagel's later contributions to logical theory, Aristotelian realism is the conspicuous element in the *Introduction*. According to Cohen and Nagel, logic is "concerned with the adequacy or probative value of different kinds of evidence" (8, p. 5). The implications between propositions comprise the subject matter of logic; furthermore, they constitute the structure of the world. Most propositions are about objects in the real world, and the implications between propositions have to do with "the possible relations between all such objects" (8, p. 18). These relations are objective and hold even when the propositions they connect are false. Hence logic deals with the possible as well as the actual and rules out what is impossible.

The development of Nagel's thought on logic is a movement

away from the Aristotelian realism of Cohen toward the naturalism of Dewey, although Nagel sometimes—as, for instance, in his polemic against Blanshard's theory of internal relations—reverts to Aristotelian modes of speech (10, pp. 266–95). Like Dewey, Nagel has addressed himself to the construction of a theory of logic within the framework of naturalism. In the probing critical essay examining Dewey's logic, which was first published in the 1940 festschrift *The Philosopher of the Common Man* (16) and was reprinted in *Sovereign Reason*, Nagel hailed Dewey's logical theory as "an impressive performance, whatever be the final judgment passed on the validity of the plan or the details of his reconstruction" (10, p. 135). At the same time he criticized Dewey for dealing too much with outmoded problems (10, p. 136), for failing to advance symbolic logic by neglecting the significance of formal systems and techniques (10, p. 137), and for "extremely vague if not ambiguous" formulation of his central technical distinctions (10, p. 138). Nevertheless, Nagel's basic orientation in logical theory reflects the influence of Dewey. To the 1935 anthology *American Philosophy Today and Tomorrow* (17) Nagel contributed an essay entitled "Notes Toward a Naturalistic Conception of Logic." Here his affinity with Dewey's general theory, expressed even before the publication of Dewey's *Logic*, is apparent. The reprinting of this essay in *Logic Without Metaphysics* confirms the continuity of Nagel's thought with Dewey's. Although Nagel places greater emphasis on symbolic logic and mathematics than Dewey would, he agrees with Dewey in conceiving logic to be an inclusive discipline which "studies the methods employed by men aiming at stable knowledge, assays their efficacy in achieving this aim, examines the role of critical thought in every department of human activity, and institutes a rigorous inquiry into the conditions upon which the significance and effective operation of discourse rest. It is a genuine organon for achieving a rational life and society" (11, p. 52).

In his famous essay "Logic Without Ontology," first published in the cooperative volume *Naturalism and the Human Spirit*, Nagel's contributions to the theory of logic reach an apex. Here he states the naturalistic conception of logic so as to discard all metaphysical presuppositions. He distinguishes three naturalistic conceptions of logic, in accord with the different ways naturalists treat, for example, the principle of noncontradiction. The first, a classical form of naturalism, defines this principle to be "a necessary truth which is descriptive of the limiting structure of everything both actual and possible. . . ." The second construes it "to be a contingent but highly reliable conclusion based on an empirical study of nature. . . ." And the third takes it "to be void of factual content and to codify an arbitrary specification for the construction of symbolic systems" (11, p. 56). Analogous differences among naturalists pertain to their interpretations of other logical principles and of mathematics. Nagel's argument is much too detailed to repeat here; it suffices to note that he subjects each conception to critical scrutiny, with the intention of demonstrating that it is inconsistent with naturalistic assumptions.

If it [naturalism] professes to accept the methods employed by the various empirical sciences for obtaining knowledge about the world, it cannot with consistency claim to have *a priori* insight into the most pervasive structure of things. If it aims to give a coherent and adequate account of the various principles employed in acquiring scientific knowledge, it cannot maintain that all of them are empirical generalizations when some are not subject to experimental refutation. And if it admits that logical principles have a recognizable function in certain contexts (namely, in inquiry), it cannot consistently hold those principles to be completely arbitrary simply on the ground that they are void of factual content when considered apart from those contexts (11, pp. 56–57).

In place of the three discarded conceptions, Nagel offers his own theory of logic. Consonant with the implications of contextualistic analysis for logical theory, Nagel interprets logico-mathematical concepts and principles in terms of the operations associated with them in specific contexts. From an examination of the laws of thought— the principles of logic—as these operate in the specific context of language, he concludes that they are not a priori structures of reality, nor empirical generalizations, nor mere formal tautologies, but normative rules, prescriptive for the use of language. "They specify minimal conditions for discourse without confusion, for they state at least some of the requirements for a precise language" (11, p. 74). They may also be employed to establish necessary connections between statements, statements which themselves need not be necessary. Thus the distinction between the laws of thought and the rules of inference, e.g., *ponendo ponens*, is contextual rather than absolute. In any event, the rules of inference serve to clarify the vague intent of ordinary language; they "help to *fix* usages where they have previously been unsettled; they serve as *proposals* for modifying old usages and instituting new ones" (11, p. 76).

The conception of logical principles in "Logic Without Ontology" differs from that in *An Introduction to Logic and Scientific Method*. In the earlier work logical principles are described as "certain *general or generic traits of all things whatsoever*" (8, p. 185). Logical principles are, therefore, principles of being. This realistic metaphysics of logic Nagel discarded once and for all in "Logic Without Ontology." This enabled him to cope more easily with the theory of symbolic logic and with the problem of construing in some coherent way the plurality of logical systems it has generated. He describes the various mathematical logics, of which the symbolic logic of Whitehead and Russell's *Principia Mathematica* is but one type, "not as accounts of the 'true nature' of an antecedently identifiable relation of 'implication,' but as alternative proposals for specifying usages and for performing inferences" (11, p. 76). The elaboration of alternative symbolic systems is tantamount to the articulation of rival sets of regulative principles for reconstructing linguistic behavior. The choice between systems, though not grounded in the putative nature of reality or of necessity, need not be arbitrary; it should be grounded "on the relatively greater adequacy of one of them as an instrument for achieving a certain systematization of knowledge" (11, p. 77).

Nagel's theory of mathematics follows the same lines. The distinction between pure and applied mathematics, which he deems to be "one of the most enlightening and fruitful contributions of modern logical research" (11, p. 83), gives rise to new problems. Perhaps most serious is the problem of relating the two, since the propositions of pure mathematics are logically necessary and are warranted without reference to empirical evidence, while those of applied mathematics relate to laboratory procedures and are empirical. This type of problem, according to Nagel, is solved by attending to the operations of mathematics in specific contexts of inquiry. For example, consider arithmetic as it operates in the context of measurement. Here its formulae "are *norms* for isolating certain properties and relations of bodies and for instituting further operations upon them" (11, p. 86). Independent of measurement, properties have no intrinsic magnitudes; stipulations appropriate to empirical properties in specific contexts invest them with arithmetically expressible magnitudes. Nagel's point is that it is not necessary to assume that mathematics mirrors the real structures of things.

Symbolism in mathematics as in logic has important functions to perform in inquiry, and the aim of Nagel's empiricism is to correct the undervaluation of formal symbolism and symbolic manipulations fostered by traditional empiricism. Symbolism, however, does not reflect any supposed necessities of thought or structures of reality. Thus Nagel attains his objective—"to make plausible the view that the role of logico-mathematical disciplines in inquiry can be clarified without requiring the invention of a hypostatic subject matter for them; and to suggest that a naturalism free from speculative vagaries and committed to a wholehearted operational standpoint expresses the temper of modern mathematico-experimental science" (11, p. 57).

Scientific Method

Nagel's emphasis on the role of reason is evident not only in the place he accords formal systems in science but also in his conception of scientific method. Science is, of course, the basic institution of naturalism. However its method may be analyzed, that method is the naturalist's sole method of knowing; and whatever its findings may be, they furnish the categories of naturalism. But empiricists disagree over what science is and means, and their disagreement centers on the very conception of scientific method. Whereas traditional empiricism, beginning with Francis Bacon, tends to look upon scientific method as the strict description of facts, experimental empiricism grants the scientist a more creative office.

According to experimentalism, the scientist is engaged in the solution of selected problems by means of hypotheses which are initially suggested by intelligence and subsequently tested by facts. In *An Introduction to Logic and Scientific Method* Cohen and Nagel subscribed to experimental empiricism: "It is an utterly superficial view . . . that the truth is to be found by 'studying the facts.' It is superficial because no inquiry can even get under way until and unless *some difficulty is felt* in a practical or theoretical situation. It is the difficulty, or problem, which guides our search for some *order among the facts*, in terms of which the difficulty is to be removed" (8, p. 199). The problem, its observation and analysis, marks the first stage of scientific method. In the second stage an hypothesis, suggested by the subject matter or by previous knowledge, is constructed; it is advanced tentatively, to explain or solve the problem. "The function of a hypothesis is to *direct* our search for order among facts" (8, p. 201). Thus, instead of being dictated by the facts, the hypothesis actually determines the significance and relevance of the facts. To be sound, of course, an hypothesis must itself be relevant to its problem, and it is deemed sound when "it expresses determinate modes of connections between a set of facts, including the fact investigated" (8, p. 202). The hypothesis, moreover, must allow for testing by further facts. Here the third stage of scientific method begins. From the hypothesis deductions are made, and these deductions are to be tested by facts. At this point the systems and techniques of logic and mathematics play their important roles in scientific method. Fourth, the actual testing of the hypothesis takes place; experimentation in the restricted sense of the term occurs. Finally, the hypothesis is verified or falsified, and, when it is verified, the original difficulty or problem is explained or solved.

Scientific Explanation

Nagel's major contribution to the philosophy of science is his excellent textbook *The Structure of Science*. As he declares in the Preface, there are three areas to be studied in the logic of science: the nature of scientific explanations, the logical structure of scientific concepts, and the evaluations of the claims to knowledge in the various sciences (12, pp. viii-ix). Promising to deal with the second and third parts in a later work, Nagel devoted his energies in *The Structure of Science* to the logic of scientific explanations: "with their logical structure, their mutual relations, their functions in inquiry, and their devices for systematizing knowledge" (12, p. ix).

According to Nagel, there are four types of scientific explanation. First is the deductive type of explanation. Having the formal structure of a deductive argument, this type of explanation treats the fact to be explained as "a logically necessary consequence of the explanatory premises" (12, p. 21). Second is the class of probabilistic explanations. Lacking sufficient evidence, the explanatory premises in probabilistic explanations do not formally imply the facts to be explained, although they make them probable (12, p. 22). Third, there are, especially in the contexts of biology and social science, functional or teleological explanations. These explanations "take the form of indicating one or more functions (or even dysfunctions) that a unit performs in maintaining or realizing certain traits of a system to which the unit belongs, or of stating the instrumental role an action plays in bringing about some goal" (12, pp. 23–24). Finally, there is the class of genetic explanations. Employed in historical inquiries, genetic explanations account for certain characteristics of a given subject of study "by describing how the subject has evolved out of some earlier one" (12, p. 25).

In directing attention to the logic of explanation in science, Nagel boldly underscores that conception of science which makes explaining why, not merely describing how, central to the scientific enterprise (12, pp. 26–28). "It is," he writes, "the desire for explanations which are at once systematic and controllable by factual evidence that generates science; and it is the organization and classification of knowledge on the basis of explanatory principles that is the distinctive goal of the sciences" (12, p. 4).

Seeking explanations, scientists construct theories. Thus scientific theory, its nature and status, is one of Nagel's major preoccupations. Indeed, the early chapters of *The Structure of Science* deal with theory in general, the later chapters with particular theories and their special problems. Consideration of Nagel's remarks on the special problems, noteworthy as they are, would lengthen unduly the discussion of his thought; it suffices here to note his general analysis of scientific theory and his treatment of the problem of the cognitive status of scientific theories.

What, then, is the nature of a scientific theory? Nagel's answer to this question stresses the logico-mathematical character of science, though it is based on empirical data. There are, he writes, three components in a theory: first, "an abstract calculus that is the logical skeleton of the explanatory system, and that 'implicitly defines' the basic notions of the system"; second, "a set of rules that in effect assign an empirical content to the abstract calculus by relating it to the concrete materials of observation and experiment"; and third, "an interpretation or model for the abstract calculus, which supplies some flesh for the skeletal structure in terms of more or less familiar conceptual or visualizable materials" (12, p. 90).

What, next, is the cognitive status of scientific theories? Nagel presents and criticizes three standard answers to this question, then resolves it in an original way. The three standard answers are the descriptive view of the cognitive status of scientific theories, the instrumentalist view, and the realist view.

The descriptive view regards theory as "a compendious but elliptic formulation of relations of dependence between observable events and properties" (12, p. 118). Accordingly, the assertions of the theory, although not designatable as true or false themselves, may be translated into statements about matters of fact. In the descriptive view, moreover, theoretical terms like "electron" do not signify external physical objects but are a kind of shorthand notation for sets of observable data. The instrumentalist view maintains that "theories are primarily logical instruments for organizing our experience and for ordering experimental laws . . . . [They] function as rules or principles in accordance with which empirical materials are analyzed or inferences drawn, rather than as premises from which factual conclusions are deduced . . ." (12, p. 118). In the instrumentalist view, theories are unlike statements about observable matters of fact; they are properly describable not as true or false but rather as instrumental. Instrumentalist thinkers disagree over the reality status of theoretical entities. Realism, which is in fact the oldest of the three views, holds that "a theory is literally either true or false . . . [and] that when a theory is well supported by empirical evidence, the objects ostensibly postulated by the theory (e.g., atoms, in the case of atomic theory) must be regarded as possessing a physical reality at least on par with the physical reality commonly ascribed to familiar objects such as sticks and stones" (12, pp. 117–18).

Nagel subjects these three views to critical scrutiny and assesses the merits and defects of each. Chapter Five of *The Structure of Science* (12, pp. 106–52) marks a high point in subtlety, lucidity, and cogency. The flexibility of the method of contextualistic analysis is shown here to its best advantage. Admitting the utility of each of the standard views in given contexts of scientific explanation and theory construction, Nagel takes a standpoint of analysis which allows all three views. He resorts to a kind of principle of tolerance; he assumes the role of the linguistic philosopher who resolves the conflict between rival points of view by showing that this conflict is due not to real differences concerning matters of fact but fundamentally to misunderstandings about the uses of words. Inasmuch as the descriptive view of the cognitive status of scientific theories is, in effect, a combination of the instrumentalist and the realist views —instrumentalist in the upper levels of the theory and realist at the level of empirical statements—the basic issue seems to be one between realism and instrumentalism over the truth status of theories and the reality status of theoretical entities. Yet, according to Nagel's analysis, the basic issue, despite what it may at first seem, is actually a matter of language, of how, for example, to decide upon criteria for the employment of the word "reality." Thus Nagel concludes that "when the two apparently opposing views on the cognitive status of theories are each stated with some circumspection, each can assimilate into its formulations not only the facts concerning the primary subject matter explored by experimental inquiry but also all the relevant facts concerning the logic and procedure of science. In brief, the opposition between these views is a conflict over preferred modes of speech" (12, p. 152).

Nagel's strategy of reducing philosophical controversies to conflicts over "preferred modes of speech," exemplified in the instance of the cognitive status of theories, is employed again and again in the critique of other philosophical disputes. It involves a method of analysis which has its roots in the pragmatism of William James, who jocularly compared metaphysical disputes to verbal quibbles about squirrels running around trees, as well as in the logical positivism of Rudolf Carnap, for whom metaphysical disputes originate in confusions or disagreements about language.

THE HISTORICAL NATURALISM
OF JOHN HERMAN RANDALL, JR.

John Herman Randall, Jr., was born in Grand Rapids, Michigan, on February 14, 1899. By parentage, by education, and by profession he is a member of the naturalist community of Columbia University. He is the son of the distinguished intellectual historian who taught at Columbia through the first quarter of the twentieth century. He received his formal higher education at Columbia, where he earned his B.A. in philosophy in 1918, his M.A. in 1919, and his Ph.D. in 1922, and where he was decisively influenced by both John Dewey and Frederick Woodbridge. He joined the faculty of Columbia University as an instructor in 1920 and rose through the ranks, becoming a full professor in 1935 and Woodbridge Professor of Philosophy in 1951. Like his colleague Ernest Nagel, John Herman Randall, Jr., has served—along with Herbert W. Schneider and Justus Buchler—as an editor of the *Journal of Philosophy*. In 1956 he was elected president of the Eastern Division of the American Philosophical Association. His contributions to philosophy were recognized by his Columbia University colleagues in 1947, when he was awarded the Nicholas Murray Butler Medal in Silver.

A professed naturalist, Randall shares with Nagel and other members of the naturalistic movement the same basic principles and orientation. But his interests differ from those of Nagel. For Nagel, who has made the best account of the formal, natural, and social sciences from the naturalist standpoint, science is the paramount concern. For Randall, although science remains important, concern with culture in the broad sense takes precedence. Hence Randall's major work is in the field of intellectual history, and his primary philosophical interests, evident from his publications, are metaphysics, philosophy of history, and philosophy of religion. As a consequence of Randall's concentration on history and naturalistic metaphysics, his philosophy may be termed—to use the title of an essay first published in *American Philosophy Today and Tomorrow* (17, pp. 411–32) and later reprinted as the Prologue to *Nature and Historical Experience* (18, pp. 1–19)—"historical naturalism."

The Cultural Context of Philosophy

Randall is an historian of philosophy whose work is of the highest rank; he is, indeed, without equal among American intellectual historians of his generation. As a young man he wrote a highly successful book on the history of modern thought (19). *The Making of the Modern Mind*, despite its author's devotion to the study of the past, is firmly rooted in its own time and place—urban America in the 1920's. In the words of its subtitle, it is *A Survey of the Intellectual Background of the Present Age*, and the opening sentence of the Foreword states the author's aim: ". . . by entering sympathetically into the spirit of the past, to make the thought of the present more intelligible." Later Randall came to doubt the validity of this early work. For *The Making of the Modern Mind* divides the history of thought into periods of transition and of synthesis, and the more Randall studied modern civilization, the less he was satisfied with this sort of division. Transition, he found, is the normal state of affairs, the almost universal condition.

Randall's second book, *Our Changing Civilization* (20), focuses on the present and its problems. The subtitle underscores the basic theme: "How Science and the Machine Are Reconstructing Modern Life." Randall views cultural institutions—science, religion, art, and morality—not only in the light of modern man's development, but also with specific reference to present problems. Writing in the late 1920's, Randall grasped the significance of the recent changes in the basic concepts of science, and he concluded: "To devise an adequate philosophy of science is one of the major tasks of modern thought" (20, p. 244). Bent on research and discovery, the contemporary scientist lacks the conception of order which science has traditionally fostered. Since the scientist accepts truth as his highest value, he comes to face, when he reflects, questions concerning values which are answerable only outside of science. "To evaluate the ultimate standards of truth requires a still more ultimate ideal of life" (20, p. 254). Further, science has spawned technology, which in turn has wrought the industrial revolution. Thus the machine, more than science, has shaped the course and character of modern civilization. Indeed, religion is at odds not so much with science as with the industrial, urban civilization created by technology. As Randall comments: "Stand in the fields, look up to the hills, live amid the rain and the wind and the growing crops, and you naturally feel the religious emotions of humility and awe, reverence, and dependence and thanksgiving. Stand in a humming factory: what has this mass of moving iron to do with religion?" (20, p. 278). Recording his first-hand impressions of Europe in the late 1920's, when Italy was strongly Fascist and Germany feebly democratic, Randall apprehended that in industrial civilization nationalism, meeting the needs which religion fails to satisfy, supplants religion. And religion is not the only casualty of the combined impact of science and the machine. Art, too, has withered. Instead of being "the natural expression of man's daily life and normal activities," art has been relegated to "a realm apart, with traditions and attitudes of its own open only to the initiate" (20, p. 295). Of course, Randall notes that, when art takes the machine itself as its subject matter, as it does, for example, in the engineering of automobiles, its prospects improve. Finally, under the pressure of industrial development and urbanization, morality undergoes radical transformation. In personal life the family either breaks down or changes its character; in public life the growth of organization in economics and politics threatens individual liberty. Reconciling the demands for social organization with the values of human freedom becomes the crucial problem for contemporary man. Randall calls for an experimental moral faith in words which reflect the influence of John Dewey: "The first and most essential task is to devise more adequate means for bringing

intelligence to bear on the organization of the new civilization"
(20, p. 361).

As a human and cultural enterprise, philosophy exists in relation
to religion, art, science, industry, commerce, and politics. Identified
as "a concern with what is significant and meaningful in human experience" (7, p. 6), philosophy is both analytic and speculative.
Drawing its insights from all fields of human experience, it attempts
to present the most coherent, comprehensive vision of the world;
it is speculative. Yet, in adjusting the various parts of experience and
the beliefs they engender into a meaningful whole, it is also analytic.
Because the experiences which lie at the base of philosophies are
various, the philosophies themselves vary, though their expansion in
the quest of comprehensiveness causes them to approach each other.
Since philosophy always dwells in the context of existent cultural
institutions and social experience, the experience it receives is already organized and interpreted. Thus historically and concretely
the function of philosophy "has been not so much to organize and
interpret the social experience and institutionalized beliefs and aims
of men in a given society, as to *reorganize and reinterpret* them"
(7, p. 28). According to Randall, a profound tension or conflict at
the heart of Western civilization has been responsible for its unusually rich history of philosophy. For in Western civilization the
two principal ways of interpreting and giving significance to human
life—"the meaning expressed in its professed religious and ethical
beliefs, and the meaning implicitly embodied in the activities and
aims it actually pursued" (7, p. 32)—have been complexly related
and even divergent. The Western peoples borrowed their ethical wisdom from the ancient Greeks; then they were converted to Christianity. Meanwhile they created a new civilization, based on their
distinctive social experience and institutional arrangements as
worked out in actual practice, and culminating in science, technology, and industrialism. This tension has been a major factor in
Western civilization, instigating cultural change as well as inspiring
philosophies. Because it is implicated in culture, philosophy naturally changes as the culture changes. "Philosophical thinking is the
intellectual expression of the process of cultural change; it is the

intellectual phase of the process by which conflicts within a culture are analyzed and clarified, resolved and composed" (7, p. 35).

Intellectual History

Change for Randall is fundamental to civilization and to philosophy. But change is not abrupt and discontinuous: "In human history there are no real discontinuities; there is only more or less gradual change" (20, p. 76). This is particularly true of intellectual history. Indeed, the more Randall has studied the history of philosophy, the more convinced he has become that there are underlying continuities of thought.

In recent years Randall has undertaken to write a monumental history of modern philosophy, the greatest ever attempted in the English language, entitled *The Career of Philosophy* (21). Two massive volumes have appeared to date. The first volume, *From the Middle Ages to the Enlightenment*, which came out in 1962, displays Randall's achievements as an historian of Renaissance thought (22). It illustrates superbly why the Columbia University circle, which Paul Oscar Kristeller heads and with which Randall is affiliated, is internationally acclaimed for its researches into Renaissance thought (15, pp. 76–77). Randall's volume is also remarkable for its emphasis on the continuities of thought which stretch from the middle ages to what is customarily regarded as the beginnings of modern philosophy in the seventeenth century. In fact, Randall's narration of how the traditions of Aristotelianism, Platonism, and the nominalism of William of Ockham carried over into the modern epoch is without equal in the existing histories of philosophy. The second volume of *The Career of Philosophy*, which appeared in 1965, traces the development of modern philosophy, in the words of its title, *From the German Enlightenment to the Age of Darwin*. For this volume Randall received in 1966 the Ralph Waldo Emerson Award, given annually by Phi Beta Kappa in the fields of history, philosophy, and religion for interpretative syntheses that carry forward the great tradition of humane learning. A third volume, to tell the story up to the present, is projected.

The key to Randall's historiography of ideas is the notion of the philosophical tradition. He defines a philosophical tradition as "a persistent body of ideas tied together by subtle associations as well as by logical relations, which persists over the generations, and dominates and colors the thinking of those who for one reason or another have been brought up in it" (23, p. 47). A tradition enjoys a career; from its beginning it exhibits a kind of identity while adjusting to changing conditions. According to Randall, four main traditions have dominated Western thought: the Platonic, the Aristotelian, the atomistic, and the skeptical traditions. In deference to Richard McKeon, Randall concedes that there may be "a fifth relatively independent tradition, the Ciceronian tradition of rhetoric, immensely influential during the Renaissance" (23, p. 51). By focusing on the "tradition" as the fundamental unit of intellectual history, Randall consciously and explicitly breaks with A. O. Lovejoy, the American father of the history of ideas (24). Lovejoy conceived intellectual history atomistically; he seized upon isolatable unit-ideas as the fundamental subjects for investigation. According to Randall, Lovejoy's method cannot do justice to the continuation of the relations between certain ideas. Of course Randall, like Lovejoy, wants to employ rigorous methods of analysis in intellectual history; he rejects the view that "each philosophy is an indivisible, unanalyzable, 'organic' whole" (23, p. 55). But unlike Lovejoy he does not dissect intellectual history, including the thought systems of single thinkers, into many often incompatible and always separable ideas. As Randall says: "The intellectual unit is not an atomic idea, it is a system—an 'organic' system, not in the sense that it cannot be analyzed, but in the sense that it is growing and living, responding to the countless pressures that impinge on it from other sources" (23, p. 55).

There is at least one other major difference between Randall and Lovejoy concerning intellectual history. For Lovejoy the historical past is forever fixed, and the task of the historian is to discover it. For Randall, who here follows the pragmatists such as Dewey and Mead, the historical past changes with the present. The historian, he insists, "can not be concerned with the entire past, with all its infinitesimal detail; he is concerned only with the 'basic' or *signifi-*

cant past, with that selection from all that did happen which *has* happened—with the history of what *has* happened as significant and meaningful events. And it is precisely this 'basic' past, this *meaning* and *significance* of the past, that is continually changing, that is cumulative and progressive" (18, p. 39).

Return to Aristotle

While Randall's *Career of Philosophy* demonstrates his emphasis on tradition in the writing of intellectual history, his *Aristotle* (25) best illustrates the importance of the present in determining the selection and interpretation of the past. For Randall interprets the Greek philosopher from the standpoint, and even in the terms, of contemporary naturalism. Torn between a formalism learned from Plato and a functionalism derived from extensive investigations into nature, Aristotle moves from the former to the latter position. Hence, on Randall's reading, Aristotle is a very current thinker.

The "return to Aristotle" in contemporary thought is due, no doubt, to the influence of Frederick J. E. Woodbridge (26). Randall and Richard McKeon must be counted among Woodbridge's outstanding students. Randall has advanced the study of Aristotle at Columbia University. McKeon, along with Robert Hutchins and Mortimer Adler, played a major part in making the University of Chicago into a center of Aristotelianism during the 1930's and 1940's. But the neo-scholasticism of Chicago's Aristotle is stripped away in Columbia's Aristotle. At Columbia, Aristotle emerges as a contemporary, contextualist, functionalist, experimental naturalist. As Randall says: " 'Aristotelianism' certainly means an emphasis on the primacy of the subject matter, the experienced world encountered" (25, p. 297). It "uses a factorial analysis, and does not fall into the seductive snares of reductive analysis," since, instead of stressing basic elements in its subject matter and then constructing all others from them, Aristotelian factorial analysis "seeks for factors and structures it can distinguish within a subject matter, but understands them always in terms of the way they are found to be functioning within the context of the subject matter" (25, pp. 297–98). Aristotelianism propounds a naturalistic theory of the status of man in the world, conceiving man as "a distinctive illustration of what any natural process is like" (25, p. 298). It construes knowledge as an activity involving language, so that "knowledge is a matter of language and saying, of words and sentences, of verbalized distinctions and of precise statements" (25, p. 298). Yet "Aristotelianism means also a logical realism, a structuralism. Knowledge is a discovery, a finding of something" (25, p. 299). Finally, "Aristotelianism means a functional realism, a philosophy of process: Aristotle is the major functionalist in the Western tradition. The structures found are always those of determinate processes, functioning in determinate contexts: Aristotle is clearly a contextualist" (25, p. 299).

Of course Randall's interpretation of Aristotle has not gone unchallenged. George Boas, who inherited Lovejoy's mantle at Johns Hopkins University, has caustically observed that it is "historically unsound and artistically unwise. . . . [It] exhibits more piety to a beloved teacher, Woodbridge, than critical exegesis of a text" (27). As strong an influence as Woodbridge on the shaping of Randall's thought was John Dewey. Indeed, Randall's Aristotle looks startlingly like Dewey, although Randall himself might state the similarity in another, opposite way. In an essay devoted to a consideration of John Dewey as an historian of philosophy, Randall has suggested that it would not be difficult to "exhibit Dewey as an Aristotelian more Aristotelian than Aristotle himself" (28). And so Aristotelianism, filtered through the combined teachings of Woodbridge and of Dewey, may serve as an introduction to Randall's own constructive philosophy.

Metaphysics

Randall's philosophy just missed systematic articulation in his collection of essays *Nature and Historical Experience*. With an overriding interest in history, Randall has bent Aristotle's concepts into the contemporary notions of process, function, and context. History is, however, not a special subject matter; nor is it a single absolute embracing all processes. Rather, it is "a character, an adjective, a predicate" (18, p. 27) of all subject matters, and there is a plurality of particular histories. As Randall says: "Everything . . . is historical in character, and has an existence that can be measured in time. And this historical aspect which any particular thing has and possesses is an essential part of what it is" (18, p. 27).

Such reflections lead Randall directly to metaphysics. Nagel, as previously noted, doubted the validity and the fruitfulness of metaphysics as a theory of the basic categories of existence as existence. Despite a commitment to philosophy as a cultural enterprise which deals with problems generated by the institutions of art, science, religion, morality, and politics, Randall nevertheless has a high regard for metaphysics. Like Herbert Schneider (29) and, as will be seen, like Justus Buchler—Columbia colleagues in the naturalistic cause— Randall has devoted some of his most intense intellectual labors to the articulation of a metaphysics. For metaphysics is too important "an instrument of criticism and analysis" (18, p. 143) to be ignored.

Randall's metaphysics offers a synthesis of Aristotle (interpreted according to Woodbridge's teaching) with Dewey. In fact, Randall equates Aristotle's philosophy of being (substance) with Dewey's philosophy of experience (process). Accordingly, the subject matter of metaphysics is what is encountered in all experience; it is the pervasive category of substance. To understand this subject matter it is necessary to draw upon the teachings of both Aristotle and Dewey. "Aristotle's analysis of Substance as the operation of powers, and Dewey's analysis of the Situation, mutually illuminate each other" (18, pp. 148–49). By this mutual illumination the opposition between the philosophy of being based on substance and the philosophy of experience founded on process is overcome. Substance, says Randall, is "what we today call 'process' "; it is "encountered and known as a complex of interacting and cooperating processes, each exhibiting its own determinate ways of cooperating, or Structure" (18, p. 152). Substance, moreover, "is always encountered by men in a *specific* transaction, a *specific* cooperation" (18, p. 154).

While substance is the context or situation in which experience occurs and is encountered most revealingly "in acting and being acted upon, in making and doing, in manipulation and experimentation, in τέχνη, art" (18, p. 153), it possesses structure, which reflective experience discovers. Structure, the analyzed attribute of substance, is formal or functional. Formal structure is "the way things are put together," the mechanisms and means internal to the thing's constitution or makeup; "it is invariant through a range of different contexts" (18, p. 163). Functional structure is the way things behave, "the structure of their *functioning as* means and materials *for a* determinate process, the structure of their way of cooperating in a specific context, their way of interacting in a particular situation"; thus it "is 'relative' to the process and its field, to that situation" (18, p. 163).

Randall's analysis of substance and structure introduces his set of metaphysical categories (18, p. 176). In accordance with the functionalistic conception of metaphysics, these categories are not kinds of being but the ways things or factors function in situations. They are, furthermore, closely linked to the parts of speech discriminable in discourse. Below is Randall's table of categories:

Category	Part of Speech	Mode of Encounter
Operations	Verbs	Direct Experience
Powers	Nouns	Reflective Experience
Ways of Operating	Adverbs	As Functional Structures in Reflective Experience
Kinds of Powers	Adjectives	As Formal Structures in Reflective Experience
Connectives	Conjunctions	

The fifth category deserves separate attention. For connectives "pervade the experienced world," (18, p. 194) and are "human ways of cooperating with other human processes" (18, p. 196). Randall distinguishes three principal types of connectives and many subtypes (18, p. 262). The main types are linguistic systems, symbols, and myths. Myths are historical or metaphysical, while symbols may be cognitive—as in the case of science, mathematics, and logic—or noncognitive—as in the case of legal systems, moral codes, art, and religion. Connectives perform a most important function in Randall's metaphysics: they institute objective relations among the factors of substance. Substance, let us recall, is always encountered in some specific context. The world, or nature, is always given as a plurality.

To unify, or at least to relate the determinate situations, the specific things and facts, is the job of the connectives. Man undertakes the invention, the institution, and the employment of connectives to bring unity to his experience, to nature.

Philosophy of Language and of Religion

Among the connectives, language and religion have received Randall's most serious consideration. In recent years more attention on the part of young American philosophers has been devoted to the philosophy of language than to any other field, except possibly ethics. This development has no doubt been due to Wittgenstein at Cambridge and the ordinary language analysts at Oxford, to the analytic philosophers at Cornell University led by Max Black and Norman Malcolm, to formal logicians like Rudolf Carnap, Willard Van Orman Quine, and Alfred Tarski, semanticists like Charles Morris, and linguists like Benjamin Whorf and Noam Chomsky. Randall's own interest in the field, however, harks back to the teaching of Woodbridge; in particular he has been openly hostile to the British analysts and their American followers. In his presidential address before the Eastern Division of the American Philosophical Association, an address barbed with *ad hominem* arguments, he wittily stated his opposition to ordinary language analysis, on the ground that the practitioners of that method overlook some basic facts about reality and knowledge. Language, according to Randall, is about some extra-linguistic subject matter, and looking, an activity which for Randall occurs in scientific observation and experimentation, is a better way to know this subject matter than mere talking (30). Later, on the occasion of the publication of *Nature and Historical Experience*, he asserted that he was postponing the publication of his philosophy of language "in the hope that Oxford in its wild gyrations will eventually and speedily come closer to his own functional and realistic approach" (18, p. 262).

Perhaps abandoning all hope for Oxford, Randall has recently come forth with his theory of language (31). It is a naturalistic theory, to which he has given the name "functional realism." According to this theory, language is "one natural process involved in a broader context of natural processes interacting and cooperating with each other" (31, p. 29). It is an activity, an art, which involves four factors: first, a subject matter, consisting of the traits of the universe of action which are discriminated and selected for the universe of discourse; second, a product—statements, etc., whether spoken, written, or internal; third, an instrument to make discourse, i.e., a language in the sense of a specific set of linguistic habits; and fourth, the ends, or purposes, of the discourse, to signify. In regard to the fourth factor, signification may be representative, or indicative, in which case the language employed consists of signs; or signification may be nonrepresentative, as when the paramount concern is with the organization, reconstruction, or rearrangement of the traits of reality, in which case symbols are used. At any rate, because language has these different functions, there are different kinds of language, and Randall has prepared a chart of the kinds of language according to function: natural science, social science, poetry, metaphysics, and religion (31, p. 40). Despite these differences in function, languages are related to reality. And in Randall's theory the relation is one of correspondence as construed in accord with functional realism. "The functioning of the specific instruments of discourse, the particular sentences and other types of connected words, involves 'real' 'objective' factors in the linguistic situation, factors, that is, that are independent of that specific functional context of speaking. There is a functional 'correspondence' between factors in the instrument and in the materials. But it is not discoverable except as the instrument does what it is intended to do, as the sentence does serve its function, does grasp, convey, and appropriately reorganize some elements in the structure of operations involved in the active and linguistic situations" (31, pp. 54–55).

As regards the second connective, religion, it might be well to point out that Randall is one of the few naturalists to be genuinely interested in the subject. His theory of religion, although not much more than a sketch when compared with his ampler treatment of metaphysics, is not simply an appendix to a system. It is rather the expression of an interest that dates back to his youth. In 1929, in collaboration with his father, Randall published *Religion and the*

Modern World (32) and reached the essential Deweyan position five years before the publication of John Dewey's Terry Lectures at Yale, *Our Common Faith* (1934). For an accurate statement of their views the authors quote from Herbert Schneider's article entitled "Faith," which appeared in the *Journal of Philosophy* in 1918. "God" is "the symbol of man's supreme allegiance," and "faith in Divinity is the hope that men may see more clearly the ideal possibilities of human life, and seeing, reweave the tangled fabric of their lives" (32, pp. 247–48).

Paul Tillich, with whom Randall conducted a seminar on religion, has, along with the early influence of Santayana, molded Randall's latest thought on religion. Concentrating on the symbolic structures in religion, he holds them to be noncognitive in character. However, he does not dismiss religion as scientific naturalism usually does when it discovers that religion is noncognitive; nor does he leap irrationally into an existential religious commitment. Rather, he adopts the position that religion, while devoid of cognitive value, is *not* meaningless. Religion projects the social ideals and values of men, and, although these ideals and values do not come from reason alone, reason is significantly relevant to their emergence and evolution. Thus Randall's *Apologia pro Theologia Rationali* concludes with encouraging remarks on religion in America. "If what religion does, its function (which we can hardly hope to abolish, or transform, or even alter), is to strengthen commitment to our living faith by consecrating the genuine values of our own group, then the primary role of science and knowledge in the religious life is to clarify through intelligence the values to which we are actually consecrated. And in that process we may even hope to extend and enlarge and deepen our vision of the Divine" (33, p. 142).

THE HUMANISTIC NATURALISM OF JUSTUS BUCHLER

Allied with science and technology, naturalism has nonetheless been attentive to the broadest cultural activities of man. By its very title, *Naturalism and the Human Spirit,* the influential cooperative volume of the American naturalists, epitomizes this humanistic orientation. Beyond question naturalism in America is also humanism.

Among contemporary American philosophers the most famous humanist is Corliss Lamont, a Columbia University lecturer and widely known author of several books and articles. Lamont not only espouses humanism (34), he is also sympathetic to dialectical materialism and political socialism, including the Russian variety. A vigorous practical commitment braces his humanism, and, although in concrete specifics it may clash with liberal as well as orthodox attitudes and values, this commitment in its essentials is inspired by the hallowed humanist imperative that man abandon false gods and depend on his own powers to work out his destiny. As Lamont proclaims, "naturalistic Humanism challenges men to rely on their own intelligence, courage, and effort in building their happiness and fashioning their destiny in this world of infinite possibilities" (35, p. 47). Besides promoting the moral aims of humanism, Lamont has also recognized the need for an adequate metaphysics. To establish the metaphysical basis of humanism, he has advanced a scheme of twelve "ultimates of existence": substance, activity, dimension, quality, form, potentiality, causality, necessity, contingency, individuality, relation, and eventuation (35, pp. 45–46). He has voluntarily submitted this list of categories to the critical scrutiny of such fellow humanists as Max C. Otto, Julian Huxley, Roy Wood Sellars, Gardner Williams, and John Herman Randall, Jr. (35, pp. 45–65). Only Max C. Otto has forthrightly denied that humanism should seek a metaphysics (35, p. 48). Julian Huxley suggested that the categories are really the framework of one's own thinking and not the ultimate constituents of existence (35, p. 51). Perhaps the most astute criticism of Lamont's metaphysics was made by Randall who, though he considered it "wise and sound," yet cautioned that it requires "more precision, more careful analysis" (35, p. 62). Of course more precision and more careful analysis of Lamont's categories would, in all probability, merely lead to Randall's own metaphysics. However, humanism—if it needs a metaphysics—should have one in which man, the human self, is the crux. For such a humanistic metaphysics which yet remains naturalistic, it is necessary to look to the philosophy of Justus Buchler.

Born in New York City on March 27, 1914, Justus Buchler graduated from the City College of New York in 1934 and pursued advanced studies in philosophy at Columbia University, where he earned his M.A. in 1935 and his Ph.D. in 1939. An instructor in philosophy at Columbia University from 1937 to 1947, and at Brooklyn College from 1938 to 1943, he was appointed assistant professor at Columbia University in 1947, was made a full professor in 1956, and became Johnsonian Professor of Philosophy in 1959.

Although unusually precocious, Buchler underwent a long apprenticeship before emerging as a creative philosopher in his own right. With Benjamin Schwartz he edited Santayana's *Obiter Scripta* in 1936 (36). For his doctorate Buchler concentrated his studies on Charles Peirce, the founder of American pragmatism, and, guided by Schneider, Randall, and especially Nagel, he produced, in 1939, *Charles Peirce's Empiricism* (37). Supplemented by a one-volume selection of Peirce's writings (38), Buchler's book has been influential not only because it was the first in a growing field that at present seems to have no end (39), but also because it stressed the empirical, methodological, and scientific aspects of Peirce's thought at a time when the marriage of logical positivism and pragmatism seemed imminent. In the early 1940's Buchler collaborated with Randall to produce for the College Outline Series an introduction to philosophy from the naturalistic standpoint (7). At last, in 1951, Buchler published his first work of original philosophy—*Toward a General Theory of Human Judgment* (40). This was followed in 1955 by *Nature and Judgment* (41), in 1961 by *The Concept of Method* (42), and in 1966 by *Metaphysics of Natural Complexes* (43). Buchler's thought has already attracted enough attention from professional philosophers to become the subject of a symposium in a double number of the *Journal of Philosophy* (44).

In his works Buchler has striven to formulate a theory of judgment. By "judgment," however, he has meant more than cognition, and his enterprise should not be identified with traditional epistemology. Indeed, he has sought to offer what he has termed "a metaphysics of utterance" (40, p. vii). So far he has expounded eleven categories: proception, communication, compulsion, convention, perspective, validation, judgment, query, experience, meaning, and method, in addition to those eight ontological categories applicable to all natural complexes: integrity, scope, prevalence, alescence, ordinality, relation, possibility, and actuality. With this train of categories Buchler's metaphysics presents a philosophy of man, a theory of the self. "I mean," he asserts, "to affirm the precarious tenure of the self in the world and the indefinite boundaries of the self, not to contrast an inner and outer life or an inner and outer world" (40, p. 8). Hence Buchler's philosophy may be deemed the highest expression of humanism within contemporary naturalism.

Buchler's concern with the self is unique in contemporary naturalism. Naturalists, pragmatists, empiricists, and process philosophers have generally abandoned the problem of the self to the personalistic idealists. Naturalism, even when nonreductive, leans toward materialism or positivism in metaphysics and toward behaviorism in psychology. Consequently, the self has rarely been central to the naturalists' investigations. Sharing the naturalistic outlook, pragmatism has gone further in explaining selfhood as a product of problem-solving. Blocked action produces the reflectiveness upon which the personal self is founded. Empiricism, which has permeated naturalism and pragmatism, has looked to experience, the field of qualities and actions, and has looked away from the supposition of an agent—a self or person—somehow distinct from the field. Nor has process philosophy, which is often naturalistic and pragmatic and empirical, offered a satisfactory conception of the self, since it has been unable to account for the continuity of the self. Thus, although his heritage is naturalism, pragmatism, empiricism, and process philosophy, Buchler breaks new ground in seeking to offer a theory of the self.

Proception

The crucial concept of Buchler's naturalistic philosophy of the self is designated by a neologism—proception. "Proception is the basic relationship in which a man stands to the world" (40, p. 16). "By nature man proceives—he moves as an accumulating whole" (40, p. 6). Proception is as crucial for Buchler as experience is for Dewey, and in the definition of proception Buchler conspicuously breaks with Dewey's naturalistic philosophy of experience. Dewey described experience as a transactional process in which subject and object are discriminable aspects; he therefore sacrificed the identity of the self to a sequence of situations which take place. For Buchler the concept of "proception" alters the naturalistic interpretation of experience as transactional process in favor of the concept of the self.

What, then, is proception? For Buchler the term "proception" means "the interplay of the human individual's activities and dimensions, their unitary direction . . . ." (40, p. 4). The process of proception is, he continues, "a moving union of seeking and receiving, of forward propulsion and patient absorption. Proception is the composite, directed activity of the individual. Any instance of his functioning, any event in his history enters into the proceptive direction . . . . Proception is the process in which a man's whole self is summed up or represented. On this idea that the whole individual is the cumulative representative of the moving individual I should like to lay the major stress" (40, pp. 4-5).

Three additional concepts are needed to elucidate proception: the proceptive domain, the procept, and the proceptive direction. Let us consider each in turn.

The proceptive domain is the "content of the summed-up-self-in-process, the individual's world . . .; [it is] a part of the world and the whole of a self uniquely represented" (40, p. 6). Buchler calls the proceptive domain "gross" if it "comprises all that belongs to the individual's living make-up . . . ." (40, p. 8). The gross domain can be either a floating or an imminent domain. When it "represents the summed-up self or proceiver within a given situation," it is floating (40, p. 8); and when it slices into a minimal cross section of the gross domain and "comprises all that is present to—that is, available for—the proceiver at a given moment," it is imminent (40, p. 9). As the floating proceptive domain is spatial, involving at least the space that bounds the proceiver and that widens or contracts with his situation, so the imminent proceptive domain is temporal, centering the process at present. The total situation in process, in its spatial and temporal aspects, represents the individual. In this sense, the individual is as great or as small as his proceptive domain.

A procept is an object, or situation, which is part of a proceptive domain. Buchler defines it as "anything that is a property *of* the individual, that happens *to* him, that affects or characterizes him in any way at all, so long as it relates to him *as a proceiver* (as an identifiable and cumulative individual) and not as a mere entity in the cosmic maelstrom" (40, pp. 7–8). A procept, moreover, "is qualitatively or ontologically just what it is" (40, p. 13). It is not, for Buchler, an abstract essence, a construction, a subjective datum. In this sense Buchler is close to new realism: the procept is a real part of the world. However, for Buchler, the world is always the world of some individual proceiver.

The gross domain, as the proceiver advances, is structured by widening or shrinking floating domains and is caught up in a flux of imminent domains, as the procepts themselves qualify the world of the individual. This development exhibits what Buchler calls proceptive direction. There is, then, dynamic purpose in proception, but it is not tantamount to a teleology, since the direction is not defined in advance of the process, nor are all elements interrelated as means and ends. Buchler goes on to analyze proceptive direction in terms of manipulation and assimilation, activities which he describes as "the essential attributes of proception" (40, p. 18). As Buchler points out: "In the manipulative dimension of his being, the individual is the actor, the agent, as in the assimilative he is the spectator, sufferer, patient; and he is both actor and spectator literally and inevitably" (40, p. 18). "As assimilator, the individual is a witness, a gatherer, a patient, a recipient of the complexes of nature. As a manipulator, he is a shaper, a transformer, an initiator, an agent of these complexes" (41, p. 142). Assimilation and manipulation take place simultaneously in the same proceptive process.

Buchler's concept of proception is presented as a correction of Dewey's concept of experience as environmental transaction. In some respects it is reminiscent of Mead's distinction between the "I" and the "me" to account for the development of the self in social psychology, but even Mead's "me" was overloaded with social content, and his "I" tended to be vacuous (45). The individual self, in Mead's thought as in Dewey's, was submerged in the social, environmental process. This loss of individuality is precisely the point which critics have attacked in naturalism. But Buchler's philosophy preserves the individual without abandoning nature. Proception replaces the ambiguous concept of transaction. As Buchler conceives it, proception "is a natural process, distinguishable in specific terms from other natural processes" (41, p. 111). It is a natural process which is directive, propulsive, and cumulative. It takes place in nature, but it always refers to some individual. Individuality, moreover, is rooted in nature. "An individual is a natural complex contingently associated with, affecting, and affected by, other natural complexes" (41, p. 118). "A procept . . . is a natural complex that relates to or affects the individual as an individual" (41, p. 121). Thus Buchler's naturalism reinterprets Dewey's conception of the relation between nature and experience, a conception which has seemed to critics to be so ambiguous that it either loses the individual subject, by construing experience as objective nature and social behavior, or loses nature, by reducing it to experience. Seeking to avoid this dilemma of Dewey's naturalistic metaphysics, Buchler holds: "Nature is always the subject matter; experience is nature proceived" (40, p. 28).

Proception does not shatter nature into the experiences of unrelated individuals. Communication occurs, and perspectives are shared. The proceiver produces; his experience is an event in nature, and, when imbued with significance, it is the foundation of communication. Proception is thus a discovery, a revelation; its expression is an utterance. Man above all is an agent of utterance. In utterance he translates individuality into sociality and assimilates sociality to individuality; in utterance he transmutes raw nature into civilized nature, or, simply, nature into culture. "Utterance is a relation between proception and production" (40, p. 46).

Judgment

In developing a "metaphysics of utterance" Buchler examines communication and hence the indispensable category of communication—judgment. "The product, representing nature re-created by human nature, has a voice. Nature refashioned is nature interpreted. Every product is a judgment" (40, p. 47). Buchler's treatment of the category of judgment is as striking, novel, and crucial to his thought as is his treatment of the category of proception.

Although he attempts to show how his usage of the term "judgment" was anticipated by his philosophical predecessors and by the plain man, Buchler employs this term in a singular way. "Whatever . . . in some possible perspective, can be deemed to *be* made or *be* said or *be* done is legitimately regarded a judgment" (41, p. 19). There are, then, three modes of judgment corresponding to the three modes of human production—doing, making, and saying —and these are "designated respectively as active, exhibitive, and assertive judgment" (41, p. 20). "Assertive judgments include all products of which a certain type of question is ordinarily asked: Is it true or false? Exhibitive judgments include all products which result from the shaping or arranging of materials (and these materials include manipulatable signs). Active judgments comprise all instances of conduct to which the terms 'act' or 'action' are ordinarily applied" (40, p. 48). Thus in Buchler's philosophy the term "judgment" is applicable to the products of knowledge, of art, and of conduct.

Buchler's theory of judgment is another step in his overall strategy to heal the dualisms, divisions, and bifurcations of traditional thought. The theory of proception corrects the concept of the separation of man from nature without losing the individual self. It regards the individual as a natural complex related to other natural complexes. The production of the individual is culture, and since the individual is rooted in nature, his products—judgments, of which culture consists—are also founded on nature. Further, the traditional division of culture into separate realms of science, art, and morality is superseded in the general theory of judgment. Using the term "judgment" to designate the products of these three distinguishable dimensions of culture, Buchler holds that all the activities of men are not only natural but exhibit, despite significant differences, a common structure.

Whether in knowledge, in art, or in conduct, every judgment is, on Buchler's analysis, a pronouncement and an appraisal; it is, moreover, subject to the categories of compulsion and convention, and it seeks or claims validation. In judgment the individual proceiver pronounces his own discovery of his predicament in nature; and in judgment he appraises this predicament, articulating his response, his attitude, his evaluation, his stance in the world. Into every judgment enter the forces of compulsion—some natural, others social. No man is wholly free; he is part of the complex processes of nature, and he bends to its forces. At the same time every judgment is formed by convention—artificial, man-made rules of language, of artistic technique, of moral behavior; and the existence of these conventions reveals that the human proceiver, though a part of nature, does not conform abjectly to her. Nature herself is not homogeneous; she is a complex of processes and events, not a whole of unitary substance. The proceiver relates to this complex in a unique way. He constitutes a perspective in nature, and, while perspectives overlap, forming thereby a foundation for a common world, a community more or less inclusive, the proceiver's individual relation to the world is singular. Because of this singularity there is always the risk that the proceiver suffers isolation from others. Utterance, the production of judgment, minimizes this risk when it seeks validation. The validation of judgment depends upon the communication of meaning, which in turn is dependent on method.

Query and Method

Buchler uses the term "query" to denote "the process of ramifying judgments" (41, p. 58). Judgment, as has been pointed out, may be assertive (as in science), exhibitive (as in art), or active (as in conduct), and query is a generic concept designating processes that occur in all three areas of human experience. Inquiry, applicable to the ramification of assertive judgments in science, is only a species of query. Query is, then, the interrogative stance of the individual in regard to his procepts or his proceptive domain; it precedes, initiates, and sustains the production of judgments. "Query is that form of

human experience which originates partly in a compound of imagination and wonder. It is exemplified by philosophy, by the inquiry
of pure science, by art, by what remains of religion liberated from
the proprietary conception of belief, and by any number of informal
but not undisciplined human processes which express themselves in
some purposive pattern of utterance" (42, p. 114).

It should be no surprise that an heir to Dewey's naturalism, writing during a period of philosophical preoccupation with the problems of methods and of methodology, particularly with the range of
questions attaching to philosophical method, should devote his attention to a study of method. What in the case of other categories
could be done within the limits of a chapter required in the case of
method a separate book—*The Concept of Method*. Buchler's emphasis on the significance of method is undeniable. Query, the process of ramifying judgments, "occurs only in a methodic framework"
(42, p. 114), but it is not reducible to method. Here again Buchler's
theory is more attuned to the imaginative side of man than is Dewey's. According to Buchler, "A method is a power of manipulating
natural complexes, purposively and recognizably, within a reproduc-
ible order of utterance; and methodic activity is the translation of
such a power into the pursuit of an end—an end implied by the reproduction" (42, p. 135). A process is methodic when it "expresses
the purposive functioning of human power in an order of judgment"
(42, p. 114). Query signifies more than method; it ramifies judgments indefinitely. "Query is more prodigal than method as such.
For although it necessarily represents utterance moving toward some
end, it luxuriates and complicates. The primary effort of method is
repeatedly to complete its instances; of query, to deepen each instance" (42, p. 114).

Whereas Dewey's naturalism tends to restrict the human productive activity to the solution of problems or the satisfaction of needs,
Buchler's naturalism regards activity—utterance, or the production
of judgment—as the inescapable, unceasing expression of the human
self. At this point Buchler's naturalism draws upon Santayana's
teaching that nature in human experience luxuriates in images and
symbols. But while Santayana viewed the qualities of human experi-

ence as strangers from a realm of essence, without origin or status in nature, and so retreated to skepticism and animal faith, Buchler adheres closely to a naturalistic description and explanation, locating proception with all its procepts and judgment in all its forms strictly within nature. In Buchler's naturalism query and method are recognized to be of equal importance. In effect, Dewey's methodological discipline is combined with Santayana's speculative imagination to mark a new phase in the development of naturalism. Buchler's new creative and speculative naturalism is perhaps best discerned in these lines: "Method without query can destroy mankind and its laborious progeny. Method informed by query is the essential expression of reason. Reason is query aiming to grow and flourish forever" (42, p. 114).

NATURALISM AND RIVAL METHODOLOGIES

The most influential of current philosophies in America, naturalism embraces a variety of forms. The works of Nagel, Randall, and Buchler comprise the broad spectrum of naturalistic thought. The main trait of naturalism is devotion to science, and, in particular, to scientific method. This trait is most conspicuous in the thought of Nagel. But, as Randall's philosophy demonstrates, science is not man's sole cultural institution; the scientific inquiry into man's place in nature must be supplemented by an historical examination of the development of culture. Hence history is added to science. Whether in natural science or in intellectual history, however, methodology remains paramount. Yet, as Buchler maintains, the methodological emphasis characteristic of American thought today results in the placement of science itself, along with its methodology, within the wide context of man in nature and in culture. Scientific method becomes but one moment, and not the exclusive moment, in man's methodological understanding and control of nature.

Scientific methodology is the fixed point from which contemporary naturalists relate themselves to other methodological philosophies—pragmatism, logical positivism, linguistic analysis, phenomenology, and dialectical materialism. Mention has already been made of Nagel's assimilation, with modification, of certain tenets of logical positivism, and of Randall's repudiation of linguistic analysis because of its erroneous subordination of the investigation of things to talk about words. And yet the fact remains that some thinkers, bred in the tradition of American naturalism, still anticipate the convergence of pragmatism, logical positivism, and linguistic analysis, a convergence which has been called a "reunion in philosophy" (46).

One principle, implicitly or explicitly, guides all forms of American naturalism—the realistic principle that there is an objective subject matter to which all methods apply. This principle is most obvious when American naturalists relate themselves to their European phenomenological counterparts. To the extent that the phenomenology founded by Husserl is attentive to the totality of human experience and, by means of its doctrine of the intentionality of consciousness, is realistic in the status it assigns the objects and factors experienced, there is no quarrel between phenomenology and naturalism. In fact Buchler's naturalism, though formulated in a distinctively American idiom—borrowing terms and concepts from Peirce, Mead, James, Dewey, Santayana, and Whitehead—is close to phenomenology when the latter, though expressed in neo-Kantian terminology, is realistically conceived. To the extent, however, that phenomenology becomes subjectivist—especially in the hands of the existentialists—naturalists have denounced it. Indeed, Marvin Farber—the thinker who has done more than any other to foster the study of contemporary European philosophy in America, the author of the second book on Husserl's philosophy to be published in the United States (47), and the founder and editor of the *Journal of Philosophy and Phenomenological Research*—has pronounced the harshest criticisms of phenomenology and existentialism in his polemical *Naturalism and Subjectivism* (48).

Not a member of the Columbia University group of naturalists, Farber nevertheless underscores one aspect of contemporary naturalism. As a naturalist, Farber conceives the philosophy of the future to be materialism (49). In truth, the realistic thesis of naturalism, according to which there is an objective subject matter, nature, lends itself to materialistic interpretation, as Nagel's own philosophy reveals. Thus naturalism in America invites comparison and contrast with dialectical materialism, an invitation which is accepted *pari passu* by the philosopher under consideration in the next chapter.

NOTES TO CHAPTER IV

1 Yervant H. Krikorian (ed.), *Naturalism and the Human Spirit* (New York: Columbia University Press, 1944).
2 See Herbert W. Schneider, *Sources of Contemporary Philosophical Realism in America* (New York and Indianapolis: Bobbs-Merrill, 1964).
3 Joseph L. Blau, *Men and Movements in American Philosophy* (Englewood Cliffs, N. J.: Prentice-Hall, 1952).
4 John Herman Randall, Jr., "The Future of John Dewey's Philosophy," *Journal of Philosophy*, LVI (1959), 1005.
5 Sterling P. Lamprecht, *Our Philosophical Traditions* (New York: Appleton-Century-Crofts, 1955), 486–97.
6 John Herman Randall, Jr., "The Spirit of American Philosophy," in F. Ernest Johnson (ed.), *Wellsprings of the American Spirit* (New York: Institute for Religious and Social Studies, 1948), 122.
7 John Herman Randall, Jr., and Justus Buchler, *Philosophy, An Introduction* (New York: Barnes and Noble, 1942).
8 Morris R. Cohen and Ernest Nagel, *An Introduction to Logic and Scientific Method* (New York: Harcourt, Brace, 1934).
9 See Ernest Nagel, *Principles of the Theory of Probability*, Vol. I, No. 6 of *The International Encyclopedia of Unified Science* (Chicago: University of Chicago Press, 1939); and Ernest Nagel, with James R. Newman, *Godel's Proof* (New York: New York University Press, 1958). Nagel has also edited, with an introduction, a volume of selected texts entitled *John Stuart Mill's Philosophy of Scientific Method* (New York: Hafner, 1950); and with Patrick Suppes and Alfred Tarski he has edited a collection of papers, *International Congress for Logic, Methodology and Philosophy* (Stanford: Stanford University Press, 1962).
10 Ernest Nagel, *Sovereign Reason and Other Studies in the Philosophy of Science* (Glencoe, Ill.: Free Press, 1954).
11 Ernest Nagel, *Logic Without Metaphysics and Other Essays in the Philosophy of Science* (Glencoe, Ill.: Free Press, 1957).
12 Ernest Nagel, *The Structure of Science: Problems in the Logic of Scientific Explanation* (New York: Harcourt, Brace and World, 1961).
13 A. E. Blumberg and Herbert Feigl, "Logical Positivism: A New Movement in European Philosophy," *Journal of Philosophy*, XXVIII (1931), 281–96.
14 For a vehement denunciation of the negative antimetaphysical stance of the logical positivists, see James K. Feibleman, "Viennese Positivism in the United States," *Tulane Studies in Philosophy*, IV (1955), 31–47; reprinted in James K. Feibleman, *Inside the Great Mirror* (The Hague: Martinus Nijhoff, 1958), 137–52.

15 Roderick M. Chisholm and others, *Philosophy* (Englewood Cliffs, N.J.: Prentice-Hall, 1964).

16 *The Philosopher of the Common Man; Essays in Honor of John Dewey to Celebrate His Eightieth Birthday* (New York: Putnam's, 1940).

17 Sidney Hook and H. M. Kallen (eds.), *American Philosophy Today and Tomorrow* (New York: Lee Furman, 1935). This historically important anthology contains papers by many then-young American philosophers who state in brief compass their intellectual interests and directions. Their subsequent accomplishments may be matched against these early pronouncements.

18 John Herman Randall, Jr., *Nature and Historical Experience: Essays in Naturalism and in the Theory of History* (New York: Columbia University Press, 1958).

19 John Herman Randall, Jr., *The Making of the Modern Mind: A Survey of the Intellectual Background of the Present Age* (Boston: Houghton Mifflin Company, 1926). A revised edition was published in 1940.

20 John Herman Randall, Jr., *Our Changing Civilization: How Science and the Machine Are Reconstructing Modern Life* (New York: Frederick A. Stokes, 1929).

21 John Herman Randall, Jr., *The Career of Philosophy*, I and II (New York: Columbia University Press, 1962–65).

22 Randall joined with Ernst Cassirer and P. O. Kristeller to produce *The Renaissance Philosophy of Man* (New York: Columbia University Press, 1948). Also, prior to the publication of the first volume of *The Career of Philosophy*, several of Randall's articles on Renaissance thought were collected and published under the title *The School of Padua and the Emergence of Modern Science* (Padua: Editrice Antenore, 1961).

23 John Herman Randall, Jr., *How Philosophy Uses Its Past* (New York: Columbia University Press, 1963).

24 See Andrew J. Reck, *Recent American Philosophy* (New York: Pantheon Books, 1964), 268–74.

25 John Herman Randall, Jr., *Aristotle* (New York: Columbia University Press, 1960).

26 See Frederick J. E. Woodbridge, *Aristotle's Vision of Nature*, ed. John Herman Randall, Jr. (New York: Columbia University Press, 1965).

27 George Boas, Review of *Nature and Historical Experience*, in *Journal of Philosophy*, LVI (1959), 74.

28 John Herman Randall, Jr., "Dewey's Interpretation of the History of Philosophy," in Paul Arthur Schilpp (ed.), *The Philosophy of John Dewey* (Evanston and Chicago: Northwestern University Press, 1939), 102.

29 Herbert W. Schneider, *Ways of Being: Elements of Analytic Ontology* (New York: Columbia University Press, 1962).

30 John Herman Randall, Jr., "Talking and Looking," *Proceedings and Addresses of the American Philosophical Association*, 1956–1957, XXX, 5–24.

31 John Herman Randall, Jr., "The Art of Language and the Linguistic Situation: A Naturalistic Analysis," *Journal of Philosophy*, LX (1963), 29–56.

32 John Herman Randall and John Herman Randall, Jr., *Religion and the Modern World* (New York: Henry Holt, 1929).

33 John Herman Randall, Jr., *The Role of Knowledge in Western Religion* (Boston: Starr King Press, 1958).

34 See Corliss Lamont, *The Philosophy of Humanism* (5th ed.; New York: Ungar, 1965).

35 Corliss Lamont (ed.), "A Humanist Symposium on Metaphysics," *Journal of Philosophy*, LVI (1959).

36 George Santayana, *Obiter Scripta, Lectures, Essays, and Reviews*, ed. Justus Buchler and Benjamin Schwartz (New York: Scribner's, 1936).

37 Justus Buchler, *Charles Peirce's Empiricism*, (New York: Harcourt, Brace, 1939).

38 Justus Buchler (ed.), *The Philosophy of Peirce, Selected Writings* (New York: Harcourt, Brace, 1940).

39 So copious have been the studies on Peirce and the materials concerning his thought and his personality that the society devoted to him began in 1965 to publish semi-annually *Transactions of the Charles S. Peirce Society*.

40 Justus Buchler, *Toward a General Theory of Human Judgment* (New York: Columbia University Press, 1951).

41 Justus Buchler, *Nature and Judgment* (New York: Columbia University Press, 1955).

42 Justus Buchler, *The Concept of Method* (New York: Columbia University Press, 1961).

43 Justus Buchler, *Metaphysics of Natural Complexes* (New York: Columbia University Press, 1966).

44 *Journal of Philosophy*, LVI (1959), 193–252. The contributors and contributions to this symposium were: Sidney Gelber, "Toward a Radical Naturalism," 193–99; Jordan Churchill, "Validation," 200–208; Robert G. Olson, "Two Questions on the Definition of Man's Status in Nature," 208–14; Rudolf Allers, "Judgment, Culture, and Conduct," 214–20; Willard E. Arnett, "Reflection on Justus Buchler's Theory of Meaning," 220–33; Theodore Mischel, "Some Questions Concerning Art and Exhibitive Judgment," 233–46; and Matthew Lipman, "Natural Obligation, Natural Appropriation," 246–52. In addition, there is a noteworthy critical study of Buchler's philosophy by Charles Landesman, "Metaphysics and Human Nature," *Review of Metaphysics*, XV (1962), 656–71.

45 See George Herbert Mead's article, "The Social Self," in George Herbert Mead, *Selected Writings*, ed. Andrew J. Reck (New York and Indianapolis: Bobbs-Merrill, 1964), 142–49.

46 Morton White, *Toward Reunion in Philosophy* (Cambridge: Harvard University Press, 1956).

47 Marvin Farber, *The Foundation of Phenomenology* (Cambridge: Harvard University Press, 1943).

48 Marvin Farber, *Naturalism and Subjectivism* (Springfield, Ill.: Charles C. Thomas, 1959).

49 Roy Wood Sellars, V. J. McGill, and Marvin Farber, *Philosophy of the Future: Quest of Modern Materialism* (New York: Macmillan, 1949).

V

SIDNEY HOOK

Pragmatism and Marxism

INTELLECTUAL AND PROFESSIONAL MILIEU

Sidney Hook is the most prominent representative of pragmatism on the American philosophical scene. Born in New York City on December 20, 1902, Hook received his B.S. in 1923 from City College, where he studied under Morris Cohen; he then pursued graduate study in philosophy at Columbia University, where his mentors were Frederick J. E. Woodbridge and John Dewey. By education and orientation Hook shares common ground with the Columbia University naturalists Ernest Nagel and Justus Buchler; he differs from them in his allegiance to pragmatism, in his preoccupation with social philosophy and action, and in his flair for polemics. Hook himself throws light on how, in spite of the influence of Morris Cohen, he became a disciple of John Dewey. "Having been trained by Morris R. Cohen as an undergraduate to believe that pragmatism was a philosophy which made our wishes, which are real, into horses, which were imaginary," Hook has confided,

I constituted myself the official opposition for an entire year in one of Dewey's large lecture classes, to the annoyance not of Dewey but of my fellow students who objected to the constant interruption of their slumber. I became converted to pragmatism in the most unpragmatic way. With Dewey's encouragement I sat down to write what I thought would be the definitive refutation of pragmatism on the basis of Peirce's theory of leading principles. The argument carried me to conclusions I did not wish to reach—and protesting all the way, I went to Dewey himself, after Morris Cohen failed me, to tell me what was wrong in where I was coming out. This time, too, Dewey encouraged me with a grin. He could find nothing wrong with the argument (1, p. 1012).

After receiving his Ph.D. from Columbia in 1927, Hook joined the faculty of New York University as an instructor in philosophy. He became chairman of the department of philosophy in the Washington Square College in 1934, full professor in 1939, head of the graduate department in 1946, and head of the all-university department in 1957. From his post at New York University on Washington Square, located on the edge of Greenwich Village, the artistic and intellectual center of New York City, Hook has taken his stand on the major issues of our time. The situation and the man fit each other perfectly. Today no philosopher and few journalists can match the sheer quantity of Hook's articles and reviews in newspapers like the New York *Times,* journals like the *New Leader,* and quarterlies like the *Partisan Review.* Always a competent editor and anthologist (2), Hook in recent years has edited a series of pace-setting volumes publishing symposia given under the auspices of the New York University Institute of Philosophy (3). Brand Blanshard, whose loyalties in philosophy and in other matters lie elsewhere, has nonetheless described Hook as "that inexhaustible geyser of books, lectures, and essays, a philosopher who scents the smell of battle from afar and is soon in the midst of it, giving as well as he gets, and usually somewhat better" (4, p. ix). Working in the hurly-burly of the world's most powerful and most advanced city, Hook has no equal in contemporary American philosophy as the engaged intellectual.

As heir to the intellectual legacy of John Dewey, Hook has addressed himself to the problems of men, with the consequence that he is today America's leading social philosopher, his works touching on all the major social issues of our time. A superb expositor of pragmatism and an irascible polemicist, he has been eager to press constructively the range and import of pragmatism and to face the urgent problems of the present with a seriousness appropriate to their tragic quality and with abiding confidence in the efficacy of critical reflection. Concern for the problems of men has not dissuaded Hook from the classical conception of philosophy as the pursuit of wisdom; though a social reformer, he is not merely that. In his 1959 presidential address to the Eastern Division of the American Philosophical Association, Hook expatiates on the pragmatic interpretation of the nature and function of philosophy, and, borrowing a distinction from Santayana, he contends that the primary role of the philosopher is that of the moralist, but not by any means that of the moralizer. The difference between the moralist and the moralizer, he comments, "is a difference, on the one hand, between *analyzing* specific and basic social problems, and conflicts, and *clarifying* the issues in dispute with all the tools at one's command—and, on the other, *proclaiming* solutions and programs on the basis of antecedent commitments which one shares with some faction of his fellow-men" (5, p. 7). Thus while as a citizen Hook assumes the responsibilities of the social reformer in regard to specific social problems and their relevant solutions, as a philosopher he is steadfast in the discovery and elucidation of those general concepts which provide the rationale of social institutions and their reconstruction. As a philosopher Hook's most distinctive contribution is his theory of democracy. If a philosophical justification of democracy consonant with the scientific, pragmatic, and experimentalist temper of contemporary America is sought, it can be found in its most full-bodied expression in the writings of Sidney Hook.

In 1928–29, Hook held a Guggenheim fellowship which enabled him to study in Germany and the Soviet Union, where he resided briefly at the Marx–Engels Institute in Moscow. Hook's concern with Marxism covers half a century. So numerous are his writings on Marxism that they vie with pragmatism for central position in the structure and genesis of his thought. No doubt his study of Marxism was in the first instance triggered by his adherence to democratic socialism which, in the days before communism had taken a Stalinist form, he sometimes referred to as communism. Youthful writings burst with irrepressible enthusiasm for Marxism and passionate allegiance to its militant proposals, which he believed were ignored by orthodox social democracy. Consider this typical early pronouncement: "The revolutionary upheavals of the last decade have brought home the realization that Marxism is not so much a petrified set of bloodless abstractions as a fighting philosophy of the underdog—a flexible method of organizational struggle in the bitter

class warfare of industrial society. We have learned that its slo-
gans are battle-cries, its formulae predictions, and its wide-sweeping
generalizations prescriptions for actions" (6). Despite such strong
emotional language, Hook, even as a self-confessed revolutionary
Marxist, kept critical control of his philosophical thought, his historical scholarship, and his social purposes. Although his early writings on Marxism are fixed in large part by the passion for social
justice, their explosive potential is harnessed by the discipline not
of political party but of critical intelligence and the scientific methods of inquiry. In truth, the temper of Sidney Hook's thinking owes
more to John Dewey than to Karl Marx. But this must not obscure
the overriding significance of Hook's philosophy for contemporary
thought—a significance which resides neither in his Marxism nor in
his pragmatism alone, but in that crucial and insufficiently noted
juncture in the intellectual history of the present epoch—the confrontation of pragmatism and Marxism, an Americanized version
of democratic socialism. To an America living in the shadow of the
cold war and challenged by an enemy armed not only with nuclear
weapons but also with a well-defined ideology, what Hook says concerning Marxism and Soviet communism, concerning democracy
and totalitarianism, is vitally pertinent.

Because Sidney Hook is America's leading philosopher of democracy and her leading scholar and theoretician on the varieties of
Marxism, his thought deserves attention and consideration. First his
pragmatism, culminating in his philosophy of democracy, will be
considered. Then his treatment of Marxism and Soviet communism
will be examined.

PRAGMATISM

Sidney Hook's pragmatism is derivative, and John Dewey is its
source. For an understanding of Hook's pragmatism, then, it is necessary to look to his appreciation of the thought of Dewey. Needless
to say, limitations of space and considerations of relevance rule out
a comprehensive exploration of Dewey's philosophy. Fortunately
Hook himself has succinctly epitomized the achievement of John
Dewey as a philosopher. Dewey, he says, "has carried to completion

a movement of ideas which marks the final break with the ancient and medieval outlook upon the world. In his doctrines the experimental temper comes to self-consciousness. A new way of life is proposed to realize the ideal promise of our vast material culture. Organized intelligence is to take the place of myth and dogma in improving the common lot and enriching individual experience" (7, p. 3).

This interpretation of Dewey's contribution revolves around three interrelated tenets of his thought. First, there is the pragmatist conception of knowing, according to which knowing is experimental and ancillary to doing. An idea is construed as a plan of action and is viewed as a behavioral response to some problem; its truth value is equated with its effectiveness in solving the problem to which it is relevant. In this sense ideas are instruments, and Dewey's version of pragmatism is instrumentalism. Second, there is Dewey's special emphasis upon the problems of men, which, in contradistinction to the problems of philosophers, are practical. Because of this emphasis, Dewey became involved in the dominant social issues of his culture and his time. Almost universally he was acknowledged as the philosopher of American democracy in its industrialized, urban setting. Dewey's instrumentalist conception of knowing and his concern with the problems of men are not disparate outgrowths of his pragmatism. They are joined at root in the pragmatist conception of knowing as a form of doing, of intelligence and inquiry as the modes of human behavior best suited to solve problems. As regards theoretical problems, the experimental method of science has proved most fruitful of solutions, and consequently Dewey generalized the experimental method into *the* method of inquiry. Perhaps his most revolutionary thesis was that this scientific method is applicable to moral and social problems. Finally, there are the basic humanist values of a "new way of life," of realizing "the ideal promise of our vast material culture," of "improving the common lot," and of "enriching individual experience." All of these values may be summed up in the single concept which Hook deems to be definitive of Dewey's value scheme—growth.

Following in the footsteps of Dewey, Hook presents a pragmatic social philosophy. This philosophy is summed up in the title of the essay which he contributed in 1944 to *Naturalism and the Human Spirit* and which was reprinted fifteen years later in *Political Power and Personal Freedom* (8)—"Naturalism and Democracy." Indeed, the terms of the title—naturalism, democracy—establish the topics under exploration.

Naturalism

A Metaphysics of Pragmatism At the outset of his career Hook sought to elaborate the general metaphysics of the instrumentalism he received from Dewey. His first book, his doctoral dissertation, was published in 1927 and bears the revealing title *The Metaphysics of Pragmatism* (9). Conceiving metaphysics to be "an account of the generic traits of nature" and its method to be critical and empirical (9, p. 10), Hook viewed instrumentalism as "not an evasion of a metaphysics but a challenge to one" (9, p. 6). The crux of Hook's theory at this point in his intellectual development is the metaphysics of the instrument. From an examination of the nature of the instrument he adduces the kind of world its existence and operation disclose. Clearly the structure and role of instruments rule out both pessimistic nihilism and romantic idealism. "If a tool is a transformative agency it can neither beget nor devour the existences it modifies; and if mind is instrumental and efficient in a world scarred with stria of shifting things and events, it cannot have created that world" (9, pp. 17–18). To understand how the metaphysics of the instrument is naturalistic and humanistic, it is necessary first to grasp what the instrument is.

Hook selects three distinct traits of the instrument for consideration:

(a) It is an instrument in reference *to* some thought or intuition responsible for its construction and existence as a *tool*,—to some plan or mental blue-print which directs its exercise and measures and interprets its effects . . . . (b) It is an instrument *for* some aggregate of entities or domain of relations in which it is to be applied. The instrument and the field of its use and activity, or literally speaking, its inquiry, are given together . . . . (c) It is an instrument *in respect* and *because* of its form, arrangement or structure. Its cut and stamp condition the extent and degree of its efficacy in securing a natural leverage in the loam or rock of subject matter (9, p. 18).

The homely key illustrates this conception of the instrument, since it "(a) exists for the purpose of rendering or denying access to certain spaces, powers and prospectively enjoyed things; (b), is efficient only insofar as there are locks and mechanisms which function in a determinate way; (c) and because we live in a world of different houses and purposes, is teethed in a distinctive pattern, so that fumbling at a door in the dark we may distinguish it by sight or touch from another" (9, p. 19).

Labeled "pragmatic-realism" (9, p. 10), the metaphysics of the instrument is obviously a version of humanistic naturalism. This metaphysics is tantamount to "a reaffirmation of the naturalistic doctrine of Aristotle purified of its ethical expression" (9, p. 26). Commenting upon it in the Introductory Word to Hook's volume, John Dewey says that it accomplishes a synoptic vision of the essential factors of classic thought with the tenets of the new movement of pragmatism.

Inasmuch as the instrument testifies to "a felt lack in existence" and promises to remove or check this lack (9, p. 22), it is utilized to realize specifiable human purposes. Having a structure which limits its function and dealing with a subject matter which it cannot eliminate but whose directional forces and potentialities it may utilize, the instrument operates under strict limitations yet selects from the natural continuity of the processes those endings which specifically satisfy human interests. "Endings that are natural and casual become ends that are practical and informed" (9, p. 26). Thus the instrument is the principle of selection whereby particularly human values are installed in the processes of nature. The instrument, Hook says,

seeks to actualize only those possibilities which are natural fulfillments of the state of affairs it begins with; and from among the possibilities which are *naturally* relevant, it selects those that are *humanly* relevant— fulfillments of human preferences. Man's judgments of preference . . . are metaphysically ultimate since they can never affect the natural adaptation of means and ends, cause and effect in the objects preferred, nor can the value qualities of the judgments themselves be *derived* from the nature of the preferred objects. For if man is not the measure of all things neither are all things the measure of man (9, p. 27).

Repudiation of Ontology   Hook's disenchantment with metaphysical endeavors to formulate the presuppositions of pragmatism cannot be dated. But with the passage of years Hook's interest in metaphysics has waned, and now when he employs the terms "metaphysics" or "metaphysical," they usually carry pejorative connotations. Partly perhaps he was motivated by theoretical considerations. Certainly the experimentalist conception of knowing renounces any metaphysics which claims knowledge that transcends nature and human experience.

In 1953 Hook published in the *Journal of Philosophy* a challenging article entitled "The Quest for Being." This article has since become the title essay of a volume devoted to studies of humanism and naturalism (10). Here Hook ascribes the revival of ontology in contemporary philosophy to "the contention that it gives us a knowledge about something or everything which is not communicated by any particular science or all of the sciences" (10, p. 147). This contention Hook attacks by means of caustic criticism of the views of traditional and contemporary metaphysicians and ontologists, underscoring their verbal ambiguities and logical inconsistencies. Of Heidegger, for example, Hook says that he "is trying to say that Being is a product of a Creative Act of an anonymous undifferentiated Ego (although he does not use this term) in a process in which substantial Nothing is presupposed. It is a pagan and Teutonic rendering of the theological myth of the creation out of nothing, which turns out to be really the mythical process of the self-realization of Mind" (10, p. 150). Traditional positions, such as Thomism, receive similar treatment. After failing to make sense of being as an analogical concept and inferring from the conception of the act of being that "metaphysics apparently is the study of action *qua* action" (10, p. 153), Hook judges that "the real secret of its [Thomistic] ontology lies in its antecedent commitment to Christian theology" (10, p. 154).

Hook's conclusion, then, is that the term "ontology" should be restricted to "a collection of an indeterminately large number of commonplaces or truisms—e.g., the world is such that this, that, or something else is found in it, which has these, those, or some other characteristics—truisms which have a certain use and point when they are counterposed to absurdities" (10, pp. 169–70). Consider Hook's examples of ontological statements: "There are many colors in the world; Colors have no smell or sound; It is possible to perceive two things at the same time; There are many kinds of processes in the world; Some processes are evolutionary; Thinking creatures inhabit the earth" (10, p. 168). Thus, he dismisses transcendent metaphysics because of its incompatibility with the empirical character of knowledge, and he reduces ontology to a set of truisms which avoid utter triviality only because of the philosophers' susceptibility to absurdity.

While the experimental methods of science strike down the claim of metaphysics to provide special knowledge, according to Hook, logical considerations undermine the thesis that metaphysics is the study of presuppositions. Ambiguity ruins the very concept of "presupposition"; the term may signify many different things—from prior axiom to tacit implication—and, to contemplate but one problem, no strict relation between metaphysics and ethics can be logically determined. Here Hook's practical concerns join his theoretical considerations. The opening essay of *The Quest for Being* argues that, though a determinant in human conduct, philosophy neither logically entails any particular set of practices nor necessarily commits the individual to any particular program of action. On the contrary, the connection between philosophy and conduct is held to be psychological and attitudinal rather than cognitive; further, this connection, whenever it exists as in the case of social movements, is an empirical one, to be ascertained by empirical historical investigation. Doubting that ontological and epistemological ideas govern practice—citing as a test case the failure of the epistemology of dialectic and the ontology of materialism to provide guidelines for concrete practice in the Soviet Union—Hook therefore puts to question the method of extrapolating from practice to the tacit metaphysics upon which it is allegedly grounded.

Humanistic Naturalism   Since Hook holds that our methods of knowing do disclose the generic traits of nature, he advocates a naturalism which consists precisely in "the systematization of what is involved in the scientific method of inquiry" (10, p. 173). Primarily methodological, Hook's naturalism accepts, in addition to the scientific method, "the broad generalizations which are established by the use of it; *viz*, that the occurrence of all qualities or events depends upon the organization of a material system in space-time, and that their emergence, development and disappearance are determined by changes in such organization" (10, pp. 185–86).

Since the foe of naturalism is supernaturalism, and since supernaturalism asserts that there is a cosmic or divine purpose in nature and history, Hook as a naturalist is hostile toward religion. This hostility stems partly from his conviction that the great religions have been indifferent to or obstructive of the important liberal democratic movements in modern history, partly from his belief that men who in time of crisis experience "the new failure of nerve" and resort to religion rather than science seek a false panacea, but mainly from his contention that religions ultimately are tissues of myths devoid of cognitively respectable foundations and fraught with reprehensible moral and social consequences. As regards the cognitive aspect of religion, Hook considers himself to be a "skeptical God-seeker" who is "willing to go a long way, to the very ends of reason itself, to track down every last semblance of evidence or argument which promises fulfillment of the quest" (10, p. 115). Concerned more with "the concept of God" than with the existence of God, Hook doubts the reliability of analogical discourse in theology, because such discourse is controlled not by experimental findings but, as Ludwig Feuerbach has shown, by "man's idealized conception of himself" (10, p. 120).

Hook's naturalism is humanistic. It regards "man as an integral but distinctive part of nature, as wholly a creature of natural origin and natural end" (10, p. 197). This does not mean that Hook is willing to follow those humanists who denominate the moral enterprise as divine, although he is prepared, in the interests of human welfare, to accept what he has ironically dubbed the "ethical suspension of the theological" (10, p. 133). In effect what Hook proposes is to apply to the hitherto sacred issues of morality and society the experimental method of science, "to approach the problems of men in their natural and social contexts and to test the validity of all theoretical claims, not by examining their presuppositions but by investigating their empirical consequences" (10, p. 200).

What is the role of philosophy if the methods of science exhaust the means of knowing, whether about nature, man, or society? As Hook said in his presidential address, the aim of philosophy is wisdom, and wisdom consists in "the knowledge of the uses of life and death" (5, p. 12). Whereas the pragmatist philosopher keeps his gaze fixed on the general methodology for the solution of social problems and the realization of social ideals, he is never insensitive to the tragic sense of life—to the presence of problems that involve conflicts of goods which defy solution without unassuageable loss. Here, indeed, the basic need for philosophy is most profoundly felt, for primarily philosophy "is a way of looking at the world, a *Lebensphilosophie*, a theory of criticism, ultimately concerned with the better and worse" (10, p. 227).

Democracy

Although the term "democracy" is so laden with emotion that its meaning lies hidden in a thicket of semantical thorns and pitfalls, it is possible, according to Hook, to ferret out a definite meaning consistent with the history of democratic traditions and subject to agreement among clear-minded discussants. On occasions too numerous to count Hook has attempted to elucidate the objective meaning of democracy, to canvas the objections raised against it, to marshal the arguments in its behalf, and, as behooves the philosopher, to examine the kinds of theoretical justifications which from time to time come forth in its support. Whatever democracy may be, it calls for a kind of belief, and yet, if we are to be philosophical, we must be able to present reasons for this belief.

Primacy of Political Form   What, then, is democracy? Hook defines a democratic society as "one where the government rests upon the freely given consent of the governed" (11, p. 285). Here the term "governed" means "those adult participating members of the community, with their dependents, whose way of life is affected by what the government does or leaves undone," and the term "government" refers to "the law-and-policy making agencies, legislative, executive, and judicial, whose activities control the life of the community" (11, p. 285). The phrase "freely given consent of the governed" means that "no coercion, direct or indirect, is brought to bear upon the governed to elicit their approval or disapproval. A government that 'rests upon' the freely given consent of the governed is one which *in fact* abides by the expression of this approval or disapproval" (11, p. 285). Of all political forms democracy offers the greatest promise of realizing the public good and of solving social problems, because, as Hook repeatedly remarks, it ministers to all the interests that compete within the community, allowing each to have a voice in the final outcome. It is no surprise, then, that in the discussion of American constitutional law Hook adopts the position of Thomas Jefferson and denounces judicial review by the Supreme Court when it invalidates Congressional legislation (12, Ch. 2). Democracy as a political institution is embodied in a legislature elected by the people and representing its diversified interests.

Most striking in Hook's conception of democracy is the emphasis upon political forms. This emphasis is highly significant and deserves close attention, since it marks a change of mind on Hook's part. As a young philosopher he was often skeptical of the practical value of democratic political forms in capitalist societies because he regarded them as mere masks to disguise the real dictatorship of the propertied classes. Yet, as his knowledge of foreign totalitarianisms grew, Hook came to appreciate the centrality of political forms to democracy. "In its primary *historical* sense," he now declares, "democracy refers to a form of government and only to government" (8, p. 30). Thus he repudiates the distinction, once popular among liberals and progressives, of two kinds of democracy— economic and political. "Those who speak of two *kinds* of democracy make the fundamental error of separating what cannot be separated. Democracy is a matter of degree, not of kind. Political democracy without economic democracy is incomplete: but economic democracy without political democracy is impossible. As well say that there are two kinds of life; life with oxygen, and life with any quality you please but without oxygen. *Political* democracy is the oxygen of the democratic body politic" (8, p. 33).

Principle of Equality The political form of democracy, moreover, is grounded upon an ethical principle. This principle is the principle of equality—in Hook's words, "an equality not of status or origin but of opportunity, relevant functions and social participation" (8, p. 38). Hence democracy implicates the concept of equality.

Hook elucidates the principle of equality with seven comments. First, equality does not describe facts but prescribes policies for treating men (8, p. 38). Second, equality does not prescribe identical treatment for men who are physically or intellectually unequal, but it prescribes "a policy of equality of concern or consideration for men whose different needs may require differential treatment" (8, p. 38). Third, equality is not "a mechanical policy of equal opportunity for everyone at *any* time and in *all* respects" but is, rather, equality of opportunity "for all individuals to develop whatever personal and socially desirable talents they possess and to make whatever unique contributions their capacities permit" (8, p. 38). Fourth, equality, instead of demanding absolutely uniform living conditions or absolutely equal compensation commensurate with socially useful work, requires "that, when the productive forces of a society make possible the gratification of basic human needs (which are, of course, historical variables), no one should be deprived of necessities in order to provide others with luxuries" (8, p. 38). Fifth, equality does not restrict the freedom of being or becoming different, but *encourages* such freedom, restricting only that exercise of freedom which frustrates or injures others (8, p. 39). Sixth, it does not deny the career of leadership but insists that it be open to all and that all have a voice in the selection of leaders (8, p. 39). Seventh, equality assumes not that men are all naturally good, but that, "treated as equals in a community of persons, [they] may become better" (8, p. 39).

Principle of Freedom Besides involving the principle of ethical equality, democracy is keyed to the principle of freedom; it "is the process by which freedoms are institutionalized" (8, p. xi).

Where other thinkers have suspected a root incompatibility between equality and freedom, Hook finds that they are intimately intertwined, each essential to the other in a democracy. Founded upon the principle of equality and incorporated in political institutions which operate primarily with the consent of the governed, democratic societies are free societies, or at least they afford the best opportunity for freedom to flourish. This does not mean, however, that democratic societies must acknowledge absolute liberties which claim universal validity independently of all historical circumstances. Inasmuch as democracy reconciles and maximizes freedoms, it must also, on occasion, in some areas of life, abridge freedom. There are, in brief, no absolute rights to freedom. "A right," as Hook defines it, "is a claim which entails an obligation or duty on the part of others in specified times and circumstances to recognize it whether in fact the law does so at the moment" (12, p. 4). Regardless of what the law may legitimate, the law and the rights it guarantees are modifiable by reference to moral principles and to changing times and altered circumstances. Of course tampering with or abridging certain rights to freedom is always hazardous, but when other rights—rights perhaps more intimately linked with the public good—are abridged, it is imperative that the method of critical intelligence be utilized to solve the problem arising from a conflict of rights and interests, and to decide what, how much, and wherein curtailment of freedom is justifiable.

This democratic process "leads to the concept of strategic or preferred freedoms, on whose functioning the very processes of democracy depend" (8, p. xi). Such strategic freedoms, clustering in the political freedoms incompletely listed in the Bill of Rights, "enable us to win new freedoms and check the excesses of the old" (8, p. 59). "The profoundest lesson of our era," continues Hook, "is the fact that without political freedom there can be no other freedoms, but only an uncertain and uneasy exercise of privileges which may be terminated abruptly without anybody's having to account to those who are affected by these decisions" (8, p. 66).

The principle of equality, along with the utility of strategic freedoms to gain new freedoms, is the key to Hook's socialism. Dating back to his school days, Hook's socialism is in effect a program of economic reorganization instrumental to achieving the moral ideal of social equality. The essence of this ideal, Hook says, "is a sense of *genuine participation* among individuals, of meaningful, uncoerced contribution to the world's work, a sense of counting for something in the concerns and decisions of the community" (8, p. xvi). Far from believing at present that the economic organization of a society necessarily determines its political constitution, he accuses the new conservatives of adhering to the economic determinism of the orthodox Marxists when they condemn planned economy as inevitably totalitarian. But because the capitalist economic system is wasteful of both human and natural resources, Hook is persuaded that the democratic ideal of human personality finds its greatest opportunity for realization within the framework of a socialist economy.

Equality and freedom, thriving in a democratic society with a socialist economy, converge to promote the development of personality. "The emphasis upon respect for the personality of all individuals, the attitude which treats the personality not as something fixed but as a growing, developing pattern, is unique to the philosophy of democracy" (8, p. 39). In *Education for Modern Man* Hook presents, in concepts derived from John Dewey, the case for progressive education (13). As Hook sees it, the aim of education is the most complete development of individual personalities, in regard to growth, character, and intelligence. But, as befits the social nature of the individuals, the fullest development of individual personalities requires a society in which all individuals, realizing their own personalities to the utmost, liberate and enrich the lives of each other. Progressive education, promoting the maximum development of the individual person, is therefore education for democracy. For the value of personality is enhanced within a society in which all persons participate on terms of moral equality.

Hook's remarks on the meaning of equality in education are especially pertinent to a nation caught in the throes of a civil rights revolution. At a moment in recent history when school desegregation dominated the news, Hook asserted: "To say that all children have the same right to an education is not to say that all have the right to the same education. It does not mean that they have the right independently of their capacities to attend the same schools.

It does mean some education for all" (4, p. 16). "The doctrine of separate but equal facilities has no justification whatsoever where race is concerned, but where we segregate solely on the basis of intellectual capacity or interest, there is no reason to cry 'Havoc!' " (4, p. 23).

Justification of Democracy   Since the concept of democracy has now been clarified, the task that remains for the philosopher is to justify adherence to democracy—to adduce reasons why it is better to accept democracy than any alternative mode of social organization. In justifying belief in the democratic creed, Hook has diligently explored the arguments that have been advanced in behalf of democracy and its principles of moral equality, and he has found all these arguments, except one, to be unsound.

First to fall is the argument from theology and religion, for this argument, which asserts that "the rational foundation of democratic belief consists in a set of supernatural religious truths" (8, p. 41), is not only historically false but also logically invalid. Needing validation themselves and consequently provoking further controversy, religion and theology do not even entail a precise social philosophy. Second to be considered is the metaphysical argument, which makes the same sort of claim as the religious argument, and which, consequently, falls for similar reasons. Despite the concession that "there is a definite historical connection between the social movements of any period and its dominant metaphysical teachings," Hook nonetheless insists that "there is no necessary logical connection between a theory of being or becoming and any particular theory of ethics or politics. Stated more accurately, it seems to . . . [him] that no system of metaphysics unequivocally determines a system of ethics or politics" (8, p. 44). Thirdly, the natural law argument, a kind of mixture of the theological and the metaphysical arguments, not only fails for reasons already stated, but also introduces additional ambiguities. The concept of natural law in social philosophy, according to Hook, confuses the physical conception of law, the legal conception of law, and the conception of moral laws of what ought to be (8, p. 46). Fourthly, the preference argument, which imputes "the choice of democracy . . . [to] a nonrational preference rooted in the constitution of our natures and brought to flower by nurture and education" (8, p. 42), is rejected outright. When democracy offers no rational justification, it raises no intellectual or moral issue, so that its acceptance or rejection is left to force alone. When, however, it does offer a rational justification, it must revert to one of the three previous arguments or proceed to the next to be considered.

The fifth argument, which Hook favors, maintains that "the belief in democracy is a hypothesis controlled by the same general pattern of inquiry which we apply to any scientific hypothesis but referring to a different subject matter, i.e., our evaluations" (8, p. 42). Measured in terms of the values of security, freedom, and cooperative diversity, democracy proves to be more fruitful than its alternatives. If these social values are accepted, then there is no difficulty. The decision is always made in favor of democracy. But can such values be accepted as absolutes, or are they, too, to be regarded as hypotheses? Needless to say, Hook's answer is that they are also hypotheses. In any concrete situation rendered problematic by virtue of a conflict of interests, certain values, derived from reflection on prior experience, are tentatively accepted as binding relative to the problem. These values prescribe ways of acting so as to organize human needs and wants for the maximum available satisfaction. Since the situations actually test the values, sometimes the terminal values differ from the original values. And even the terminal values are subject to further testing by new situations. This does not mean that the validation of a value is deferred to an infinite regress; a value finds its validation within the situation to which it is pertinent. But along with new situations may arise new values.

Consider the principle of moral equality, a cardinal value in a democratic society. According to Hook, the justification of equality is found in six propositions, each referring to desired consequences. First, equality stimulates "a maximum of creative, voluntary effort from all members of the community" and "elicits a maximum of intelligent loyalty" (8, p. 51). Second, it "enlarges the scope of our experience by enabling us to acquire insight into the needs, drives, and aspirations of others" (8, p. 51). Third, it "makes it more likely that different points of view may negotiate differences and learn to live peacefully with one another" (8, p. 51). Fourth, it promotes the greatest fulfillment of the individual capacities of all and consequently makes available to all individuals the existing stores of truth and beauty; it even increases these goods (8, p. 51). Fifth, it diminishes human cruelty by making men compassionate and sensitive to each other's needs. And sixth, it promotes more reasonable and satisfying solutions of conflicts of interests than any other procedure, since it permits each interest to be heard, with all standpoints enjoying mutual consultation and free communication (8, p. 52).

Hence democracy is justified by its results. Of course, its superiority to other forms of social organization does not guarantee its acceptance. There is no historical inevitability that democracy must everywhere prevail, or, for that matter, must anywhere exist. That democracy does exist, that it may prevail, hinges upon the intelligent and courageous decisions of men. Certainly, just as there is nothing in the cosmos which necessitates democracy, there is nothing which nullifies its possibility. And that, for Hook, is enough. He writes:

Democracy needs no cosmic support other than the *chance* to make good. That chance it has, because man is part of nature. To ask for more is unreasonable as well as unworthy. The way in which man acts upon his chances is additional evidence of the objective possibilities and novelties of existence. In so far as he is caught in the flux of things, the intelligent democratic man honestly confronts the potentialities of existence, its futurities, its openness, its indeterminateness. He is free of the romantic madness which would seek to outlaw the truths of science and of the quaint conceit, permissible only as poetry, that nature is a democratic republic. He takes the world as science describes it. He employs his knowledge of the world to achieve a more just and happier society (8, pp. 56–57).

MARXISM

Sidney Hook is not only America's leading pragmatist philosopher of democracy; he is also, as has already been noted, her leading theoretician on Marxism. His early books, *Towards the Understanding of Karl Marx* (14) and *From Hegel to Marx* (15), are by far the best expository, interpretive, historical, and critical studies of Marx's thought ever written by an American philosopher. Hook's study of Marxism was fired by a passion for social justice which led him to adopt communism, though he did not become a member of the Communist Party or give his moral allegiance to the Soviet Union. Rather, he sought to propound an objective interpretation of Marxism conforming to the procedures established by scientific methodology (16). Belonging neither to the party of those who denounce Marx without studying or understanding him nor to the party of those who accept his texts as sacrosanct revelations or who distort them to accommodate particular political purposes, Hook offers an account of the true meaning of Karl Marx, including an assessment of what is valid and invalid in Marxism. Further, he examines that offshoot of, and departure from, Marxism—Soviet communism. Providing a critical estimation of its theoretical significance and practical import, Hook is prepared to make recommendations for coping with it.

The Meaning of Marx

Since the aim of this chapter is to grasp the spirit and rationale of Hook's thought, prolix, detailed consideration of Marx's thought is irrelevant. What is germane is an understanding of how Hook understands Marx's thought. To a considerable extent, the subtitle of *Towards the Understanding of Karl Marx*, "A Revolutionary Interpretation," discloses Hook's view of Marx.

A Pragmatic Interpretation   In one sense, the term "revolutionary" qualifies the thought and character of Karl Marx. At least Hook, who repudiates "orthodoxy" as alien to the life and works of Karl Marx, stresses activism. According to this interpretation, Marx's philosophy is no hard and fast system demanding inflexible allegiance. "None of his [Marx's] writings contain a definitive and finished expression of doctrine. He himself lived to say, '*Je ne suis pas un marxiste*' " (14, p. 3). The essential meaning of Marx, since it resides in no neat set of dogmas which establish absolute verbal consistency, lies in the revolutionary intent. "The purpose of Marx's intellectual activity was the revolutionary overthrow of the existing order" (14, p. 68). For Hook the "touchstone of allegiance" to Marx's thought is categorically stated to be the theory of the state, since "it is the theory of the state which is ultimately linked up with immediate political practice. . . . For Marx, every social revolution must be a political revolution, and every political revolution must be directed against the state" (14, pp. 270–71). He continues: "To be a Marxist means to be a revolutionist. The strategy and tactics of Marxists everywhere must be guided by an evaluation of the consequences of any proposed course of action upon the conquest of political power. When conditions are different, methods of procedure will be different, but the use of one method rather than another is determined by a revolutionary purpose which is constant in all situations" (14, p. 273). This conception of Marx's thought, moreover, becomes an effective instrument for grasping an underlying unity regardless of the variations in formulas within Marx's writings. When the thought of Karl Marx is interpreted to be "a philosophy of social action; more specifically, *a theory of social revolution*" (14, p. 9); the various dissident orthodoxies which have sprung up in the wake of Marx—"the ambiguous legacy," in Hook's own phrase (17)—are seen to be rooted in Marx's responses to different thinkers and programs in their struggles to dominate the politico-economic scene. Indeed, Hook's *From Hegel to Marx* has as one of its avowed purposes to corroborate, through historical studies of Marx's contemporaries—such as D. F. Strauss, Bruno Bauer, Arnold Ruge, and Ludwig Feuerbach—the thesis that "the apparent contradictions in Marx's thought, for example between his social determinism and class teleology, his theoretical analyses and his revolutionary activism, could be interpreted as relative emphases arising in the course of criticism of opponents whose positions are antithetical to each other" (15, p. 11).

In another sense, the term "revolutionary" qualifies the nature of Hook's interpretation. In a review of *Towards the Understanding of Karl Marx*, Max Eastman sarcastically described the book as "a delightfully intelligent day-dream of what Marx might have thought and said had he been a pupil of John Dewey" (18). In spite of Eastman's irony the fact remains that, once the evidence is examined, Hook's case for the pragmatic elements in Marx's thought is persuasive. As a revolutionary Marx naturally stressed action and tested theories and programs by the success of the actions they initiate. "For Marx and for those of his followers who have been faithful to his revolutionary ideal, it is history and action that are the matrix of intelligibility. . . . To understand is to act" (14, p. 183). To this Hook adds: "If practice and successful action are criteria of intelligibility, then critical intelligence may be defined as an awareness of the technique, procedures and instruments involved in all directed activity. There is no directed activity outside of the realm of history. All genuine problems become problems of ways and means, and although there is no assurance that they can be solved, the necessary conditions of their solutions are already known" (14, p. 184).

Hook's pragmatist interpretation of Marx's theory of understanding is most clearly borne out in the concluding chapter of *From Hegel to Marx*, where, in an unsurpassed commentary on Marx's theses on Feuerbach, he singles out Thesis II and remarks that "these sentences suggest pragmatism" (15, p. 281). Summing up Marx's theory of truth, Hook says: "The truth of *any* theory depends upon whether or not the actual consequences which flow from the *Praxis* initiated to test the theory are such that they realize the predicted consequences" (15, p. 284).

Shortly before the Second World War Hook said: "The most outstanding figure in the world today in whom the best elements of Marx's thought are present is John Dewey" (11, p. 132). Yet, in a symposium on Marxism published in 1934, John Dewey—along with Bertrand Russell and Morris Cohen—rejected communism, in an essay entitled "Why I Am Not a Communist" (16, pp. 54–56). In the concluding sentences Dewey did admit that what he was rejecting was orthodox communism—i.e., official communism, organized in the Communist Party and the Soviet Union, and not communism with a small *c*. This provided Hook with the opportunity to link Dewey's pragmatism with the communism of Karl Marx, for what Hook means by Marxism is its emphasis upon scientific method in the study of society and its goal of the classless society in which democratic ideals are fulfilled. In the 1934 symposium Hook defined Marxism as "the theory and practice of achieving communism or a classless society" (16, p. 63). And more than two decades later, in 1955, in confirmation of the reputed centrality of science and democracy to the true meaning of Marx, Hook said: "What remains perenially valid in the ambiguous legacy of Marxism is dedication to the scientific spirit and the democratic faith" (16, p. 130). By this time Hook had realized that the term "communism," even in lower case, was hopelessly compromised by association with the political program of the Communist Party. He also wryly observed that according to his conception of Marx, he was the only Marxist left in the world.

Arguments for Communism Throughout the years, despite shifts of emphasis and ideas, Hook has remained loyal to the essential democratic content of Marxism. In the 1934 symposium, in reply to Dewey, Russell, and Cohen, Hook advocated "communism without dogmas." Why, then, does he accept communism as he defines it? What are the dogmas he discards?

Hook's acceptance of communism—or of democratic socialism, more properly called—is predicated upon five arguments. First, according to the argument from efficiency, the failure of capitalism to keep industry working at full capacity in order to minister to human needs leaves only the alternative of the socialist (or communist) planned economy (16, pp. 64–65). Second, according to the argument from democracy, the classless society stands as a democratic society in stark contrast with the capitalist order wherein the ruling economic classes dictate to the working masses. A revolution which is based upon the will of the majority and which overthrows the capitalist class structure is also deemed democratic (16, pp. 65–68). For Hook the revolutionary tradition of the Declaration of Independence with its enshrinement of rights to life, liberty, and the pursuit of happiness finds its culminating realization in the struggle for a classless society (19). Third, according to the argument from morality, especially when counterposed to the morality of abstract formal obligations or the social goals of the propertied classes, Marx's ideal proves to be truly moral, for it is "the ideal of a society 'in which the free development of each individual is the condition for the free development of all' " (16, p. 69). Fourth, the argument from art compares the situation of art in a capitalist society, where hostility and indifferent support weaken and destroy it, with its condition in a communist society, where, because art will be drawn into the natural life of the people, artists will participate in the productive processes of society and flourish (16, p. 71). Fifth, according to the argument from necessity, "the existing situation in the world today, which must always be the point of departure for realistic analysis, narrows 'the vital option' mankind can exercise, to a choice between war and social revolution" (16, p. 72).

Repudiation of Communist Dogmas   Even during this unguarded period when Hook could youthfully declare that "the only valid criticism of the Communist Party is that it is not communist enough," he nonetheless insisted that the time had come "to build a new organization which will represent in philosophy and action the genuine ideals of communism" (16, pp. 73–74). Viewed in historical perspective, the use of the term "communism" was unwise. Hook's motivation in employing it, however, was to win over the more intelligent and more idealistic individuals within the Communist Party and its large network of organizations whose sympathies really lay with basic democratic values. What he sought to discard as dogmas are four principles closely bound up with Soviet communism and the Communist Party.

First, he denies that communism is inevitable, that it is fated by ironclad historical laws which prevail regardless of what men do (16, pp. 74–78). Persistently criticizing the historical determinism of orthodox Marxism, Hook argues that history contains the contingent and the unforeseen and, further, that individual men play important roles in the making of history. Though he is aware of the preponderant evidence (upon which orthodox Marxists have perhaps focused exclusively) that social forces wield a determining influence in history, he rightly insists that individual men also make a difference in history. His sprightly prize-winning volume *The Hero in History* (20) is devoted to this topic. Hook defines "the hero in history" as "the individual to whom we can justifiably attribute preponderant influence in determining an issue or event whose consequences would have been profoundly different if he had not acted as he did" (20, p. 153), and he is confident that such heroes have existed. To clarify the character and function of the historical hero he offers the illuminating distinction between the *eventful* man and the *event-making* man. He writes: "The *eventful* man in history is any man whose actions influenced subsequent developments along a quite different course than would have been followed if these actions had not been taken. The *event-making* man is an eventful man whose actions are the consequences of outstanding capacities of intelligence, will, and character rather than of accidents of position. This distinction tries to do justice to the general belief that a hero is great not merely in virtue of what he does but in virtue of what he is" (20, p. 154). Ironically Hook presses his case for the existence of historical heroes into the very area of Russian history. Of the Russian revolution Hook states "that had it not been for the work of one man we should be living in a vastly different world today" (20, p. 184). He cites Lenin's historical performance to refute the historical determinism of orthodox Marxism.

The second dogma which Hook discards is dialectical materialism; he denies that communists must be dialectical materialists (16, pp. 78–84). Hook's conception of the relation between metaphysics and social philosophy undermines the dogma of dialectical materialism. Moreover, while attributing dialectical materialism to Engels rather than to Marx, Hook specifically condemns it as the new obscurantism (11, Chs. 9–11). The third dogma Hook rejects is the view "that the state will necessarily wither away and that any automatic guarantees can be provided against the abuse of power by those who constitute the leadership of the Communist Party during the transitional period" (16, pp. 85–86). In the early thirties Hook perceived the menace of the Communist Party and the party domination of the Soviet Union and foresaw the frustration of the democratic aspirations of the workers. More on this point will be considered when Soviet communism is examined.

Finally, Hook had no patience whatever with the communist dogma of the "collective man." So far as communism fulfills American ideals, it must promote individuality and individual development; and for Hook the essential meaning of communism or democratic socialism consists in the realization of American democratic ideals. "It cannot be too much stressed, therefore, that communism is hostile to individualism, as a social theory, and not to individuality, as a social value. It seeks to provide the material guarantee of security without which the free development of individuality is an empty or impossible ideal. But the *free development of personality remains its ideal* . . ." (16, p. 88).

Soviet Communism

Although he is sympathetic with Karl Marx's advocacy of the humanitarian ideals of social equality and of the application of scientific method to the study of society, Hook has nonetheless engaged in unrelenting opposition to Soviet communism. At the twelfth International Congress of Philosophy, which met in Venice in September, 1958, he played a prominent role as critic of the representatives of the Soviet Union. In the aftermath of the Congress he challenged the judgment of John Herman Randall, Jr., who claimed that philosophy as developed in the Soviet Union today has much in common with America's pragmatic naturalism (21). Hook, whose most distinctive contribution to recent American thought has been the confrontation and reconciliation of pragmatism and Marxism, would have no part of this alleged common outlook between naturalism and Soviet communist dialectical materialism (22).

Hook's opposition to Soviet communism, his firm position on America's role in the cold war, has incited the antagonism of intellectuals; yet, a generation earlier, when the enemy was Hitlerite Germany, these same intellectuals favored strong policies for America (23). Hook's attacks on the Soviet Union have often been attributed to his alleged Trotskyism. Contrary to widespread suspicions, however, he was never a Trotskyite, although he did deplore the unjust treatment which members of the Communist Party and so-called liberals meted out to Trotsky and his followers. Early he detected that, in principle, "Trotskyism is Stalinism *manqué* (11, p. 179). Hook's hostility to Soviet communism springs from his astute assessment of the communist movement in its march to power. The key to understanding this movement, its strategy and its tactics, is an understanding of its ideology. An ideology is, according to Hook, "the fundamental beliefs about nature, society, and man which any group offers in justification of the direction and goal of its *political* activity" (8, p. 108); and the ideology of the Soviet Union is "not Marxism as much as it is Bolshevik–Leninism" (8, p. 111). Expounded in the writings of Lenin and Stalin, the ideology of Soviet communism contains three basic propositions which, marking it off from Marxism, assert the dependence of the welfare of humanity upon the victory of the proletariat, the dependence of the victory of the proletariat upon the dictatorship of the Communist Party, and the dependence of the efficient functioning of the Communist Party upon dictatorship by its leaders (8, p. 115).

From the outset, according to Hook, the Bolshevik revolution betrayed the teachings of Karl Marx. Hook imagines a conversation with Marx in Limbo, in which Marx repudiates the ideology and conduct of the Soviet Union (8, pp. 332–38). The betrayal does not consist so much in the national chauvinism and imperialism of the U.S.S.R. as in the establishment of a totalitarian regime dominated by the Communist Party. As Hook remarks: "*Culturally*, Leninism must be regarded in the light of its development, as the first Fascist movement of the twentieth century" (8, p. 379). Instead of realizing or approximating the ideal of a classless society, the Bolshevik revolution placed absolute ownership of the entire property of Russia, including the citizenry, and the control thereof in the hands of the Communist Party. "In the most unbridled capitalist democracy there are many things that the Rockefellers and the Morgans and their interlocking directorates cannot do. As directors of the incorporated economy of the U.S.S.R. the hierarchy of the Communist Party is all powerful" (11, p. 164).

The crucial difference between the teachings of Karl Marx and the reality of Soviet communism is mirrored in the stark contrast between humanitarian social democracy and an implacably ruthless dictatorship. This difference is perhaps crystallized in the determination of the economic life of society by political fiat on the part of the Communist Party. In this sense, Hook observes: "The orthodox Marxist theory of social development has received its definitive refutation at the hands of those who flaunt their Marxism to the world" (8, p. 142). And this refutation redounds to the credit of Karl Marx and not the Soviet communists, because, as Hook points out, it was Marx's humanism which ruled out the rapid industrial development of a society at the cost of excessive human suffering.

A totalitarian system bent on world conquest, Soviet communism constitutes a special menace for democratic societies. Defining "the fundamental conflict of our age" as "not between capitalism and collectivism but between democracy and totalitarianism" (8, p. 75), Hook has shrewdly apprehended and analyzed the nature of the Soviet threat and how to meet it. "Bolshevism," he says, "is the greatest movement of secular fanaticism in human history" (8, p. 422). When its professed ends are clearly grasped in the light of its practical instrumentation of these ends, it is possible to forge an effective policy to meet the threat. In broad terms what Hook proposes is a policy of "competitive coexistence"—that is to say, "the presence of peaceful relations between the free and the Communist world which permit each to preserve its own system and to strive by all means, short of war, to make its ideals prevail" (8, p. xiii). Hook amplifies:

The only coexistence acceptable to us should be one which does not diminish the area in which free institutions exist. The Soviet concept of coexistence is that of a breather, or truce from armed struggle, which will enable their Communists by propaganda or subversion to expand their empire until it absorbs the entire globe. In this sense coexistence has always been conceived of as competitive by the Communists. . . . My view is that for us, too, coexistence, which we have faithfully practiced, should be competitive, which until now we have failed to make it. The goal of *our* competition should be, by all means short of war and with the explosive bombs of truth, to expand the world sector of freedom (8, p. xiii).

Competitive coexistence must be implemented by a domestic policy and a foreign policy.

The crux of the domestic policy to cope with the threat of Soviet communism is, in addition to living up to our own ideals, the institution of a program to safeguard strategic freedoms and at the same time promote national security. Among contemporary American philosophers Hook has been the most cognizant of the realities and potentialities of the Communist Party for espionage and subversion. He has consequently defended the establishment of a just but adequate security program, scrutinized the issues of academic freedom, and criticized the appeal to the Fifth Amendment in investigations.

In *Heresy, Yes!—Conspiracy, No!* (24), written when McCarthyism was at its height, Hook argues vigorously for a security program which, though adequate to cope with the threat of Soviet communism, is still compatible with liberalism. Nothing less than the survival of free society is at stake. Defining liberalism as an attitude or temper of mind toward all programs, Hook borrows the words of Justice Holmes to describe the liberal as one who, above all, believes "in the free world of ideas—that the test of truth is the power of thought to get itself accepted in the competition of the market" (24, p. 19). Such a free market, he adds, operates within the framework of two presuppositions: "that the free expression and circulation of ideas may be checked wherever their likely effects constitute a clear and present danger to public peace or the security of the country" (24, p. 20), and "that the competition will be honestly and openly conducted" (24, p. 21). Hence a liberal society, according to Hook, should tolerate heresy but not conspiracy. While heresy consists in "a set of unpopular ideas or opinions on matters of grave concern to the community" (24, p. 21) and is essential to liberal society, which "can impose no official orthodoxies of *belief*, disagreement with which entails loss of liberty or life" (24, p. 22), a conspiracy "is a secret or underground movement which seeks to attain its ends not by normal political or educational processes but by playing outside the rules of the game. Because it undermines the conditions which are required in order that doctrines may freely compete for acceptance, because where successful it ruthlessly destroys all heretics and dissenters, a conspiracy cannot be tolerated without self-stultification in a liberal society" (24, p. 22). In terms of this definition, communist ideas are heretical, but the communist movement, carried out by the Communist Party under the dominion of the Kremlin, is conspiratorial.

A sane security program, considerate of the principles of a liberal society and consequently tolerant of heresy, must guard against conspiracy. The two dominant social groups, which Hook has dubbed "the cultural vigilantes" and "the ritualistic liberals," fail to appreciate the sort of program required for security in a liberal society. Thriving not as much in government as in "certain pressure groups in education, religion, national and economic affairs" (24, p. 38), the cultural vigilantes so completely misunderstand the character and importance of heresy in a liberal society that they suppress it along with conspiracy. Though sensitive to the dangers of cultural vigilantism, liberals have unfortunately been less perceptive of the menace of the communist conspiracy, and so have more often been ritualistic than realistic. Ritualistic liberals, misreading the character of the communist movement, too readily stand upon allegedly absolute rights which, protecting conspirators along with heretics, enable the conspirators to subvert and undermine institutions. The worst consequence of ritualistic liberalism is that it provides fuel for the cultural vigilantes. As Hook remarks in his brilliant analysis of the psychology of the fellow traveler, "the gravest evil for which the Communist fellow-traveler can be held responsible [is] that of giving all dissent an appearance of treason" (8, p. 185).

Unless liberalism is to lose out to cultural vigilantism, it must exercise more realism in regard to the communist movement. Because it is Hook's conviction that realistic liberalism offers the best prospects for democratic ideals in the future development of our society, much of what he has written, especially during the trying fifties, is inspired by a desire to stimulate liberals to be realistic and thus win the confidence of the community. In *Common Sense and the Fifth Amendment* (25) Hook challenges the ritualistic liberals' defense of the invocation of the Fifth Amendment by respondents before investigative committees. He does not argue that the invocation of the privilege against self-incrimination entails the legal guilt of the person who invokes it. But, adopting the standpoint of common sense—defined not as "the logic of the syllogism but [as] the logic of inquiry which is derived altogether from experience and from reflection upon it" (25, p. 15)—Hook contends that, "although it [invocation of the Fifth Amendment] is a very good shelter for the guilty because it suppresses evidence of guilt, it is a very poor shield for the innocent because of the presumption of guilt which invariably attends its use wherever common sense has not abdicated" (25, p. 63).

It should be noted that Hook's "original concern with the question of the Fifth Amendment arose, not in conjunction with strictly legal issues, but with the implications of its use outside the courtroom, especially in its bearings on professional qualifications in filling positions of trust" (25, p. 48). In particular, Hook has been concerned over the penetration of education by the communists. While no one surpasses Hook in the defense of academic freedom, which he defines as "the freedom of professionally qualified persons to inquire, discover, publish and teach the truth as they see it in the field of their competence, without any control or authority except the control or authority of the rational methods by which truth is established" (24, p. 154), he is firm in his judgment that members of the Communist Party, because of their commitment to dogmas and tactics regardless of the verdicts of reflection and experience, because of their allegiance to the intellectual discipline of the party, and because of their obligation to recruit members from among their students, are by presumption unfit to teach on grounds of professional ethics. However, aware of the complexities and injustices of various programs to ferret out and dismiss communist teachers, Hook concludes that "the best safeguard against indoctrination and related dishonorable practices is not prying supervision of teachers, subtle interrogation of students, foolish and needless imposition of loyalty oaths, but the recruiting of competent men and women sufficiently dedicated to the ideas of teaching and scholarship to recognize that such practices are incompatible with professional integrity" (24, p. 192). In addition he has stressed his opposition to automatic dismissals of any kind. The person identified as a member of the Communist Party or of any other organization which gives him instructions to violate his professional trust is presumptively unfit, but it is a rebuttable presumption. The burden of proof rests upon one who has voluntarily accepted membership in an organization which instructs him to violate the ethics of his profession; he must show that he has disregarded these instructions.

The domestic scene bursts with complex issues of security and freedom. These issues must be resolved if the menace of Soviet totalitarianism is to be met and turned back. No American thinker measures up to Hook for his courageous confrontation, sober analyses, and sane solutions of these issues. Since, moreover, the source of the threat is foreign, a sound domestic policy must be accompanied by a sound foreign policy if the free world is to survive and halt or reverse the chain of losses it has suffered since the end of World War II.

According to Hook, the failure of our foreign policy vis-à-vis Russia has been due to two crucial mistakes: "the underestimation of the significance of Communist ideology as a determinant of Soviet behavior" (8, p. 422); and "the failure to understand that, despite this unappeasable fanaticism, the Soviet Union really did not desire a general war" (8, p. 422). Basing his judgments upon the knowledge of communist ideology and upon the conviction that the Soviet Union does not really want war and will back away from it whenever the free world decides to fight rather than sacrifice its interests, Hook has sought to gird the courage of America and the free world to stand firm in the defense of freedom. Taking issue with Bertrand Russell, who on occasion has gone so far as to propose unilateral disarmament by the West in order to avoid a nuclear war (8, pp. 429 ff.), Hook has argued that the best defense of the West is its readiness to fight in behalf of freedom, even if this means nuclear war. Hook has devoted a great deal of energy to trying to put to rest the fears among Western intellectuals that reliance on nuclear weapons as a deterrent to communist aggression will lead inevitably to world holocaust. For example, he has treated the reception of the sensational best selling novel *Fail-Safe* as "evidence of a widespread syndrome of political defeatism. It sees in the deterrent shield of defense, behind which the main centers of free culture have until now survived, an instrument not of safety but one that insures a world-wide calamity" (26, p. 8). He has scrutinized the novel to show "that the story of *Fail-Safe* rests on a conjunction of unrelated improbabilities which would lead to the conclusion that the event the authors fear is extremely unlikely to occur" (26, p. 11).

As Hook says: *"The ultimate weapon of the West is not the hydrogen bomb or any other super-weapon but the passion for freedom and the willingness to die for it if necessary"* (8, p. 426). This view is eloquently summed up in the epigraph to *Political Power and Personal Freedom:* IT IS BETTER TO BE A LIVE JACKAL THAN A DEAD LION—FOR JACKALS, NOT MEN; AND . . . THOSE WHO ARE PREPARED TO LIVE LIKE MEN AND, IF NECESSARY, TO DIE LIKE MEN, HAVE THE BEST PROSPECT OF SURVIVING AS FREE MEN AND ESCAPING THE FATE OF BOTH JACKALS AND LIONS.

NOTES TO CHAPTER V

1 Sidney Hook, "John Dewey—Philosopher of Growth," *Journal of Philosophy,* LVI (1959), 1010–18.
2 See the following anthologies and symposia edited by Sidney Hook: with H. M. Kallen, *American Philosophy Today and Tomorrow* (New York: Lee Furman, 1935); with Milton R. Konvitz, *Freedom and Experience: Essays Presented to H. M. Kallen* (Ithaca, N.Y.: Cornell University Press, 1947); *John Dewey: Philosopher of Science and Freedom* (New York: Dial Press, 1950); *Marx and the Marxists: The Ambiguous Legacy* (Princeton: Van Nostrand, 1955); and *American Philosophers at Work* (New York: Criterion Books, 1956).
3 Hook has edited the following symposia based on the annual proceedings of the New York Institute of Philosophy and published by New York University Press: *Determinism and Freedom in the Age of Modern Science* (1958); *Psychoanalysis, Scientific Method, and Philosophy* (1959); *Dimensions of Mind* (1960); *Religious Experience and Truth* (1961); *Philosophy and History* (1963); *Law and Philosophy* (1964); *Art and Philosophy* (1966); and *Human Values and Economic Policy* (1967).
4 Brand Blanshard (ed.), *Education in the Age of Science* (New York: Basic Books, 1959).
5 Sidney Hook, "Pragmatism and the Tragic Sense of Life," *Proceedings and Addresses of the American Philosophical Association,* 1959–1960.
6 Sidney Hook, "Marxism, Metaphysics and Modern Science," *Modern Quarterly,* IV (1928), 388. This article is a highly critical review of Max Eastman's *Marx, Lenin, and the Science of Revolution.* An acrimonious debate ensued. See Max Eastman, "As to Sidney Hook's Morals," *ibid.,* V (1928), 85–87; and Sidney Hook, "As to Max Eastman's Mentality," *ibid.,* V (1928), 88–91. Both toughminded controversialists exchanged sharp words through the years, the personal bitterness abating in time and yielding to mutual respect. For an account of the Hook-Eastman controversy in *Modern Quarterly,* see Daniel Aaron, *Writers on the Left* (New York: Harcourt, Brace and World 1961; Avon Books, 1965), 335.

7 Sidney Hook, *John Dewey: An Intellectual Portrait* (New York: John Day, 1939).

8 Sidney Hook, *Political Power and Personal Freedom* (New York: Criterion Books, 1959).

9 Sidney Hook, *The Metaphysics of Pragmatism* (Chicago: Open Court, 1927).

10 Sidney Hook, *The Quest for Being and Other Studies in Naturalism and Humanism* (New York: St. Martin's Press, 1961).

11 Sidney Hook, *Reason, Social Myths, and Democracy* (New York: John Day Company, 1940).

12 Sidney Hook, *The Paradoxes of Freedom* (Berkeley and Los Angeles: University of California Press, 1962).

13 Sidney Hook, *Education for Modern Man* (New York: Dial Press, 1946; rev. ed. New York: Random House, 1963).

14 Sidney Hook, *Towards the Understanding of Karl Marx: A Revolutionary Interpretation* (New York: John Day, 1933).

15 Sidney Hook, *From Hegel to Marx: Studies in the Intellectual Development of Karl Marx* (New York and London: Reynal and Hitchcock and V. Gollancz, 1936; New York: Humanities Press, 1950).

16 Sidney Hook, "The Meaning of Marx," in Sidney Hook (ed.), *The Meaning of Marx: A Symposium* (New York: Farrar and Rinehart, 1934), 32. With an introduction by Sherwood Eddy and papers by Bertrand Russell, John Dewey, and Morris Cohen bearing the title "Why I Am Not a Communist"—as well as Hook's reply article, entitled "Communism Without Dogmas"—this symposium first appeared in the *Modern Monthly* in April, 1934. All references are to the Farrar and Rinehart publication.

17 Sidney Hook, *Marx and the Marxists: the Ambiguous Legacy* (Princeton: Van Nostrand, 1955).

18 Max Eastman, Review, *Books* (April 16, 1933), 6. See also Max Eastman, *The Last Stand of Dialectic Materialism: A Study of Sidney Hook's Marxism* (New York: Polemic Publishers, 1934).

19 Sidney Hook, "The Democratic and Dictatorial Aspects of Communism," *International Conciliation* (December, 1934), 463. For Hook's latest views on revolution, see *The Paradoxes of Freedom*, Ch. 3.

20 Sidney Hook, *The Hero in History: A Study in Limitation and Possibility* (Boston: Beacon Press, 1943; New York: Humanities Press, 1955).

21 John Herman Randall, Jr., "The Mirror of USSR Philosophizing," *Journal of Philosophy*, LV (1958), 1019–28.

22 Sidney Hook, "J. H. Randall, Jr., On American and Soviet Philosophy," *ibid.*, LVI (1959), 416–19.

23 See Christopher Lasch, *The New Radicalism in America 1889–1963* (New York: Alfred A. Knopf, 1965), 306–307, 322–33.

24 Sidney Hook, *Heresy, Yes!—Conspiracy, No!* (New York: John Day, 1953).

25 Sidney Hook, *Common Sense and the Fifth Amendment* (New York: Criterion Books, 1957).

26 Sidney Hook, *The Fail-Safe Fallacy* (New York: Stein and Day, 1963).

VI

F. S. C. NORTHROP

Philosophy as Ideology

INFLUENCES

"The essence of man as a moral and spiritual being is that he is a knowing being" (1, p. 45). In these words F. S. C. Northrop, Sterling Professor of Philosophy and Law Emeritus at Yale University, has delineated the nature of man. Both scientifically and spiritually, he continues, man is "a walking philosophy" and, he adds, "the cause of the unity of a culture is the philosophy which its people by intercommunication hold in common" (1, p. 37). Northrop has devoted his life to the pursuit of knowledge as few men in his generation have; science, culture, law, international politics have fallen under his philosophic scrutiny. Since, for Northrop, knowing is intrinsic to human nature, and since it is expressed in beliefs about facts and values which govern man's outward conduct and which shape his cultural formations, philosophy as the critique of such knowledge is inherently practical. Thus, like Sidney Hook, who has followed in the footsteps of John Dewey, Northrop has addressed himself to the problems of men—in particular to those all-embracing problems of international law and order upon which the issue of peace or war hangs. Unlike the pragmatists, however, Northrop has insisted upon the primacy of knowing over acting. Ideas, then, are central to human conduct and human culture, not because their meaning consists in their practical effects, but rather because they determine and evaluate such effects. Hence in assessing the tensions and the conflicts that prevail in international politics, Northrop has directed his attention to ideology—though without minimizing the role of political, economic, and military power.

Born in Janesville, Wisconsin, on November 27, 1893, Northrop studied at Beloit College, where he received his B.A. in 1915 and an honorary doctorate in 1946. There he studied history under Professor Robert Kimball Richardson and natural science under Professor George Clancy (1, p. 9). In 1919 Northrop received his M.A. in economics from Yale, having begun there before World War I to study Greek philosophy under Professor Charles Montague Bakewell (1, pp. 9–10). In 1922 he earned a second M.A., this one in philosophy from Harvard, where he studied with William Ernest Hocking and Henry Sheffer. In 1924 he received his Ph.D. from Harvard with a dissertation in philosophy on the problem of organization in biology, a topic which brought him under the joint supervision of Hocking and the noted American physiologist L. J. Henderson (1, pp. 14–15). Earlier he had studied in England, with John McTaggart at Cambridge and with Alfred North Whitehead at London. The association with Whitehead proved most fruitful.

In 1924 Whitehead joined the faculty of Harvard University, where by virtue of the merits of the works he wrote in the United States he won a permanent place as an American philosopher of the first rank. His influence on American thought in philosophical cosmology, in logic, and in the philosophy of culture is second to none. Northrop's own debt to Whitehead is considerable, as Northrop has admitted: "(1) He directed my philosophical analysis of the theory and method of 20th-century mathematical physics. . . . (2) Whitehead made it unequivocally clear to me that there must be a reconstruction of not merely the scientific but also of the humanistic, including the religious and aesthetic, philosophical assumptions of the modern world. . . . The third thing he impressed upon me, both the first time we met and the last time before he died, is that in either science or philosophy one cannot be too suspicious of ordinary language" (1, pp. 15–16, 19). The intellectual closeness of Northrop's association with Whitehead is borne out by Northrop's testimony that in the early 1920's Whitehead took him "page by page and chapter by chapter through *The Principles of Natural Knowledge* and *The Concept of Nature*" (1, p. 175). However, although he has promoted Whitehead's works (2), Northrop is not a disciple of Whitehead. On the contrary, Northrop developed a theory of the meaning of scientific concepts quite different from Whitehead's. Befriending Albert Einstein in Berlin in 1927, Northrop came under the influence of the German physicist, an influence nurtured by numerous visits to Princeton after Einstein came to the United States. As Northrop has said, he "left Whitehead's epistemological philosophy of both common sense and physics for that of Einstein" (1, p. 211; 3).

Northrop's emergence as ideologist occurred after long years spent in the study of the sciences, years in which the influences of Whitehead and of Einstein, not altogether harmonious, were paramount.

PHILOSOPHY OF SCIENCE

Northrop's first book, *Science and First Principles,* is a remarkable critique of the foundations of science (4). Theories of relativity physics, quantum mechanics, and physiology, which the scientists were then presenting to clarify the areas of physical nature and life, meanwhile confounded common sense and perplexed the philosophical imagination. Before Einstein had shifted toward the field theory in physics in 1929, Northrop had independently discerned the need for a unitary frame to which all relative motion of matter refers. Since Einstein's relativity physics had removed absolute space as the referent for atomicity and motion, Northrop had argued that "either the traditional physical kinetic atomic theory must be radically amended to provide a new referent for atomicity or motion, or the science and civilization of our own day must be reared upon entirely different philosophical foundations from those of the last three centuries" (4, p. 50). Because relativity physics defines space-time in terms of matter and motion and so cannot consistently employ space-time as the referent for atomicity and motion, Northrop did not consider an objective chrono-geometrical field to be an adequate frame of reference.

Hence he postulated the macroscopic atom: "This universe must be constituted not only of the moving microscopic atoms of the traditional atomic theory but also of one large physical macroscopic atom, spherical in shape and hollow in its interior except for its inner field, which surrounds and congests them" (9, p. 120). Whether the macroscopic atomic theory is a tenable hypothesis or not, it may be viewed as an ingenious attempt to overcome difficulties in Einstein's physics prior to the development of field theory concepts. It also promised to assimilate and reconcile discoveries in quantum mechanics, thermodynamics, and biology, thereby guaranteeing the order and uniformity of nature in general and of biological organisms in particular without recourse to any principles except matter and motion. It should perhaps be noted in passing that Whitehead himself esteemed Northrop's doctrine of a macroscopic atom to be the only alternative to his own cosmology of microscopic atomic occasions (5, p. 508).

However, Northrop's scientific materialism, which envisages one macroscopic atom enframing swarming myriads of microscopic atoms, was eventually superseded by Einstein's field theory. In the case of Northrop, as in the history of science, it was not the particular results reached, but the methods utilized, which proved most fruitful for his future intellectual progress. Northrop has outlined these methods in *The Logic of the Sciences and the Humanities* (6).

Drawing upon expert interdisciplinary knowledge of the arts, the sciences, and the humanities, Northrop defines logic broadly "to include any form of knowing in religion and art as well as the sciences," closely linking it with epistemology, which examines the relation between the knower and the subject matter as known (6, p. viii). The starting point of knowing, moreover, is always some problem in the subject matter under investigation. But problems differ in type: some pertain to logical consistency or mathematical precision and call for formal logic or mathematics; others concern factual matters and are resolved by empirical observation and experiment; still others arise from conflicts of values and are dealt with by the methods of normative social science. It follows, then, that the methods of inquiry must differ, and Northrop adopts a methodological pluralism. "There is no one scientific method" (6, p. ix). Rather there are several methods, each appropriate to specific problems or to particular stages in the treatment of specific problems. Northrop's general theory of methods embraces the rival methodologies of Francis Bacon, René Descartes, Morris Cohen and John Dewey, by assigning each to a distinct stage in the total process of inquiry. This general methodology displays a pluralism and an irenicism characteristic of his entire philosophy.

Scientific inquiry passes through several discernible stages, each of which involves distinctive methods. The first stage is the analysis of the problem which starts the inquiry. The method of analysis detects the problem and uncovers its components, stating clearly the set of conceptions and factors which generates it and translating it into a relevant factual situation.

After the analysis of the problem follows the second stage of scientific inquiry—namely, the natural history stage. Here three Baconian methods of induction—observation, description, and classification—come into play. Although the second stage of scientific inquiry opens with pure fact under observation, it terminates with described fact or classified fact, fact no longer pure but altered by concepts. Pure fact, "defined as that which is known by immediate apprehension alone" (7, p. 39), is "a continuum of ineffable aesthetic qualities, not an external material object" (6, p. 4). The bedrock of empirical knowledge is drenched with intuited quality, evincing an essential relation between fact and the sort of values mirrored in impressionistic art.

In the third stage of scientific inquiry hypotheses are constructed; this stage is dominated by hypothetico-deductive methods. Whereas at the second stage every element under consideration may be expressed by what Northrop calls "a concept by intuition"—i.e., one "which denotes, and the complete meaning of which is given by, something which is immediately apprehended," such as, for example, the concept "blue" to denote the sensed quality (6, p. 82)—at the third stage there are in the hypotheses concepts which refer to unobservable entities, e.g., electrons. Each such concept Northrop terms "a concept by postulation"—i.e., "one the meaning of which in whole or part is designated by the postulates of some specific deductively formulated theory in which it occurs" (6, p. 62).

The hallmark of Western science and philosophy, according to

Northrop, is the employment of hypothetico-deductive theory containing concepts by postulation which refer to nonobservable but systematically designated entities. Such theory, furthermore, requires empirical verification to reconnect it with the experience from which it originally came. Of course, when the concepts by postulation in a deductive system are identified with concepts by intuition, there is no difficulty. "In this case [there] obtains *abstractive deductively formulated theory*, which because of the concepts out of which it is constructed, permits direct empirical verification of its postulates" (6, p. 109). But if the deductive theory is constructed of concepts by postulation which are not identical with intuited concepts but instead refer to concepts of imagination—e.g., the atoms of classical particle physics—and concepts of intellection—e.g., the space-time continuum of Einstein's field physics—it is *"hypothetically inferred deductively formulated theory,"* its postulates being testable only indirectly through their deductive consequences (6, p. 109).

To bridge the gulf between unobservable entities designated by concepts by postulation and the immediately apprehended items of experience, as the verification of hypothetically inferred deductively formulated theory requires, Northrop distinguishes a technical epistemological operation which he names "epistemic correlation." "An epistemic correlation is a relation joining an unobserved component of anything designated by a concept by postulation to its directly inspected component denoted by a concept by intuition" (6, p. 119). Although epistemic correlation is exemplified in the sciences in linkages between, say, the length of an electromagnetic wave and a sensed color, it is not restricted to such applications; it becomes in Northrop's usage an important instrument for the meeting of diverse cultures.

For Northrop the epistemology of natural science—the methods of inquiry and the clarification of the components of knowledge—is applicable to social science. He has, indeed, insisted that it is indispensable to anthropology, the social science to which he has contributed his energies in recent years (7, p. 8). Northrop has distinguished two methods in social science: the descriptive method and the normative method. "The one type, appropriately termed 'factual or descriptive social theory,' attempts, after the manner of natural science, to obtain an empirically verified deductively formulated theory of society as it is in fact. The other type, appropriately called 'normative social theory,' attempts to specify a deductively formulated theory of society as it ought to be" (8, p. 95). Both methods are assimilated in philosophical anthropology as Northrop conceives the discipline. Because men as members of society share beliefs about values, have norms and ideals, anthropology has these values as part of the facts, the data, with which it deals. In addition to the descriptive method, anthropology should employ what Northrop has called the "evaluative method." This method "is not merely a standard for measuring traditional moral and political goal-value philosophies and norms of the *de facto* nations. It also prescribes what to do to determine the ideal nation" (8, p. 118). Thus the evaluative method in philosophical anthropology is, in Northrop's eyes, an important tool of practical politics.

PHILOSOPHY OF CULTURE

Northrop's most widely known book, *The Meeting of East and West*, is an extended application of the methods of scientific inquiry to the pressing ideological problems of our time (9). As a quick glance at the present international and national scene and a brief review of recent history reveal, our epoch is fraught with conflicts between East and West, between segments within the East and within the West, and even between regions and factions within individual states. Sidney Hook's stance vis-à-vis Soviet communism, discussed in the preceding chapter, illustrates the exceptional alertness of one American philosopher to the ideological elements in the conflicts of our time. Hook, however, centered his attention on Marxism and Soviet Russia. In view of America's postwar emergence as a global power committed in Asia and Africa as well as in Europe and Latin America, and twice entangled in wars on the Asiatic mainland—first in Korea and now in Vietnam—an adequate account of contemporary ideological forces must stretch beyond the confrontation between the United States and the U.S.S.R. Northrop offers just such a global account of ideologies. By "East" he means the Far Eastern Orient, and not the Soviet Union, which he treats as a branch of the modern West.

Northrop has focused the analytic methods of science upon recent conflicts and has ascertained that ideology is a causative factor. Ideologies, systems of basic beliefs concerning reality, knowledge, and value, while perhaps not wholly determining what men do, greatly influence their actions. Consequently, world peace hinges upon the ability of men to understand the differing ideologies which motivate the behavior of nations, in order to reconcile them when they are compatible and to correct them in consonance with impartial criteria when they are incompatible.

Philosophy therefore plays two significant roles in resolving the problems that menace the peace of the world. First, so far as philosophies are ideologies, cultures may be regarded as overt, concrete embodiments of philosophical systems. Here it is relevant to note that Northrop naturalistically bases the ideas and values which define human cultures. Leaning heavily on the contributions of Warren S. McCulloch and Walter Pitts to neurophysiology, he offers a theory of "trapped universals." This theory correlates introspected universals (ideas or values) with a regenerative loop in the brain which continuously transmits impulses to act so long as neural energy is in supply. In this sense, ideological man is natural man: "Literally, moral, thoughtful, choosing, purposeful individual and social man is the scientifically verified and conceived natural neurological man" (10, p. 426).

Second, so far as the explication and criticism of fundamental presuppositions are philosophical tasks, philosophy is best suited to explore and examine the ideologies which underlie cultures. This philosophical inquiry into the philosophical presuppositions of cultures falls within the second stage of scientific inquiry, for it involves the observation, description, and classification of ideologies. The philosophy of culture is at the outset an empirical investigation which treats philosophies as empirical data, and the main body of The Meeting of East and West consists in an empirical, inductive exploration of the ideologies of the major cultures of the contemporary world. When, however, Northrop undertakes to mollify ideological conflicts by reinforcing common or complementary cultural elements and by recommending the rejection of elements discordant with the findings of the sciences, his philosophy of culture extends beyond the limits of strictly descriptive science and utilizes the methods of normative science.

Western civilization exhibits a pluralism of cultures, each embodying a distinctive ideology or cluster of ideological convictions. Northrop's delineation of these ideologies is enhanced by his technically acute understanding of the sciences and philosophy, his critical appreciation of artistic and religious values, and his discerning sensitivity to social, economic, and political forces and trends. The "rich culture" of Mexico, grounded in the aesthetic naturalism of the Indians in combination with Roman Catholicism and passionate Spanish individualism, schooled in French positivism and swayed by both Anglo-American ideals of political democracy and Russian ideals of communism, now moves in the direction of a dynamic humanism. The "free culture" of the United States, based upon Protestant individualism and Locke's natural law philosophy of inalienable rights and constitutional government, its economy sustained by an efficient scientific technology neglectful of all values except material production and property, evinced new orientations toward aesthetic values and social concerns for the welfare of men. British democracy, with its strong sense of community, derives its ideals from the familial, status-stressing, hierarchical polity of Richard Hooker and from Cromwellian Protestantism; while it fosters nonconformist individual rights, it nevertheless engages in thoroughgoing socialist reconstruction of its economy. German idealism since Kant has divorced morality from science and has increasingly lent itself to fanatic, nationalistic philosophies; when unchecked by rational control it engenders political totalitarianisms. Russian Communism, explicitly founded upon the dialectical materialism of Marx, Engels, and Lenin, adopts a policy entailed by its conviction that economic forces determine that history will unfold from the present contradictions embedded in capitalist society and destined to erupt into class warfare and world revolution until inevitably through the dictatorship of the workers as guided by the Party a classless society is attained. Meanwhile, the entire history of the West manifests disruption and discontinuity, as the culture of Greek science is discordant with the culture of the Christian Middle Ages, which in turn is contradicted by the contemporary West, itself shattered by conflicting ideologies.

Is there a common factor which groups together the divergent ideologies of the West? Is there a basic idea or value which persists through and imparts unity to all the Western ideologies? According to Northrop, there is such a common factor: it is utopianism. "This utopianism . . . is not a purely modern phenomenon of the European imagination. It goes back behind Marx and Hegel, Hume and Locke, Descartes and Las Casas, St. Thomas and St. Augustine, and even behind Aristotle, to Plato and Democritus. Full-born, it shows itself in the vision of the 'New Atlantis' in the *Dialogues* of Plato. Here we find the meaning of Western civilization, both in its origin and in its American manifestations, in its roots" (9, p. 292). Accompanied by ideological differences and cultural discontinuities, this utopianism springs from a Western rationalism which, by acknowledging inferred nonobservable entities designated by the postulational concepts of hypothetico-deductive theories, imputes primacy to the theoretic component in knowledge. Since these entities cannot be reduced to the sensed objects of immediate intuition, they testify to a domain of ideal reality distinct from sense experience and wider than the imaginations of men, and since these concepts by postulation are verifiable only indirectly, they are tentative and prone to revision, instigating the drastic ideological shifts that shatter the cultural unity and continuity of the West.

In contrast with the rationalistic emphasis common to the ideologies of the West is the positivism of the Orient. The religions of Buddhism, Hinduism, Taoism, and Confucianism, which undergird the traditional Eastern cultures, share a basic unity by virtue of their common stress on the aesthetic component in knowledge. Of prime significance to the Easterner, then, are not the inferred nonobservable entities that are the glory of Western scientific mentality and political idealism; rather, what is primary is the aesthetic continuum.

As Northrop says: "This complex aesthetic continuum is made up of two factors; one the determinate sensed or introspected differentiations which are transitory; the other, the undifferentiated aesthetic continuum within which the determinate differentiations come and go. Since time has to do with the transitory differentiations, the Oriental affirms the undifferentiated aesthetic continuum to be outside time and hence not transitory" (9, p. 460). First attending to the particular qualities revealed by the various senses, the Oriental mind apprehends the fragile transiency of these particular differentiations and consequently comes to concentrate on the universal, unifying, abiding undifferentiated aesthetic continuum which encompasses all differentiations. Thus the radical positivism of the Orient balances a stark realism concerning the transitory particular values, which in effect are deemed relative, with a mysticism which takes "the indeterminate *tao, jen,* Nirvana or Chit as not merely primary, but as the source of the creation and the receptacle at the death of all transitory differentiated things" (9, p. 396).

After analyzing the problem which besets the contemporary world and finding it to be ideological, and after observing, describing, and classifying the component ideologies, Northrop ventures a solution to the problem. He writes: "The task of the contemporary world falls into four major parts: (1) the relating of the East and the West; (2) the similar merging of Latin and Anglo-Saxon cultures; (3) the mutual reinforcement of democratic and communistic values; and (4) the reconciliation of the true and the valuable portions of the Western medieval and modern worlds" (9, p. 436). Difficult as the task may have seemed, it did not appear hopeless. Just as science, by means of epistemic correlations, bridges the rift between the aesthetic and theoretic components in knowledge without reduction, so, from Northrop's irenic standpoint: "East and West can meet, not because they are saying the same thing, but because they are expressing different yet complementary things, both of which are required for an adequate and true conception of man's self and his universe. Each can move into the new comprehensive world of the future, proud of its past and preserving its self-respect. Each also needs the other" (9, pp. 454–55). As no imponderable obstructs the marriage of East and West in a richer, total world culture, it seemed plausible, in the atmosphere of optimism that reigned at the close of World War II, that even Russian communism and the traditional democracies of Europe and America could be reconciled (9, pp. 465–72). Guided by the example and the findings of science, the nations of the twentieth century, Northrop argued, can establish institutions and pursue actions which "would be valid for everybody," if only they modify their ideologies to conform to "the conception of man and nature as determined by immediate apprehension with respect to the aesthetic component and by the methods of natural science with respect to the theoretic component" (9, p. 470).

Thus, providing the continuous intuitive factor in the aesthetic, and the systematic unifying factor in the theoretic parts of our nature, which make all men and things one, are fostered, so that the equally real and important differences between men do not lead them to their mutual destruction, it should eventually be possible to achieve a society for mankind generally in which the higher standard of living of the most scientifically advanced and theoretically guided Western nations is combined with the compassion, the universal sensitivity to the beautiful and the abiding equanimity and calm joy of the spirit which characterize the sages and many of the humblest people of the Orient (9, p. 496).

PHILOSOPHY OF LAW

Northrop's conception of the world as a plurality of cultures, each with its own ideology, does not justify the conclusion that the only policy to peace among nations is that of power politics. On the contrary, Northrop has consistently advocated policies which, while not shying away from the employment of power, nevertheless utilize existing ideological factors to build toward an order among nations, toward a system of international law. From his chair in the Yale Law School Northrop has wielded immense influence in directing the minds of his students, foreign as well as American, to a theory of law adequate to the needs of the international situation.

The Complexity of Legal and Ethical Experience is comprised mainly of papers which Northrop had published previously in legal and philosophical journals; only the first chapter and last two chapters appear in print for the first time. Despite the repetition to be found in such a collection, this work offers a consistent, comprehensive legal theory (11). Northrop engages primarily in the criticism of existing legal theories, but not only does he cast upon existing jurisprudence light usually absent from the writings of legalists and philosophers, he also constructively sketches a scientifically grounded jurisprudence containing validated normative methods. For Northrop comes to legal theory with a dispassionate, objective, scientific methodology as well as an intense practical concern for the resolution of ideological conflicts.

Northrop's grasp of methodology proves useful both in the elaboration of his own theory and in the understanding of existing legal theories and systems. As he points out, epistemological conceptions profoundly affect the character of legal systems. The Oriental, who focuses on the aesthetic component in experience and who ignores abstract universal principles, tends "to push legal codes into the background, preferably dispensing with them altogether, and to bring the disputants into a warm give-and-take relationship, usually by way of a mediator, so that previously made demands can be modified gracefully, and a unique solution taking all the exceptional circumstances of the case into account is spontaneously accepted by both disputants" (11, pp. 184–85). Besides the Oriental's "intuitive mediational type of law," there is "the natural history type of law," which consists of codes expressed in ordinary language and which describes "the biologically conceived patriarchal or matriarchal familial and tribal kinship norms of the inductively and sensuously given status quo" (11, p. 186). Before the time of the Stoic Romans, all codified ancient law was of this type. In sharp contrast to both of these types of law is "the abstract contractual type of law," which the Westerner, who concentrates on the theoretic component in knowledge and who consequently leans toward hypothetico-deductive theory, has adopted. Replacing commonsense language with a technical terminology, abstract contractual law permits "the construction of legal and social entities different from any which are observed in any traditional society" (11, p. 188). Thus Westerners readily appeal to codes for the settlement of disputes and also acknowledge for their laws ethical norms other than those of the immediate status quo, so that their legal systems exhibit progressive dynamism and universal application.

Just as Northrop's study of scientific methods prepares him uniquely for legal theory, so also his conception of ideologies as basic sets of philosophical beliefs and norms underlying cultures has given him a special perspective on legal theory. All major contemporary conflicts, whether international—as, between democratic liberalism and Soviet communism—or domestic—as between the Supreme Court and Southern segregationists—display an "inescapably ideological character," since they stem from the clash of divergent sets of norms (11, pp. 16–18). Moreover, existing jurisprudence cannot resolve these disputes because it presupposes the very norms which the ideological conflicts put to question. It is necessary, therefore, to develop a legal system based on a scientifically grounded legal science capable of evaluating existing norms.

Such a legal science must begin, as all science does, with problematic experience, although legal experience is "much more complex than any traditional theory . . . would suppose" (11, p. ix). Like science in its natural history stage, legal theory must proceed with inductive methods, adhering closely to the complexity of legal experience and intent upon an analysis of its multiple facets. Traditional legal theories—legal positivism, sociological jurisprudence, intuitive ethical jurisprudence, and natural law jurisprudence—emphasize one or another of the facets of legal experience, but they reveal, upon analysis, inadequacies remediable solely by an irenic legal philosophy which, embracing the traditional theories in a more general theory, remains true to the complexity of legal experience. Yet, Northrop maintains, this new legal science cannot be purely descriptive, because its subject matter is not purely descriptive. Whereas natural science restricts itself to describing what is and ethics focuses on what ought to be, Northrop writes:

In law . . . the "is" of the most sordid and vile conduct comes face to face in fact before a bar of judgment which passes a sentence in terms of norms with specific content that presuppose and prescribe an "ought."

What the world would be were there no Sundays and what Heaven is where there are only Sundays combine in human legal experience. And in this meeting of the "is" with the "ought" in which the de facto sordidness of the defendant's act is measured against the normative "ought" of the law's prescriptive precedents and principles, for all the shortcomings and the miscarriages of justice, it is the "ought" that wins. In legal experience Cinderella wins her Prince (11, p. 4).

Thus as law involves ethics and is normative, legal theory, inasmuch as it compares and evaluates legal systems and theories, does not merely describe but also assumes a normative function. In fact, Northrop examines rival legal theories by reference to their performance of this normative function.

Legal positivism maintains that the "subject matter of legal science is the positive law" (11, p. 26). Derived from John Austin in England, transmitted to America by J. B. Thayer during his professorship at Harvard in the late nineteenth century, extended by C. C. Langdell's introduction of the case method, and present in modified form in the writings of Hans Kelsen, legal positivism emerges in the decisions and writings of jurists, such as Justice Felix Frankfurter and Judge Learned Hand. In epistemology legal positivism is radically empiricist; in ethics it is subjectivist; in political philosophy it is inspired by the Hobbesian and Austinian notions that the power of the sovereign is the sanction of the law. Viewing ethical judgments as expressions of personal wants, aversions, and preferences, legal positivism undertakes to separate legal science from ethics, prescribing that the role of the judge is to apply the law, not to judge it. Thus the law made by the sovereign will of the legislature is not challengeable by appeal to any higher, constitutional principles, but rather constitutional principles—as, for example, the Bill of Rights—are regarded to be, at most, admonitions of forbearance to the legislature.

According to Northrop, legal positivism is shot through with serious defects. Because a radically empiricist epistemology is cognizant only of immediately sensed objects, it suffices neither for hypothetico-deductive natural science nor for legal systems in which contractual law is fundamental. Contractual law wrenches men from the immediately apprehended condition of status in which they appear and, despite obvious empirical differences, treats them as equal entities. Further, the ethical subjectivism of legal positivism, originating in the crude psychological ethics of David Hume and Jeremy Bentham, both impugns the role of the judge in judicial review and undermines the entire framework of legal obligation. If values are wholly subjective, then, as Northrop observes, it is impossible to justify legal obligation when obedience to the law violates one's own scale of preferences and aversions, as indeed Kelsen's grappling with the problem evinces (11, pp. 66–67). Besides, by equating justice with the will of the legislature, this subjectivism destroys the very possibility of judicial review. In making the power of the sovereign the ultimate sanction of the rightness of existing law, legal positivism is incompatible with the American constitutional system with its guarantees of individual rights and balance of powers. Finally, by equating the actual positive law with what ought to be, legal positivism is contradicted by any judge who, despite adherence to it in past cases, strikes down federal or state legislation in the name of civil rights, thereby making clear that there are outside the positive law norms by means of which this law should be criticized.

In Northrop's more recent work his attacks on legal positivism, noticeable in the early papers included in *The Complexity of Legal and Ethical Experience*, have been muted. After all, legal positivism in the West studies Western law, and Western law is the law of contract. Here Northrop follows the lead of Sir Henry Maine. Contractual law, Northrop holds, was the invention of the legal theorists and practitioners of Stoic Rome, and although it dominates the West, having replaced the law of status in most communities and nations there, it has not yet penetrated the East. He writes:

According to this contractual theory, a person's social, religious, moral, legal and political rights and duties have nothing to do with sex, the temporal order of one's birth, or the color of skin of the tribe of one's ancestors. Instead, since legal and political obligations, rights, duties and privileges arise, in contractual law, only when human beings reach the maturity to enter into contractual relations with one another, it follows that all human beings the world over are born free and equal before the law and with respect to their legal and political rights and duties. This is what the Stoic Roman lawyers and philosophers meant when they said that moral, legal and political man is universal, ecumenical or cosmopolitan human being (8, p. 10).

The persons who enter into these contractual relations, the relations themselves, the rights and obligations involved are all, on Northrop's analysis, concepts by postulation. So far as Western legal science, even legal positivism, studies Western contractual law, it does therefore furnish norms, although the best formulation of these norms is to be found not in Austin's positivism but in Kant's categorical imperative and the neo-Kantian legal formalism.

When Northrop at first failed to find in legal positivism the norms to criticize positive law, he turned to sociological jurisprudence, for sociological jurisprudence claims to uncover these norms in the living law. Defined by the Austrian sociologist of law Eugen Ehrlich as "the inner order of associations" prevalent in a community, the living law corresponds to what the anthropologists call "patterns of culture" (11, p. 52). Consequently, the sanction of positive law is its correspondence to the living law. When, as in the instance of Prohibition, the positive law violates the living law, it proves ineffective and breaks down.

Roscoe Pound of Harvard introduced sociological jurisprudence to American legal circles, but Underhill Moore at Yale rendered it scientific. With sympathy and praise Northrop describes Moore's endeavors to convert sociological jurisprudence into an exact legal science on equal footing with physics and with Clark Hull's behaviorist psychology (11, pp. 31–36). Moore had equated the living law with the objectively observed spatio-temporal behavior of the members of society. But, as Northrop remarks, Moore's rigorous yet restrictive method cannot be applied to detect the living laws of a mass society of, for example, 350 million Indians. In such cases it is necessary to rely upon the methods of the philosophy of cultures, for uncovering the ideology of a people, as *The Meeting of East and West* demonstrates, is tantamount to detecting the norms that dominate their behavior. Thus Northrop's book on European union, in which the positive laws of constitutions, statutes, and treaties establishing an organization of European nations are tested by reference to the actual ideologies of these nations, is, as its subtitle states, "a study in sociological jurisprudence" (12). Thus, also, in his discussions of world law Northrop insists that unless the positive international law is in accord with the actual pluralism of living laws it cannot succeed.

But sociological jurisprudence is unsatisfactory, because it assumes that the living law is right, and this assumption collapses whenever, as in Hitler's Germany, the living law is palpably not what it ought to be. Even Moore perceived this shortcoming, and he attempted to remove it by taking tomorrow's living law as the standard for the criticism of today's law. He failed, however, to devise a method for predicting what the future living law will be. Sociological jurisprudence therefore, confined to the actually existing living laws of a given society, cannot continue to function normatively and still escape what Northrop calls "the culturalistic fallacy" (11, pp. 239–40), the fallacy of identifying the good with what a given culture condones. However, when there are several cultures, each with a distinctive living law, and when these laws conflict, as in the contemporary world, it becomes imperative to locate norms outside the living laws so that these laws may be evaluated and criticized.

Intuitive ethical jurisprudence also fails. Represented in the writings of Morris Cohen and his son Felix, intuitive ethical jurisprudence invokes as the standard for the criticism of laws the ethical good as intuited, but since the intuitive conception of the good changes from culture to culture and from individual to individual in the same culture, it cannot operate as a reliable, objective norm.

Although cognizant of the relativity of natural law conceptions to the cultural biases of individual authors, Northrop has inclined toward a natural law jurisprudence (11, p. 253). If legal science is to contain objective norms for the criticism of living laws, it must include natural law ethics and natural law jurisprudence. To clarify and justify this claim Northrop distinguishes between "first-order" and "second-order" facts. "First-order facts are the introspected or sensed raw data antecedent to all theory and all cultures, given in anyone's experience in any culture. Second-order facts are cultural artifacts; that is, they are the result in part at least of human theory of first-order facts. Nature and natural law are the names for all first-order facts and their relations. Culture and living law are the names for all second-order facts and their inner order" (11, p. 254). On the next page he continues: "Stated more precisely, therefore, natural law jurisprudence is the thesis that scientifically verified theory of the 'is' of first-order facts provides the cognitive standard for measuring the goodness or badness of second-order artifacts. Thus just as sociological jurisprudence uses the scientifically verified theory of the 'is' of the living law to judge both legislation and the cases of the positive law, so natural law jurisprudence uses the empirically verified theory of the 'is' of first-order facts to judge the goodness or badness of the living law" (11, p. 255).

Hence Northrop's legal theory contains an argument for natural law, although it is wrong to suppose that natural law jurisprudence is the whole of his legal theory. Nature, disclosed in experience and scientific theory, and existing independently of and prior to cultures, is the objective standard of living laws. Furthermore, as knowledge of nature alters with scientific progress, ideologies and laws must alter to keep pace with these changes. Stoic or Christian natural law jurisprudence was suited to the theory of nature afforded by science in the natural history stage, and the Lockean natural law jurisprudence of inalienable rights inherent in atomistic mental substances was appropriate to classical Newtonian hypothetico-deductive physics. But now, it should follow, a new natural law jurisprudence is demanded by the conjunction, on the one hand, of the hypothetico-deductive theory of nature represented in the quantum mechanics and relativity physics of the West, and, on the other hand, of the immediately intuited aesthetic continuum mirrored in the art and religions of the East. Perhaps just as Lockean natural law jurisprudence has provided the ideological and legal foundations of the Western constitutional democracies, so Northrop's natural law jurisprudence may well contribute the sorely needed ideological and legal foundations of world order.

PRACTICAL APPLICATIONS

Northrop has brought his knowledge of science, of cultures, and of law to bear on the solution of the practical problems of world peace. He has employed philosophy in the service of practical politics. To date Northrop has written three books which focus on the practical problems of international politics. In 1953 he published *The Taming of Nations* (13), in 1954, *European Union and United States Foreign Policy* (12), and in 1960, *Philosophical Anthropology and Practical Politics* (8). Of course all of Northrop's major philosophical works are made relevant to the practical problems of international politics. Insights gathered from *The Meeting of East and West* and *The Complexities of Legal and Ethical Experience* facilitate a diagnosis of the world situation.

As Northrop writes in *The Taming of Nations*:

A nation is a society responding as a unit. What is it that gives a society this national unity? The answer is common norms. Except as the people of a society agree upon at least some common norms that society cannot respond as a national unit. The key, therefore, to the understanding of any nation and to the specification of those of its properties which will determine its international reactions is to be found when the major common norms of its people are determined. For unless the people of a nation have a dominant ideology there is no consistent dominant purpose (13, pp. 3–4).

In the final analysis, then, national policies spring from ideologies, so that understanding ideologies becomes an instrument of effective foreign policy. Soviet Russian communism repudiates the rule of international law because, as one of the authoritative Soviet writers (Mintauts Chakste) on international law has said, "an intercourse on the basis of intellectual unity (ideological solidarity) between countries of bourgeois and socialist cultures, cannot exist as a rule, and hence the rules of international law covering this intercourse become pointless" (13, pp. 254–55). Ideological differences account for the most prominent international disagreements. Not only, for example, are they at the root of the rupture between Hindu–Buddhist India and Mohammedan Pakistan; they also crop up in such irritating international situations as the neutrality of Nehru's India with respect to the United Nations police action in Korea. In fact, according to Northrop's analysis, the neutralist standpoint of the Orient originates in the Easterner's basic cultural attitude toward law. Whereas Westerners, accustomed to universal principles reached by hypothetico-deductive theory, are loyal to universal law backed by force against its violators, Easterners, persuaded that all distinctive values are transient and relative, look not to enforced universal law but rather to the mediator who, instead of applying laws to particular cases, endeavors to arrange a compromise between the clashing demands of particular claimants. When the incapacity of the East to comprehend international law supported by police action is added to what Northrop has called "the modern fragmentation of Western civilization" into a plurality of conflicting ideologies (13, pp. 214–26), the logical result is the ineffectiveness of international institutions, such as the United Nations and the League of Nations, which assemble together nations with different ideologies.

However, instead of despairing, Northrop discerns that the United Nations type of world organization represents but one path to world order; actually there is a second, more promising movement. He writes: "This movement, which is occurring before our very eyes, consists in starting with the absurdly large number of present national political units and stepping first to a relatively small number of cultural political units. What makes this possible is the fact, upon which we have come again and again, of the decline of nationalism and the rise and resurgence of culturalism" (13, p. 277). Accordingly, seven major cultural political groups are demarcated:

(1) The Asian solidarity of India, Ceylon, Tibet, Burma, Thailand, Indo-China, China, Korea and Japan rooted in the basic philosophical and cultural similarity of non-Aryan Hinduism, Buddhism, Taoism, and Confucianism. (2) The Islamic world rooted in the religious and philosophical faith and reconstruction of a resurgent Islam. (3) The non-Islamic, non-European African world rooted in its lesser known culture. (4) The continental European Union grounded in a predominantly Roman Catholic culture with a secular leadership that has passed through the liberalizing influence of modern philosophical thought. (5) The British Commonwealth with its predominantly Protestant British empirical philosophical traditions combined with the bond of unity derived through classical education, English law, the Church of England and its Royal Family from a Stoic Christian Rome that has passed through Hooker, the Tudors and Cromwell's versions of the Protestant

Reformation. (6) Pan America rooted in the liberal constitutionalism of the common law of the United States on the one hand and the modern equivalent of Cicero's liberal Stoic Roman legal universalism on the other hand as expressed in governments, and even education, under secular leadership. (7) The Soviet Communistic world comprising U.S.S.R., her Eastern European satellites, mainland China and North Korea (13, pp. 286–87).

In *European Union and United States Foreign Policy*, Northrop discusses the movement toward European union, assessing the practicality of positive laws, constitutions, statutes, treaties, and proposals pertaining to the establishment of an organized community of European states, by reference to the actual ideologies of the peoples of these states.

Northrop has also applied his descriptive and evaluative methods in philosophical anthropology to the Soviet Union and Red China. The descriptive method uncovers the basic postulates of the Soviet Union to be: the dominance of the law of contract, the epistemology of naïve realism, and the dialectical theory of history with economic determinism and class warfare. The evaluative method detects contradictions in these basic postulates—for example, between the contractual law postulate and the historical determinism (8, pp. 277–78). Similarly, years before the current crisis in Red China, Northrop showed that Red China is at best a "remarkable short-run success," since it exhibits a contradiction between the Confucian-Taoist-Buddhist beliefs of the Chinese people and the Communist Marxist ideology. Mao is caught in a grave dilemma. Either he "remains a Marxist . . . and . . . runs the very serious and real risk of failing to carry his people with him" or "his dialectical way of thinking . . . triumphs over the determinism of his Marxism . . . and his Marxist goal-value aim has to be thrown away" (8, p. 296). These weaknesses in the ideologies of America's foes offer genuine opportunities for a successful American foreign policy.

Clearness about the democratic values as well as an understanding of the ideologies of other nations are prerequisite to the formulation of American foreign policy if it is to succeed in winning peace and establishing international law. Such a policy should avoid the pitfalls of Republican Eisenhower–Dulles–Goldwater moralism with its "go-it-alone-to-the-brink" implications and also the Democrat Niebuhr–Kennan–Rusk–Johnson realism with its preoccupation with power politics. Northrop has recommended the positive program of "an objectively and scientifically grounded foreign policy," which, instead of relying upon economic and military power alone, "must root itself in the principle of living law pluralism and in the precise distinction between international federal unity and states' rights plurality which the living movements from nationalism to world law and culturalism specify, . . . [and] also it must participate in the movement now starting with the few cultural political units and proceeding toward a single common world ideology" (13, p. 308). Northrop, therefore, concludes that "the major department in the Department of State or the Foreign Office of any government must be not its liaison connection with the Department of Defense, its Information Service or its Program of Economic Aid, but its Division of Cultural Relations" (13, p. 308). To a nation entangled in the confused war in Vietnam, with internal factions fighting with each other as much as with the external foe, Northrop's demand that American foreign policy be made on the basis of a sure knowledge of the cultures involved seems particularly timely. In this fundamental sense philosophy, as the study of ideologies, becomes indispensable to the education of statesmen and experts in international affairs. In a world rent by ideological differences, philosophers may well be the best diplomats and soldiers.

NOTES TO CHAPTER VI

1 F. S. C. Northrop, *Man, Nature and God, A Quest for Life's Meaning* (New York: Simon and Schuster, 1962).
2 F. S. C. Northrop and Mason W. Gross, *Alfred North Whitehead, An Anthology* (New York: Macmillan, 1953).
3 See F. S. C. Northrop, "Whitehead's Philosophy of Science," in Paul Arthur Schilpp (ed.), *The Philosophy of Alfred North Whitehead* (Evanston, Ill.: The Library of Living Philosophers, 1941), 165–207; and "Einstein's Conception of Science," in Paul Arthur Schilpp (ed.), *Albert Einstein: Philosopher-Scientist* (Evanston, Ill.: Library of Living Philosophers, 1949), 385–408.

4   F. S. C. Northrop, *Science and First Principles* (New York: Macmillan, 1931).

5   Alfred North Whitehead, *Process and Reality: An Essay in Cosmology* (New York: Macmillan, 1929).

6   F. S. C. Northrop, *The Logic of the Sciences and the Humanities* (New York: Macmillan, 1947).

7   See F. S. C. Northrop and Helen H. Livingston (eds.), *Cross-Cultural Understanding: Epistemology in Anthropology* (New York: Harper and Row, 1964).

8   F. S. C. Northrop, *Philosophical Anthropology and Practical Politics: A Prelude to War or to Just Law* (New York: Macmillan, 1960).

9   F. S. C. Northrop, *The Meeting of East and West: An Inquiry Concerning World Understanding* (New York: Macmillan, 1946).

10 F. S. C. Northrop, "Ideological Man and Natural Man," in *Ideological Differences and World Order* (New Haven: Yale University Press, 1949).

11 F. S. C. Northrop, *The Complexity of Legal and Ethical Experience: Studies in the Method of Normative Subjects* (Boston: Little, Brown, 1959).

12 F. S. C. Northrop, *European Union and United States Foreign Policy: A Study in Sociological Jurisprudence* (New York: Macmillan, 1954).

13 F. S. C. Northrop, *The Taming of Nations: A Study of the Cultural Bases of International Policy* (New York: Macmillan, 1952).

VII

JAMES KERN FEIBLEMAN

Axiological Realism and Ontological Positivism

INTRODUCTION

"I was born," James Feibleman relates, "into the middle of the first decade of the twentieth century in the United States, evidently, as I have discovered, in order to seek an answer to the question which the English philosopher, Whitehead, has framed so simply, 'What is it all about?'" (1, p. 1). For Feibleman the discovery of the philosopher's vocation came neither early nor directly.

Born on July 13, 1904, in New Orleans, Louisiana, Feibleman graduated from the Horace Mann School in 1924 and later spent less than a year at the University of Virginia. While other contemporary professional philosophers were preparing for academic positions by studying in colleges and graduate schools in the United States and abroad, Feibleman spent his days in business and his leisure hours on literature. The family business, a Southern chain of department stores, imposed responsibilities. For several years Feibleman served as the assistant manager of one of the major department stores in New Orleans. In 1930 he became vice-president and general manager of the James K. Feibleman Realty Co., Inc., and in 1954 a partner in the Leopold Investment Company.

Literature attracted Feibleman more than business when he was a young man. In the period between the world wars New Orleans was a literary center, where Feibleman befriended and associated with prominent and soon-to-be prominent literary figures—Sherwood Anderson, William Faulkner, Roark Bradford, and others (2). He wrote poems and short stories for the little magazines that bloomed in the 1920's and published one volume of poetry in 1931, *Death of the God of Mexico* (3). Since then he has published four others: *The Margitist* (4), *Journey to the Coastal Marsh* (5), *Trembling Prairie* (6), and *The Dark Bifocals* (7). In 1948 he published a moderately successful novel, *The Long Habit* (8), and in 1952 the first part of his autobiography, *Philosophers Lead Sheltered Lives* (1). These works establish Feibleman as a minor literary figure. Beyond that, he is the head of Louisiana's leading literary dynasty: his son, Peter S. Feibleman, is a successful novelist and playwright, and his second wife is the Pulitzer prize-winning novelist Shirley Ann Grau.

Long years in the service of literature laid the ground for a prose style which nimbly combined lucidity and suggestiveness, but, paradoxically, it was as a businessman that Feibleman discovered his vocation as a philosopher. Because of his unusual initiation into academic philosophy, Feibleman has suffered an extreme degree of isolation within the community of professional philosophers. He never attended graduate school and, until recently, rarely participated in the meetings of the various philosophical societies and associations. Sometimes this isolation has resulted in a lack of communication between him and other philosophers at work on the same problems, often producing defects in Feibleman's own work due to ignorance of what others have already accomplished, and causing astonishing ignorance on the part of other philosophers concerning Feibleman's genuine contributions. On the other hand, the isolation may have compelled Feibleman to philosophize in greater independence than that enjoyed by any thinker of his generation. Just as Sidney Hook personifies the American philosopher as engaged intellectual, so James Feibleman exemplifies the American philosopher as creative thinker.

In 1943 Feibleman joined the faculty of Tulane University as acting assistant professor of English. In 1945 he transferred to philosophy, becoming in 1946 a full professor in the graduate school. In 1951 he was appointed head of the philosophy department in the College of Arts and Sciences, and in 1958 chairman of the University department. Meanwhile, he has published twenty books on philosophy and has served formerly as co-editor with H.

N. Lee and now as editor of the annual *Tulane Studies in Philosophy*. Although Feibleman's philosophical works have not yet found their audience, interest in them is awakening (9).

In recent years Feibleman has sought to explain philosophy in terms of an experimental theory of human behavior, a theory which he has elaborated by extending and generalizing the results of the investigations of I. P. Pavlov, Clark Hull, and their followers (10, p. 5). While a philosophy, according to Feibleman, is a "system of ideas more general than any other," it is also "an orienting response system, a kind of doubly-condensed set of knowings, condensed once by the process of abstraction and again by the systematic relating of the abstractions. Philosophies behave in psychological contexts like security systems. The holding of a philosophy is the acquisition of a security system as the goal object of the need to know. In the ordinary course of relative events, it is followed by need-reduction" (10, pp. 168–69).

Feibleman's own career as a philosopher concretely illustrates his behavioral theory of philosophy. As a businessman without formal education in philosophy he set out to defend values, particularly aesthetic values, in a world dominated by business practice and the scientific outlook. In the process he discovered the ancient metaphysics of Platonic realism. The professor succeeded the business man, and in the second phase of his career Feibleman formulated his system of axiological realism. But logical positivism and analytical philosophy, both spawned by theories of natural science, repudiate the kind of speculative ontology his realistic theory of values involved, and he had to adapt his thought to their strictures. Consequently his version of axiological realism became an ontological positivism. At present, in the third phase of his career, Feibleman is busily working out what was begun earlier—the application of his system to concrete fields, in particular to social institutions, to ethics, and to man.

PATHFINDING: TOWARD AXIOLOGICAL REALISM

The call to philosophy came gradually and circuitously. A longtime friendship with Julius Friend, a local businessman who was co-founder of *The Double Dealer*—a New Orleans little magazine which published Feibleman's first poems—grew into a philosophical collaboration. Drawn together by their common interest in the defense of the objects of the businessman's scorn—the objects of art and the values of the good life—Friend and Feibleman published three "pathfinding" volumes of philosophy. Initially intent upon criticizing the businessman for his philistinism, they were soon led to examine the principles of business itself. Since modern business is based upon technology, they studied technology, and since technology depends upon physics, they proceeded to physics. Reading backwards from practical physics to pure physics led them inescapably to philosophy. As Feibleman recounts the adventure: "From our start in the most practical kind of problem conceivable, that of how to remedy the shortcomings of the conduct of business in the United States in 1929, we finally emerged into the abstract and eternal air of Greek philosophy" (1, p. 142). And there a proposition which was to influence all of Feibleman's subsequent thinking was discovered: "All practice is the application of pure theory" (1, p. 141).

In 1929 "the business world had suddenly fallen apart" (1, p. 143). When the collapse of the stock market, signaling the advent of the Depression, shattered the spirits of the business community, Friend and Feibleman literally rushed to their typewriters. Their first book, called *Alicism* because it "dealt with the brittle, unreal, looking-glass world of the United States at that time" (1, p. 143), they considered unsuccessful and consequently tore up. They then wrote a second volume, *Science and the Spirit of Man* (11), which was published in England in 1932.

The central thesis of *Science and the Spirit of Man* is "to show the subjective aspect of physical relations and the objective aspect of the human values, reverse epistemological views from the then currently accepted conception" (1, p. 144). Influenced by Whitehead, its authors reject the bifurcation of the world into subject and object, the separation of values from primary qualities. This dualism, they held, stems from abstractions which distort the basal unity of experience, and it is responsible for the scientific cosmology which assigns values a secondary status. Above all, they were concerned to establish the objectivity of values on a footing equal in reality to that accorded to the entities with which the sciences deal. Convinced that "the key problem of entire man is the problem of value" (11, p. 254), they described the empirical world as "a world of values" (11, p. 257) and equated "the stuff of the universe" with "infinite value" (11, p. 315).

Following Emile Meyerson, they conceived scientific thought to consist in the discovery and representation of identities, which they also termed "universals." In neo-Kantian fashion they came to regard the world studied by science to be nothing more than a system of percepts and concepts. Their theory would have collapsed into idealism except that, having repudiated the dualism from which idealism could issue, they believed that "the mind can no more exist without an object than the objective world can exist without a subject" (11, p. 58). Although the percepts were seen to be located in the concrete experience which they constitute, concepts, abstract identities, universals had a far more problematic status.

Science and the Spirit of Man is an immature work, but, having established the objectivity of values and moving in the direction of an argument for the objectivity of universal concepts, the authors were definitely on the track of axiological realism. "In so far as we deny the ultimate reality and absoluteness of concepts," they declared, "we are nominalists; although we reject the setting up of particulars as being in any sense more real than concepts, since both partake of the same reality but belong to different categories of value. In so far as we admit that on the plane of experience universals have exactly the same reality as particulars, and in so far as we claim an objectivity for both, we are realists. We therefore maintain that reason can asymptotically approach ultimate truth, and is effective and valid, yet not absolute in the sense that it can deal with ultimates" (11, p. 84).

Feibleman has described *Science and the Spirit of Man* as "the cry of a humanist against what the terrific accomplishments of physical science had done to man's other aspects; it was a pathfinding attempt" (1, p. 143). And he added:

We went into the writing of that book humanists and emerged from it realists, in the medieval and Platonic sense of the latter term. We started out in an effort to show that physics had distorted mankind, and to do this we had planned to demonstrate how everything that physics regarded detachedly really belonged to the human being as an attribute. But we ended in a different corner; we actually finished the book having convinced ourselves that nothing that exists within the human being originated there; everything subjective and mental had to be located and accounted for as a property of the objective world (1, pp. 143–44).

The reorientation was almost tantamount to a rebirth. "In place of the popular division of the mental and the physical, . . . we substituted an older one, namely, the division of the actual and the possible, which assumes that all that was actual must have been possible or it could not have become actual, but that all that was possible was never actual altogether or there could not be new things coming into the actual world" (1, p. 144). Plato's realism with its two levels of being, once recovered, constituted the foundation of a philosophical system with considerable promise for expansive applications.

In the interval between the completion of *Science and the Spirit of Man* and the beginning of a second volume with Friend, Feibleman was introduced to the philosophy of the then obscure American C. S. Peirce. A representative sample of Peirce's writings was at the time available only in Morris Cohen's *Chance, Love, and Logic* (12). After the publication of the first six volumes of Peirce's writings by Harvard University, under the editorship of Charles Hartshorne and Paul Weiss, Feibleman wrote a book on Peirce's philosophy interpreted as a system of realistic metaphysics (13). As Feibleman claims: "The key to the whole philosophical position of Peirce lies in the realism-nominalism controversy" (14, p. 33). Whether or not this is the key to Peirce, it is the key to the development of Feibleman. For in the second Friend–Feibleman volume, *The Unlimited Community* (15), the very title of which is derived from Peirce, the authors at last attained in unambiguous terms the position of axiological realism. According to axiological realism, universals and values comprise a separate order of being equally as real as the order of physical particulars. All Feibleman's later philosophical works extend and intensify this position.

In *The Unlimited Community*, Friend and Feibleman imputed the breakdown of social theory and practice, everywhere evident in the fourth decade of the twentieth century, to a nominalistic philosophy which impugns the reality of values and universals and affirms solely the reality of physical particulars or subjective minds; they maintained that sound social science and practice depend upon the thesis of axiological realism, upon the objectivity and commensurability of values. If value is an objective property of the world and is measurable by exact quantitative methods, then social science is truly possible. Thus a valid social science presupposes an ontological realism which posits the independent being of a domain of values and universals apart from the historical order of actuality. In *Science and the Spirit of Man* Friend and Feibleman depicted the culpable scientific cosmology as nominalistic, but they were persuaded that science is ultimately realistic. In *What Science Really Means*, the last volume of the collaboration, they spelled out the ontological realism of modern science. Here they maintained that the subject matter of science is comprised of functions which are independent of mind and of actuality and so are nonmental and nonactual. These functions are, they held, "the inexorable conditions of knowledge and actuality. The analysis of the scientific subject-matter shows it to be not the content of actuality but conditions abstracted from actuality, conditions which are purely formal. And thus science reaches and strives to make manifest an unchanging hierarchy of functions which is through and through logical" (16, p. 192).

A persistent concern with values, defended first against the philistinism of American business culture and then against the nominalistic cosmology seemingly fostered by modern science, led Friend and Feibleman to the positive advocacy of axiological realism. The practical program suggested in the title of *The Unlimited Community* is the logical consequence of this concern. Following in the footsteps of Peirce, Friend and Feibleman discerned, in the historical order of actuality, a definite pattern of direction. "It consists in the greater and greater organization of any actuals considered as unities toward the greatest organization, in which each is subordinated to the next higher in an irrefrangible and mathematical order" (15, p. 307). This cosmic pattern in actuality is pregnant with practical implications.

Progress cannot stop with any finite society; each society must be transcended and subsumed by a larger and larger society. . . . That human society conceived by itself is not the final organization, the final end, is inescapable. The final end can only be ideally postulated as the organization of a greater and greater society which transcends all actual societies, and does not stop until it includes and organizes in the logical order all existence. From the standpoint of human actuality, this means the reaching out toward a greater and greater community of interests directed by greater and greater knowledge. Its goal is the unlimited community (15, p. 308).

While working out the position of axiological realism with Friend, Feibleman also began to write and publish philosophical works independently of the collaboration. During the pathfinding years these independent works concentrated upon aesthetic and practical values, always within the metaphysical framework of axiological realism.

In *Christianity, Communism, and the Ideal Society*, which appeared in 1937, Feibleman focused on the metaphysical issues without being blind to the actual forces running through practical affairs (17). Although the daily successes of fascism tended to confirm its claim to be the new order of politics, Feibleman perspicaciously saw that it was at best a temporary affair (17, p. 76). Consequently, he restricted the real political alternatives for modern man to three: Christianity, communism, and a third position called the ideal society. And he analyzed these alternatives by recourse to metaphysics. Defining nominalism as the negative doctrine which places its emphasis "not only on the reality of physical particulars but also on the unreality of universals" (17, p. 26), Feibleman condemns it as "the ancient philosophic error" and "the single comprehensive idea" which, though scarcely noted because it operates in concealment deep within, is at the root of all crises—economic, political, and cultural—that menace contemporary men and institutions (17, p. 25). Social reconstruction under the aegis of the ideal society requires the metaphysics of axiological realism, a metaphysics which affirms that the timeless, logical order of universals and values and the actual, temporal order of physical particulars and subjective minds are equally real.

It is Feibleman's contention that Christianity and communism depart from axiological realism in different ways. Of Christianity he says that it "has always existed as a study of the logical order, to the complete neglect of the study of the conditions of actuality" (17, p. 136). In reifying universals and values and deeming them more real than physical particulars, Christianity commits the fallacy of crypto-materialism. At the conclusion of his critical scrutiny of Christianity, Feibleman presents a balance sheet which recommends, on the one hand, the abandonment of the institution of the Christian Church, prayer as supplication, the fallacy of crypto-materialism, the shadow version of realism, the doctrine of transcendence, and the neglect of the logic of actuality, and, on the other hand, the retention of the infinite worth of the individual, prayer as adoration, the validity of independent reason, the "fragment" version of realism, the doctrine of immanence, and belief in the triumph of justice over force (17, p. 198).

Feibleman deals with communism in similar fashion. "Contrary to the emphasis of Christianity," he points out, "communism concentrates upon the historical order of actuality, to the complete neglect of the logical order of possibility" (17, p. 199). To suppose, in the fashion of communism, that physical particulars alone are real is to commit the nominalistic fallacy of materialism. Once again, after critical scrutiny, Feibleman draws up a balance sheet for communism, recommending, on the one hand, the abandonment of the nominalistic philosophy of dialectical materialism, the scientific claims of Marxism, the program of hatred and bloody revolution, the determinism of class distinctions, the religion of Marxism, and the belief in actuality as solely real, and, on the other hand, the retention of the Marxist analysis of industrialism, exact social science, the recognition of actuality as brute and irreducible, the realistic existence of ideals, the dialectic logic of actuality, and the idea of society as the individual's goal (17, p. 272).

What remains, then, is the possibility of an ideal society, firmly grounded on the metaphysics of axiological realism. This ideal society must be "capable of embodying the valid elements which can be saved from both Christianity and Communism," and, since communism is close to the ideal society in the practice of economic reform, the ideal society could perhaps arise from the synthesis of liberalism and communism (17, p. 341). The basis of the ideal society is, of course, Peirce's idea of the unlimited community. It is the most rational and scientific of societies, guided by a scientific philosophy which apprehends in precise concepts the values and universals which lawfully govern life and conduct.

Feibleman's name for the ideal society, presented in the title of a book which he finished just as World War II broke out in Europe, is "positive democracy." While negative at present, democracy can become positive if it meets certain conditions (18, pp. x–xi). Spelling out these conditions is tantamount to preparing the theory and program of social reform. That society is an entity as real as the individuals who compose it must be recognized. The majority which rules should acknowledge the higher authority of reason. The advance of science should be promoted in an atmosphere of intellectual freedom. Property rights ought to be interpreted functionally to promote the welfare of the citizenry. Civil rights must be broadened. The welfare of the individual citizens as well as that of the society as a whole must be considered. These conditions for positive democracy reveal that the ideal society is more than a remote utopia; it is a practical program.

Feibleman the poet did not disappear in Feibleman the metaphysician. His interests in aesthetic values continued, converging upon the literary art of comedy. The result was the publication in 1939 of In Praise of Comedy. This book is Feibleman's most successful, and, within its limits, his best one. After concentrated study upon complex and abstruse problems, comedy promised welcome relief, and that is perhaps why Feibleman was attracted to it. But there is another reason for his consideration of comedy. Like tragedy, comedy testifies to the metaphysical framework of axiological realism with its ideal, logical order of being. Unlike tragedy, which is a matter for feeling, however, comedy is an affair of reason. As Feibleman says, "Comedy consists in the indirect affirmation of the ideal logical order by means of the derogation of the limited orders of actuality" (19, pp. 178–79). Art, science, and politics, therefore, all presuppose and confirm the metaphysics of axiological realism. The pathfinding years were over; the mature system was at hand.

THE SYSTEM OF AXIOLOGICAL REALISM

Axiological realism receives its most adequate systematic presentation in the *Ontology* (20), published in 1951, followed eleven years later by the second volume of the system, *Foundations of Empiricism* (21). Still a third work on epistemology has been promised. In these works Feibleman seeks to define the ultimate categories of reality—called the universes of essence and existence in the *Ontology*, the worlds of logic and substance in *Foundations of Empiricism*—and to specify the connections of the two worlds through the universe of destiny.

What is most notable in Feibleman's version of axiological realism, which owes so much to Plato among the classics and to Whitehead among the moderns, is how he fashions it to become, in the title of the introductory chapter of *Foundations of Empiricism*, "a metaphysics for empiricists." Where other speculative thinkers have either ignored or rejected logical positivism, empiricism, and linguistic analysis, Feibleman has attempted to work out a speculative systematic philosophy within the limitations they have imposed. He occupies a unique position in recent American thought—the point of confrontation between the antimetaphysical logical positivism and analytic philosophy, on the one hand, and the metaphysics of axiological realism, on the other.

Feibleman's confrontation of logical positivism and analytic philosophy has two sides. On one side he attempts to prove how these antimetaphysical doctrines really presuppose elements of the metaphysics of realism. In *Inside the Great Mirror* (22), Feibleman examines the philosophy of Russell, Wittgenstein, and their followers; he argues that, despite the antimetaphysical posture of the followers,

Russell and Wittgenstein manifest in their works the saving elements of metaphysical realism. This brilliant little book, which may unfortunately be neglected because of the ponderous amount of logically tidier material on the subject, contains the first commentary on Wittgenstein's *Tractatus* to appear in print; it also astutely points out the common features in the philosophies of Whitehead and Wittgenstein, features historically rooted in the usually overlooked common source—Bertrand Russell.

On the other side Feibleman strives to present axiological realism within the limits of logic and of fact—"in short to produce a system of ontology which might, to make a rough analogy, restrict Whitehead by means of Wittgenstein" (21, p. 150). The upshot is that Feibleman's philosophy is an "ontological positivism" or a "finite ontology." It is our aim here to delineate the major outline of axiological realism as an ontological positivism, as a finite ontology.

But before proceeding a cautionary word is in order. The structure of Feibleman's philosophy reflects the influence of Peirce, who in turn was indebted to Kant and Hegel. As is well known, these philosophers were deeply concerned with architectonic—the construction of a system of philosophy by analogy with the erection of a massive building. Unfortunately the architecture of such theories is often merely confused Gothic. Even worse, the edifice, which is constantly under construction and reconstruction, is sometimes lost in the scaffolding. Such defects mar Feibleman's philosophy. Terms serving one function in one segment of the whole are used in other parts with different functions. Ordinarily in Feibleman's writings, for instance, the term "metaphysics" denotes a field divided between the fields of ontology and epistemology, although quite often, especially in its adjectival and adverbial forms, it is used interchangeably with ontology. However, in *Foundations of Empiricism*, "metaphysics" designates a separate field. "Ontology is the theory, or system, of being, and metaphysics is the criticism of ontology. To argue for (or against) a certain position in ontology, then, would be a metaphysical undertaking. The method is metaphysical, but what the method seeks to accomplish concerns ontology" (21, p. 3). Pursuing the implications of conceiving metaphysics as the criticism of ontology, Feibleman subdivides metaphysics into seven parts, which provide the organizational structure for the *Foundations of Empiricism*: categorematics, axiomatics, systemics, ethics, practics, historics, and epistemics (21, Ch. 8). Impressed by the structure of the entire work, one reviewer remarked that "such a formal framework keeps the argument neat and tidy" (23). Limitations of space prevent detailed examination of Feibleman's ventures into architectonic; this brief mention must suffice to underline their existence and importance.

Ontological Positivism, or Finite Ontology

Feibleman's philosophical system is firmly founded upon ontology. The purpose of a philosophy, he says, "is to find the nature of the universe of all universes while at the same time saving the facts, to account for every type of detail in the world as well as to seek out reasons for the very existence of such details. A philosophy is a scale-model of all that we can describe from our experience or imagine, a model based upon an ontological system" (20, p. 3). The primacy of ontology, sustained in large measure by Feibleman's realism, signifies the subordination of epistemology, the theory of knowing, just as realism rules out the subjectivism and the idealism associated with excessive emphasis upon knowing. Ontology is the science of being, the widest of the categories, of which knowing, the topic of epistemology, is but an instance.

While Feibleman stresses the primacy of ontology, he nonetheless endeavors to assimilate the impact of the empirical and mathematical sciences upon philosophy. Indeed, he meets the indictment of ontology by "the scientific philosophers" by showing ontology to be positivistic and finite (24). The contemporary gravamen against ontology, he notes, "rests on the arguments that it is (A) dogmatic, (B) absolutistic, (C) undemonstrable, (D) dispensable, (E) nonempirical, (F) opposed to common sense, and (G) inapplicable" (20, pp. 95–96). Each charge is examined and rejected. Historically, he concedes, ontology may have been guilty of these charges singly or severally, but logically there is no reason why it must be so.

Ontology need not be dogmatic; on the contrary, it may be provisional, tentative, and revisable. Nor need it be absolutistic in any pejorative sense of the word "absolute." Granted ontology seeks the widest system of knowledge of all being, it may be tentatively held as an hypothesis open to modification and even to rejection. "Ontology," says Feibleman, "is the search for the widest true system, and deals with the most general categories, a subject-matter which is admittedly absolutistic; but the point is that theories of ontology do not have to be *held* absolutely" (20, pp. 98–99). Here Feibleman adopts a principle he learned from Peirce—the principle of fallibilism. This principle, involving a partial skepticism and a minimal dogma concerning reason and fact, is summed up in the proposition that "propositions may be demonstrated false" (20, p. 34). So long as the philosopher holds his ontology in strict recognition of the claims of fallibilism, ontology is neither dogmatic nor absolutistic in any bad sense of these terms.

Meanwhile, ontology is freed of the charge that it is undemonstrable. To the argument that ontology is undemonstrable because science alone provides demonstrable knowledge, Feibleman replies that science itself involves ontological assumptions. Science needs ontology; but ontology does not need science. If, in addition, ontology is held to be undemonstrable because the language it employs reduces to nonsense and has no extra-linguistic reference, Feibleman's rejoinder is that language itself, as well as this restrictive theory of language, involves ontological assumptions. That ontology is inescapable is further borne out by the distinction between implicit and explicit ontologies. Since everyone holds, consciously or unconsciously, a set of beliefs about being and value—in other words, an ontology—and since this set of beliefs governs conduct, ontology is implicated in the structures of human and institutional behavior.

The assertion that ontology is nonempirical in character is refuted by the fact that ontological entities such as qualities and relations are given in experience. The tentative ontology Feibleman proposes is empirical. Moreover, it is not inflexibly pitted against common sense. After all, common sense is the residue of scientific theories, and so long as it keeps abreast of science, it is compatible with the ontology which science implies. If common sense loses pace and falls behind science, then it should be abandoned or amended. Finally, although the abstractness of ontology makes its applications exceedingly difficult to trace, ontology is applicable. Because implicit ontologies influence human and institutional behavior, as previously noted, Feibleman goes so far as to regard cultures as applied ontologies.

Since ontology is as indispensable as food and sex, it is imperative to formulate an ontology which, bypassing the errors of traditional ontologies, measures up to the demands of modern science. Such an ontology is precisely what ontological positivism promises to be. Confronting the anti-ontological tenets of the logical positivists, Feibleman maintains: "The systematic relatedness of empirical findings cannot be extended beyond the confines of a single science without seriously involving the implications of metaphysics. In other words, it does not appear to be possible to operate consistency-rules between divergent sets of empirical data without calling in the aid of ontology" (20, p. 164). Feibleman presents ontological positivism as a revision of the postulate set that comprises logical positivism. The postulate set of logical positivism is as follows:

1. Elementary propositions have just an empirical reference.
2. This empirical reference yields to logical analysis.
3. Metaphysics is nonsense.
4. The sciences can be unified.
5. The physical language is the universal scientific language (20, p. 165).

Ontological positivism results from substituting for proposition 3 the following proposition: "3A. It is not the case that metaphysics is nonsense," and by adding the following proposition: "6. Ontology is defined by consistency-rules between divergent sets of empirical data" (20, p. 166).

Whereas logical positivism dismisses as nonsense any proposition which belongs neither to the class of logical and mathematical tautologies nor to the class of empirical statements, the referents which reduce ultimately to the field of physics, ontological positivism relies upon the most adequate postulate set to embrace all the propositions of all the sciences and of all other areas of human experience.

Ontological positivism, therefore, is emphatically not a reduction-ism. It abides by a modified version of Ockam's razor: "Entities must *not* be multiplied *beyond* necessity, but principles *must* be multiplied *to* necessity" (20, p. 116). Hence ontology becomes the widest system of knowledge available to men.

Reflection on the meaning of the concept of the widest system leads to a recognition of additional factors about the nature of on-tology. First, the system is finite. As Feibleman says: "Ontology, which is the heart of philosophy, is equivalent to the widest of any finite set of systems of knowledge. It aims to be a description in finite terms of the universe. The widest system must be the widest of a finite set only, for the widest of an infinite set is a contradiction" (20, p. 121). Second, ontology is or proposes to be a system. As a system, ontology "must have at least the minimal requirements of two elements: postulates and deductions from postulates," though "the system of ontology itself, considered from the viewpoint of the whole of being, consists in a postulate-set from which the deductions are all that is. Ontology itself is a postulate-set, the meta-systematic postulates of all systems" (20, p. 132). It is from this that Feible-man's most startling thesis arises—namely, that ontology constitutes "an all-presumptive calculus."

Ontology proposes the most adequate, simple, consistent postu-late set to unify all the propositions of the sciences and of human experience. In brief, the problem of the ontologist is: "Given all the theories and facts of modern knowledge, to find the explanatory sys-tem which could best account for them" (20, p. 126). "The onto-logical problem," in other words, "is then the discovery of the proper number of primary categories into which can be classified all kinds of being. Such categories must be the fewest allowable and the most necessary" (20, p. 127). Within the system of ontological positivism there are three orders or categories comprehending the elements taken from ordinary experience: "a transient order, the selection of whose elements is governed by empiricism alone"; "a persistent or-der, the selection of whose elements is governed by a combination of empiricism and mathematics"; and "the order of intent, governed by the principles of inquiry, specifically the scientific method, which seeks the links between the other two orders" (20, p. 168). We turn now to the exploration of these three primary categories or universes of being.

The Universes of Being

Comprising a set of primary categories which encompass all beings, the widest finite system of ontology requires a definition of what being is. Such a definition, anterior to the formulation of the primary categories, belongs to what Feibleman has called "the prelogical ontology." Here being is defined as "power in itself" and is that which can exist within itself (20, p. 190). In addition to defining being, the prelogical ontology also provides the primal postulate from which ontology proper, with its primary categories, proceeds. The primal postulate asserts that "there is a unity of being" (20, p. 190). Immediately, by means of concepts drawn from the dialectics of Parmenides, Plato, and Hegel, two primitive antinomies crop up. First, there is the antinomy of total unity of being: the contradiction between the boundary required by unity and the boundlessness implied by totality (20, pp. 190–91). Second, there is the antinomy of all-inclusive value: the contradiction between the existence-in-itself of being and the existence-for-other of value (20, p. 193). Yet the primal postulate, with its antinomies, serves an important and indispensable function in ontology. It is the ground from which the primary categories arise as parts, and it is the whole to which they belong; at the same time it is "a goal which is forever approachable but likewise forever incapable of attainment" (20, p. 195).

To move from the primal postulate of the unity of being—the prelogical ontology of an immobile monism—to ontological positivism with its three primary categories, Feibleman relies upon the science of geology for the concept of the geological fault. Just as rocks and minerals exhibit potential fractures and cleavages, so the unity of being of the prelogical ontology manifests an ontological fault. "An ontological fault is a potential fracture or fold in the whole which would cause it to be capable of breaking into certain, well-defined parts. . . . Being has cleavage planes, dependent upon the axial functions of its constituents" (20, p. 196). Thus being splits into parts in certain definite and determinate ways, and logic and value arise—logic "from the way in which the wholes analyze into parts," and value "from the way in which parts require the wholes" (20, p. 196). Systematic ontology proper hereupon emerges within the prelogical ontology.

The postulates and theorems of logic and value become central to Feibleman's discussion of being, because logic and value are ultimately ontological. Indeed, he goes so far as to assert that logic "*is* primary being in so far as primary being admits of identity and difference" (20, p. 198), while the total unity of being is a unity of value. The logical postulates of inclusion, noncontradiction, and excluded middle and the axial postulates of continuity, plenitude, and gradation, along with their theorems, are ontological. The logical postulates assert whole-part relations within being; and the axial postulates posit a graded series, or hierarchy, of values. The architectonic of Feibleman's entire ontology pivots on the distinction between the whole-part relatedness and the hierarchical series, a duality which generates both tension and equilibrium.

The ontological fault divides the unity of being into the primary categories of essence, existence, and destiny. The immobile monism of being in the prelogical ontology yields to a pluralism in which permanence and change intermingle.

Essence　The realm of essence has occupied a prominent place in the thought of American realists. It has received its most complete statement in Santayana's system and, after Santayana, in Feibleman's.

Following Plato in the *Sophist*, Feibleman defines essence as "the power to affect or be affected" (20, p. 212). Essence, moreover, comprises a "universe of possibility" (20, p. 213). The universe of essence is not part of actual existence, nor is it dependent upon it. "Possibility means possibility of actualization. But possibilities do not ever have to become actualized in order to be possible or in order to prove that they are possible. What is possible remains possible" (20, p. 213). Thus Feibleman often speaks of the universe of essence as the widest universe, equating essence with being. However, the universe of essence is neither in physical space nor in time. As regards space, the universe of essence is located in real, abstract, mathematical space—i.e., "a field determined by objects in the field having common properties, which are known as the structure of the space" (20, p. 213). As regards time, the universe of essence, so far at least as it involves universals, is held to be impervious to "the influence of time, exemplification and change" (20, p. 236).

Although Feibleman's conception of the universe of essence owes much to Plato's theory of ideas, it avoids the Platonist crypto-materialistic reification of essence by clearly emphasizing that the universe of essence is a universe of possibility, not of perfect actuality. This emphasis is reflected by the Principle of Actuality and its corollary the Principle of Perfervidity. The Principle of Actuality asserts: "No claim can be made for the being of any essence for which there is not some evidence in existence" (20, p. 278); while the Principle of Perfervidity maintains: "Nothing would be vivid and reasonable (axial and logical) without existence. Existence, then, is a value without which essence would be incomplete and imperfect" (20, p. 280).

As a universe of possibility, the universe of essence consists of two kinds of elements: values and universals.

The equation of being and value, posited by the primal postulate, is crucial to Feibleman's ontology; it justifies the label axiological realism. But what specifically does the term "value" mean? Though analyzable in terms of whole-part relatedness, value is a serial concept connoting a graded hierarchy, much as the sciences make up a graded series according to the complexity of the levels with which they deal. Approached from the perspective of whole-part relations, value is defined as "the election of part for whole" (20, p. 210). Value may be intrinsic, extrinsic, or symbolic. Beauty exemplifies intrinsic value, defined as "the election of part for whole of the whole" (20, p. 211), for "beauty is the quality which emerges from the perfect relation of parts in the whole" (20, p. 231). Goodness exemplifies extrinsic value, defined as "the election of part for the whole of the part" (20, p. 211), for "goodness is the quality which emerges from the perfect relation of any whole to other wholes, the

extrinsic elections of wholes" (20, p. 231). Holiness is symbolic value; it is "the quality which emerges from the perfect relation of all
parts and wholes in the largest finite whole of being as symbolized
by any part or whole" (20, p. 231). Though defined formalistically
in terms of whole-part relations, "values are affective and ineffable"
(20, p. 232).

In contrast to values, "universals [are] rational and relational"
(20, p. 232). Universals are equated with classes based upon the
observed similarities of particular things, except that in addition to
a definite number of actual things every universal is "a class having
an unlimited indeterminate number of possible members and a definite number of actual members" (20, p. 235). Because there are
classes of different orders, it follows that there are universals of different orders. A first-order class is a class "whose members are actual
things"; a second-order class is one "whose members are classes"
(20, p. 234). Among universals "redness" belongs to the first order,
number to a higher order. Thus universals, depending upon their
range of generality, make up a hierarchy. This suggests that the
complex structure of essence contains many levels. "The universals
[or classes] of the universe of essence thus give evidence of a highly
structured system requiring immense investigation" (20, pp. 234–
35).

One final word on the universe of essence: universals and values
are not two wholly different kinds of entities. Rather the same entity, the essence or the possibility, is both a universal and a value.
Whether its universal character or its value character is uppermost
depends upon the vantage point in the hierarchical structure of essence from which it is viewed. "The axiologic system or, in other
words, the value-logic order of possibility is a consistent system of
values and universals in a graded series, such that viewed up it yields
values and viewed down universals" (20, p. 225).

Existence   Feibleman describes existence as "the temporal and
historical dialectic of actuality" and defines it as "whatever affects
or is affected" (20, p. 215), or, in other words, "as that which elects
or is elected" (20, p. 284). Like essence, existence comprises a separate universe of being—a universe which Feibleman identifies with

nature (20, p. 282). Nonetheless, existence is not so broad a category as essence, since it "is made up of a selection from among the possibilities of essence." And in a fundamental way existence is dependent upon essence, "for were there no whole, there could be no parts. Existence may be compared to a changing participation in the fixed, a theatre consisting of the comings and goings of essences which, like meteors flaring up when they plunge into the earth's atmosphere, enter existence and become vivid" (20, p. 215).

Consider the dependence of existence upon essence for its elements—the universals and the values which, prior to actualization, are possibilities in the world of essence and which, once actualized, are incomplete and fragmentary. From Plato, Feibleman borrows the concept of parousia to express the relation of how existent singulars derive their being from the universe of essence. He speaks of "the positive content of existence as broken fragments of essence which, taken together with their limitations and their positive effects, account for all that existence contains" (20, p. 360). And he stresses: "The only difference between essence and existence is brought about by limitation, severe limitation, it is true, but solely limitation none the less, and nothing else but limitation" (20, p. 360).

Hence the properties peculiar to existence in contrast with essence, formulated as the Postulates of Actual Conditions, are privation, discontinuity, and inequality. Against the plenitude of essence is the privation in existence. Indicating a lack of being and a dependency upon essence, privation is yet indispensable to the existence of any value whatsoever. "Every value which does exist exists in virtue of the privation of those values which do not. Hence existence requires limitation" (20, p. 286). Against the continuity of essence stands the discontinuity of existence. Though dependent upon the continuity of essence, the discontinuity of existence is not merely negative. Difference and contrast, diversity and plurality, are due to discontinuity, which consequently "accounts for vividity, for the eventfulness, for the very life of this universe" (20, p. 287). In contrast to the gradation of essence, whereby a hierarchical order assures that at every level only entities of equal value or being are allowed,

existence is disorganized and chaotic, so that at the same level unequal elements exist and come into conflict. Privation, discontinuity,
and inequality characterize existence, and disvalues result. "Ugliness,
evil, unholiness, error and conflict are peculiar to existence; they
have no place in the universe of essence" (20, p. 288).

Despite the dependence of existence on essence and despite its
privative aspects and imperfections, Feibleman consistently regards
existence as a universe separate from essence and sharing equal reality with it. For if existence manifests wants and privations as regards
essence, it also exhibits ontological attributes which essence lacks.
Unlike essence, existence is a field in which interaction takes place;
the power to affect or be affected, which constitutes essence, is acti-
vated in existence into the actions and passions of individual things
and processes. Whereas essence is the abstract space of possible values and universals in a logical hierarchy, existence is the field of interacting individual things and events occurring in a dialectical flux.
The basic elements of existence are individual things and events. "A
thing," declares Feibleman, "is nothing but the field of existence
whose force is strong at a spatio-temporal point. Waves of probabili-
ties are concentrated in the field, and the concentration is called a
thing" (20, p. 292). A thing is unique through its locus, for "its
uniqueness is primarily a function of its space-time reference" (20,
p. 293). No mere collection of universals or values suffices to make
a thing. "For it is not the values or universals that constitute a singular but their intersection at a certain date and place, an intersection
which occasions their limitation and distortion as well as their actualization. The vividity of a thing in existence is like a meteor
which suddenly flames up and burns more rapidly when it encounters the resistance of the earth's atmosphere" (20, p. 295).

Viewed in the light of its dynamics, existence is an ongoing process of action and interaction. It is a flux of events. An event, indeed,
is a thing viewed dynamically, just as, conversely, a thing is an event
viewed statically. But through the change there is a quasi-identity
which is changing. "An event is an occasion of change with recognizable identity, that is, with an unchanging aspect, an aspect which
enables us to regard it separately, as though it were a thing" (20,
p. 300).

Because existence is a field of interacting things and events, incompletely embodying values and universals and caught up in a spatio-temporal system whereby they are limited yet made unique, it is a field of incessant conflict. "Conflicts are the most omnipresent phenomena of existence. . . . Existence is a tissue of conflicts and positive values" (20, p. 376). Influenced by Hegel, Feibleman construes existential conflict as incarnate logical contradiction and so construes the flux of existence as a dialectical movement, each thing moving in a course which brings it into conflict with other things, veering somewhat and taking then a modified course to survive. The result is a zigzag movement which Feibleman calls dialectical. The dialectic of existence, with its own logic of events, is "a succession of disturbances-and-returns, an alternating rhythm which exhibits some similarity but which also develops fundamental changes" (20, p. 386).

But the dialectical logic of events is not a hard and fast logic, not a rigid causal determinism which locks all things and events in an absolute sequence of formal implications drawn out over a time line. On the contrary, Feibleman is too much a disciple of Peirce to be unappreciative of the objectivity of chance. Feibleman readily acknowledges that change is fundamental to existence, but he also insists that the processes of existence require identities supplied by the universe of essence as well as a matrix of spatial and temporal relations and the governance of causal laws. Within the ordered continuity of nature, moreover, there are spontaneous and novel occurrences which are not reducible to any known regularities. The source of such occurrences is objective chance. Indeed, Feibleman considers objective chance to constitute the ultimate substrate of all becoming—the true substance of nature.

Thus the universe of existence adds its complement to being on a par with the contribution of essence. The equal reality of essence and existence is borne out by the twin principles of possibility and actuality. Mention has already been made of the Principle of Possibility. Here we need only note what the Principle of Actuality asserts: "Given the equality of all other considerations, it is better for a possibility to be also actual than merely to remain a possibility" (20, p. 392).

Destiny   The universes of essence and existence are related through a third, subordinate universe—the universe of destiny. "Destiny is the direction of existence toward essence. Otherwise expressed, it is the essence-vector of existence. More fully, destiny is the direction which the temporal and historical dialectic of actuality follows in its efforts to get back to the perfect conditions of the axiological order of possibility" (20, p. 215).

Essence may be related to existence in two ways. First, essence may spill over into existence. According to this way, "destiny is the abundance of the completeness of essence declaring itself even in the incompleteness of its part" (20, p. 400). It is the traditional theological way of accounting for existence. It is not, however, Feibleman's way.

The second way in which essence and existence may be related is for destiny to be subordinate to the universe of existence. "Destiny . . . is the drive within existence toward essence; . . . the bottom pushes up" (20, p. 400). Although the universe of essence never exerts any force upon elements of existence or of destiny, with every closer approach of destiny to essence, the push of existence "turns into a pull" (20, p. 493). Leaning upon Plotinus, but with modifying restrictions, Feibleman invokes the concept of "epistrophe" to denote this phenomenon of destiny. "Epistrophe," he remarks, "is the urge of the part to return to the whole, where bits of existence are considered to be parts and the corresponding segments of the universe of essence the wholes. . . . epistrophe is a drive compelling things in existence to a certain kind of feeling toward essence" (20, p. 494).

In describing the universe of destiny Feibleman draws upon conceptions derived from Greek tragic drama. Impressed by the logic of events which regulates the dialectical flux of existence, Feibleman sketches the frames of destiny in Greek terms: moira, success, hubris, nemesis, and ruin. The movement of existence toward essence is governed by a life cycle (20, pp. 417 ff.). The cosmic principle of moira, which legislates that everything has its due proportion, is also a moral principle. And so far as anything exists as an individual thing, it has succeeded, at least in having come into existence and having survived for a while. Success is actually the first moment of the life cycle. Then hubris sets in, springing directly from the existent thing's claim to endure and involving a subsequent violation of the principle of moira. The disturbance in the cosmic, moral order brought about by hubris has its reverberations, and nemesis sets in, for nemesis "is the spirit of retribution belonging to all those natural forces which witness, or are more actively affected by, the acts of hubris" (20, p. 419). The result is ruin. "Ruin is the end of things in existence— death.... The meaning of ruin is that essence cannot be approached through the existence of a fixed number of things and/or events; destiny works *through* things and events in a chain series, not exclusively *with* them" (20, p. 420).

The frames of the life cycle, the initial frames of destiny, then, bear witness to another set of frames—the ultimate frames whereby through destiny existence approaches essence. These ultimate frames are moira, dike, and soteria. Elevated to a higher dimension than in the frames of the life cycle, moira now is the ultimate demand that everything have its due proportion in the sense that the final valuation of everything takes precedence over all immediate or proximate valuations. "Dike is the demand for justice, that everything be treated according to its acts" (20, p. 421). "Soteria is the salvation which greets the existing thing after its career in certain cases" (20, p. 422). Whereas dike serves the ethical demands of value, soteria is more concerned with the aesthetic—with the guarantees that whatever is of positive value may be saved.

What is the practical significance of these frames of destiny? Uppermost in Feibleman's mind is his conviction that individual things and events move toward essence but cannot attain it by themselves. "Existing things serve a final end but only by means of a number of proximate ends, each of which is a means to a further proximate end, and so on until the final end is reached" (20, p. 420). This is a tragic interpretation of existence, but one which allows for salvation. This Greek conception of human existence has profoundly impressed Feibleman; his novel *The Long Habit* is the *Oresteia* set in the Louisiana coastal marsh. The values which men seek and which individually and in the long run each loses because he loses his own life are, also in the long run, served and attained. But their achievement implicates culture and its higher institutions: art, science, religion, and philosophy.

APPLICATIONS AND COMPLETIONS

Feibleman's system of axiological realism is a comprehensive philosophy, accounting for every area of experience and every possible subject of knowledge. *Foundations of Empiricism* opens with a table of contents for "A System of Philosophy." The system is divided into twelve parts: Logic, Ontology, Metaphysics, Epistemology, Ethics, Aesthetics, Anthropology, Sociology, Philosophy of Science, Theology, Philosophy of Education, and Philosophy of Law. All parts of the system have already been covered in separate volumes, in published essays, in chapters of published books, or in book-length treatises. It is Feibleman's intention to write and publish individual books on those parts of the system which have not yet been treated in separate volumes. Recently he has published his work on ethics (32). Moreover, he has completed volumes, as yet unpublished, on the philosophy of science (the first part treating scientific method), on the philosophy of technology, and on the philosophy of education; and he plans to write volumes of epistemology, politics, and philosophy of law. Central to this unfolding system, of course, is the ontology of axiological realism with its three domains of being—essence, existence, and destiny—conceived in accord with the principles of ontological positivism as the widest postulate-set verifiable by empirical data. Indeed, the other parts of Feibleman's philosophy may all be regarded as applications of the ontology. Limitations of space preclude exploration of the entire system; it is possible here only to sample parts.

We focus on Feibleman's theory of culture, not only because he has been persistently concerned about culture, but also because culture as a complex of institutions—of which art, science, religion, and philosophy are the highest— will serve to organize the discussion. Situated in the universe of destiny, culture and social institutions look up to and strive after the universe of essence. Thus in the ontological space between the two worlds, "there is no emptiness after all. A genuine separation does not have to provide a no man's land where forces strive mightily to bring the two worlds into some concord. The most logical of abstractions depend from their position, the most substantial of concretions propel themselves upward, and in this way the two worlds shade off into one another" (21, p. 116).

Feibleman subsumes the theory of culture and of social institutions under the philosophy of man, for men as institutionalized throng the universe of destiny. The philosophy of man includes three fields. Listed in order of increasing complexity and in the reverse order from that in which Feibleman treated them, they are: biopsychology, which is treated in *Mankind Behaving* (10) and *Biosocial Factors in Mental Illness* (25); sociology, which is dealt with in *The Institutions of Society* (26); and anthropology, which is covered in *The Theory of Culture* (27). Feibleman's biopsychology, incomplete at present, undertakes to explain man and all his activities in terms of tissue needs and instinctive drives for feeding, breeding, and inquiring in behavioral response to environmental and social stimuli. From the vantage point of a scientific philosophy of man it is possible to look up toward the structures of being, especially toward the universe of essence. Now concentrating his investigations upon the philosophy of man and its ramifications in the various social institutions, Feibleman is in a real sense not merely elaborating the applications of the ontological structures to concrete cases, but rather assessing the full meaning of these structures from the striving levels below.

From the outset of his philosophical career, Feibleman has considered ontology central to culture. In this respect Feibleman and Northrop hold similar theories. Often referring to culture as applied ontology, Feibleman defines culture as "the actual selection of some part of the whole of possible human behavior considered in its effect upon materials, and according to the demands of an implicit dominant ontology and modified by the total environment" (27, p. 76). The unique element in this definition is represented by the phrase "implicit dominant ontology." Usually abbreviated I.D.O. in Feibleman's writings, the implicit dominant ontology is "the subconsciously accepted belief of the majority of the members of a social group respecting the ultimate nature of reality"—that is to say, "a set, more or less consistent, of logical premises concerning the nature of ultimate being capable of being put into practice in proximate existence by the members of a social group, so that the resultant beliefs, tools and practices constitute what is known as culture" (27, p. 75). The meaning of the I.D.O. is sharpened by comparison with the ethos and the eidos of culture. The ethos is defined as "the qualitative aspect of the social group [which] resides in the subconsciously held beliefs of the individual psyche, or organization of the human individual, and [which] constitutes the substance of the bonds between the members of a social group" (27, p. 7). The eidos is equated with common sense, which is tantamount to the I.D.O. For the eidos is "a subconsciously held body of systematic rational beliefs having the traditional stamp of approval which consists in being held by most of the individual members of a social group" (27, p. 48). Its main features are: first, "that it is subconsciously held," (27, p. 39); second, "that we tend to act from it" (27, p. 41); and third, "its lack of consistency" (27, p. 44).

To deal with the implicit dominant ontology and its impact upon social and individual behavior, Feibleman proposes two types of analysis, similar to psychoanalytic methods of therapy. First, there is the analysis of a culture to elicit its dominant ontology. Whenever a culture is operating from an inconsistent ontological postulate-set, it is pathological, and then analysis and criticism of its ontology is practically invaluable. Second, there is the analysis of the individual member of society. Feibleman describes the implict dominant ontology clinically as the "public retention schemata" of the individuals making up the society and the basic beliefs of the individuals as "private retention schemata" (25, p. 48). Mental health hinges upon correspondence between public and private retention schemata. A deviation spells mental illness, and Feibleman proposes transfer matching as a new method in psychotherapy (25, Ch. 3). This method calls for the application of electric shock and other techniques to rid the patient of the deviant beliefs; afterwards—and this is the unique element in Feibleman's theory—other beliefs consistent with the public retention schemata and with each other are fed into his mind.

Reaching down into the inner recesses of individual minds, the implicit dominant ontology represents the role of ideas and beliefs in human behavior, but without excluding the importance of material factors. Not only is Feibleman's psychology founded upon biological and behavioral facts; his sociology focuses on institutions, granting prime consideration to material artifacts. Defining an institution as "an established social group working in customary ways with material tools on a common task" (26, p. 21), Feibleman analyzes institutions structurally and functionally. Structurally, institutions are organizations of personnel with definite procedures and equipment (26, Ch. 11), while functionally they contain as goal-directed elements myth, symbol, style, and charter (26, Ch. 12). The myth of an institution is particularly pertinent, because it is "a qualitative presentation of certain philosophical propositions concerning reality" (26, p. 168); the implicit dominant ontology is the myth of the leading institution. But it is the artifact which usurps the foreground of Feibleman's social theory (28). After all, institutions themselves are artifacts produced by men, along with other physical tools and instruments, by means of which they cope with their environment the better to satisfy their basic needs. Always there is the hazard of too much preoccupation with artifacts, the result of which is institutional pathology. "Instead of the production of artifacts as a mere extension of his working methods, man now has the production of artifacts as the end-product of his working methods" (26, p. 111). The terrible consequence is expressed in the myth of Frankenstein, the tale of an artifact out of control and wreaking havoc upon its creators.

Feibleman draws a distinction between the service institutions and the higher institutions, granting the importunateness of the former while insisting upon the importance of the latter. Among the higher institutions are the sciences, the arts, philosophy, and religion. Since Feibleman's conception of philosophy as "that institution which furnishes the criticism of the presuppositions to other institutions" (26, p. 220) has been dealt with throughout this study, the remainder of the discussion will concentrate on science, art, and religion. "The sciences are those institutions which furnish information concerning the laws governing segments of the natural world to other institutions" (26, pp. 215–16). "The arts are those institutions which furnish the values to other institutions" (26, p. 218). Religion is "that institution which furnishes the salvation from suffering to other institutions" (26, p. 222). All the higher institutions, as noted previously, are agents of destiny striving through existence to actualize the universe of essence.

According to Feibleman, science "conducts the search among facts through the method of hypothesis, experiment and verification, for tendencies, laws and causes, leading to the prediction of events and the control over phenomena, at advanced stages of development involving mathematically formulated theories to account for instrumentally-discovered data" (20, p. 431). This compact statement of Feibleman's conception of scientific method is elaborated in a forthcoming volume on science. His entire philosophy, in fact, so profoundly affected by high regard for the scientific method and its accomplishments, seeks to be speculative without being unscientific. For science itself is interpreted ontologically. What science seeks to discover are the constant functions and laws of natural things, and these laws and functions are universals which belong to the logical order of essence. Hence Feibleman locates science within the universe of destiny, "the interim realm which seeks to weave together the universes of essence and existence by directing existence toward essence" (20, p. 440).

Art, too, is a cultural institution which belongs to destiny. Here it should be remembered that artistic concerns—mainly literature, but painting, sculpture, music, and architecture as well—first moved Feibleman away from business. In addition to poetry and fiction, Feibleman has tried his hand at painting, and he even designed the home in which he lives—a spacious modernistic structure. It is no wonder, then, that his *Aesthetics* (29) is replete with illustrations drawn from an intimate connection with the arts. As Feibleman writes: "Art is that division of culture which aims at the deliberate apprehension of beauty" (29, p. 37). Further, he says, "beauty is the value emanating from any actual organization when its parts approximate a perfect relation to the whole organization" (29, p. 30). Because beauty signifies a perfect harmony of parts, it belongs to the universe of essence; the work of art "is a symbol of the absolute perfection, the perfect unity, of all being" (29, p. 45). Since he sees the value the artist symbolizes by means of his art as subsisting independently of the artist and his method, Feibleman describes the artistic method as a process of discovery rather than of creation. "The ultimate aim of all art is to discover a symbol for the widest possible value, for the universally valuable" (20, p. 462).

Religion, like art and like science, is a higher social institution, and its office is to offer salvation from suffering. Just as an entire culture is an applied ontology, the dominant institution imposing the dominant ontology, so religion presupposes ultimate beliefs about the ultimate nature of things and is, in Feibleman's words, "applied theology" (20, p. 510). For science the value is truth, for art beauty, and for theology holiness. "The holy is defined as the symbolically universal value of all things. The holy is the value of anything representing total value" (20, p. 506). Since anything may represent total value, anything may be holy. Herein is entailed a special view of religion.

Feibleman's discussion of religion, scattered through all his works, comes to focus in two recent books: *Religious Platonism* (30) and *The Pious Scientist* (31). As would be expected, religion is defined in relation to the universes of existence and essence posited by axiological realism and is therefore located within the universe of destiny. As an essay on the history of Western religious thought, *Religious Platonism* argues that the sort of objective idealism found in Plato and exploited by the neo-Platonists has exerted a determinant influence upon Western religious thought, but that, unfortunately, the valid Platonic realism of two equally real universes of being has never found expression. *The Pious Scientist*, for all its brevity, is a highly personalized, provocative confession of a religion based upon the valid realism, a creed that is tentative and naturalistic. Its first principle is the maintenance of half-belief through "the balancing of attachment with non-attachment" (31, pp. 14-15). Its second principle, which in effect defines the purpose of religion, is to seek "the unaffiliated truth" (31, p. 16). So stated, the principles of Feibleman's religion are identical with his practice of philosophy. Hence, his religion is tantamount to his vocation as a philosopher.

Feibleman's religion is a religion within the limits of reason and of science, of logic and of fact. "Active non-interference" is its practical recommendation; its command is: "Do what is necessary in order to cause as little change as possible" (31, p. 19). This results in the meditative attitude appropriate to the philosopher, with reverence for all existence. Such reverence is consonant with the universality of holiness, which is radically stated thus: "Every act is a sacrament" (31, p. 43). This religion clearly requires no church or ritual. "Religion," Feibleman declares, "is anything ordinary, pursued with detachment. Work done in an art, in a science, or in philosophy, is enough, provided it be pursued for its own sake and not for some personal end" (31, p. 49). Its creed, expressed in the words of the title, is that of the pious scientist.

No mystical escape from nature into the arms of God is permitted; on the contrary, "nature mediates between God and man" (31, p. 54). As Feibleman says: "If God is the reason for the world, then we are always talking about God when we talk about the world; yet we can talk only about the world. It is all God—a name we should never use. For just because it is all equally His business, our business is not with Him. Our business is with nature, and science is the name of that business" (31, p. 76). With a tentative creed, without a church, and within the limits set by science, this religion nevertheless claims for its membership nothing less than the unlimited community with its aspiration for the unaffiliated truth. This religion, the vocation of the philosopher, has "no dogma but that of fallibilism; no feeling but one of humility; no attitude but that of acceptance; no rules but only safeguards; no beliefs but in inquiry" (31, p. 68).

NOTES TO CHAPTER VII

1   James K. Feibleman, *Philosophers Lead Sheltered Lives: A First Volume of Memoirs* (London: Allen and Unwin, 1952).

2   James K. Feibleman, "Literary New Orleans Between World Wars," *Southern Review*, I (new series, 1965), 702–19.
3   James K. Feibleman, *Death of the God in Mexico* (New York: H. Liveright, 1931).
4   James K. Feibleman, *The Margitist* (New Orleans: River Press, 1944).
5   James Feibleman, *Journey to the Coastal March* (Cummington, Mass.: Cummington Press, 1946).
6   James K. Feibleman, *The Trembling Prairie* (Lexington, Ky.: Hammer Press, 1952).
7   James K. Feibleman, *The Dark Bifocals* (Lexington, Ky.: Hammer Press, 1953).
8   James K. Feibleman, *The Long Habit* (New York: Duell, Sloan, and Pearce, 1948).
9   Huntington Cairns has selected from Feibleman's voluminous writings a thick but manageable anthology, *The Two Story World* (New York: Holt, Rinehart and Winston, 1966). See also John G. Fuller, "Trade Winds," *Saturday Review*, XLIX (July 16, 1966), 16–17.
10 James K. Feibleman, *Mankind Behaving: Human Needs and Material Culture* (Springfield, Ill.: Charles C. Thomas, 1963).
11 Julius W. Friend and James Feibleman, *Science and the Spirit of Man: A New Ordering of Experience* (London: Allen and Unwin, 1933).
12 Morris Cohen (ed.), *Chance, Love, and Logic* (New York: Harcourt, Brace, 1923).
13 James Feibleman, *An Introduction to Peirce's Philosophy Interpreted as a System* (New York: Harper and Brothers, 1946; London: Allen and Unwin, 1960).
14 James Feibleman, *The Revival of Realism: Critical Studies in Contemporary Philosophy* (Chapel Hill: University of North Carolina Press, 1946).
15 Julius W. Friend and James Feibleman, *The Unlimited Community: A Study of the Possibility of Social Science* (London: Allen and Unwin, 1936).
16 Julius W. Friend and James Feibleman, *What Science Really Means: An Explanation of the History and Empirical Method of General Science* (London: Allen and Unwin, 1937).
17 James Feibleman, *Christianity, Communism and the Ideal Society: A Philosophical Approach to Modern Politics* (London: Allen and Unwin, 1937).
18 James Feibleman, *Positive Democracy* (Chapel Hill: University of North Carolina Press, 1940).
19 James Feibleman, *In Praise of Comedy: A Study in its Theory and Practice* (New York: Macmillan, 1939; reprinted by Russell and Russell, 1962).
20 James K. Feibleman, *Ontology* (Baltimore: Johns Hopkins Press, 1951).
21 James K. Feibleman, *Foundations of Empiricism* (The Hague: Martinus Nijhoff, 1962).
22 James K. Feibleman, *Inside the Great Mirror: A Critical Examination of the Philosophy of Russell, Wittgenstein, and Their Followers* (The Hague: Martinus Nijhoff, 1958).
23 F. I. G. Rawlins, *Nature*, CXCV (September 8, 1962), 931.
24 See Gustav Bergmann, *The Metaphysics of Logical Positivism* (New York: Longmans, Green, 1954).
25 James K. Feibleman, *Biosocial Factors in Mental Illness* (Springfield, Ill.: Charles C. Thomas, 1962).

26 James K. Feibleman, *The Institutions of Society* (London: Allen and Unwin, 1956).

27 James Feibleman, *The Theory of Human Culture* (New York: Duell, Sloan, and Pearce, 1946).

28 See James K. Feibleman, "Artifactualism," *Journal of Philosophy and Phenomenological Research*, XXV (1965), 544–59.

29 James K. Feibleman, *Aesthetics: A Study of the Fine Arts in Theory and Practice* (New York: Duell, Sloan and Pearce, 1949).

30 James K. Feibleman, *Religious Platonism: The Influence of Religion on Plato and the Influence of Plato on Religion* (London: Allen and Unwin, 1959).

31 James K. Feibleman, *The Pious Scientist: Nature, God and Man in Religion* (New York: Bookman, 1958).

32 James K. Feibleman, *Moral Strategy* (The Hague: Martinus Nijhoff, 1967).

VIII

JOHN WILD

From Realism to Existentialism

INTRODUCTION

"The only truth to which we have any access," John Wild writes, "is a human truth that lives and grows in history. We no longer expect a human philosopher to bring this history to a close. We expect him to give us insight into the world in which we live" (1, p. 178). Wild exemplifies the type of human philosopher he describes. Enthusiastic in style and provocative in content, his thought dynamically oversteps all fixed loci, moving in recent years from the advocacy of classic realism to the espousal of a phenomenological philosophy of existence. His earnestness has inspired the cooperation of other thinkers, at one time to form an association for realistic philosophy and at another time to establish a society for phenomenology and existentialism.

Born in Chicago on April 10, 1902, Wild received his Ph.B. and Ph.D. degrees from the University of Chicago in 1923 and 1926. In 1927 he was appointed instructor of philosophy at Harvard University, where he had earned his M.A. degree in 1925, and he remained there until 1961 when he resigned his professorship. He then became chairman of the department of philosophy at Northwestern University, which was at the time initiating a policy to become a center for the study of existentialism and phenomenology. In 1963 he left Northwestern to join the faculty of Yale University as professor of philosophy.

John Wild, though controversial, is an outstanding scholar and creative thinker. Editor of the writings of Spinoza for Scribner's

Modern Student's Library (2), and author of a detailed biography of Berkeley's intellectual development (3), Wild has thoroughly studied the two dominant pre-Kantian philosophical movements —rationalism and empiricism. Wild's book on Berkeley is as noteworthy for its author's asides on the nature of philosophy and philosophical issues as for its scholarly investigation of its subject. It marks a major revolution against the prevalent interpretation of Berkeley's thought. Tracing "the concrete logic" of Berkeley's thought—a logic moved as much by urgent existential concerns as by abstract dialectical considerations—Wild unveils a Berkeley who transcends the spiritualistic empiricism of *The Principles* and who abandons this truncated Humean empiricism for the more profound neo-Platonism of the *Siris*. This early book is harbinger of Wild's own subsequent intellectual development in two directions: toward a deep-seated interest in Platonism, in metaphysics and practical philosophy, and toward a passionate preoccupation with the structure of concrete, individual, dynamic existence.

Platonism comes to the fore in Wild's next book, *Plato's Theory of Man* (4). Published in 1946, when postwar America cheerlessly faced an atomic age and the communist threat, *Plato's Theory of Man* admittedly uses scholarship primarily for philosophical enlightenment concerning urgent contemporary problems of culture. Research on Plato is instrumental to introducing, in the words of the subtitle, "the realistic philosophy of culture." In the style of neo-Platonism, Wild concedes the validity of Aristotelian realism in the theoretical sciences of metaphysics and logic, the philosophy of nature, and natural theology, but he insists upon the superiority of Plato's doctrines in ethics, politics, and the philosophy of culture. Guided in part by the synthesis of St. Thomas Aquinas, Wild presents the philosophies of Plato and Aristotle as a unified system in textbook format for undergraduate students in his *Introduction to Realistic Philosophy* (5).

These works unmistakably identified Wild with classical realism. Founder of the Association for Realistic Philosophy, Wild edited the major publication of the society, *The Return to Reason* (6). In addition to containing Wild's important essay "Phenomenology and

Metaphysics," this cooperative volume includes the contributions of twelve other professional philosophers—Harmon M. Chapman, Oliver Martin, Jesse De Boer, Manley H. Thompson, Jr., Francis H. Parker, Henry Veatch, Eliseo Vivas, William A. Banner, John Ladd, Robert Jordan, Harry S. Broudy, and J. Arthur Martin—as well as a paper by Charles Malik, then Minister of Lebanon and Chairman of the United Nations Human Rights Commission. At the end of the volume appears the platform of the Association, which, in four parts, treats metaphysics, epistemology, practical philosophy, and the history of philosophy and which clearly defines the realism advocated. This realism, in contradistinction to the neorealism and the critical realism which flourished in the United States several decades ago, is the classical realism of Plato, Aristotle, and St. Thomas Aquinas, updated to take account of contemporary intellectual issues and practical problems. Wild's group, then, constituted part of the widespread revival of realism in Europe and America.

A major factor in this movement has of course been the role of the Roman Catholic Church in propagating neo-Thomism, a role now diminishing as members of the Church are increasingly allowed to look beyond St. Thomas for philosophical inspiration. Wild's group, however, remained secular, or at least unaffiliated with any particular religious institution. Thus the Association for Realistic Philosophy represented an outlook shared by other centers of classical realism, such as the University of Chicago during the 1930's and 1940's. This outlook is still perpetuated in the Institute for Philosophical Research headed by former University of Chicago professor Mortimer Adler. The Institute was once located in San Francisco and is now in Chicago. As noted in the preceding chapter, Feibleman at Tulane University, though an independent, may also be counted as a member of this realist movement. No doubt the need for universal and rational moral standards to guide and evaluate practical affairs has stimulated the renascence of classical realism in our troubled times, as the expectation of satisfying this need has crystallized in the revival of natural law theory. In response to this situation Wild offers his *Plato's Modern Enemies and the Theory of Natural Law* (7).

Wild's advocacy of realistic philosophy has been characterized by strict attentiveness to contemporary modes of thought. Distressed by recent Anglo-American analytic thought which, in repudiating metaphysics, has trivialized philosophy and neglected burning practical issues, Wild has hastened to denounce this alleged breakdown of thought and has sought nurture from the European currents of existentialism and phenomenology. Although Wild's interest in existentialism and phenomenology goes back several decades (8), it has been intensified of late. In *The Challenge of Existentialism* (9) Wild elucidates the main doctrines of the existentialist thinkers, highlighting their strength, exposing their weaknesses, and concentrating on their potentialities for alignment with realism. Convinced that realistic philosophy must meet the challenge or perish, Wild has responded with his *Human Freedom and Social Order* (10) and *Existence and the World of Freedom* (11).

REALISM

The Association for Realistic Philosophy sharply defined its position by proposing a set of carefully stated theses on metaphysics, epistemology, practical philosophy, and the history of philosophy. Since this philosophy stems from the classical realism of Plato and Aristotle, it affirms, as regards the history of philosophy, the principle that "important truths are contained in the classical tradition of Platonic and Aristotelian philosophy." Hence the Association called for, first, the recovery of "the living truth" of the classical texts through philosophical, rather than purely philological or antiquarian, study; second, the "inductive clarification of basic concepts," to take account of modern knowledge and experience and to avoid dogmatic theological intrusions; third, the preparation and publication of better translations of the classical texts and of the important commentaries, of anthologies, and of systematic textbooks suitable for contemporary students (12); and fourth, the investigation of historical problems, such as the relation of Plato to Aristotle (6, pp. 362–63).

Here Wild's conception of how to amalgamate or synthesize the theories of Plato and Aristotle is germane. In metaphysics and epistemology Wild's thought bears the imprint of traditional Aristotelianism, flexed to handle the issues of our times, but in practical philosophy it turns to Plato for inspiration. In this way Wild sidesteps the timeworn issues between Aristotelianism and Platonism, construing them as complementary theories which, with differing emphases, elaborate the same fundamental philosophy. He writes: "Aristotle is a speculative theorist, Plato a practical philosopher. One is like a map-maker with a purely topographical interest, interested only in the formal correctness of his map in every detail. The other is like the roadbuilder who, it is true, has to have *some* knowledge of the topography, but whose primary aim is rather to build a satisfactory road to a given destination" (4, p. 11). Seen in this light, the contrast between Platonism and Aristotelianism is not an irresolvable opposition between two divergent philosophies, but "rather two distinct though inseparable phases of one and the same philosophy" (4, p. 16). As Wild says: "One essential part of philosophy is to discover the theoretical truth concerning being. If you need this, turn to Aristotle! The other essential part of philosophy is to arouse yourself and others to act in the light of this truth, choosing the particular means which will lead to the end revealed only by such theoretical light. If you need this, turn to the dialogues of Plato for protreptic inspiration and practical guidance in the confused flux of concrete history! Every man really needs both" (4, p. 17).

In accordance with this conception of Plato and Aristotle as complementary and of their urgent contemporary relevance, the realistic platform systematically expounds theses on metaphysics, epistemology, and practical philosophy. Fleshed by Wild's writings, these theses make up the skeleton of a significant and full-bodied philosophy. First we shall explore what this philosophy teaches as regards phenomenology, metaphysics, and epistemology, and then we shall discuss the practical philosophy.

Phenomenology

Convinced that the method of phenomenology is the only method which affords an adequate and accurate description of the immediate data of experience upon which metaphysics must be based, Wild joins realism with phenomenology. He accepts the empiricist demand that theory be checked by the data of immediate experience, but where empiricists are convinced that all such data fall within the fields of the special sciences, Wild contends that there are immediate data outside the scope of the special sciences which comprise the subject matter of philosophy.

An immediate datum is "any empirical item which is thrust upon awareness with constraining evidence" (6, p. 38). Wild finds these immediate data to be much wider and richer than the prevailing theories allow, and he proceeds to examine critically and reject five philosophical theories which narrow down the data to the detriment of metaphysics. In contrast with the repudiated theories, Wild's theory maintains that the immediate data comprise a structuralized yet differentiated field, amenable to description (6, pp. 39–40); that they must not be conceived merely as essences but are pervaded with existence (6, pp. 40–42); that they are not distinct unrelated atoms but contain elements of dynamism, continuity, tendency, potency, and interrelations (6, pp. 42–43); that they are not merely subjective, since no priority of the inner subjective side of experience is presented over the outer objective world (6, p. 44); and that, further, they disallow the reduction of consciousness to its content because they actually manifest a bipolarized structure involving intentional consciousness and object intended (6, pp. 44–47). Thus Wild concludes that the immediate data divide into two basic kinds: "(1) a vast field of existent objects including the extended, measurable entities of physical science, and the personal objects of the social sciences; and (2) many different levels of awareness, including sense, imagination, memory, and rational acts of defining, judging, and arguing" (6, p. 47).

No matter how thoroughly and rigorously the sciences cast their specialized hypotheses over the given data, some data escape, and, when clarified and explained, they become the bedrock of metaphysics. Prior to metaphysics, however, is phenomenology, which takes up the task of carefully scrutinizing and describing these data. As Wild declares: "Before we speculate, let us first describe!" (7,

p. 190). Phenomenology is defined as "that basic, noetic discipline whose function is to describe the structure of the immediate data of experience, to classify their different kinds, and thus, in brief, to clarify what is vaguely and loosely referred to as experience" (6, p. 48). A wholly descriptive method, phenomenology clarifies "those recurrent structures which, though capable of indefinite variation, are themselves constitutive of any concrete datum whatsoever" (6, p. 49). Such descriptions make up the propositions that serve as the basis of knowledge. Among these basic propositions is a special class which Wild has ventured to term philosophical or metaphysical protocols (6, p. 52; 7, p. 185). Because phenomenology lays bare the recurrent structures embedded in immediate experience, Wild has equated it with Plato's method of dialectic (8c, pp. 85–86).

Philosophical protocols are different from the protocols of the special empirical sciences because their data differ. Whereas the scientific data are restrictive and nonpervasive, quantitative and measurable, partial and dependent upon unobservable causal entities for their explanation, and relatively simple, the data to which philosophical protocols refer are *pervasive* in that they are implicated in every datum, *nonquantitative* and consequently not amenable to physical measurement, and extremely *complex* and difficult to describe, though fully observed (6, pp. 53–54). These philosophical data constitute the bedrock of realistic metaphysics. Inasmuch as phenomenological research reveals the structure of experience to be bipolar, there are two major philosophical data: existence (the object of metaphysics) and awareness (the object of epistemology). "Existence is an immediate datum which permeates every phase of concrete experience" (6, p. 49); and awareness "necessarily belongs to the experience of any object, in some one of its many modes. No datum can be given which is not given to some level of awareness" (6, p. 54).

Metaphysics

Wild locates "the heart of realism" in metaphysics (13, p. 150). And in metaphysics the platform of the Association of Realistic Philosophy asserted three basic theses:

1. Being cannot be reduced to either material being or to immaterial being.
2. Empirical evidence shows that both modes of being exist in the cosmos.
3. This cosmos consists of real, substantial entities existing in themselves and ordered to one another by real, extramental relations (6, p. 357).

Wild focuses these three theses upon two fundamental principles: the unique concept of being and the radically empirical, or phenomenological, method. Inasmuch as we have already considered the role of phenomenology in Wild's realism, we turn now to the concept of being and the other metaphysical concepts it entails.

To metaphysics falls "the task of describing, analyzing, and explaining" the most pervasive datum of experience—being (6, p. 55). The concept of being encloses essence (that which can exist) and existence (that which brings essence into act), but because essence apart from existence is nothing, Wild often uses the terms *being* and *existence* interchangeably (6, p. 55, n. 27). The general science of metaphysics reports that the fundamental traits of being are universal in scope. "What belongs to being as such will belong to everything whatsoever, whatever and wherever it may be" (6, p. 55). Only nonexistence, impossibility, or nothing is excluded from being as such. This absolute exclusion, according to Wild, is the ontological foundation of the law of noncontradiction; and that law, applying universally to being, sets a standard to which thought must conform if it is to grasp being. Another trait of being is its intelligibility: "Being contains its sufficient reasons within itself" (6, p. 56). Here is the ontological foundation of the principle of sufficient reason which, like the law of contradiction, applies universally to being. After a consideration of the two basic principles of contradiction and sufficient reason as indicators of the universal traits of being as such, whether finite or infinite, changing or immutable, multiple or one, Wild concentrates his analysis upon the finite, changing, multiple, existential entities of immediate experience.

He first takes up change, which, though not all-pervasive, does pervade all the data of immediate experience. In Book III of *Physics*, Aristotle defines change as "the actualization of that which is potential, in so far as it is potential" (5, p. 320). In this conception, Wild observes, three principles are involved: two structural principles having to do with the fact that a thing changes from one state (the privative principle) to another (the formal principle), and one material principle of potentiality. Without the principle of potentiality change would be simply the exchange of one specific determinate state for another equally determinate state; the process would be characterized by discontinuity. With the principle of potentiality, however, change is a continuous process whereby a thing develops from one state into another.

As in the definition of change, so in the demarcation of the kinds of change, Wild follows Aristotle. Germane to this demarcation is the distinction between substance and accident. Since knowledge of substance or of accident is impossible unless both are known, the distinction does not rest upon epistemological considerations but rather upon the structure of change, particularly so far as change involves continuity (6, p. 59). And substance and accident do not refer to separable entities. On the contrary, they are correlative principles which exist only in fusion, substance affording the continuity and individuality of the thing and accidents providing novelty and discontinuity (6, p. 60). So far as change takes place only in the accidents, the substance in which these accidents inhere remains constant, so that discontinuity as regards accidents is matched by continuity as regards substance. However, whenever an entire substance comes to be or passes away, the change is more radical than the mere change of accidents; it is a change of substance, and its explanation requires the Aristotelian hylomorphic theory of finite substances. According to the hylomorphic theory, a finite substance consists of form and matter. On the question whether there are forms apart from matter, Wild accepts the Aristotelian position which locates forms within matter, arguing that Plato, in his maturity, did not posit their separate existence (4, Ch. 6). As Wild says: "Matter and form are correlative principles, each of which exists only by virtue of the other. . . . Each is a vectorial principle, intrinsically correlative to something distinct from itself, and each contributes something to the whole concrete entity which is thus constituted. The matter sustains the entity and gives it an individual position in nature, while the form specifically characterizes the entity as a whole" (6, p. 61). Since the theory of change is worked out in terms of the theory of substance, the claims of process are reconciled with those of substance, claims ordinarily regarded to be contradictory.

Still another aspect of change invites attention—the disclosure of multiplicity and unity. In the case of accidental change the unity of the substance stands over against the multiplicity of its accidents, and this unity is expressed temporally by the continuity of a process actualizing potentiality. In the case of substantial change the unity is the continuity of matter, evident in the order of nature, and the multiplicity is manifest in the plurality of species and individuals. Unity, then, involves multiplicity, at least as regards finite, changing things. To elucidate this point Wild cites the self. The self is at once aware of itself as distinct from others, and yet, so far as it is an existent, it is aware also that it shares existence in common with others (6, p. 62). Here, in truth, is an intimate experience of the problem of the one and the many.

How does Wild cope with the problem? Again he resorts to an analysis derived from classical realistic philosophy which further stresses the complexity of being. Every being is made up of the correlative principles of essence and existence. Essence is what a thing is; existence is what makes a thing be rather than not be. Essence separates a thing from other existents; existence, separating a thing only from nothing, is that which it shares with other things (7, p. 199). Denouncing the essentialist trend in Western philosophy, Wild, like the existentialists, regards existence to be "more ultimate and more perfect than essence" (6, p. 63). Though easily understood by the mind apart from existence, essence is nothing without existence, since existence alone makes essence cease to be nothing and emerge into being. Hence existence is "active and diffusive" (6, p. 63).

At this point in Wild's discussion, activity gains the center of attention. Activity which originates and is partially completed in an entity is termed "tendency" (6, p. 64). Tendency is either immanent or transitive. When a tendency is wholly completed within the substance in which it originates, it is immanent; otherwise it is transitive, and transitive tendency is the ontological basis of efficient causation (6, p. 65). Change, therefore, involves causation. And while Wild accepts the Aristotelian doctrine of final, formal, material, and efficient causes (5, pp. 298–302), and consequently castigates modern philosophers for their reduction of causation to efficient causation and thence to temporal sequence (14), he also specifically stresses the element of tendency in causal efficacy (15). Indeed, he considers tendency to be "a third ontological category distinct from both essence and existence but equally wide in range .... [A]ctive tendency ... arises primarily from the act of existence but ... is determined to proceed in a certain direction by the limiting essence" (7, p. 199). As he says: "Tendency is an urge that reaches out beyond essence to more being not yet possessed" (6, p. 64).

One further word on the realistic metaphysics. As Wild surveys the world of finite, changing, multiple entities with the complexities of substance-accident, form-matter, essence-existence, he concludes that, since such complex yet finite and mutable being cannot account for itself, there is sound argument to warrant the assertion that there exists an infinite, perfect, first cause of all being—God (6, pp. 65–67).

Epistemology

In epistemology the platform proclaimed: "These real entities (substances) and relations together with human artifacts can be known by the human mind as they are in themselves and can be aesthetically enjoyed" (6, p. 360). Wild's epistemology is derived from Aristotle and St. Thomas Aquinas, and while it is not necessary here to examine it in any detail, it is worth noting that, in its formulation, Wild and his realist associates rely upon the classical and medieval texts rather than upon the hypotheses and theories of contemporary symbolic logic and experimental psychology. Moreover, this realistic epistemology, termed "natural realism," is presented in contradistinction to both neorealism and critical realism.

Neorealism is dismissed as an epistemological monism which wrongly identifies the mental representation (the species) by which we know an object with the existent object, and critical realism is rejected as a dualism which separates the species from the object and neglects to find means to bridge the gap between them.

Natural realism affirms the existential separateness of the species as a mental representation by which the thing is known from the thing as a real being outside the mind. Yet it also asserts the formal identity of the two. The form within the real being is grasped in intellectual abstraction, and consequently it is possible to know the thing truly through its species. A basic feature of this cognitive process is intentionality. "Natural realism defends knowledge as an intentional relation terminating in the externally existent thing" (6, p. 360). The importance of intentionality in the realist conception of the cognitive process cannot be overestimated. In fact, the medieval distinction between first and second intentions is the basis for the most brilliant achievement in the realistic effort to reinstate an Aristotelian logic in opposition to symbolic logic—namely, Henry Veatch's *Intentional Logic* (12).

REALISTIC PRACTICAL PHILOSOPHY

The theoretical sciences of metaphysics and epistemology, according to Wild, are not pursued simply for their own sakes, although the knowledge they afford is an end in itself. They are also foundational to practical philosophy and moral action. For it is the conviction of the realists that, in the words of the platform: "Such knowledge [of reality], especially that treating of human nature, can provide us with immutable and trustworthy principles for the guidance of individual and social action" (6, p. 361). And certainly, in Wild's case, the return to classical philosophy, the "return to reason," is permeated with burning practical zeal. While practical philosophy is only part of the realistic platform, coequal with metaphysics, epistemology, and history, it is Wild's main preoccupation, if one is to judge from the amount and quality of the work he has devoted to such practical questions as the nature of human culture and of natural law. In the practical field, based as it is upon the foundations of metaphysics, lies the passionate center of Wild's intellectual career.

Wild's contributions to practical philosophy may be divided into three phases. The first phase, in which the influence of Plato is predominant, focuses on the theory of culture and on the concept of anatropism, presented in *Plato's Theory of Man*. The second phase, in which Wild still centers on Plato as leading moral philosopher, concentrates on the concept of natural law, a concept which is attributed to Plato. The second phase is amply expounded in Wild's book *Plato's Modern Enemies and the Theory of Natural Law*. The third phase develops out of Wild's encounter with existentialism, and to a remarkable extent it marks, if not a new direction in his thought, conspicuously new emphases.

Theory of Culture

In *Plato's Theory of Man*, Wild professedly seeks to be more than a scholarly interpreter of his subject; he intends to elicit from Plato's texts a coherent theory of culture and to project an ideal standard for cultural aspiration and evaluation. Consequently, what Wild says about Plato reveals not only his interpretations of Plato but also, and more importantly, what Wild himself believes concerning the philosophy of culture. Plato emerges as the austere moralist who in his infallible wisdom offers a program for the true cultural order. Wild never doubts that there is only one true, or natural, order of life and that deviations from it are false, unnatural, even unreal. He describes this new order in metaphysical language, identifying it with "the actual causal order of reality" (4, p. 41), with "the true hierarchical order of things as they proceed from their ultimate source, being itself" (4, p. 204).

This true order is, moreover, a hierarchy consisting of higher and lower levels. The higher is more real than the lower, and the highest is equated with the self-sustaining cause of being. Although the hierarchy is objectively necessary in that the lower is the means to the higher as the end, it is not practically necessary (4, p. 43). No compulsion forces men to choose what is objectively necessary. Consequently, every level of the hierarchy affords opportunities for inversion, for the domination of a higher by a lower level. Wild invents the neologism "anatropism" to denote the reversal of the hierarchy. Anatropism is defined "as the miscarriage of human action involving misapprehension of the hierarchical structure of means and ends" (4, p. 36). With Plato as his guide, Wild pursues anatropism in the arts, in life, in individual behavior, in society, in ontology, and in knowledge, tracing it to its roots in sophistry.

The arts illustrate the concept of order and the susceptibilities to anatropic decay. An art works on a matter which is given to it, and under the guidance of its peculiar insight into the structure of the matter, it shapes the matter into some form or end. Art involves, besides its own set of operational techniques, a material principle and a final-formal principle. So long as the true order prevails, the arts are "guided *from ahead* according to plan," but once inverted they are "pushed *from behind* by material pressure" (4, p. 78). As a consequence of inversion art degenerates into routine, and regardless of initial successes routine eventually breaks down because it can not cope with new contingencies.

As soon as inversion attacks the arts, it spreads like an infection over all the levels of the hierarchy. In the true order, "each art is *conditioned* by the lower arts which provide it with matter and *determined* by the higher arts which provide it with an end" (4, p. 88). But when inversion occurs, this arrangement is upset and higher arts fall under the domination of the lower ones. With the consequent obscuring of the system of ends which the arts should subserve, instrumental arts tend to arrogate a spurious autonomy, and such false arts as cookery, flattery, quackery spring up. When disruption overwhelms the higher arts, "philosophy loses control of its matter, and the various sciences decompose into the anarchy of special techniques" (4, p. 80). Education deteriorates. Instead of fulfilling its higher function of attending rationally to the rational needs of rational animals, education degenerates to its lower function of admonition, of indoctrinating children with existing customs, habits, and beliefs (4, pp. 69–70). Statesmanship declines. As Wild says: "Without adequate guidance, supplied by education and philosophy, the statesman is at sea. He does not dare impose any rational pattern on the whole community. Indeed he is not cognizant of any such pattern. He must yield to the pressure of this subordinate interest or that, and thus materialize his statesmanship" (4, p. 80).

Inversion in the arts is paradigmatic of other types of inversion. Anatropism materializes the natural hierarchy, distorting and suppressing form, and induces irrational blindness to the standards, or ends, for social and personal action. Just as the hierarchy of the arts is an order in which rational form dominates matter, so in the order of an integrated society rational form rules. And just as inversion occurs in the hierarchy of the arts, it occurs in politics, with the subordination of the rational and the formal to the pressures of the material. Anatropism in society, evident in the numerous blatant defects of modern culture, furnishes Wild the opportunity to pronounce jeremiads. Like Plato, he denounces the prevailing democratic conception of the best government as the one founded on public opinion, but he endeavors to retain the ideal of democracy by an unusual interpretation of its import. True democracy, he says, is "movement in the direction *away from* tyranny and private opinion *towards* the classless theocracy of the *Republic*, or at least *towards* some society actually integrated, as our present day 'democracy' only pretends to be, by a common reference to the stable, and therefore superhuman, source of all genuine science and wisdom" (4, p. 111). Arguing from "the phenomenology of public opinion," Wild contends that public opinion is too incomplete, partial, and wavering to support the broad structure of political society (4, pp. 125 ff.). When force or public opinion dominates wisdom in the governance of society, political anatropism results, with concomitant deformations of the public life. True democracy, the only alternative to the tyranny of force or of public opinion, is tantamount to theocracy.

Wild's theocratic conception of true democracy is, however, hostile to totalitarianism. Indeed, he has bent every effort of scholarship to refuting the charges of those recent scholars, "Plato's modern enemies," who claim that the *Republic* is the original pattern of the closed society (7, Chs. 1 and 2). The ideal of democracy, as Wild points out, is a complex concept, containing elements derived from Greek realistic philosophy and the Judaeo-Christian religious tradition. Although modern skepticism has played an historically significant role in the rise of democracy by inducing those rebellious attitudes of mind which have struck down feudal and class oppression, the Judaeo-Christian religious tradition has contributed essential elements to the ideal of democracy. For democracy, regarded not merely as a negative but primarily as a positive ideal, involves "an appreciation of the dignity and worth of human existence and a trust in the common man, derived primarily from Christianity; and . . . the concept of natural law as equally binding upon all men everywhere, and a respect for reason and rational education, contributed by Greek philosophy and its later developments" (7, pp. 58–59). Thus Plato's *Republic*, construed as Wild suggests, not only is consonant with the ideal of modern democracy but even historically foreshadows this modern ideal.

Above all, within a society organized along the lines of the *Republic*, the individual plays a cardinal role. Against all totalitarians Wild argues: "For the achievement of reliable guiding insight the state must call upon the individual intellect for guidance or perish" (4, p. 124). To suppress the individual's freedom of inquiry, as totalitarianism does, is to undermine the ideal hierarchical polity. "The state cannot reason and plan for itself effectively unless there is present in it some single individual who has achieved some stable understanding of the permanent idea of the pattern of the state as a whole" (4, p. 124). Further, Wild expressly rejects the Hegelian theory which makes society more substantial than the individuals. While he grants that "neither community nor individual can exist actually without the other," he perceives that the relation is hierarchical rather than symmetrical, the individual being the higher element (4, p. 132). He writes: "The state supplies the material and certain of the efficient conditions without which individual life is impossible. But the individual supplies knowledge of the formal and final causes of the state. Hence the state is even more dependent upon the individual than the individual upon the state" (4, p. 132). Reinforcing the metaphysical ground of the argument, he adds: "Only the individual man is a substance, existing in his own right. Society is a composite, being made up of many individual men living together at one time, and succeeding one another in different times" (4, p. 133). The ideal state depends upon "the puny, evanescent individual," who alone is capable of grasping the single truth indispensable to a just social order.

Individual human life too is characterized by an order—the rule of the appetites by reason—which is susceptible to inversion. When the appetites gain the upper hand, the individual is pushed from behind, his reason is rendered ineffectual, and the result is psychological and moral decay. Such failure in the human individual is the basis of anatropism not only in the individual human life but also in society and in the arts. This failure is, in essence, a failure of understanding. As Wild puts it: "The *final* source of human evil lies in the disordering of human knowledge" (4, p. 174). Wild apprehends in Plato's image of the cave the theme of the individual's reparation of his misunderstanding by the strenuous effort of turning around from the shadows on the wall and coming face to face with the rational forms. Correlating Plato's passages on the myth of the cave and the divided line, Wild argues that each level of the line marks off a distinctive level of being and of knowing, making up a natural hierarchy: imagination and images, opinion and physical things, mathematical knowing and mathematical objects, knowing proper and the intelligible forms, and at the top the Good, or God. Summing up the significance of these passages of Plato, Wild defines "the nature of education" as "the revolution of the soul away from the less intelligible things (subjective sense data in us) which happen to be better known *to us*, towards more intelligible things (existing in themselves) which are less well known to us. In this moving process the human soul passes from a social or individual subjectivism, in which man seems the measure of all things, to a realism, in which man, both social and individual, is allotted his proper subordinate station, and God, not man, is finally known as the measure of all things" (4, p. 204).

According to Wild, the ultimate cause of all anatropism is sophistry. Recovering the meaning of Plato after centuries of the history of philosophy had concealed it, Wild lays bare the malevolent magnitude of sophistry. "Sophistry," he declares, "is not the inversion of this philosophy or that philosophy, but something far more fundamental, the inversion of philosophy itself" (4, p. 273). It is "a unitary inversion of order, a descent from understanding to opinion, from personal life to social life, from art to the accidental domination of nature. To ascend out of the Cave is to be a philosopher; to descend is to be a sophist" (4, p. 273). Unlike the philosopher, who is concerned with being, the sophist, following the downward path, is concerned with nonbeing (4, p. 240). And this is, for Wild as for Plato, no mere abstruse ontological topic divorced from practical considerations. "To misunderstand being is to misunderstand everything" (4, p. 241), so that in the last analysis civilization pivots upon ontology, or, to be more precise, upon adequate and accurate knowledge of ontology. As in ontology, hierarchy prevails in knowledge, ranking cognitive faculties in an order, which unfortunately is susceptible to anatropism too.

Sense perception, opinion, and knowledge have definable functions to perform, and as long as knowledge dominates, there is no difficulty. But when knowledge, which is supposed to grasp the intelligible forms, is undermined by skepticism or is distorted by the imaginative faculty, the upshot is anatropism, fraught with all kinds of undesirable practical consequences. As Wild remarks: "Idealism lies at the root of *Machtpolitik*, and humanism is the next step to barbarism" (4, p. 254). And here again the culprit is the sophist. Sophistry, then, is no superficial activity confined in its impact to small coteries of philosophical discussants. Rather it is the original germ of all individual and social moral ills. No fleeting social phenomenon, sophistry is found to be a constant temptation for human nature. In the final analysis, sophistry resides in a "fabricative tendency in man which leads him to confuse his own constructions with real being, the fabrication of God" (4, p. 310).

Theory of Natural Law

Projecting a system of ideals for modern man and modern culture from a consideration of Plato's philosophy, Wild does not propose a revolution which appeals to force; on the contrary, he recommends the rule of reason. As he says: *"Either reason or force must control human affairs.* These alternatives are always open" (7, p. 23). Consequently, Wild's revolution, like Plato's, seeks to turn the souls of men away from illusions toward intelligible realities through education. For right practice depends upon reason about reality, and ethics is based upon metaphysics. In practical philosophy this realist outlook entails the doctrine of natural law. Wild defines natural law as *"a universal pattern of action, applicable to all men everywhere, required by human nature itself for its completion"* (7, p. 64). From the outset, moreover, he stresses the ontological meaning of this formula. Opposed to the modern separation of facts and values, Wild repeatedly defends their interrelatedness and emphasizes the grounding of norms within reality. "Value," he says, "is realization or activation of being" (7, p. 212). Although he recognizes that no present condition of finite existence is absolutely good, nevertheless he regards good as a mode of existence and evil as a mode of nonexistence. So long as an existent is finite, it suffers privation; as it tends toward completion, it finds goodness in the realization of its tendencies and evil in their frustration (7, p. 65).

Through an analysis of the multiple senses of the term "nature," Wild illuminates the ontological foundations of natural law. Whereas A. O. Lovejoy had detected in the shifting meanings of the concept of nature a manifestation of unconscious inferences and associations and of intellectual irresponsibility (16), Wild detects a relatedness of meanings signifying a basic metaphysical unity (7, p. 149). He notes five meanings of the term "nature": first, "the general relation of fitness, and the dynamic entities ordered into a world or cosmos by this normative relation"; second, "the form or definite structure of a finite entity which determines its basic tendencies, and the kind of activity which will fittingly complete these tendencies"; third, "the tendencies determined by this form"; fourth, "the fitting direction of these tendencies in such a way as to lead them towards fulfillment"; and fifth, "the good or fitting condition of existential fulfillment" (7, p. 108).

From a consideration of these five senses of the term "nature"

Wild sharply formulates the ontology of natural law in five principles:

1. The world is an order of divergent tendencies which on the whole support one another.
2. Each individual entity is marked by an essential structure which it shares in common with other members of the species.
3. The structure determines certain basic existential tendencies that are also common to the species.
4. If these tendencies are to be realized without distortion and frustration, they must follow a general dynamic pattern. This pattern is what is meant by natural law. It is grounded on real structure, and is enforced by inexorable moral sanctions.
5. Good and evil are existential categories. It is good for an entity to exist in a condition of active realization. If its basic tendencies are hampered and frustrated, it exists in an evil condition (7, pp. 132–33).

From these five ontological principles three ethical principles are derived:

1. From the second (2) it follows that the common traits of human nature, the tendencies determined by these traits, and the laws governing the fitting realization of these tendencies are the same for all men everywhere.
2. From the third and fourth (3 and 4), it follows that certain modes of action commonly called virtues or obligations must be pursued if frustration is to be avoided. These modes of action are not due to arbitrary decree, or preference, but are founded on human nature itself.
3. From the fifth (5) it follows that the good for man is the activation of his nature, the most complete and intensive living of a human life (7, p. 133).

Because the tradition of natural law theory goes back to Plato and Aristotle and has been continually restated in medieval and modern thought (7, Chs. 5, 6 ff.), Wild makes no claim to originality; in fact, he has on occasion condemned spurious originality in philosophy as a symptom of sophistry (4, pp. 310–11). But there is an original element in Wild's realism—namely, his demarcation of tendency as a category on an equal footing with the categories of essence and existence. This category of tendency strengthens noticeably the realist justification of the moral categories and of natural law. When it is understood that "reality is not made up of properties alone but of existent properties with active tendencies" (7, p. 217), then the moral categories—good, evil, right, wrong, obligation—are defined in terms of this ontology. Thus obligation, a moral category around which so much recent ethical discussion revolves, is an existential category grounded in active tendency. Each kind of entity has its own active tendencies for the fulfillment of its being and is urged to realize itself (7, p. 173). Deepened in man, this urge assumes the form of moral obligation. "Obligation is a peculiar datum of human experience which includes a factor of apprehension together with a subjective feeling of urgent tendency toward what is apprehended" (7, p. 213). If tendency is followed to its fulfillment, the concept of goodness is analyzed. If fulfillment is traced back to its tendency, the concept of rightness is analyzed (7, p. 217).

Besides affording the bases for the clarification of moral concepts, the realist metaphysics, amplified by the recognition of the categorial import of active tendency, buttresses the defense of natural law theory against its detractors. Wild examines the five arguments leveled against the natural law theory, and, finding that they rest upon misconceptions, he repudiates all five. First, against the charge that the natural law theory, founded upon an allegedly "dubious inferential teleology," attributes to the universe as a whole anthropocentric characteristics of purposiveness, Wild argues that, once one accepts change as a primary fact of nature, it follows that tendencies must in fact inhere in the dynamic entities that throng the world, although it is not necessary to ascribe consciousness to every tendency (7, pp. 73–76). Second, against the allegation that natural law is "a vague and indeterminate moral standard," Wild replies that through disciplined understanding it is possible to grasp the essence that marks off a species and the realization toward which an existent member moves, so that definite moral norms may be discovered and established (7, pp. 76–81). Third, against the thesis that natural law doctrine confuses descriptive with prescriptive law, Wild answers that, while natural law philosophy distinguishes existence from value, it does not make them utterly separate. The absolute equation of existence and value excludes the need for moral choice, but the absolute divorce of the two also undermines such choice, since it rules out the possibility of the realization of value (7, pp. 76–85). Fourth, against the claim that natural law theory, in committing the so-called naturalistic fallacy by its reduction of the simple putative property of goodness to a complex natural property, impugns the autonomy of ethics, Wild replies by rejecting the conception of goodness as an unanalyzable property, by defining good "as the realization of natural tendency," and by applying it "throughout all the categories of being" (7, pp. 85–93). Finally, against the contention that natural law has exerted "a reactionary influence upon history," though he concedes that individuals and institutions may have abused natural law, Wild emphatically denies that it is intrinsically reactionary. On the contrary, he cites natural law as the source of man's most progressive moral ideals, for, as he points out, it "is founded on tendential facts of human nature" (7, p. 96).

It should be clear that, for Wild, the metaphysics of essence, existence, and tendency not only supports the moral validity of natural law but also satisfies the dynamic demands of the philosophy of flux. In this respect it awakens memories of one of Wild's earliest published essays on the strategy of evolution, written when he was deeply influenced by the naturalism and instrumentalism of the Chicago school. Viewing the pervasiveness of purpose in nature, Wild then envisioned a grand strategy which, going beyond the dualism of life and matter and even beyond the dualism of the temporal and the eternal, reveals the emergence of the timeless from the temporal. With youthful enthusiasm Wild proclaimed:

The grand strategy of evolution is nothing more than what we notice constantly in the inner life of man, the devolution of the physical, coordinate with evolution of the spirit, till perhaps it develops beyond development, and matter disappears. I do not know what other worlds or realms of existence there may be, but this world seems to be a self-transcending process, ultimately achieving oneness with that absolute and changeless Being, of which we catch glimpses in the universal promptings which lie back of the moral strivings of men, and particularly in the space-and-time transcending flights of knowledge (17, p. 312).

No equation of Wild's early conception of the strategy of cosmic evolution with his more mature conception of nature as tendential is intended. But an affinity may be noted. There is no pattern stored up in heaven for the guidance and judgment of human choice and action, but there is a goal. And this goal constitutes the natural law as the moral law. It denotes no cosmic necessity but represents the rational aspiration of natural man. By virtue of their nature men elect this goal and pursue it through the vicissitudes of existence. As Wild says: "Man is as much a part of nature as the tiger and the snake. But his nature is rational. He can understand his end or misunderstand it; and he can choose alternative ways of realizing it. He is not automatically propelled toward the goal like subrational beings. Hence, the natural law of human action is a moral law and hypothetical in character" (7, p. 23).

EXISTENTIAL DIRECTIONS

On the contemporary scene classical realism confronts two opposed philosophies: the analytic and the existentialist. Dominant in the Anglo-American world, analytic philosophy represents for Wild "the breakdown of modern philosophy," because of its incapacity to be truly empirical and to provide a phenomenological description of all the data of immediate experience. As Wild writes: "Modern philosophy has paid too much attention to the tools of logic and analysis and the building of vast constructive systems, and far too little to the wide ranges of immediate data that lie beyond the province of the restricted sciences. This is a primary reason for the breakdown of philosophy" (9, pp. 15–16). The breakdown is evident in all the major philosophical sciences. In metaphysics a flight from ontology has transpired because existence, the most pervasive datum of immediate experience, has been dismissed as an empty epithet and ontological distinctions have been treated as empirically meaningless verbalisms. In epistemology and logic the neglect of the intentionality of thought is linked with the repudiation of ontology, and the upshot has been subjectivism, or phenomenalism, or skepticism, or linguistic conventionalism, all philosophies which deny or doubt that there is an objective reality to which knowledge and logic are anchored. In ethics knowledge has been divorced from practice, just as it has been separated from reality, and this divorce, betrayed by the prevalence of noncognitivist theses in contemporary ethical theories, in effect condones moral blindness unilluminated by the guidance of reason.

Were analytic philosophy the only alternative to classical realism on the contemporary scene, Wild's stance would be wholly direct and simple. There would be nothing left for philosophers to do but to return to the wisdom of classical realism. However, at present still a third philosophy is thriving, though it is confined mainly to Europe. Commonly termed existentialism, this philosophy is not simply a movement of "rebellion and reconstruction" in the face of modern philosophy; it is also a revitalization and renovation of classical wisdom. From existentialism Wild, like many other contemporary thinkers, derives "new inspiration and real hope for the revival and reconstruction of philosophy in our time" (9, p. 26).

Existentialism as a Philosophy

Wild examines existentialism by tracing its history back to its origin in the thought of Søren Kierkegaard, by elucidating the central doctrines of Karl Jaspers, Martin Heidegger, Jean-Paul Sartre and Gabriel Marcel on a set of major questions in metaphysics, epistemology, anthropology, and ethics, by scrutinizing their writings to uncover common themes, and by evaluating them critically to pinpoint their strengths and weaknesses. Wild's aim is that of the philosopher: to discover the truth about existentialism and to ferret out the leads it may afford for positive philosophical endeavor.

Tracing the origin of existentialism back to Kierkegaard, Wild ascribes Kierkegaard's achievements to "a triumph of rational description and analysis—the revelation of new fields of experience hitherto buried in deep obscurity. Inspired by classical and Christian sources, he recovers many insights of this tradition, applying them in novel ways to modern problems and correcting many basic errors of modern philosophy. Instead of wasting his time on constructive

interpretation and system building, he devotes himself to the accurate description of facts as they are given in the concrete" (9,
p. 54). In this sense Kierkegaard sets the stage for existentialism. For
in the hands of thinkers like Jaspers, Heidegger, Sartre, and Marcel,
existentialism is simply radical empiricism in metaphysics, anthropology, and ethics, centered upon phenomenological ontology. Wild
not only departs from the standard interpretation of the history of
existentialism in the way he treats the European founders and leaders of the movement, he also pioneers a point of view in maintaining that existentialism has at least one set of American roots, in the
philosophy of William James, whom he calls "the first American
existential philosopher" (11, p. 17). and whom he credits with having "contributed to every one of the major phases of existentialist
thought" (11, p. 29; 18).

The revival of ontology, whether in existentialism or in realism,
is rooted in phenomenological descriptions of immediate experience
productive of metaphysical protocols. But existentialism, unlike
classical realism, focuses its phenomenological investigations upon
human experiences that are usually neglected—upon awareness and
its structure, upon moods of feeling, such as care and guilt, upon the
phenomena of choice and its conditions—in short, upon human existence and its situation. Setting out from these newly disclosed data,
the existentialist advances his ontology-based philosophy. The successes of existentialism Wild readily acknowledges. Its probing
analyses of awareness, care, and time, elements found in everyone's
experience simply by virtue of his humanity, turn up phenomenological data upon which a novel and profound ontology of man, a
philosophical anthropology, may be erected. Similarly, existentialism
directs the phenomenological method upon the human phenomena
of choice and decision, engendering vital ethical theories firmly
rooted in the existence of human freedom. Like awareness, care,
and time, freedom is looked upon as a mode of existence—a way
of being-in-the-world. Consequently, existentialism inaugurates intensified investigations into topics central to philosophical theory
and ethical practice yet often ignored by traditional thinking.

Despite a high regard for the worth of existentialism, Wild is
cognizant of its weaknesses. Although, for example, he has cited

Heidegger's theory of time and history, based upon a phenomeno-logical scrutiny of human existence, as "certainly one of the most profound and original expressions of existentialist phenomenology" (9, p. 115), he argued in his presidential address to the Metaphysi-cal Society of America that this conception of time, profoundly perti-nent to human experience, needs supplementation by world time, a cosmic dimension which establishes an order of succession and an objective real framework in which change with all its novelty occurs. Wild says: "The greatest defect in Heidegger's analysis is his ten-dency to neglect the omnipresent flow of world time, and even at certain points to interpret it as a mere unauthentic mode of time as existence" (19, p. 555). Wild systematically spells out the major de-fects of existentialist thought. As regards method, the existentialists, though right in their emphasis upon phenomenology, have so far restricted this method "to *human* existence alone, and have paid relatively little attention to other levels and manifestations of being. They have given us no philosophy of nature, but only an anthro-pological fragment" (9, p. 179). As regards metaphysics, the existen-tialists rightly deplore the traditional exaggeration of the inactive, timeless structure of essence and stress instead the importance of the existential categories, but unfortunately they tend to slur over es-sence and even sometimes to abandon it. "Essence," Wild remarks, "is coordinate with existence; one is never given without the other" (9, p. 181). As regards epistemology, the existentialist is right in call-ing attention to human moods and feelings and thereby in avoiding a confining detached intellectualism, yet with his attacks upon reason and systematic thinking, he has fallen into the opposite error of anti-intellectualism. As regards ethics, the existentialists are right in their attentiveness to human freedom, so often overlooked by phi-losophers under the influence of scientific determinism, but unfor-tunately they sometimes "press their assertion of freedom to such lengths that it becomes fantastic and unbelievable" (9, p. 183).

Exploration of the Lebenswelt

According to Wild, the most significant contribution of existen-tial philosophy is the exploration of the *Lebenswelt* (life-world).

Not mentioned as such in Wild's first writings on existentialism, the term has cropped up in several of his recent articles, was used in his book *Human Freedom and Social Order,* and served as the topic of his 1960 presidential address to the Eastern Division of the American Philosophical Association (20), which was reprinted in revised form in his latest book *Existence and the World of Freedom.* The *Lebenswelt,* current in contemporary European thought and derived from Husserl, who employs the concept in his *Krisis der Europaischen Wissenschaften,* "is the world of history into which we are born, in which we exist and engage ourselves in our chosen projects, and in which we die. It is the world of ordinary language with its wealth of concrete usage, its obscurities, and ambiguities" (11, p. 60). According to Wild, the concept of the *Lebenswelt* promises a meeting place for the Continental existentialists and the British analysts of ordinary language (11, pp. 41 ff.).

Wild regards the exploration of the *Lebenswelt* to be "the most noteworthy philosophical achievement of our time" (10, p. 90). Although in *Plato's Theory of Man* Wild accepted the verdict of Plato on the phenomena of concrete life in contradistinction to the intelligible entities accessible to objective mathematical reasoning and dialectic, he has since undergone a radical change of mind. Wild once stressed the message of the allegory of the cave, esteeming it to be sound advice for leading man out of confusion and error on the way up to the most intelligible entities that guide sound moral practice and social policy; he now condemns this image as indicative of the traditional philosophers' disparagement of the *Lebenswelt.* "On this point," remarks Wild, "Plato made a mistake from which the West has not yet recovered. The universe of science does not encompass and precede the world of life" (10, p. 65). In a brilliant tour de force Wild contends that the real truth is portrayed by the inversion of Plato's image of the cave. He writes:

If we were to give a picture of *these* facts [of the *Lebenswelt*] in terms of Plato's famous myth, we would have to invert the image. . . . The world that is already there in the first place is not the underground cavern but the vast upper region where men work and struggle out of doors in the light of the sun. It is here that human life and history begins. Rational thinkers and scientists are a special group of men. In this respect Plato was right. But they do not climb up. They descend into a gloomy, cavernous region of their own, more adapted to the weakness of their eyes (10, p. 63).

Under the spell of Plato's mistake philosophy has become abstract, academic, sterile; it can be cured only by the phenomenological exploration of the *Lebenswelt*.

Following the lead of French thought, Wild distinguishes primary thinking from secondary reflection. He writes:

Primary thought is spontaneous, always concerned and interested, often creative, but uncritical. It is to this type of thought that we owe the first original answers that have been given to the ambiguities and agonies of life. But when left to itself, without criticism, this style of reflection becomes provincial, fanatical, and closed to what is universally human. Secondary reflection, on the other hand, is reflective and disinterested, self-conscious, critical, and open to the universal. It is through this type of secondary reflection, when it is in touch with the former, that fanaticism is avoided, and our existence in the life-world is kept open and free. When left to itself, however, it becomes abstract, sterile, and uncreative (11, p. 62).

Both types of thought are indispensable to philosophy; and the phenomenological exploration of the *Lebenswelt* heals the breach between the two, or at least connects secondary reflection intimately with primary thought—the creative source in experience of our fundamental concepts and values.

Wild considers the *Lebenswelt* to be the most inclusive, unlimited horizon of lived fact and value from which the objective fields of the special sciences are but impoverished abstractions. The *Lebenswelt* is sharply demarcated from the objective universe of science and rational understanding. Whereas the objective universe is a partial horizon abstracted from the world as lived, the *Lebenswelt*, expressed by the revealing power of ordinary language, is a total horizon, spatial and temporal, subjective and objective, factual and value-rich.

At several levels of analysis and description the central significance of the *Lebenswelt* is illuminated by contrast with the objective universe of the sciences. At the level of fact, which is defined as "any bit of evidence that is forced upon our attention whether we will or no" (11, p. 66), world facts are marked off from scientific facts. World facts, or historical facts, are complex, including physical, sociological, and subjective factors. "World facts . . . are temporal and existential,—always open to the global world horizon which is beyond the range of objective reason and science," while "scientific facts are abstract; they reveal human existence and its global meanings only in so far as they can be objectified and thus deprived of their ambiguities and openness" (11, p. 67). At the level of meaning, scientific meanings, which deal with abstract essences or causal laws that afford a measure of control over the individual events they subsume, are distinguished from world meanings, described as interpretations which, permeated with subjective concerns, place facts in a broader field of meaning, which we at least dimly understand and seem to share in common.

The intent of world meaning is understanding rather than the control over facts sought by scientific meaning. But understanding, according to Wild, may be either objective understanding or world understanding. Objective understanding operates upon the limited horizon of scientific facts and meanings, and while it provides a mastery over nature, manifest in technology, it fails to comprehend the thinker himself as a dynamic existence. This is a grave omission, testifying to the glaring defectiveness of objective understanding. For, as Wild has argued, existence is known immediately in the first act of one's own existing awareness (21). Since world understanding penetrates to the existence of the individual dynamic thinker, it grasps all facts, subjective and objective, in their concrete wholeness. Radiating from the individual existent consciousness which erupts into "this darkness of beings" and which brings them "into a world of meaning which was not there before" (21d, p. 414), world understanding is the mother of world meanings.

According to Wild, who refuses to accept the positivist restriction of truth to the facts and meanings of objective scientific understanding, these world meanings, or interpretations, stemming from the *Lebenswelt* are capable of attaining truth. Although the evidence of the *Lebenswelt* does not suffice to establish exclusively one single ontology, it does rule out many as egregiously false. Despite variant human interpretations, Wild is still convinced that the world is a unity. He concedes that philosophy is involved in an incessant dialectic, but this dialectic, he says, testifies to the exercise of human freedom in the interpretation of the world. As he puts the matter: "Philosophy is the discipline of freedom, and her first responsibility is to keep freedom alive. But this does not mean that all interpretations can be dismissed as subjective opinions on the same plane. Some express lasting types and structures of the world, and call forth authentic existence. Others are false to the world as it is. They enslave, disintegrate, and dehumanize man" (11, p. 75).

Toward a Christian Philosophy

Between the *Lebenswelt* and the objective universe a struggle ensues at present—in Wild's phrase, "the war of the worlds" (11, p. 80). The resolution of this war, according to Wild, requires not only the concession of the primacy of the *Lebenswelt* but also the possibility of a Christian philosophy. Amid the conflicting interpretations which unsettle all meanings and values and menace the pacific order of human life, the test of Christian faith is crucial. Stimulated by Emile Brehier's challenging judgment that a Christian philosophy has never been formulated (22), and relying upon the phenomenological exploration of the *Lebenswelt* for insights, Wild sketches in *Human Freedom and Social Order* what an authentic Christian philosophy is and indicates how it assists in the solution of moral and political problems both in theory and practice. Wild explores the development of Christian thought from myth to reason, examines the failures of rationalism—i.e. gnosticism—surveys rival conceptions of the relations of faith and reason, and offers his own idea of Christian philosophy to fill the void noted by Brehier which had been approached but not filled by Augustine, Pascal, and Kierkegaard. From a consideration of the import of Christian philosophy, Wild proceeds to discuss Christian ethics and social philosophy, differentiating the methods and contents of classical and Christian ethical theories, clarifying the gulf between the morality of Christian persons and the immorality of social and political groups, and proposing to bridge this gulf.

According to recent anthropology and phenomenology, myth is the first answer man has for the disturbing questions concerning his existence and destiny when his earliest efforts to transcend his natural situation result in a sense of alienation and danger. Although myth suffices originally by projecting an atemporal, immutable, tribal world which consumes the individual in the group and freezes change in ritual, it readily crumbles under the scrutiny of reason, historically exemplified by Socrates. Gnosticism then arises, promising complete objective scientific systems to supplant the deteriorating tribal *Lebenswelt* crystallized in myth and to unify the multiple conflicting perspectives of individual experiences. But since gnosticism's neglect of subjectivity deprives it of firm anchorage in subjectively lived experience, it becomes a doctrine in the history of philosophy and therefore succumbs to the incessant strife of philosophical systems. Mythological as well as rational, religion in its Christian form exhibits man's "ultimate devotion to a transcendent mystery directly encountered in the world of concrete existence" (10, p. 34). It focuses on the individual person; it employs the language of human experience; it points to historical events; it acknowledges the primacy of change in the possibilities of personal conversions and persistent reorientations toward God. But Christianity has so far failed to generate its own philosophy.

Wild's proposal of a Christian philosophy pivots on his interpretation of the relation between Christian faith and philosophical reason, necessitated partly by the alleged collapse of all traditional treatments of this relation, but suggested primarily by the phenomenologists' rediscovery of the *Lebenswelt*. Faith, construed as "the ultimate concern for which we are ready to make real sacrifices in ordering our existence," and reason, defined as "the exact understanding of things around us and of our changing situation in history" (10, p. 85), must be reconciled by mutually constituting "a flexible, dialectical tension with each other." Wild continues: "Like the two sides of the arch, each is dependent on the other, and yet at the same time independent, making its own contribution in its own way" (10, p. 91). Reason proceeds only on evidence and produces science and philosophy; but philosophy is more than science, because it "envelops all human existence, including science" (10, p. 88), and deals not merely with objects but with "lived experience which is neither exclusively subjective nor exclusively objective, but both together in one" (10, pp. 88–89). Philosophical investigations, however, are incomplete, since they revolve around "basic concepts like being, truth, value, and meaning which are partially indeterminate." The clarification of these concepts, Wild contends, "must rest on faith in a guiding image of some sort that cannot be conclusively confirmed by any available evidence" (10, p. 90). "As other philosophers have taken their basic assumptions from images current in the culture of their times, the Christian philosopher openly accepts the guiding image of his faith in making ultimate clarifications where the evidence falls short" (10, p. 92).

Wild's conception of the dialectical interplay of faith and reason in true philosophy signifies no abrupt break in his intellectual development, but rather represents a recovery of a conception expressed in his work on Berkeley. "Just as faith is the inescapable 'refuge' of reason, so is reason the inescapable 'refuge' of faith, and we are forced inevitably from the one to the other. There can be no 'blind' faith, for not to see is to see nothing. Before we can reason we must have faith in reason" (3, p. 389). Accordingly, Berkeley is rated a philosopher in the full sense of the term only when he has reached the point—beyond skepticism, beyond rationalism— at which faith and reason cooperate in dialectical equilibrium.

When philosophy becomes Christian, it does not merely satisfy the intellectual yearnings of man; it also contributes an invaluable element to moral and political thought and action. Whereas the classical ethic of happiness depicts the moral agent as a static self rationally deliberating the choice of courses of action presumably most instrumental to the realization of ends fixed by its own nature prior to any activity, the Christian ethic of love focuses on the radical freedom of the individual person to break with his past and to sacrifice himself to God. The classical ethic of self-realization, therefore, does not apply to Christian men oriented toward God; rather, it is descriptive of human behavior of social and political groupings.

Wild undertakes to define the distinctive idea of freedom entailed by Christianity and allegedly confirmed by phenomenological investigations of the *Lebenswelt*. Freedom, he writes in *Human Freedom and Social Order*, is "being-open-to-otherness. It is a capacity for self-transcendence-to" (10, p. 180). In *Existence and the World of Freedom* Wild elaborates his case. Freedom, he maintains, consists in spontaneity, activity, and indeterminacy. And, he continues, it "is an act of self-transcendence, or, as we may say, an active-being-open-to-what-is-other. . . . Freedom is this openness to what is other" (11, p. 127). Moreover, it is indispensable to responsibility, the foundation of morality. And as the openness-to-other, freedom is the ground of understanding in general; the understanding, when employing the determinist categories of science, cannot legitimately deny freedom.

Intrinsically free acts are "acts of giving." The genuinely free act is "that total sacrifice of the self to the transcendent which is the central act of Christian faith" (10, p. 181). In this sacrifice, moreover, all is gained, since personal freedom mediates nature and Grace: "through this fragile channel of personal freedom . . . Grace first enters human history" (10, p. 216). Wild's conception of freedom is explicitly intended to avoid both the subsumptions of freedom within objective frames that lean toward determinism and the absolute humanistic freedom propounded by Sartre. Personal freedom, Wild insists, is "socially conditioned, not unlimited" (10, p. 232). By entering through the freedom of the individual, Grace elevates this individual to a plane of existence higher than that occupied by individuals who are wholly immersed in nature. Thus Wild strives to attenuate the classical distinction between nature and Grace, since it is "oversimplified and fails to focus the intermediate world of human freedom which lies between, or rather brings these two together in the sweeping horizon of the world of man" (10, p. 215). Although it is the unity of God which guarantees the harmony of the two orders of Grace and nature, the efficacy of Grace in human history is wholly dependent upon the exercise of human freedom: "Grace must first be received into the heart of man and exercised by free decision" (10, p. 216).

Wild's exploration of the *Lebenswelt* results not only in a conception of freedom as openness-to-others, as self-transcendence, but also in a new approach to the ancient question concerning proofs for the existence of God—or, in the new language, "an existential argument for transcendence." The "world fact" with which the existential argument starts is "the restlessness of existence-in-the-world, which drives us beyond any fixed form or pattern, and works in us as a first, creative ferment in our human history" (11, p. 206). This restlessness drives man from one limited perspective to another, taking him beyond any human achievement. It is an urge toward self-transcendence, or, in Wild's words, "the image of the divine in man" (11, p. 215). Thus from the world fact of restlessness Wild concludes that "there is a transcendent unity, which is the ultimate, creative source of meaning and being, and of the unity of the world" (11, p. 219). Alluding to the affinity of his argument to the ontological argument Wild identifies this "transcendent unity" with God.

Further, Wild's identification of freedom with being-open-to-otherness provides a foundation for Christian social order. Kierkegaard has no social philosophy, and some existentialist thinkers, like Niebuhr and Berdyaev, because of the blatant division between private Christian morality and public immorality, have come to hold that there are two ethical standards. Wild, however, stands apart from such views. Urging adherence to the idea of Christian philosophy in order to close the gap between the two moral universes and establish a social order which maximizes human freedom, Wild resorts to natural law. As noted above, natural law is founded upon the essential nature of man and the dynamic tendencies to satisfy the needs that spring from this essential nature. This law, moreover, is rational and consequently accessible to reason. In fact, the doctrine of natural law is an integral part of classical realism. With the rise of existentialism the ethical situation, for which formerly natural law was sufficient, has become more complex, involving existential as well as natural norms. In this respect the fundamental contribution of existentialism is its lucid and profound analysis of human freedom. As Wild observes: "Freedom is not a natural but an existential norm. It is not an ordered set of determinate tendencies but a way of realizing them in the concrete that is peculiar to man" (9,

p. 262). Hence neither classical realism nor contemporary existentialism alone affords an adequate ethics, for, in Wild's words: "Natural law must be reconciled with existential freedom" (9, p. 267).

In the past decade Wild has devoted himself to the fusing of realism with existentialist themes, though the success of his efforts at synthesis is at present indeterminate. Rich in ideas and learning, Wild has the intellectual and moral passion to address himself to the pressing problems of an epoch which seem to go unnoticed in the logically tidy writings of many American professional philosophers. Persuasively suggestive rather than cogently systematic, Wild's work is critically portentous. Not only does it promise to synthesize rational classical realism with a dialectically tense Christian existentialism, it also reveals how the return to classical reason, when goaded by narrow analytic strictures in Anglo-American circles and challenged by existentialist movements in Europe, may find support in the embrace of faith.

NOTES TO CHAPTER VIII

1   Sydney and Beatrice Rome (eds.), *Philosophical Interrogations* (New York: Holt, Rinehart and Winston, 1964).
2   John Wild (ed.), *Spinoza: Selections* (New York and Chicago: Scribner's, 1930).
3   John Wild, *George Berkeley: A Study of His Life and Philosophy* (Cambridge: Harvard University Press, 1936).
4   John Wild, *Plato's Theory of Man: An Introduction to the Realistic Philosophy of Culture* (Cambridge: Harvard University Press, 1946).
5   John Wild, *Introduction to Realistic Philosophy* (New York: Harper, 1948).
6   John Wild (ed.), *The Return to Reason: Essays in Realistic Philosophy* (Chicago: Henry Regnery, 1953).
7   John Wild, *Plato's Modern Enemies and the Theory of Natural Law* (Chicago: University of Chicago Press, 1953).
8   See, for example, the following articles by John Wild: (a) "Kierkegaard and Classic Philosophy," *Philosophical Review*, XLIX (1940), 536–51; (b) "Husserl's Critique of Psychologism: Its Historic Roots and Contemporary Revelance," in Marvin Farber (ed.), *Philosophical Essays in Memory of Edmund Husserl* (Boston: Harvard University, 1940), 19–43; (c) "On the Nature and Aims of Phenomenology," *Philosophy and Phenomenological Research*, III (1942–43), 85–95. As early as 1936, Paul Weiss, a longtime friend of Wild, described Wild's mind as "seared by Kierkegaard," in his review of *George Berkeley* in *New Republic*, LXXXVIII (August 19, 1936), 52.
9   John Wild, *The Challenge of Existentialism* (Bloomington: Indiana University Press, 1955).

10 John Wild, *Human Freedom and Social Order: An Essay in Christian Philosophy* (Durham: Duke University Press, 1959).

11 John Wild, *Existence and the World of Freedom* (Englewood Cliffs, N. J.: Prentice-Hall, 1963).

12 Henry Veatch, a former student of John Wild at Harvard, formerly Distinguished Service Professor of Philosophy at Indiana University and professor of philosophy at Northwestern University, has reported that, in response to Wild's call to write a textbook on realistic logic, he set out to do so only to discover that it was necessary first to write a more technical treatise on the nature of logic in consonance with the tenets of realism and in opposition to the new mathematical logic. See Veatch's *Intentional Logic: A Logic Based on Philosophical Realism* (New Haven: Yale University Press, 1952), vi–vii. Veatch's textbook on logic came later, in collaboration with his former student Francis Parker, now professor of philosophy at Purdue University. See their *Logic as a Human Instrument* (New York: Harper and Row, 1959). More recently Veatch has prepared a realist ethics. See his *Rational Man: A Modern Interpretation of Aristotelian Ethics* (Bloomington: Indiana University Press, 1962). Veatch served as editor of the interrogation of John Wild, but because of Wild's change of beliefs during the course of the interrogation, Veatch has denied responsibility for the final product (1, p. 5).

13 John Wild, "What Is Realism?", *Journal of Philosophy*, XLIV (1947), 148–58.

14 John Wild, "Cartesian Deformation of the Structure of Change and Its Influence on Modern Thought," *Philosophical Review*, L (1941), 36–59.

15 John Wild, "A Realistic Defence of Causal Efficacy," *Review of Metaphysics*, II (June, 1949), 1–14.

16 See A. O. Lovejoy, *Essays in the History of Ideas* (Baltimore: The Johns Hopkins Press, 1948).

17 John Wild, "Grand Strategy of Evolution," in T. V. Smith and W. K. Wright (eds.), *Essays in Philosophy* (LaSalle, Ill.: Open Court, 1929).

18 John Wild, "William James and Existential Authenticity," *Journal of Existentialism*, V (1965), 243–56.

19 John Wild, "The New Empiricism and Human Time," *Review of Metaphysics*, VII (1953–54), 537–57.

20 John Wild, "The Exploration of the Life-World," *Proceedings and Addresses of the American Philosophical Association*, 1960–1961, pp. 5–23.

21 (a) See John Wild, "Contemporary Phenomenology and the Problem of Existence," *Philosophy and Phenomenological Research*, XX (1959–60), 166–80. See also the discussion this article provoked: (b) Frederick J. Adelmann, S.J., "The Root of Existence," *ibid.*, XXII (1961–62), 405–408; (c) Calvin O. Schrag, "John Wild on Contemporary Philosophy," *ibid.*, XXII (1961–62), 409–12; and (d) John Wild, "Reply to Father Adelmann and Professor Schrag," *ibid.*, XXII (1961–62), 412–15.

22 Emile Brehier, "Y a-t-il une philosophie Chrétienne?" *Revue de Métaphysique et de Morale*, XXXVIII (1931), 133–62.

IX

CHARLES HARTSHORNE

Process Philosophy, Panpsychism, and Panentheism

INTRODUCTION

"A metaphysics of becoming and relativity is," writes Charles Hartshorne, "the modern task" (1, p. 191). "Metaphysics seeks," he
continues, "the essential nature of becoming which does not itself
become and cannot pass away; or, it seeks the universal principle of
relativity whose validity is absolute. 'Nothing is absolute but relativity'—this saying, which I heard as a student, and which meant
nothing much to me at the time, I have come to see as, properly
construed, the secret of secrets . . ." (1, p. 192). This metaphysics
of becoming and of relativity, this process philosophy, is, moreover,
a metaphysics of love. As Hartshorne writes: "A metaphysics of love,
that is, of socially structured, or relative, creative experience is what
we need, whether in ethics, religion, or politics—indeed, in all our
basic concerns" (1, p. 210).

Charles Hartshorne is without question the most persuasive living
spokesman of the philosophy of creative process. Born in Kittaning,
Pennsylvania, on June 5, 1897, Hartshorne was educated at Harvard
University, where he received his B.A. in 1921, his M.A. in 1922,
and his Ph.D. in 1923. He also studied at the German universities
of Freiburg and Marburg, where he became directly acquainted with
the phenomenological philosophy of Husserl (2). From 1925 to
1928 he was a member of the department of philosophy at Harvard
as an assistant in philosophy and a resident fellow. At Harvard he
came under the influence of Alfred North Whitehead. He also began to edit for publication the writings of Charles Sanders Peirce.

Some years later Paul Weiss joined him, and together they succeeded in bringing out the standard edition of Peirce's works (3).
In 1928 Hartshorne joined the faculty of the University of Chicago
as an instructor in philosophy, and in 1948 he became a full professor. In 1955 he was appointed professor of philosophy at Emory
University in Atlanta, and since 1962 he has been Ashbel Smith
Professor of Philosophy at the University of Texas. He has also
served as a Fulbright professor in Australia and in Japan. The high
regard in which he is held by his colleagues is evident in the fact
that he has been elected president of several professional organizations: the Western Division of the American Philosophical Association, the Peirce Society, the Metaphysical Society of America, the
Southern Society for the Philosophy of Religion, and the Southern
Society for Philosophy and Psychology. And in 1964 friends, colleagues, and former students gathered together to present him with
a distinguished *Festschrift* (4). In addition to his work as a professional philosopher, Hartshorne has found the leisure to contribute
numerous papers to ornithology (4, p. 591).

Two philosophers have had a great influence on the thought of
Charles Hartshorne. Peirce, whose impact is evident in the works of
Columbia naturalists, of James Feibleman, and of Paul Weiss, has
also affected profoundly the thought of Charles Hartshorne. But
deeper and broader than Peirce's influence on Hartshorne has been
Whitehead's. There should be nothing startling in the fact that both
Peirce and Whitehead could shape a philosopher's thought. Other
commentators have concurred with Hartshorne in perceiving "as-
tounding" similarities between the philosophies of Whitehead and
Peirce (5). Still, Hartshorne has rated the influence of Whitehead
higher. He confesses that he has "no doubt" that Whitehead has
"achieved the major metaphysical synthesis of our day" (6, p. 212).
Perhaps no contemporary thinker has gone as far as Charles Hartshorne in the adoption, adaptation, elaboration, and defense of
Whiteheadian ideas (7). Neither limiting the source of his ideas
to Whitehead nor refraining from novel variations on his own,
Hartshorne has nonetheless insisted that there is a present convergence of views in metaphysics, constituting in effect a consistent yet

viable movement, and that this movement is most adequately and coherently articulated in the philosophy of Whitehead. "I take it," Hartshorne writes, "that Bergson, James, Fechner, Alexander, Whitehead, Varisco, Scheler, Ward, Boutroux, Montague, Parker, Garnett, Hocking, Boodin, and others, including the present writer, are in a certain rough agreement that is somewhat more striking and representative of metaphysics since about 1850 than is any other trend" (8, p. 131). Of this new trend, which is epitomized in the title of one of his books, *Reality as Social Process*, Hartshorne remarks: "Whitehead is its Einstein, Leibniz was its Newton . . ." (8, p. 31).

Hartshorne's philosophy may be viewed as a creative variation of the new trend in metaphysics. His first book, *The Philosophy and Psychology of Sensation*, introduces into psychological theory principles of continuity and aesthetic feeling espoused by the new metaphysics in the philosophy of mathematics and of nature, and the upshot is the novel doctrine of the affective continuum (9). Hartshorne's next book, *Beyond Humanism*, announces the movement as "a genuine integration of all the modern motifs" culminating in a new theology, which he designates "theistic naturalism or naturalistic theism," and which he presents in contrast with and in opposition to its great contemporary rival, "non-theistic" humanism (10, pp. viii–x). *Man's Vision of God* undertakes to formulate the logic of the new theism and to demonstrate its superiority to the classical synthesis of Thomas Aquinas (11). In these works Hartshorne expounds and defends a metaphysics of panpsychism; he also suggests what he subsequently develops more fully as a theology of panentheism. In his Terry Lectures at Yale, later expanded and published as *The Divine Relativity* (12), Hartshorne systematically formulates the panentheistic conception of deity, a conception which owes much to Whitehead (13). *Philosophers Speak of God*, which Hartshorne edited with William Reese, presents and discusses all the important possible conceptions of deity; Hartshorne argues in the comments and in the opening and concluding chapters for the validity of panentheism (14).

For his book *The Logic of Perfection* (15), Hartshorne won the

Lecomte du Nouy prize. Like *Reality as Social Process*, it is primarily a collection of scattered essays which amplify and extend his philosophy. However, the second essay, the monograph which occasioned the publication of the volume, breaks new ground in the development of recent theology, for it offers the most technical and profound restatement of the ontological argument for the existence of God in modern philosophy and theology. Hartshorne's book *Anselm's Discovery* (16) offers, as the subtitle states, "A Re-examination of the Ontological Argument for God's Existence"; it is divided into two parts: first, an extensive consideration of Anselm's proofs in the new perspectives of logic and history, and second, a critical survey of the responses to Anselm's proofs from Gaunilo to Frederick Fitch. Further amplification of Hartshorne's theology is found in his book on natural theology for our time (19). Hartshorne has come to term his position in metaphysics and theology "neoclassical." Classical metaphysics posits a statically perfect God, predicated upon a philosophy of substance. Neoclassical metaphysics posits a perfect God who surpasses himself, includes temporal entities and events, and so possesses a relative changing aspect, predicated upon a metaphysics of social process. At present Hartshorne is writing a massive system of metaphysics to sum up his point of view.

This chapter will explore the three main aspects of Hartshorne's thought: the affective continuum, panpsychism and social realism, and panentheism. Although it has been suggested that these ideas are specifications and variations of themes characteristic of the new trend in philosophy of which, admittedly, Whitehead is the leading exponent, this does not mean that Hartshorne's thought is merely derivative. Hartshorne is a creative metaphysician of extraordinary ability, remarkable for his speculative originality as well as for his logical rigor.

THE AFFECTIVE CONTINUUM

In *The Philosophy and Psychology of Sensation* Hartshorne investigates the concept of sensation in the light of ideas which, despite fruitful employment in the interpretation of the physical sciences, had not yet been applied to psychological science. Unfortunately obsolete concepts, incompatible with the philosophical principles required by the recent revolutions in the physical and biological sciences, still held sway in psychology, particularly as regards sensation. Hartshorne's theme, therefore, is that "the application of scientific and rational principles to the sensory qualities results in a new theory of these 'immediate data of consciousness,' considered both in themselves and in relation to their physical stimuli, organic conditions, biological significance, and evolutionary origin" (9, p. 6).

Against Materialism

To this new theory of the immediate data of consciousness the prevailing alternative, an alternative continued in psychology in spite of its obsolescence in physics, is materialism. In the modified sense Hartshorne accepts, materialism supposes that "matter in what may be called the 'bad' sense, exists" (9, p. 11). Materialism posits the existence of atoms, discontinuous, discrete, independent bits of matter, devoid of feeling and life, isolated except for accidental external relations, timeless and unchanging with respect to internal constitution and hence without growth or evolution. This conception of matter, fostered by Newtonian physics, has been rejected as a result of the recent revolutions in physics, which, according to Hartshorne, give "more encouragement in detail to the Whiteheadian conception of events composed of aesthetic feeling as the materials of all nature than Newtonian physics could give to Leibnizian monadology" (9, pp. 16–17). But if materialism is repudiated in physics, it must also be repudiated in psychology, where materialistic modes of thought still linger, not only, as is obvious, in the rise of behaviorism but also in the theories of sensation. As long as psychologists adopt theories of sensation which treat sensations as discrete data, separated from each other, sharply distinguished from feeling, and isolated on the one hand from the internal neural processes of the sentient organism and on the other hand from the external physical stimuli, they are, unwittingly perhaps, adhering to an outmoded materialism.

But what theory does the application of the new principles in physics and philosophy to the psychology of sensation suggest? Hartshorne's answer is the theory of the affective continuum. According to this theory, "the contents of sensation form an 'affective continuum' of aesthetically meaningful, socially expressive, organically adaptive and evolving experience functions" (9, p. 9). The immediate data of consciousness comprise an ever-changing field of interpenetrating qualities, the qualities differentiated against a background of feelings socially involved with the feelings of others. The continuum is *affective*, since it is generated from contrasts of joy and sorrow, liking and disliking, etc., characteristic of feeling, and since the discrimination of contents within the continuum depends upon their comparison with recognizable forms of affectivity (9, pp. 9–10). Affection, or feeling, then, forms a *continuum*. Although holes do exist in any experienced continuum of sensory qualities, they may be construed in such a way that the continuum is unimpaired. Regardless of its seemingly hypothetical character, the continuum of affection is empirically significant "not only in its enlightening us with regard to what may exist even though as yet unobserved by us, but also in the fact that measurement of degrees of difference can take place as it were over the holes" (9, p. 10).

Elucidation of the Affective Continuum

The theory of the affective continuum centers upon five conceptions.

The first conception involves the application of mathematical continuity to sensation. As Hartshorne puts it: "The type of relation existing between colors, whereby one is connected with or shades into another through intermediaries, can be generalized so as to connect qualities from different senses (e.g., a color and a sound) or from different elementary classes (e.g., secondary and tertiary qualities)" (9, p. 6). Mathematical philosophy, in accord with Whitehead's method of extensive abstraction, considers points not as elements of which the continuum is composed but rather as ideal limits of abstraction from the continuum. And physics, in line with Whitehead's criticism of the fallacy of simple location, views its ultimate physical elements of analysis as wave-packets into which the entire physical system focuses. Similarly, psychology may regard sensations as discriminable aspects of a continuum of felt quality. The point is illustrated by the color scale, which "is not an aggregate of colors, but a qualitative unity" (9, p. 42). "Colors are thus aspects of the one fact which is 'color' " (9, p. 43). What is true for color is true for all sensations and for all feelings as well. Citing empirical evidence which Berkeley had noticed long ago, Hartshorne observes: "Heat passes into practically pure pain as orange into red. . . . Thus, qualities from two senses, one of them by all natural human conviction akin to the 'tertiary' or affective factor of sense experience, have observably the same continuity of nature as qualities from one sense" (9, p. 50).

The second conception is the primacy of aesthetic meaning, or affective tone (Whitehead's "feeling-value"). "The 'affective' tonality, the aesthetic or tertiary quality, usually supposed to be merely 'associated with' a given sensory quality is, in part at least, identical with that quality, one with its nature or essence. Thus, the 'gaiety' of yellow (the peculiar highly specific gaiety) is the yellowness of yellow" (9, p. 7). Viewed as a subclass of feeling tones, sensory qualities are species for which feeling is the genus (9, p. 179). Moreover, the development of sensations out of feeling is, for Hartshorne, tantamount to asserting that "sensation is what feeling becomes when externally localized in phenomenal space," an assertion which he claims is supported by empirical evidence (9, p. 135).

The third conception emphasizes the fundamental social character of experience. "Experience," maintains Hartshorne, "is social throughout, to its uttermost fragments or 'elements.' Its every mode is a mode of sociability" (9, p. 8). Since, for Hartshorne, the sociality of experience entails panpsychism, this conception of the social structure of experience will be considered again when panpsychism and social realism are discussed. Here it suffices to state that the sociality of experience signifies, in Whitehead's phrase, "the feeling of feeling" (9, p. 193). Just as within the individual self simple memory testifies to the feeling of past feeling, so the self, according to Hartshorne, feels the feelings of the cells that comprise its organism (17). The extension of the principle of "the feeling of feeling" beyond human selves to God gives rise to the speculation that God in his self-enjoyment feels the feelings of all creatures. In this sense, "the world may be conceived as the necessary specifications of the theme 'feeling of feeling' " (9, p. 208).

The fourth conception has to do with biological adaptiveness. "The intrinsic natures of sensory qualities, and not merely the order and correlations in which they occur, express organic attitudes, or tend, of themselves, to incite modes of behavior; and these modes may be appropriate or useful, in relation to the physical circumstances generally accompanying the occurrence of the stimuli productive of the respective sensations" (9, p. 8). That sensations of pleasure and pain play a significant role in the adaptation of the organism to its environment is a commonplace, though the role of other sensations—e.g., sensations of color—is less clear. Hartshorne points out that these other sensations are also triggers to modes of behavior. Indeed, he argues that definite associations hold between particular modes of feeling and behavior and particular sensations of color or sound, and he concludes from this that psycho-physical associations are more fundamental in the life of the organism than associations of ideas (9, pp. 250 ff.).

The fifth conception pertains to evolution from a common origin. "The first appearance of a given quality at a certain stage in evolution is not a pure 'emergence' (though it has an emergent aspect) of the quality, unrelated to the previous state of nature, but is intelligible in much the same fashion as the appearance of a new organ" (9, p. 8). On this point—the evolution of sensory qualities from a common origin—Hartshorne's indebtedness to Peirce's category of firstness is pronounced. Thus a continuum of sheer, undifferentiated, indeterminate, vague feeling becomes determinate and specified, through a process of objectification, into particular sensory qualities (9, pp. 207–208).

PANPSYCHISM AND SOCIAL REALISM

The theory of the affective continuum, an elaboration of the Whiteheadian metaphysics of events as feelings of feelings, is linked in Hartshorne's thinking with the advocacy of panpsychism. Here the

influences on Hartshorne's philosophy are Leibniz as well as Whitehead, and to a lesser extent Gustav Fechner.

Meaning of Panpsychism

In its simplest form panpsychism asserts that "all the pronounced
units of matter are living" (10, p. 166). The plausibility of panpsychism hinges in large measure upon the discarding of the concept
of dead, static matter in physics, and, applying a concept from biological science, upon the general adoption of the cell theory of
reality. The discovery that the individual organism consists of living
cells becomes the principle, which Leibniz employed first with considerable success, whereby material objects at the macroscopic level
are construed to be colonies or aggregates of sentient microscopic
monads. Within the organism, it is held, "a cell is not only a living
but a sentient organism" (9, p. 244). Against the prospective objection that the cell cannot feel because it has no nervous system,
Hartshorne's retort is straightforward: The cell performs functions
of digestion and reproduction without the appropriate organs. Similarly, it may feel without the nervous system. "Lack of explicit organ
does not spell lack of function, but primitive form of the function"
(9, p. 244). The ascription of sentience to cells within the organism
suggests, furthermore, the consideration of the simplest physical
entities—electrons and other atomic particles—as centers of feeling
(9, pp. 249–50). That such entities are simple compared with higher
animals does not preclude that they possess mind and will and feeling; "it merely means a low degree of complexity, and hence it
is contrasted, not to mind and feeling and will in general, but to
complex types of mind and feeling and will" (11, p. 214).

The Leibnizian-Whiteheadian principle of interpreting macroscopic objects and organisms and even persons as societies of simpler,
microscopic sentient beings is the key to Hartshorne's advocacy of
social realism within the framework of panpsychism. Despite the
advances Fechner made, he failed to grasp the societal principle, a
failure that led him to treat composite organizations devoid of
personal order as "compound individuals," resulting in the bizarre
and discredited panpsychism which attributes souls to plants and

other macroscopic physical objects such as planets (14, p. 255a). The societal principle in Hartshorne's philosophy, by contrast, signifies that feeling, identified with the very stuff of consciousness and universally attributed to all being, is social. The feelings of an organism comprise complex feelings of the simpler feelings of the particular sentient beings, cells, that make up the organism; and these feelings in turn are feelings of the feelings of the yet simpler physical entities that constitute the external environment stimulating the cells of the organism. There is, then, a steady flow of feelings from the lower to the higher orders of organisms, even though some organizations of cells fall short of the high degree of unity necessary for personal order and integral consciousness.

The social structure of feeling is well illustrated by a consideration of color perceptions. The perception of a specific color—red, for instance—involves the supposition that the nerve cells are qualified by this color. But what can a nerve cell so qualified be like? In answer to this sort of question Hartshorne, like Whitehead, breaks with the bifurcation of nature into objective physical primary qualities and subjective mind-dependent secondary qualities. Adhering to a social realism which imputes a continuity of felt quality between the organism and its environment, he writes: "Red is a mode of feeling value, describable in terms of the dimensions of social affectivity as such. The nerve cells have feelings also determinable on these dimensions. The relation between red as we see it and red as it is in the nerves is the relation between the individual units of a complex of feelings and the complex as a single over-all quality" (9, p. 248).

Arguments for Panpsychism

In Hartshorne's philosophy the case for panpsychism rests upon six arguments.

The first argument is the argument from *causality*. According to this argument, the relations between past events and present ones, relations exemplified by causality, require the persistence of the past into the present. This persistence can be understood and the causal order in nature guaranteed, Hartshorne claims, only if we suppose the pervasive presence of experiences akin to memory, either in the form of rudimentary memory experiences in seemingly physical entities or in the form of an absolute cosmic memory which forgets nothing. The only alternative to this supposition is, Hartshorne insists, the positivistic denial of causality (8, pp. 78–79).

The second argument is the argument from *unity within diversity*. According to this argument, "apart from subjects" there is no principle for the one-in-the-many. Space and time and physical matter fail to provide the requisite unity (8, pp. 78–79).

The third argument is the argument from *contrast between particular and universal, actual and potential*. Although this contrast or polarity is a dominant characteristic of all being, it is intelligible, Hartshorne contends, only with respect to subjects with desires and consummations (8, pp. 79–80). This argument is closely related to the fifth argument.

The fourth argument is from *the nature of quality* and involves concepts related to the affective continuum. Briefly, this argument maintains that, since qualities qualify the object perceived and the nerve cells of the percipient organism, they indicate the presence of modes of feeling in both. "Thus all *known* qualities are actually qualities of feeling, whatever else they may be, and all knowable qualities are potentially qualities of feeling" (8, p. 80).

The fifth argument is the argument from *the realization of possibilities*. Realization is a process of deciding between possibilities, of choosing some and rejecting those which are incompatible with the ones selected. This process, prevalent throughout the natural cosmos, is tantamount to creative choice, and as Hartshorne insists, creative choice "seems totally unintelligible in the mere non-subject" (8, p. 82).

The sixth argument is the argument from *intrinsic value*. According to this argument, intrinsic value inheres in beings with lives and feelings that may excite the interest of others and be enjoyed by them. Such beings must be subjects in the panpsychical sense. To be interested, even in what common sense presumes to be dead matter, is, tacitly perhaps, to assume that values inhere in it, that, in other words, it is alive and feels. "The only intelligible conception of direct derivation of value from an object is," observes Hartshorne, "that the object has value to give, and this means, has its own values, its own life and feeling, and thus is some sort of subject" (8, p. 82).

Science, Knowledge, and Ontology

In addition to these six arguments which clarify and justify panpsychism, three important implications of the doctrine are discernible: in the philosophy of science, in the theory of knowledge, and in the ontology of individuality.

In the philosophy of science panpsychism means the unity of the sciences, but it is an unusual kind of unity. "Panpsychism is the doctrine that comparative psychology as psychophysiology . . . will ultimately include physics as the simplest branch" (10, p. 179). The mind-body interaction and the subject-object relation, which since Descartes have given rise to baffling philosophical problems, are dealt with effectively by Hartshorne in his treatment of these relations as consisting in bonds of organic sympathy, inasmuch as mind and body, subject and object are societies of sentient entities sharing each others' feelings. This solution to what has been in effect *the* problem of modern philosophy is a form of idealism, since it requires subsumption of the allegedly physical under the psychical. This idealism is consistent with Hartshorne's speculative method. Being is regarded as a system of infinite variations, the values of which are concretely described by the psychological concepts of feeling, willing, thinking, and remembering (10, pp. 115–18). As Hartshorne puts it: "We can generalize beyond human experience only by generalizing 'experience' itself beyond the human variety" (10, p. 122). Of course, it should be made clear that Hartshorne intends not to eliminate physics, but to retain it as a science confined to the simplest entities. "Physics is only the behavioristic aspect of the lowest branch of comparative psychology," while in view of the societal structure of reality "all psychology is in some sense social psychology, so that the final empirical science will be generalized comparative sociology" (11, p. 160).

In the theory of knowledge panpsychism means realism, but this realism is epistemological, and paradoxically it is compatible with and even culminates in metaphysical idealism. This theory, tantamount to a synthesis of idealism and realism, consists in the joint assertion of four theses:

(i) The principle of *Objective Independence*: "An 'object,' or that of which a particular subject is aware, in no degree depends upon that subject" (8, p. 70).

(ii) The principle of *Subjective Dependence*: "A 'subject,' or whatever is aware of anything, always depends upon the entities of which it is aware, its objects" (8, p. 70).

(iii) The principle of *Universal Objectivity*: "Any entity must be (or at least be destined to become) object for *some* subject or other" (8, p. 70).

(iv) The principle of *Universal Subjectivity*: "Any concrete entity is subject, or set of subjects" (8, p. 70).

Following Whitehead, Hartshorne calls the theory which asserts these four theses "reformed subjectivism"; he also calls it " 'societism' for it amounts to a social theory of reality" (8, p. 71).

In ontology panpsychism means the doctrine of "the compound individual." Whitehead's reformed subjectivist principle, adopted by Hartshorne, entails the consideration of macroscopic entities as consisting of microscopic subjects. Formulating a defensible theory of substantial individuality, while at the same time acknowledging a plurality of individuals both internally and externally related some to others, involves difficulties which are writ large over the history of philosophy. It is customary to locate the source of these difficulties in the alleged incompatibility between substance and process, an incompatibility which Hartshorne denies repeatedly. But the difficulties really stem from the historic inability of philosophers to conceive how simpler substances are related—i.e. compounded—to form more complex substances without either losing the individuality of the components or attenuating the individuality of the compounds. Throughout the history of philosophy there have been two opposing solutions to this problem: on the one hand, a pluralism of discrete, unrelated individualities, atoms, or monads; and, on the other hand, a monism of absolute, undifferentiated substantial being. Neither alternative can be tolerated by immediate experience, which, according to Hartshorne, is social in structure and involves the feeling of feeling, evincing the togetherness of microscopic individuals within more complex organisms. Although some organizations of simple individual entities—e.g., plants and stones—do not have the high degree of personal order and consciousness requisite for true individuality and are consequently mere composites, there are, Hartshorne maintains, compound individuals. But compound individuals were not acknowledged until Whitehead's philosophy. As Hartshorne writes: "In the 'cell theory' or 'philosophy of organism' of Whitehead we have nothing less than the first full-blooded, forthright interpretation of the cellular model (passing over the not much less adequate version found in Peirce's theory of the categories, and his doctrine of synechism, both of which conceptions have advantages not entirely paralleled in Whitehead's system). The theory of the enduring individual as a 'society' of occasions, interlocked with other such individuals into societies of societies, is the first complete emergence of the compound individual into technical terminology" (6, p. 211).

PANENTHEISM

From the idea of the compound individual to the idea of God the transition is rapid and direct, for God is the maximal compound individual. "The idea of God is the idea of a 'supreme' or 'highest' or 'best' individual (or superindividual) being. As a minimal definition, God is an entity somehow superior to other entities" (11, p. 6). Theology demands at least this much, while religion adds that God must be a being worthy of worship. To be adequate, then, theology must expound and defend a concept of God which preserves the values which religion emphasizes; it must "express and enhance reverence or worship on a high ethical and cultural level" (12, p. 1). According to Hartshorne, only panentheism affords a theological concept of God which possesses the desired religious value. Although Hartshorne credits many ancient and modern philosophers —including Plato, Sri Jiva, Schelling, Fechner, Peirce, Iqbal, Berdyaev, and Weiss—with shaping theological panentheism, he holds

Whitehead in especially high esteem. Commenting on Whitehead's theory in *Philosophers Speak of God*, Hartshorne says: "It is impossible to avoid a feeling of impertinence in attempting to comment on thinking so great as this. Not in many centuries, perhaps, has such a contribution been made to philosophical theism" (14, p. 282b).

Concept of God

By means of a consideration of the primary attributes predicated of God, Hartshorne defines panentheism in such a way as to distinguish it from its major rivals, of which the foremost were traditional theism and pantheism. There are five major questions pertaining to the concept of God: "Is God eternal? Is he temporal? Is he conscious? Does he know the world? Does he include the world?" (14, p. 16b).

Hartshorne's panentheism answers: first, that God is "Eternal—in some ... aspects of his reality devoid of change, whether as birth, death, increase, or decrease"; second, that God is "Temporal—in some ... aspects capable of change, at least in the form of increase of some kind"; third, that God is "Conscious, self-aware"; fourth, that God is "Knowing the world or universe, omniscient"; and fifth, that God is "World-inclusive, having all things as constituents" (14, p. 16b). God, therefore, is "The Supreme as Eternal-Temporal Consciousness, Knowing and including the World" (14, p. 17a). This conception of deity not only guarantees the values upon which religion insists but also conforms to the most rigorous logical analysis and finds empirical confirmation in the theories of nature supported by contemporary science.

Rival conceptions of deity are differentiated from panentheism by their omission of one or more of the five attributes ascribed to God. The history of philosophy has witnessed eight alternatives to Hartshorne's panentheism: first, God as an eternal consciousness, neither knowing nor including the world, as in Aristotelian theism; second, God as an eternal consciousness that knows but excludes the world, as in the classical theism of Philo, Augustine, Anselm, Aquinas, and Leibniz; third, God as "the Eternal beyond consciousness and knowledge," as in Plotinus' emanationism; fourth, God as "Eternal Consciousness, Knowing and including the World," as in the classical pantheism of Spinoza and Josiah Royce; fifth, God as "Eternal-Temporal Consciousness, Knowing but not including the world," as in the temporalistic theism of Faustus Socinus and Jules Lequier; sixth, God as "Eternal-Temporal Consciousness, partly exclusive of the World," as in the limited panentheism of William James and Edgar Sheffield Brightman; seventh, God as "wholly Temporal or Emerging consciousness," as in the cosmology of Samuel Alexander; and eighth, God as "temporal and non-conscious," as in the theology of Henry Nelson Wieman (14, p. 17).

Hartshorne's conception of God, unlike its alternatives, fastens on the juxtaposition of predicates representing eternity and omniscience and of those representing temporality and world-inclusiveness. It is unquestionably the most comprehensive conception of God, but its comprehensiveness heightens the contrast within God between an aspect which is absolute and unchanging and an aspect which is relative and changing. This contrast, akin to Whitehead's distinction between the primordial and consequent natures of God, entails, as Hartshorne contends, "Divine Relativity." In this sense, panentheism is Surrelativism, with God the Compound Individual conceived as the Process. According to Surrelativism, "the 'relative' or changeable, that which depends upon and varies with varying relationships, includes within itself and in value exceeds the non-relative, immutable, independent, or 'absolute', *as the concrete includes and exceeds the abstract*" (12, p. vii). From this "it follows that God, as supremely excellent and concrete, must be conceived not as wholly absolute or immutable, but rather as supremely-relative, 'surrelative,' although, or because of this superior relativity, containing an abstract character or essence in respect to which, but only in respect to which, he is indeed strictly absolute and immutable" (12, p. vii).

For Hartshorne none of the eight conceptions of God described above quite equals his own panentheistic conception of God as the supreme eternal-temporal consciousness, knowing and including the world. None attains the fullness of being crystallized in the dipolar theory of divine relativity. It is no surprise that the history of theology is divided between classical theism and pantheism, both of which regard God in monopolar terms. Classical theism stresses the absoluteness and transcendence of God, radically separates God from the world, and guarantees his immutability by excluding all passivity and becoming from him; pantheism, on the other hand, identifies God with the total system of all changing things and consequently denies any absolute, transcendent, or independent side to his nature. Thus while classical theism favors a conception of God which fails to portray his supreme perfection adequately, since the cosmos is greater than God in that it contains God and the world; pantheism never succeeds in grasping that aspect of God's nature which is absolute in its perfection and independent of the vicissitudes of becoming. The pantheist and the traditional theist seize upon one set of contrary attributes and disregard the other set. As Hartshorne says: "Common to theism and pantheism is the doctrine of the invidious nature of categorical contrasts" (14, p. 2a). Pantheism and classical theism have, in effect, generated an artificial dilemma for theology, because both "have assumed that the highest form of reality is to be indicated by separating or purifying one pole of the ultimate contrasts from the other pole" (14, p. 2a).

The way out of the dilemma, Hartshorne argues, is to abandon the principle of monopolarity upon which it is based and to substitute the principle of polarity. This principle, borrowed from Morris Cohen (18), dictates that "ultimate contraries are correlatives, mutually interdependent" (14, p. 2b). The adoption of the principle of polarity in theology signifies that "all contrasts . . . fall within God (since, in one aspect of his reality, he is the most complex and inclusive of all beings), but each contrast is in God in its own appropriate way" (14, p. 15a). For Hartshorne dipolarity points the way beyond pantheism and traditional theism to the doctrine of panentheism. In panentheism God is immanent in and contains the world of changing, individual, dependent beings, and is at the same time an eternal, absolute, independent being transcending the world (12, p. 90).

Furthermore, God is at last conceived to be both personal and social, a being who changes yet has absolute, eternal aspects. Indeed, the personality and sociality of God are mutually implicative, since to be a person is to be "qualified and conditioned by social relations, relations to other persons" (13, p. 25). Traditional attributes, such as omniscience and love, make sense for God only if he is a social being related to others. Paradoxically, the traditional presumption that God knows and loves other beings but is unrelated to them, although they in their dependent status are related to him, contradicts the ordinary view that the objects of knowledge and of love make a difference to the knower and lover, perhaps more difference than the knower and lover make to them. Common sense tells us the denial that God is related to his creatures is equivalent to the denial that he knows or loves them. To know and to love are to be related, and the relation involved in this case is the relation of inclusion (12, pp. 16–18). When God knows or loves his creatures, he includes them eminently, not in his essence of course, but within his total being.

At this point a serious problem arises: If God includes imperfect beings, then he is imperfect and so not worthy of worship. On the other hand, if he excludes any beings, then the totality which includes them and him is greater than he, and he is no longer supreme. The solution Hartshorne offers is effective and novel. The perfect being is defined as a being which is unsurpassable except by itself (11, pp. 8 ff., 342 ff.). The perfect being, God, is a being for whom "self-superiority is not impossible," so that "the perfect is the 'self-surpassing surpasser of all' " (12, p. 20). God embraces all the value there is; he lacks none. This does not mean, however, that more value will not come to be in the future; but if and when it does come to be, God will embrace this value, too. God, therefore, changes, not in those abstract aspects which are eternal, but so far as he is related to and includes changing things.

Here the attribute of omniscience illuminates the dipolar nature of God. Basically, the omniscience of God is eternal, and God always knows all there is to know—whatever was and whatever is. But in addition to this absolute aspect of God as eternally omniscient, there is, according to Hartshorne's analysis, a relative, changing aspect. Though God is eternally omniscient, his knowledge changes. As new events occur each moment, he knows them;

but prior to their occurrence, when they are not yet actual, God's knowledge does not grasp them as actual, since to do so would be to falsify them. God does know them as possibilities, but as possibilities they subsist within an indefinite range of indeterminate alternatives. No possibility is definitely actual before it is realized, and nothing destines one set of possibilities rather than another for realization prior to the actual, concrete course of becoming (11, pp. 99 ff.). Hence God, though eternally and absolutely omniscient, does not know what will happen tomorrow until it *does* happen, and his omniscience has both an eternal, absolute and a temporal, relative aspect. Since what is found true for omniscience is true also for the other attributes of God, it follows that God, a perfect being, yet is a changing being.

Arguments for God's Existence

To the problem of demonstrating the existence of God Hartshorne has devoted considerable thought. It should be obvious that the arguments for panpsychism are germane, insofar as they point to the existence of a universal subject. The pages of Hartshorne's writings are dotted with passages which reflect the perspective afforded by panpsychism in demonstrating the existence of God. The following passage is illustrative:

How do we know that God exists? The universe must have some primordial and everlasting character, as the ultimate subject of change. The past being immortal, there must be a complete cosmic memory, since the past in the present *is* memory. The future being predictable, there must be a world anticipation; for the future as fact in the present is anticipation. Also, action implies the faith that at no time in the future will it ever be true that it *will* have made no difference whether the action was well-motivated or ill. This condition is met by the affirmation of a God who will never cease to treasure the memory of the action and of its results (6, p. 218).

Later in his career Hartshorne remarked that all the arguments for God's existence "amount to this: that the proposition, 'There is a supremely excellent being, worthy of worship,' expresses fundamental or categorical aspects of experience and thought, while the denial of this proposition contradicts such aspects. There can be as many arguments for God as one can distinguish fundamental aspects of experience and thought" (14, p. 24b). Hartshorne suggests a list of six arguments: "the aesthetic argument, the ethical argument, the epistemological ('idealistic') argument, the design argument, the cosmological argument, and the ontological argument" (14, p. 25a). Although these arguments have been used since the beginning of theology, and although they have been corrupted by their connection with the artificial dilemma between traditional theism and pantheism, they can, Hartshorne believes, "be given a more exact and perspicuous form than has hitherto been given them" (14, p. 25a).

At least in regard to the ontological argument for God's existence, Hartshorne has demonstrated that traditional proofs for God's existence may be given more exact and perspicuous form within the context of panentheism than they have so far been given within the context of classical theism. In *The Logic of Perfection*, by means of exact analysis of symbolic logic, Hartshorne translates the ontological argument into modal proofs for God's existence. The resurrection of the ontological in symbolic logical expression superbly illustrates Hartshorne's "neoclassical" turn of thought. The rejection of the ontological argument on the ground that existence cannot be inferred from an idea apparently entails the modern principle that existence is always contingent, and this principle Hartshorne explicitly repudiates. The root argument of the modal proofs for God's existence is that if perfect existence is possible, then, since it is necessary, it is. The argument presupposes that perfect existence belongs to a logical type quite distinct from ordinary existence, which is contingent.

While Hartshorne claims, according to the title of his essay, to offer ten ontological or modal proofs of God's existence, he presents his case in such a way that it is not easy, if indeed it is possible, to mark off ten proofs. Nevertheless, there are several peaks of clarity. In one memorable passage (15, pp. 50–51), the logical structure of St. Anselm's second ontological argument receives mature symbolic formulation, with elements of theology and of mathematical logic drawn together in mutual support. The argument is quoted in full:

'q' for '(Ex) Px' There is a perfect being, or perfection exists
'N' for 'it is necessary (logically true) that'
'~' for 'it is not true that'
'V' for 'or'
'p→q' for 'p strictly implies q' or 'N~(p and ~q)'

1. $q\rightarrow Nq$	"Anselm's Principle": perfection could not exist contingently.
2. $Nq V \sim Nq$	Excluded Middle
3. $\sim Nq \rightarrow N \sim Nq$	Form of Becker's Postulate: modal status is always necessary.
4. $Nq V N \sim Nq$	Inference from (2,3)
5. $N \sim Nq \rightarrow N \sim q$	Inference from (1): The necessary falsity of the consequent implies that of the antecedent (Modus form of modus tollens)
6. $Nq V N \sim q$	Inference from (4,5)
7. $\sim N \sim q$	Intuitive postulate (or conclusion from other theistic arguments): perfection is not impossible.
8. Nq	Inference from (6,7)
9. $Nq \rightarrow q$	Modal axiom
10. q	Inference from (8,9).

One further remark on Hartshorne's treatment of the ontological proof is in order. Recall that God for Hartshorne is dipolar. The ontological proof, then, serves only for the absolute eternalistic side of God, but, because of criticisms directed against Anselm's argument, it is necessary to acknowledge another side of God which is contingent. Going beyond the traditional distinction between essence and existence, Hartshorne also draws a distinction between existence and actuality, between the fact *that* a being is and *how* it is (16, p. 131). Accordingly, "any individual, no matter how superior, exists by virtue of contingent concrete states; but whereas with you and me it is always possible that there should be no such states at all, with God, though any such state is contingent, that there is some such state is necessary" (16, p. 40). Great as Anselm's discovery was, it was, in Hartshorne's view, less than final. He writes: "Anselm discovered, and really discovered, the modal uniqueness of God. What he overlooked, and nearly all his critics equally fail to see, is that, since actuality cannot be necessary, there must be a real duality in God, as in no other being, between necessary existence and contingent actuality" (16, p. 134).

The panentheistic conception of God, argues Hartshorne, is not only logically exact and theologically full; it is also the only conception of God worthy of inspiring man's worship. At last man's vision of God in religion is fulfilled in his vision of God in theology. "Divine Relativity" introduces a God who is active and passive, who creates and enjoys his creatures but suffers and sorrows with them as well. "Here," Hartshorne comments with a nod to Berdyaev, "the Christian idea of a suffering deity—symbolized by the Cross, together with the doctrine of the Incarnation—achieves technical metaphysical expression" (14, p. 15b). God, then, is both personal and social. Hartshorne relates that once in private conversation Whitehead described God "as a 'society of occasions' (with personal order)" (12, pp. 30–31); from this description of God to the panentheistic conception of God as the most perfect compound individual the distance is short. Or, to put it another way, the conception of God Hartshorne offers, in accord with "Whitehead's supreme conception . . . of a society of actual occasions, related one to another by the sympathetic bond of 'feeling of feeling'" (12, p. 29), has as its reverse side the panpsychical conception of the world as the divine organism. The doctrines of the affective continuum, of panpsychism and social realism, and of panentheism are expressions in technical philosophy which translate St. Paul's dictum: "We are members one of another" (10, p. 123).

NOTES TO CHAPTER IX

1 Charles Hartshorne, "Present Prospects for Metaphysics," *Monist*, XLVII (1963), 182–210.
2 Hartshorne was a contributor to the American *festschrift* for Husserl. See Charles Hartshorne, "Husserl and the Social Structure of Immediacy," in Marvin Farber (ed.), *Philosophical Essays in Memory of Edmund Husserl* (Cambridge: Harvard University Press, 1940), 210–30.

3 See Charles Hartshorne and Paul Weiss (eds.), *The Collected Papers of Charles Sanders Peirce*, I–VI (Cambridge: Harvard University Press, 1931–36).

4 William L. Reese and Eugene Freeman (eds.), *Process and Divinity, The Hartshorne Festschrift* (LaSalle, Ill.: Open Court, 1964). This work also contains an excellent bibliography of Hartshorne's writings.

5 See, for example, James K. Feibleman, *An Introduction to Peirce's Philosophy Interpreted as a System* (New York and London: Harper and Brothers Publishers, 1946), 459–63.

6 Charles Hartshorne, "The Compound Individual," *Philosophical Essays for Alfred North Whitehead* (London, New York, and Toronto: Longmans, Green and Co., 1936).

7 See, in addition to those papers by Hartshorne on Whitehead which will be cited in separate references, the following: "On Some Criticisms of Whitehead's Philosophy," *Philosophical Review*, XLIV (1935), 323–44; "The Interpretation of Whitehead," *ibid.*, XLVIII (1939), 415–23; "Is Whitehead's God the God of Religion?" *Ethics*, LIII (1943), 219–27; "Ely on Whitehead," *Journal of Liberal Religion*, V (1943), 97–100; "Das Metaphysische system Whitehead," *Zeitschriff fur philosophische*, III (1949), 566–75; "Whitehead's Metaphysics," in Victor Lowe, Charles Hartshorne, and A. H. Johnson, *Whitehead and the Modern World* (Boston: Beacon Press, 1950), 25–41; "Le principe de relativité philosophique chez Whitehead," *Revue de Métaphysique et de Morale*, LV (1950), 16–29; "Whitehead's Philosophy of Reality as Socially-Structured Process," *Chicago Review*, VIII (1954) 60–77; "Whitehead and Berdyaev: Is There Tragedy in God?" *Journal of Religion*, XXXVII (1957), 71–84; "Whitehead on Process: A Reply to Professor Eslick," *Philosophy and Phenomenological Research*, XVIII (1958), 514–40; "The Buddhist-Whiteheadian View of the Self," *Proceedings of the Ninth International Congress for the History of Religions* (Tokyo, 1958), 298–302; "Whitehead and Contemporary Philosophy," in Ivor Leclerc (ed.), *The Relevance of Whitehead* (London: Allen and Unwin, 1961), 21–43; "Whitehead the Anglo-American Philosopher-Scientist," *Proceedings of the American Catholic Philosophical Association* (Catholic University of America, 1961), 163–71; "Whitehead's Novel Intuition," in George L. Kline (ed.), *Alfred North Whitehead: Essays on His Philosophy* (Englewood Cliffs, N. J.: Prentice-Hall, 1963), 18–26; and "Whitehead's Conception of God" and "Whitehead's Prehension," *Actas Segunda Congreso Extraordinario Interamericano de Filosofia* (San Jose, Costa Rica, 1963), 163–70.

8 Charles Hartshorne, *Reality as Social Process: Studies in Metaphysics and Religion* (Glencoe and Boston: Free Press and Beacon Press, 1953).

9 Charles Hartshorne, *The Philosophy and Psychology of Sensation* (Chicago: University of Chicago Press, 1934).

10 Charles Hartshorne, *Beyond Humanism. Essays in the New Philosophy of Nature* (Chicago and New York: Willett, Clark, 1937).

11 Charles Hartshorne, *Man's Vision of God and the Logic of Theism* (New York: Harper and Brothers, 1941).

12 Charles Hartshorne, *The Divine Relativity: A Social Conception of God* (New Haven: Yale University Press, 1948).

13 See Charles Hartshorne, "Whitehead's Idea of God," in Paul Arthur Schilpp (ed.), *The Philosophy of Alfred North Whitehead* (2d ed., New York: Tudor, 1951), 515–59.

14   Charles Hartshorne and William L. Reese, *Philosophers Speak of God* (Chicago: University of Chicago Press, 1953).

15   Charles Hartshorne, *The Logic of Perfection and Other Essays in Neoclassical Metaphysics* (LaSalle, Ill.: Open Court, 1961).

16   Charles Hartshorne, *Anselm's Discovery: A Re-examination of the Ontological Argument for God's Existence* (La Salle, Ill.: Open Court, 1965).

17   Charles Hartshorne, "The Social Structure of Experience," *Philosophy*, XXXVI (April and July, 1961), 97–111.

18   Morris Cohen derived the principle of polarity from Wilmon H. Sheldon in the latter's seminars at Columbia University in the late 1890's. For a discussion of the role of polarity in Sheldon's thought, see Andrew J. Reck, "Wilmon H. Sheldon's Philosophy of Philosophy," *Tulane Studies in Philosophy*, VII (1958), 111–28. Hartshorne is sympathetic to Sheldon's philosophy. See his review of Sheldon's *God and Polarity* in *Philosophical Review*, LXIV (1955), 312–16.

19   Charles Hartshorne, *A Natural Theology for Our Time* (La Salle, Ill.: Open Court, 1967).

X

PAUL WEISS

Systematic Metaphysics and Open Thinking

Paul Weiss has described the philosopher as "an individual in his errors and a *Weltgeist* in his truth. If successful he has presented a myth; if not he has ventured outside the ordinary reaches and ended with something close to a wrong-headed perverse doctrine" (1, I, p. 168). While most Anglo-American thinkers today have sought to escape "wrong-headed perverse doctrine" by retreating to philosophical analysis, Weiss has proposed a new system of speculative philosophy which is unstintingly metaphysical. In a caustic note Weiss has compared those "modern philosophers who have eschewed metaphysics" to "men practicing to sit in the air. . . . But for the rest of us," he says, "a chair is what we want. It does not demand of us that we learn odd ways of manipulating our bodies, but it does demand that we know what is at our rear" (1, I, p. 704).

Weiss's ambition is undeniably to construct a great system of philosophy, without equal since the days of Hegel. And Weiss has striven tirelessly to realize this ambition. He was born on May 19, 1901, in New York City. Too poor to pursue the ordinary program of studies leading to a professional career in philosophy, he went to work without graduating from high school. Years later, his intellectual curiosities aroused, he learned that it was possible for an adult without a high school diploma to attend the City College of New York in the evening. In 1927 he received the B.B.S. degree from City College. There the influence of Morris Cohen, under whom he studied philosophy, proved decisive—Weiss was set on a career in philosophy. Though short of funds, he entered graduate school at Harvard University. From Harvard, where he did his major work under Whitehead, Weiss received an A.M. in 1928 and a Ph.D. in 1929. After a year in Europe as a traveling fellow at German universities, Weiss returned to Harvard in 1930 as an instructor in philosophy. During his Harvard years he joined Hartshorne in the preparation of the standard edition of Peirce's collected papers (2). Work on Peirce profoundly affected the development of his thinking. Recently Weiss admitted: "I have learned more from Peirce than from anyone else" (3, p. 139).

In 1931 Weiss joined the faculty of Bryn Mawr College, where he taught until 1945, taking leave one year to study on a Guggenheim fellowship. In 1945 he was invited to Yale University, where he is now Sterling Professor of Philosophy. An indefatigable promoter of philosophical causes, Weiss was the founder and the first president of both the Peirce Society and the Metaphysical Society of America. In 1965 he was elected president of the Eastern Division of the American Philosophical Association.

In 1947 Weiss founded the *Review of Metaphysics*, which he served as editor until 1964, when Richard J. Bernstein assumed full editorial responsibilities. This journal has played a significant and as yet not fully assessed role in the development of contemporary American philosophy. An organ for metaphysics at a time when positivism and linguistic analysis have tended to suppress speculation, the *Review of Metaphysics* has furnished a publishing outlet for speculatively inclined philosophers, including such thinkers as Wild, Hartshorne, and Feibleman as well as numerous younger men. It has also attempted to represent continental European philosophical developments. Finally, it has encouraged contributions from philosophers affiliated with religious groups, particularly Roman Catholic philosophers, and has thus widened the scope of the philosophical dialogue in America.

In a perceptive critical study published in the *Review of Metaphysics*, James Collins, professor of philosophy at St. Louis University, ventured to classify Weiss's publications into three broad phases: doctrinal formulation, systematic formalization, and concrete reflection (4, p. 302). Weiss began as a logician, moved into metaphysics and cosmology, struggled with the root problems of philosophical anthropology and ethics, eventually formulated a complete system of ontology, and then proceeded to elaborate his philosophy in the concrete fields of politics, law, art, history, religion, and education.

Weiss's first book (5) and early papers (6) revealed a penchant for logic. His accomplishments as a symbolic logician did not, however, restrict him solely to the technical manipulation of formal symbols. *The Nature of Systems,* his doctoral dissertation, explores existing symbolic systems of logic and mathematics. It manifests his early preoccupation with the genuinely speculative problem of discovering and formulating a general theory descriptive of all systems and explanatory of their interrelations. Incisively critical and perceptively creative in his early writings, Weiss was seeking both to formulate the system which underlies and embraces all systems and to suggest a scheme for possible future advances in the field of logic.

Weiss moved cautiously from logic into metaphysics, as his numerous transitional articles reveal (7). In 1938 he published *Reality* (8), in which he treated that category or mode of being which he later termed Actuality. Afterwards, he examined the nature of man as one type of real being; the result was the publication in 1947 of *Nature and Man* (9). A work in philosophical anthropology, *Nature and Man* was foundational to Weiss's ethics; at the same time it uncovered a dimension of reality beyond Actuality, a dimension or mode of being which he later called Ideality. In 1950 Weiss published his ethics under the title *Man's Freedom* (10). Increasingly aware of the inadequacies of the original metaphysical scheme, Weiss felt the theoretical need not only for Ideality to supplement Actuality but for other categories as well.

In 1958 Weiss's *Modes of Being* (11) appeared. Circulated in multilithed form to students, former students, and colleagues in the years preceding its publication, *Modes of Being* underwent revision in the course of the discussions it stimulated; it also won a small but appreciative audience even before its printing. The climax of Weiss's quest for a systematic formulation of his philosophy, *Modes of Being* presents a fourfold ontology of Actuality, Ideality, Existence, and God. The presentation is unique for contemporary philosophy. Weiss divides the book into four major parts—one for each of the four modes—and advances each proposition as a numbered thesis. Each numbered thesis is elucidated and demonstrated in a subordinate paragraph. The structure of the system, in which each thesis receives support from and renders support to the other theses, is made plain by the fact that in clarifying or maintaining every thesis Weiss cites by number the relevant theses in an elaborate cross-reference system. Winning praise even from unsympathetic critics—one of whom, in his survey of American metaphysics from 1930 to 1960, conceded that it is "an impressive work" (12, p. 149)—*Modes of Being* immediately established Weiss as America's foremost living speculative philosopher. In 1961 a group of his friends, colleagues, and former students presented him with a collection of essays to honor him on his sixtieth birthday (13).

Since the publication of *Modes of Being* Weiss has engaged in concrete reflection. In consequence he has produced a spate of works, perhaps too rapidly for proper assimilation by the community of philosophers. Following the procedure employed for *Modes of Being*, Weiss has circulated several of his recent works in multilithed form in order to stimulate and take account of discussion and criticism prior to publication. On politics and law he has written *Our Public Life* (14); on art, *The World of Art* (15) and *Nine Basic Arts* (16); on history, *History: Written and Lived* (17); on religion, *The God We Seek* (18); and on education, *The Making of Men* (19). In addition, since 1955 he has written notes each morning, running from brief paragraphs to essays of thousands of words, to record the thoughts that have passed through his mind, typing as rapidly as he thought, in order to capture his mind's contents and flow. Since 1963 these notes have been published quarterly in fascicles of approximately sixty-four pages; in 1966 they were collected and published in book form. This work, *Philosophy in Process*, is a unique venture in the history of philosophical publication (20). Since it presents Weiss's unrevised thinking, exposing the character of his mind, his ideal aims and root concepts, his doubts and hesitations, his inconsistencies, and clarifications, his evasions and self-corrections, it is nothing less than "an exhibition of an effort at 'open thinking' " (1, p. 186).

Systematic metaphysics and open thinking, speculation and concrete reflection—these features, so often at odds in lesser thinkers, are interrelated, each supplementing the other, in Weiss's creative and original philosophy. To grasp in some measure the structure and movement of his thought it is necessary to explore each of his modes of being.

ACTUALITY

Weiss's first efforts to engage directly in the root questions of metaphysics crystallized in his book *Reality*. Although he was somewhat influenced by his teacher Whitehead, he departed from Whitehead's process philosophy on basic issues—particularly on the question of the reality of substance. Further, Weiss offered in *Reality* an intricate descriptive, explanatory system of sixty-six categories to embrace all knowledge and all reality. The merit of this book, however, does not stem from the comprehensive list of categories it presents. Indeed, in critical remarks on Whitehead, Weiss has confessed misgivings concerning any list of fundamental categories that is so long and is not through dialectic reduced to a manageable set (15, p. 159). *Reality* is significant for its novel perspective on the basic issues of philosophy and for the audacity of its dialectical method. The result is a system in which being and knowing are interlocked—a theory of knowing which reconciles realism and idealism in a new theory of judgment, and a theory of being which, confronting process with substance, unfolds a richer conception of reality.

Epistemology and Ontology

Weiss insisted that neither epistemology nor ontology alone exhausts philosophy, and that neither is logically prior to the other. Ontology, which inquires into the nature of being, presupposes that there are valid ways of knowing, while epistemology, which investigates the processes, range, and validity of cognition, presupposes that knowing is a real activity occurring in a real world. Epistemology without ontology cannot mark off the real from the unreal and consequently cannot focus cognition on its proper object, while ontology without epistemology is blind, since it lacks the requisite criteria of meaning and truth. An ontological inquiry necessarily assumes what epistemology validates, and conversely. This circularity of ontology and epistemology offers a "check against dogmatism and sterility" (8, p. 10); just as the detection of tacit assumptions makes the inquirer critical toward all theories, so the discovery of the way the assumptions of one branch of philosophy are implied in another spurs him to elaborate an increasingly comprehensive philosophy. Weiss's acknowledgment of the circularity of epistemology and ontology led, therefore, to the development of both disciplines to the fullest, generating a total yet critical system in which being and knowing are wedded.

Weiss's theory of knowledge reflects the influence of Kant, modified by the philosophical logic of F. H. Bradley and sharpened by the semiotic of C. S. Peirce and the symbolic logic of Whitehead and Russell. The Kantian element in Weiss's epistemology does not consist in a divorce of knowledge from reality, nor in the reduction of knowledge to a product of the imposition of mental forms upon brute, heterogeneous content. On the contrary, his position is fundamentally realistic. Perception reveals the objective world. Indeed, even perceptual error evinces the veridical disclosure of reality by true perceptions, inasmuch as the analysis of error shows its content to be generically similar to the object it specifically mistakes (8, pp. 26–27).

According to Weiss, a perception, from which all nonperceptual knowledge originates and to which it is related (8, p. 83), is a judgment composed of three elements: an indicated, a contemplated, and an adumbrated. The indicated is the subject of the judgment, that to which it points or that which it denotes (8, p. 33). The contemplated, as perceived, is "a present, sensuous, intelligible, extensive, intensive unity" (8, p. 41). The contemplated is the predicate which with the indicated articulates the nature of the perceived object. The subject and predicate—the indicated and contemplated—are synthesized in a judgment, and this judgment itself, as expressed by the copula, synthesizes the conjoined indicated and contemplated with a reality beyond, which Weiss calls the adumbrated. As perceptual the adumbrated is "the correlate of the indicated and the perceptual contemplated, the third factor in judgment which prompts us to unite the other two, makes their union possible and provides an objective substantial body for both together" (8, p. 58). "Perception is the wedding of an interpreted contemplated with an objective indicated to form an articulate object of knowledge, which itself merges into an adumbrated as a more substantial but unarticulated version of it" (8, p. 32).

In addition to the perceptual adumbrated, there is what Weiss calls a recessive adumbrated: "No matter how far we probe in judgment, no matter how much we accrete to what we articulately know, there is always an adumbrated lying beyond" (8, p. 58). This "adumbrated lying beyond" comprises a domain of ignorance, the inescapable awareness of which inspires metaphysical speculation. Weiss's theory of the recessive adumbrated has affinities with Kant's doctrine of the transcendental object. Like Kant's transcendental object, the recessive adumbrated is the ever-transcending limit of judgment, an object which both lures and eludes thought and which, because of its perpetual elusiveness, justifies the view that knowledge is fallible. Still Weiss did not succumb, as Kant apparently did in *The Critique of Pure Reason*, to skepticism about metaphysical speculation; nor did he appeal, as Bergson deemed necessary, to a quasi-mystical intuition to make contact with the real. For unlike Kant's transcendental object, the recessive adumbrated is not an unknowable thing in itself; on the contrary, it is cognizable, although cognition never embraces the vast extensiveness or plumbs the intensive privacy of beings. In this sense, the adumbrated is analogous to Bradley's absolute subject; it is the ultimate subject of which the subjects and predicates within a judgment are abstractions, a subject which retrieves the contents abstracted from it by thinking through true judgments which, in effect, attribute the abstracted contents back to it. But where Bradley adhered to an absolutistic monism and recognized but one metaphysical adumbrated, Weiss is an epochal pluralist. He acknowledges a multiplicity of adumbrateds. Different judgments are linked with different adumbrateds according to variations in the conditions of the making of the judgments; regardless of what knowledge has been attained, there always remains a domain of ignorance thronged by beings still to be known. Admission of this domain of ignorance is the confession of intellectual deprivations which the activity of inquiry promises to satisfy.

Substance and Process

Weiss's *Reality* presents an ontology of realistic pluralism focused on substantial actualities and creative processes, thereby reconciling the great tradition of substance philosophy stemming from Aristotle with the recent process philosophy advocated by Bergson and Whitehead. *Reality* explores the nature and roles of actualities within the cosmic process. Like Aristotle's substances, actualities are both realities correlated with the adumbrateds of judgmental syntheses and ontological, concrete individuals which persist through change. Weiss was disturbed by Whitehead's conception of actualities (8, pp. 207–208). By taking all actual occasions to be temporally atomic, Whitehead had to suppose them to perish as soon as they came to be. The seemingly stable entities of experience were thus reduced to societies whose members flash into existence momentarily, perish instantly, and are succeeded by others. Weiss accused Whitehead of committing the fallacy of supposing that to be is to be complete. Weiss wrote: "*To be is to be incomplete.* . . . No reality is completely confined within the span of a moment and it cannot therefore perish with the passage of that moment. Realities persist while they change because, though they are wholly present as actual, as virtual they are still future, unaffected by the adventures of that moment of time which is then present" (8, p. 209).

Equating being with becoming (thereby excluding persistent substances), Bergson had brilliantly shown that the past is never lost, that it is efficacious in present being, and Whitehead had insisted on the objective immortality of past entities in the present. But neither Bergson nor Whitehead had appreciated fully the ingredience of the future in the present. Their entities, though as present they are enriched by the past enfolded within their natures, are divorced from the future.

Weiss in effect preserves substantialist modes of thinking by developing the temporalism upon which process philosophy depends. Influenced by Aristotelian hylomorphic conceptions of substantial realities as proportionalities of act and potency, Weiss maintained that every actual entity possesses virtual features not yet actualized. What it does and how it acts is determined by its concern for completion. But whereas for Aristotle these virtual features testify to potentialities inherent in the matter of substances, for Weiss the virtual character of an actuality is a relational aspect terminating in its possible future. The actuality, then, is inseparable from its future. By thus expanding the temporalism of process philosophy until the future is included in the nature of a being to guarantee its persistence, Weiss reconciles substance and process. In consequence, the future is rendered efficacious in the present, an efficacy which Weiss called "mellontological causation" (8, pp. 245 ff.). Since actualities in their quest for completion seek realities which other existent actualities possess, what they do is determined by what they need and by what the future promises once they reach the realities they seek.

As Weiss came to see, the ontology of *Reality*, despite its remarkable achievements, is glaringly defective. To some extent *Reality* rests, as Weiss now admits, on misinterpretations of Whitehead and Aristotle, misinterpretations which "make Aristotle and Whitehead have better systems than otherwise" (1, p. 32). Still worse, the ontology of *Reality* shatters the cosmos into a plurality of actualities, each bent on devouring the others. A cosmos of unrelieved strife engendered by unmitigatable selfishness is the result. Knowledge alone offers refuge from frustration: "Man," Weiss remarked, "is capable of a vicarious completion through the medium of knowledge, for to know is to possess in the mind those things which one in fact lacks" (8, p. 294).

Yet even knowledge does not suffice for man. For, as Weiss continued: "Until his knowledge seeps through his being, it is not he, but part of himself that is complete. . . . To be actually, formally and materially, though still vicariously complete, he must, through the agency of virtuous acts, integrate his knowledge with his being" (8, p. 294). However, Weiss soon found, in his endeavors to formulate the ontological conditions of the moral life, that a cosmos without real contemporaries and hence without unity must be discarded for a cosmos in which all actualities are united by reference to a common, possible good. But this was tantamount to acknowledging another mode of being—the Good, or Ideality.

Although *Reality* does not clearly delineate the modes of being distinguished in Weiss's mature system but instead blurs such fundamental categories as Actuality and Existence, it nevertheless contains several basic tenets pertinent to Actuality which are retained in the mature system. Actualities are spatial beings with bodies (11, p. 21). Because of their physical properties, actualities are related to each other, and out of the web of relations emerges the derivative being of space (11, pp. 26–27). Actualities are simple beings or compounds of simple beings (11, p. 23). Actualities that are active are primary actualities (11, pp. 22–23). Compounds are active primary actualities when the whole determines the behavior of the components (11, pp. 23–24). The activity of primary actualities is causality (11, pp. 23, 29). Since activity involves a temporal sequence of cause and effect, it follows that actualities are temporal (11, p. 24). Spatial and temporal, actualities are physically extended and durationally complete (11, pp. 25–26). Within the universe of actualities dwell men, a domain of special actualities. Indeed, it is the human actuality which discerns additional, nonactual modes of being. The first of these in Weiss's order of discovery is Ideality.

IDEALITY

Although Weiss's aim in *Reality* was to present a speculative theory interlocking epistemology and ontology and to formulate the framework of categories requisite for a coherent, comprehensive description of being and knowing, he recognized there that the fruits of pure theory are partly gathered in moral action. Knowledge, to be integral, must not be divorced from action. Like C. S. Peirce, Weiss stressed the pragmatic determinant in all theory without impugning the integrity of thought itself. Weiss came to center his metaphysical analysis and speculative talents on the practical dimensions of human reality.

Theory of Man

Weiss's topic in *Nature and Man* is philosophical anthropology. Building on the naturalistic foundations of *Reality*, Weiss takes man to be a naturally evolved being. Man possesses common ontological features with other beings, but he is nonetheless distinctive. Although he originates and dwells in nature, he has qualities which point toward a supernatural function and destiny.

All beings, Weiss argues, have an inside and an outside, a private nature and a public nature (9, pp. 39–41). Furthermore, all are free (9, pp. 20 ff.): "An activity is a free occurrence which, over and above what the past determines, is self-determined. . . . The agent is compelled to act by what has gone before, but the action is his own, then and there made to be what it is" (9, p. 33). And all beings are *concerned*. "Each being," Weiss writes, "has a *concern*, a way of reaching from the concrete present into the abstract future"; and he adds: "From the inside, to be is to be concerned with a pertinent good" (9, p. 53).

With other natural beings man has privacy, publicness, and freedom. But man emerges with a concern whose expression, requiring alterations in the structure of the body and its organs, is directed toward the realization of a good pertinent to others (9, p. 138). At this juncture in evolution the self comes into being: "The self is the self of a natural yet ethical man. It is (1) constant, (2) active, (3) concerned, (4) unique, (5) beneficial to the body, (6) responsible, and (7) sensitive to values" (9, pp. 252–53). Thus each man has a self, a constant individual agency which possesses the body and expresses itself as mind and which consists in the concern for others' as well as one's own good.

Upon the self, moreover, hinges immortality. As Weiss later explicitly argued: "The death of the body does not demand the death of the self. . . . At death it [the self] cuts off and holds to itself that portion of Existence which once characterized it as the self of the body. It has a natural origin, exists in this life in the body, and yet has a capacity to act and eventually to exist apart from that body" (11, pp. 51–52).

Freedom

In the preface to *Nature and Man* Weiss promised an ethics and a politics based upon his philosophical anthropology. The ethics appeared soon afterward with the publication of *Man's Freedom*. Pursuing the themes of freedom and concern for the good advanced in *Nature and Man*, Weiss showed how man is free yet responsible in a context of obligation to realize the good. Like Bergson, Weiss locates the presence of freedom in the duration, the temporal span, in which an act is performed (10, pp. 3 ff.). The specific, detailed, concrete character of the act and its result are unpredictable prior to the action, although the possible courses are foreshadowed. But unlike Bergson, Weiss does not propose an anti-intellectual indeterminism. On the contrary, the conditions that precede an action, the productive activity of the agent, and the time taken to perform the action together entail a result which, despite its antecedent indeterminacy with respect to detail, is necessitated and intelligible.

According to Weiss, freedom "is an intelligible process by which the indeterminate, the possible, the future, the good, is made determinate, actual, present; it is an activity by which the general is specified, specialized, delimited, given one of a number of possible concrete shapes" (10, p. 71). As a process freedom is pointed toward possible goals. Men are free to choose among alternative ends for their actions (10, p. 116), and they are also free to prefer some means over others for the realization of the same goals (10, p. 118). But because men are ontological selves defined by a concern for the all-embracing, absolute Good, human freedom is exercised within a framework of obligation to creatively will the Good (10, p. 201).

The Good

This absolute Good serves as the ideal standard of perfection which, by transcending individual attainments and social arrangements, is the perennial lure of all human action (10, pp. 102 ff.). As the harmony of goods sought by all beings, it is the future (10, p. 176). Weiss defines "the summum bonum, the greatest good" as "a totality in which each being was at its best in perfect harmony with all the rest. Such a cosmos," he adds, "does not now exist. It is an ideal, an excellence applicable to all that is or can be, an absolute 'ought to be,' *the* good, enabling us to judge what is good and bad, right and wrong, virtuous and vicious. Every single 'ought to be' specializes and is subordinate to it" (10, p. 199).

Weiss's conception of the absolute Good is metaphysical, and yet it departs from the ontology depicted in *Reality*. His venture into philosophical anthropology and ethics, instead of merely working out the practical implications of the early metaphysics, resulted in the recognition of a mode of being distinct from Actuality. In *Reality* the good sought by an actuality is nothing more than the values other actualities now have; it promises primarily to satisfy the needs and wants of the actuality that seeks it. There is in the early ontology no universal Good but a plurality of goods. However, Weiss's conception of the Good in *Man's Freedom* becomes the idea of a nonactual, universal objective and norm for action. It is therefore able to do what had to be done to complete the cosmology of *Reality*—namely, to integrate all actualities within one cosmos by virtue of their common direction toward the realization of the Good.

Ideality in the Mature System

In *Modes of Being* Weiss provides a formal theory of Ideality. Ideality is possibility. All possibility is internally coherent (11, p. 105), but real possibility must be more than coherent; it must, though independent of what does exist, be capable of being in fact (11, pp. 106–107). Real possibility is thus relevant to actualities (11, p. 108) and changes because they do (11, p. 109). It also imparts intelligibility to the actualities which stand over against it and realize it (11, p. 111). Weiss here reconciles elements of the philosophies of Plato and Aristotle (11, pp. 111–12). With Plato he holds that possibilities are exterior to and independent of actualities, and with

Aristotle, that possibilities are relevant to actualities. In fact, the discussion of the Good and its relevance to man underscores Weiss's theory of real possibility and illuminates the connection between morality and ontology. As Weiss succinctly put it: "The Good is a possibility which ought to be realized" (11, p. 112). Weiss's doctrine of Ideality in *Modes of Being*, moreover, gathers together the seemingly inconsistent or at least unrelated suggestions concerning the nature and function of the Good in the previous books and shapes these suggestions into a coherent concept.

As depicted in *Modes of Being*, Ideality is considered in three guises: the Good, the Future, and the Principle of Perfection. First, with respect to actualities, and first in the order of discovery by Weiss, Ideality is the Good, "an all inclusive possibility, or Ideal" (11, p. 120). Second, with respect to Existence, Ideality is the Future. The Good, as the Ideal in relation to actualities, "is continuous with itself in the guise of the Future, i.e., in relation to Existence. When the Ideal acts to encompass Actualities, it also functions as a Future which, by giving direction to Existence, controls it" (11, p. 122). Third, as relevant to God, the Ideal is the Principle of Perfection. "When the Ideal acts to subjugate Actualities," Weiss writes, "it also functions as a principle of value which, as accepted by God, evaluates him. The effect of this twofold effort is, on the one hand, to make actualities subject to an evaluation, and thus to be ordered in a hierarchy, and on the other hand to make God a being concerned with the fulfillment of the Good" (11, p. 123).

Weiss had put the Good on so absolute a footing with respect to the obligations it imposes upon man that he was forced in *Man's Freedom* to conclude: "Man is the guilty creature, a being who can never entirely live up to his obligations, and knows it" (10, p. 259). Absolute ontological human guilt was the consequence of the fact that the Good is independent and transcendent. Consideration of the paradox of human guilt issuing from man's inability to meet the obligations of the Good upon which his universal ethical nature hinges prompted Weiss in his mature system to acknowledge the two additional modes of being—God and Existence. For although "ought" does not imply "can" for men and men are consequently necessarily guilty, "ought" does imply "can" cosmically. The other modes of being make it possible to realize the Good which man alone never succeeds in realizing.

EXISTENCE

Just as Weiss's metaphysics assimilates the classical Western ontologies through the modes of Actuality and Ideality, it is keenly attuned to those currents in contemporary thought which, stirred by process philosophers and existentialists, have revolved around Existence as an equally important, if not paramount, mode of being. Weiss early apprehended creative process as a significant aspect of reality. This awareness is expressed as a distinctive mode of being— i.e., Existence—only in the mature system of *Modes of Being*. Here Weiss writes: "An irreducible mode of being, Existence is sheer vitality, forever passing from one position or guise into another. By encapsulating a portion of Existence within the confines of its own nature, each entity is enabled to stand away from all others at the same time that it is caught inside a wider realm of Existence, where it is kept at a distance from others" (11, p. 185).

Creative Vitality

Existence is both the field embracing all actualities and the internal vitality of each being. Space, Time, and Energy are the main features of Existence. As the field, Existence constitutes "a cosmos of energy," "a whole of time," and "a cosmic contemporary world" (11, pp. 186–87). As the internal vitality of each being, Existence is "in perpetual inward tension": "Existence perpetually divides" (11, p. 186). Dynamically extensive, Existence is implicated with Ideality in the cosmic process, thereby establishing "a whole of time" which not only interlaces all actualities in a contemporary world but also guarantees the possibility of history.

Existence in this view is analogous in nature and function to the principle of creativity in process cosmologies. But where process philosophers have merely suggested discriminable modes of being, Weiss has clearly demarcated Existence from the other modes while at the same time explicitly showing how it interplays with those modes. Existence is "the spatial field" of actualities (11, p. 190), the "causal ground" for Ideality (11, pp. 190–91), and "the cosmic vitality" of God (11, pp. 191–92). It makes actualities "contemporaries" (11, p. 192), adds implications to Ideality which otherwise would be a mere possibility (11, pp. 193–94), and comprises the dynamics of coming to be and passing away over against the eternal self-identity of God (11, pp. 195–96). Moreover, just as Existence derives characteristics from the other modes, the other modes take on characteristics from the standpoint of Existence. "From the perspective of Existence, Actualities are focal points, the Ideal is future and God is essence" (11, p. 196).

This conception of Existence as creative vitality, sharpened by contrast and relation to other well-defined modes of being, is superior in clarity to the concepts afforded by rival process cosmologies; it also escapes the objection to speculation raised by existentialism, which insists that existence is absurd. For Weiss, Existence is intelligible. Despite the dynamic divisiveness of Existence (which seems to deny the unity necessary for understanding), its interplay with other modes imparts unity to it. More important is the argument that if Existence were not intelligible, "we would not know what it was for something to exist rather than not exist" (11, p. 198). Existence has an essence, an intelligible unity expressible as a predicate. Existence "marks the fact that an entity . . . (a) is present, (b) is in a process of becoming, or (c) has more implications than those that follow from an idea of it" (11, p. 200). There is, therefore, no unbridgeable gulf between ideas and Existence; in fact, ideas themselves *exist* as occurrences, as meanings carried by the occurrences, and as meanings within cognitive wholes (11, p. 203).

The interplay of Existence and Actuality encompasses all actualities in a frame which makes each determinate in respect to the others, and which makes all actualities concordantly effective (11, p. 223). It also discounts the theological conviction that actualities

depend upon God for their Existence: "Each actuality has its own Existence" (11, p. 222).

The Past

Actualities can lose their Existence, pass away, become de-existentialized, be reduced to fact (11, pp. 224–25). "The past is a tissue of exhausted, dead, desiccated Actualities, without vitality because no longer possessing Existence. It is a realm of facts, sheer phenomena, without power or energy or movement" (11, p. 227). "It is a world where determinism holds full sway" (11, p. 228). Although present actualities exist without dependence upon God, the past exists through God. As Weiss says: "God gives the past an existence, not by making its items stand on their own feet with a genuine existence in them—for . . . this would make them all present —but by making them all possess the present existence at greater, or less remove, as more or less immediate" (17, p. 224). Like Actuality and like Ideality, Existence needs, at least as regards the past, that mode of being which Weiss calls God.

GOD

Weiss's theory of God was perhaps induced by reflection on the moral problem in which his philosophy issues: the inevitable failure of men to realize the obligations imposed upon them by the Good. Since the Good prescribes that the values of all beings be maximized, and since men are compelled to make choices which always derogate from the goods of some beings, men are ontologically guilty (11, pp. 101–103). Though obligated, they are unable to meet their obligations. For man, "ought" does not imply "can." However, according to Weiss, "ought" does imply "can" cosmically: " 'One can because one ought' is not true; but 'This can be because this ought to be' is necessarily true. What ought to be is that which can be, because what ought to be is the Good, and this is possible. Or, to put it another way, the Good is cosmic in import; its 'can be' has cosmic range" (11, p. 104).

Unless other modes of being within the cosmos can realize the Good when men fail, the normative possibilities made obligatory

by the Good for all actualities, once passed over, would cease to be and would no longer operate as standards for assessing the failures of actualities. Moreover, unless these normative possibilities are realized in some way other than in Actuality or Existence, the cosmos, having rejected these possibilities in its existential course, would suffer the continuous dissipation of the Good. To offset the annihilation or dissipation of the Good, Weiss insists that what Actuality or Existence fails to realize of the Good is left over for God to realize. "There is always a residuum which no action in time could ever exhaust" (11, p. 183).

The Nature and the Needs of God

Although Weiss introduces God in order to meet the needs of nondivine modes of being, he nevertheless maintains that God is a mode of being with a nature and needs of his own. He contends that "each mode of being needs the others" (11, p. 277). "All [modes of being] are on a footing, independent, irreducible, final. Because each lacks the reality which the others possess, each is imperfect. And since there are four modes of being, each is triply imperfect, imperfect from three sides. Each expresses a three-pronged need for the others which are outside and independent of it, defining it to be incomplete because it lacks their reality. Each needs the others, not consciously or biologically, but ontologically, as external conditions outside its control, determining it to have the status of a being which is not and cannot be the whole of being" (11, p. 278). Despite the fact that, like the others, God is independent, irreducible, and final being, He is imperfect and ontologically equal with the modes of Actuality, Ideality, and Existence.

So far at least Weiss agrees with the new theologians who argue for a finite or relative God. His theory, however, is superior to theirs, for his God and the modes of being and their interrelations are more sharply defined. At the same time Weiss is careful not to deprive God of that transcendent identity upon which more traditional theologies have rested.

Distinct from Actualities, Ideality, and Existence, God lacks the essential features of these. Singular, he is, despite his individuality, no

contingent, striving Actuality. Determinate and inward, he is, despite his perfection, no mere Ideal. Not spatiotemporal, he is, despite his Existence, simple. . . . Undivided, the counterpart of our idea of him, God's being is distinct from his actual individuality, his ideal essence and his vital existence. His being is all of these together, one and un-distinguished. Absolute in comprehensiveness, he is limited in excellence, since he is without the reality which the other modes possess. Finite, since there are others, he is yet internally infinite, able to encompass all (11, p. 331).

God therefore has a nature distinct from that of the other modes, and although Weiss describes this divine nature by means of ap-parently contradictory attributes which seem to be primarily onto-logical, he approaches God as a person who is accessible to volition and emotion as well as understanding.

It is in relation to Actuality that God emerges as Absolute Other. As Weiss puts it:

Since to be Actual is to be 'other than', and since 'other than' is a re-ciprocal relation, requiring its terms to be equally effective, the correlate of an Actuality must be at least as real as it is. Each Actuality therefore must be other than some being which is unaffected by the fact that there might be this or that Actuality in the world. That being is the other of Actuality. As such it must continue to have being at least as long as there are any Actualities at all. It must therefore be another mode of being, as fundamental, as irreducible, as indestructible as Actuality (11, p. 288).

Since Ideality has no inwardness and Existence lacks the necessary unity, neither Ideality nor Existence can serve as the Absolute Other. Only God can have this function. Because "God is all inwardness as it were," he alone can be "the Absolute Other of all Actualities" (11, p. 289).

The aspect of God as the Evaluator, or Judge, appears most clearly in connection with Ideality. Ideality faces actualities as a relevant yet exterior Good. But actualities can never wholly realize that Good, and what remains unrealized is left to God and Existence. Because actualities never bring into Existence all that the Good demands, the Good remains basically exterior. If the residual, unactualized, nonexistent Good is sheered off as irrelevant possibility, the failures of Actuality and Existence would be annulled, since no standard with which to judge these failures would remain. "God alone has the power and dignity to keep exterior a relevant norm in terms of which the worth of the universe and the things in it are evaluatable as defective" (11, p. 292).

God is also the Effective. This is most obvious in connection with Existence. Existence, let us recall, is sheer vitality, and as such it is self-divisive. It is necessary that its self-opposition, which imparts momentum to it, be restrained by a unifying essence. Neither actualities, because "they are too limited in range and power," nor Ideality, because it "is at the border of Existence, serving as its Future," can provide this unifying essence. "Only God has the power to make the essence of Existence one with it, hold Existence together with its own essence so as to constitute a unified being with a nature" (11, p. 295).

The Proofs for God's Existence

This discussion simplifies Weiss's conception of God and takes out of context the dense, interlocking, mutually modifying statements of a difficult doctrine which synthesizes traditional and contemporary elements in a novel theology worthy of serious, intensive study and analysis. Blending together traditional and unorthodox conceptions in a brilliantly original way, Weiss's theory of the proofs of God is especially noteworthy. Although for Weiss proof of God is required no more than proof of any other being, since "each mode of being provides as good a beginning, as good a relation, as good an agency, and as good a terminus of a proof as any other" (11, p. 276), Weiss's argument proceeds in consonance with the traditional preoccupation with proving God. All proofs start with testimony of modes of being for each other. This testimony consists of nonessential yet descriptive features which each mode possesses—i.e., "features, not implicated in the idea of it [a mode of being], without which it would not be a real being in this cosmos" (11, p. 280). "These features provide evidence that the object is partly determined from the outside, that there is something other than it which makes those features descriptive of it" (11, p. 281). The basic proofs of God depend upon such testimonies. The inwardness and otherness of actualities, the Ideal as the principle of perfection, the unity of Existence—all testify to the being of God; the individuality, perfection, and power of God testify, in turn, to Actuality, Ideality, and Existence.

A proof starts from testimony, then proceeds to relate the mode of being giving the testimony to the mode to which the testimony points, and finally terminates in the other mode which is thus established as an independent, irreducible, final being (11, p. 286). Proving God, therefore, involves three kinds of approaches, construed as steps in a unified approach: the teleological, the cosmological, and the ontological. The teleological approach accepts the evidence of direct and indirect testimony and undertakes to find their explanation in God (11, pp. 286–97). The cosmological approach traces the routes from other modes of being to God (11, pp. 287–306). And the ontological step detaches the being of God from the structure of the proof and establishes God as an independent, irreducible, final being (11, pp. 306–18). For Weiss, then, "a proof of God begins teleologically, is validated cosmologically, and terminates ontologically" (11, p. 319). In the twenty-seven proofs he offers, Weiss accepts as testimony, as routes, and as modes of ontological detachment factors other than simple logical evidence and argument: there are nine proofs through faith (11, pp. 319–21), nine through logical inference (11, pp. 321–23), and nine through work (11, pp. 323–24). Since for Weiss God underlies all arguments as the principle of identity and is assumed by all proofs— including those germane to his own existence—as "a power capable of identifying the possible and actual conclusion of a proof" (11, p. 325), it follows that, in a real but not embarrassing sense, all the proofs of God's existence, as well as proofs of anything else, are "circular and question-begging" (11, p. 324).

Togetherness: God and the Other Modes

In *Modes of Being*, Weiss cuts through the medley of categories delineated in *Reality* and presents in sharpened, well-defined form four basic realities. These four modes of being are not simply a kind of shorthand to describe the vague complexities of human experience; they are embedded in the structure of the cosmos and in the normative laws of logical thinking. The principles of identity, noncontradiction, excluded middle, and logical inference are logically expressed correlatives to God, Actuality, Ideality, and Existence (11, pp. 92–94).

The descriptive features of the modes are not simply the bases of the proofs of one mode from another; they also comprise the interrelations which integrate the modes into a single cosmos without shattering their ontological autonomy. For Weiss these interrelations spell out the togetherness of the modes. This togetherness does not merge the plurality of beings into a substantial One which absorbs everything as an attribute of itself. Even God, though he is eternal unity, is not the Absolute Substance. On the contrary, God is one mode of being in a cosmos involving the three other modes on an equal footing. Nevertheless, the modes are not so independent of one another that they never come together within a unified whole. For Weiss the cosmos exhibits the togetherness of the modes. "The togetherness of beings is the being of them together. . . . The being of the four modes together is the four of them together. Such a togetherness is not a new, distinct entity; it is a fact constituted by the demands or thrusts of each to the others as met by their counter-demands and counter-thrusts" (11, p. 514).

THE SYSTEM AND CONCRETE REFLECTION

Weiss's devotion to his system of philosophy is accompanied by an awareness that there are rival systems. "The existence of warring philosophic systems," he declares, "is proof enough that no one of them says all that needs be said"; and, he continues, "rejection of the rest by each is what one might expect from partial systems falsely claiming to be all-inclusive" (11, p. 381). Weiss's strategy in the face of the warfare of systems is not to deny dogmatically the claims of the others, but to include them all as "partial illustrations" of his own system (11, p. 381). He devotes a major part of *Modes of Being* to showing that his system includes and is illustrated by other systems. This highly original approach to the problem of disagreement in speculative philosophy has instigated sharp criticism (12, pp. 150–52; 21). Only his recent forays into concrete reflection match Weiss's attempt to capture all other systems of philosophy in the formal embrace of his own system.

The abstract, skeletal nature of Weiss's system of metaphysics should not obscure the fact that the flesh of this philosophy is every area of knowledge, experience, and reality. Metaphysics is not simply a logically controlled scheme of sharply defined and keenly articulated concepts; on the contrary, it is immersed in the dense contents of the widest possible experience.

Philosophy of Law and Politics

In his Mahlon Powell Lectures at Indiana University, Weiss expounded his political and legal philosophy. These lectures were published in 1959 as *Our Public Life*, which deals with the region in which Actuality and Ideality interact. Reliance on conclusions arrived at in the earlier works is evident. Because men have public as well as private sides, social groupings arise as natural to the realization of human excellence (14, p. 32). Governed at first by social law, a mosaic of inherited customs (14, p. 44), men enter into political groups which, centralizing sovereignty in the state, institute positive laws that guide actions toward the attainment of public goods (14, p. 118). Yet because independently of these groups men have natures, they have native rights, each right being in essence a claim to satisfy their bodies, wills, emotions, or minds (14, pp. 62–72). Although these rights vary in their expressions and are separately alienable according to mutable social circumstances, they are collectively inalienable (14, pp. 89–93). Weiss's theory of native rights welded together into one inalienable right to benefit from social existence is tantamount to a renovated doctrine of "natural rights."

In a similar flexible way Weiss advocates a unique theory of natural law. Natural law is defined as an actual law of nature, a relation between possible present action and a presently desired, publicly acknowledged future good (14, Ch. 6). Like positive laws, natural laws vary from society to society, since the public good varies; but for any society the natural laws formulate the most effective means for realizing the socially posited goods (14, p. 184). Since man has a concern for an absolute Good which is both the standard of excellence normative for all action and a positive lure, a harmony of all values to be realized, there is no need to accept relativism. Beyond the social laws and positive laws, and even beyond the natural laws, there is an everlasting law which expresses this Good in its public form—namely, the law of civilization. This is the measure of all existing political establishments and the goal and guiding light of all international political action (14, p. 184). But even the law of civilization does not exhaust the Good for man; for the whole Good pertains to man's private side as well as to his public side (14, p. 243). Politics does not exhaust human nature but must be supplemented by other regions of concrete experience.

Philosophy of Art

In personal terms Weiss's venture into the concrete field of art has proved most radical. For a while he became a painter, so good a painter, in fact, that he won national recognition and critical acclaim (22). But the encounter with art had reverberations affecting Weiss's entire intellectual posture. When he began working on art, he now confesses, he "seemed to have started only with a suggestion of an idea derived from the *Modes*; this, when faced with actual works of art, with writings on art, with reflections on the nature of beauty, etc., became something I never had even surmised" (1, I, p. 752). In 1961 Weiss's philosophy of art appeared in two volumes: *The World of Art* and *Nine Basic Arts*. "*The World of Art* seeks to isolate the general principles which are exemplified in art, to discover what problems art confronts, what claims it makes, and how its activities and products contrast with those exhibited in other enterprises. The sequel, *Nine Basic Arts*, is devoted to distinguishing and characterizing the major arts" (15, p. 5).

The region of experience which concerns art has to do with the mode of being called Existence. As Weiss asserts, "existence, speculatively dealt with in *Modes of Being*, acquires concreteness and human pertinence when portrayed and mediated by art" (15, p. viii). Like natural beings, works of art, Weiss argues, are substances (15, p. 63), although they are "partly constituted by our emotions" (15, p. 75). "Works of art are created works, with their own space, time and dynamics" (15, p. 156). Weiss expounds the sense in which art, as man's most concrete way of dealing with Existence, involves its own space, its own time, and its own energy. He also proceeds to show how each of the nine basic arts he distinguishes copes with space and time and energy. "Architecture, sculpture, and painting are arts which create a space iconic of existing space. Musical compositions, stories, and poetry create a time having the texture and meaning of existing time. Becoming is creatively presented in musical performances, in the theatre, and in the dance" (15, p. 9).

Philosophy of History

Just as Weiss's philosophy of art is a study of the world of art, so his philosophy of history is a study of the historic world. Whereas art is the way man privately deals with existence, history, according to Weiss, is "concerned with man's public use of existence" (17, Preface). Furthermore, like his theories of law and of politics, his theory of history draws upon the positions attained in *Modes of Being*.

History: Written and Lived sums up in its title the two problems of the philosophy of history: 1) "to understand what historians ideally do and accomplish" and 2) "to provide an account of the world about which the historian discourses" (17, p. 4). It would be too much to detail here Weiss's conception of history as written. It is sufficient to remark that the writing of history, like all other human enterprises, originates in man's need to complete himself, and that history-writing has its own subject, methods, and norms. What for our purposes is noteworthy about Weiss's theory of history as written is his contention that the historian assumes that there are pasts at various temporal distances from the present and that these pasts have an exterior being which is not only inferred but encountered. "The past," writes Weiss, "is at once outside the present and in it. As outside, it can be reached by inference; as inside, it can be reached in an encounter. When the historian both infers and encounters that to which he infers, one of his inquiries is over. But he still has to write down his results, and describe a course of history from the inferred past to the encountered evidencing present, or to some point in between. It is an essential part of his task to provide an historical narrative" (17, p. 94).

Weiss's philosophy of history in *History: Written and Lived* adds to the treatment of history provided in *Modes of Being*. In *Modes of Being* Weiss distinguished epistemic and ontologic history. Ontologic history is a tissue of facts in the past; epistemic history is the historian's account and is "reconstructive" (11, p. 245). "The historian attempts to retrace in his mind the steps by which the present came to be" (11, p. 246).

Weiss's philosophy of history at one end reflects upon actualities which are past and thus no longer exist, and at the other end contemplates objective, ideal norms. In *History: Written and Lived* Weiss defines the historic world as "a reality, having a distinctive temporal direction, spatial unity, and intelligible career" (17, p. 119). He treats it as "one product resulting from an interrelating of the basic realities which make up the universe"—Actuality, Ideality, Existence, and God (17, p. 119). It is, he adds, "the outcome of a juncture of nature and a human realm, the one a large but limited part of Existence, the other itself a sub-region which had already been produced by an interplay of men with a small limited part of Existence" (17, pp. 120–21). "It is a world with its own characteristic space, time, and causation, each with its own units, divisions, rhythms, nature, and power. Most of it has already passed away" (17, p. 216). Yet the past is not simply preserved in the present as that part of present existence which the historian encounters as relevant to the past about which he discourses; it has a being outside the present. This exteriority of the past is guaranteed by God.

Philosophy of Religion

The God We Seek is devoted to religion. Its "major topic . . . is the experience of and concern with God in privacy and in a community. . . . It is essentially a phenomeno-analysis, which is to say an account of the nucleal, normative dimensions of private and public religious life" (18, p. 8). Like history, religion is a region produced by the interplay between man and a mode of being. In the preface to *History: Written and Lived*, Weiss clearly states his conception of the regions treated by his works. The way men privately and publicly interplay with Actuality is treated in *Reality* and in *Nature and Man*; with the Ideal, in *Man's Freedom* and in *Our Public Life*; with Existence, in the works on art and in *History: Written and Lived*; and with God, in *The God We Seek*. In *The God We Seek*, Weiss deals with man's private and public experience of God, considering religion both as personal experience and as institutional.

Of course, Weiss's philosophy of religion builds on the principles established in the *Modes of Being*. His original interpretations of the proofs for God's existence, though omitted from *The God We Seek*, are not contradicted but rather supplemented by the views presented. However, the metaphysical and theological principles do not occupy the foreground of Weiss's attention. Experience of God in private and in institutions is foremost. Faith, hope, and love take precedence over rational argumentation, although the discussion of these virtues of religious experience is clear and sharp. The religious life, moreover, is seen to involve relations to other men as well as to God. Religion meets in practical terms the basic human need "to be loved and to love, and yet to be free. . . . The religious affirmation that there is a God is one with the affirmation that all beings are loved for what they are, by a single, constant lover. God alone always loves without compromise or hesitation; only His love is absolutely appropriate to the beings that receive it" (18, pp. 239–40).

An Open System

Better than any of his contemporaries, Weiss has articulated a metaphysical system of philosophy. It is a common objection against such philosophies that they are dogmatic, dictating a priori what experience must reveal and excluding or distorting those reaches or items of experience which refuse to conform. But reflection on Weiss's system puts the lie to this objection. His philosophy has manifested from the beginning the dynamic movement of inquiry toward the truth which is consistent with and often demands that specific theses be revised or discarded. Indeed, throughout *Philosophy in Process* Weiss returns to his scheme of Actuality, Ideality, Existence, and God, examining the togetherness of these basic modes, questioning their interconnections, viewing each from the standpoints of the others, and exploring an unmeasured range of topics from the multiple perspectives they afford. In fact, every objection which the critics have leveled against Weiss's metaphysics has at one time or another received his consideration, and this has taken place not because of the critics' promptings but because of the internal momentum of thought toward coherence and truth.

Weiss has remained steadfast in his adherence to the principle that philosophy ought to be systematic. To reverse Nietzsche's aphorism, the tendency toward system signifies for Weiss the expression of intellectual integrity. To philosophize systematically is not necessarily to dogmatize; rather it is to think every problem through to its solution as interrelated with all other solutions of all other problems. It is to push inquiry forward and backward relentlessly until a unified coherent explanation of the initial problem and its endless ramifications results. Accordingly, the true dogmatist is not the system-seeking philosopher; on the contrary, it is the skeptical adversary who denies the worth of systematic philosophizing as consisting in the grasp of a particular conclusion in the light of all other conclusions. In a real way the metaphysical skeptic is the vicious dogmatist, for it is he who blocks inquiry. No one who has worked his way through the argument of *Modes of Being* can ignore the unique intellectual flexibility afforded by a metaphysics which requires that each topic be faced from the perspective of four ontological modes and their relations to each other. Weiss's work is a singular intellectual experience without comparison in recent philosophical literature. The system itself is an exhibition of open thinking.

NOTES TO CHAPTER X

1   Paul Weiss, *Philosophy in Process*, Vol. I: 1955–60 (Carbondale: Southern Illinois University Press, 1966). Vol. 2: 1960–64, published late in 1966, originally appeared as one book.

2   Charles Hartshorne and Paul Weiss (eds.), *The Collected Papers of Charles Sanders Peirce* (Cambridge: Harvard University Press, 1931–35), I–VI. A. W. Burks has edited *The Collected Papers of Charles Sanders Peirce*, VII–VIII.

3   Paul Weiss, "Charles S. Peirce, Philosopher," in Richard J. Bernstein (ed.), *Perspectives in Peirce* (New Haven: Yale University Press, 1965).

4   James Collins, "Weiss's Exploration of Religion," *Review of Metaphysics*, XIX (1965), 301–28.

5   Paul Weiss, *The Nature of Systems* (La Salle, Ill.: Open Court, 1929). This book also appeared in *Monist*, XXXIX (April and July, 1929), 281–319, 440–72.

6   Paul Weiss, "Theory of Types," *Mind*, XXXVII (1928), 338–48; "Relativity in Logic," *Monist*, XXXVIII (1928), 536–48; "Entailment and the Future of Logic," *Seventh International Congress of Philosophy* (Oxford, 1930), 143–50; "Two-Valued Logic—Another Approach," *Erkenntnis*, II (1931), 242–61; "The Metaphysics and Logic of Classes," *Monist*, XLII (1932), 112–54; "On Alternative Logics," *Philosophical Review*, XLII (1933), 520–25. Weiss's letter, "A Home for Logic," *Philosophy of Science*, I (1934), 238, was helpful in the establishment of the *Journal of Symbolic Logic*.

7   As transitional articles, see Paul Weiss, "The Metaphysical and the Logical Individual," *Journal of Philosophy*, XXX (1933), 288–93; "Metaphysics: The Domain of Ignorance," *Philosophical Review*, XLIII (1934), 402–406; "A Memorandum for a System of Philosophy," in H. M. Kallen and Sidney Hook (eds.), *American Philosophy Today and Tomorrow* (New York: Lee Furman, 1935), 488–98.

8   Paul Weiss, *Reality* (Princeton: Princeton University Press, 1938; New York: Peter Smith, 1949).

9   Paul Weiss, *Nature and Man* (New York: Henry Holt, 1947).

10 Paul Weiss, *Man's Freedom* (New Haven: Yale University Press, 1950).

11 Paul Weiss, *Modes of Being* (Carbondale: Southern Illinois University Press, 1958).

12 Manley Thompson, "Metaphysics," in Roderick M. Chisholm and others, *Philosophy* (Englewood Cliffs, N. J.: Prentice-Hall, 1964).

13 Irwin C. Lieb (ed.), *Experience, Existence, and the Good: Essays in Honor of Paul Weiss* (Carbondale: Southern Illinois University Press, 1961).

14 Paul Weiss, *Our Public Life* (Bloomington: Indiana University Press, 1959).

15 Paul Weiss, *The World of Art* (Carbondale: Southern Illinois University Press, 1961).

16 Paul Weiss, *Nine Basic Arts* (Carbondale: Southern Illinois University Press, 1961).

17 Paul Weiss, *History: Written and Lived* (Carbondale: Southern Illinois University Press, 1962).

18 Paul Weiss, *The God We Seek* (Carbondale: Southern Illinois University Press, 1964).

19 Paul Weiss, *The Making of Men* (Carbondale: Southern Illinois University Press, 1967). See also Paul Weiss and Jonathan Weiss, *Right and Wrong, a Philosophical Dialogue between Father and Son* (New York: Basic Books, 1967).

20 See my review of *Philosophy in Process*, "Open Thinking," *Yale Review*, LV (Winter 1965–66), 432–35.

21 John Wild, "Weiss's Four-fold Universe," *Review of Metaphysics*, XI (1958), 610–36.

22 "Philosopher in Oils," *Newsweek* 53:83 (February 2, 1959).

EPILOGUE

American philosophy today is rich, vital, and diverse. The new American philosophers testify to a plurality of views. As Sidney Hook has pointed out, there "is no state philosophy in America and no authority is recognized except good argument and cogent evidence" (1, p. 13). This situation, Hook insists, "proves that American philosophers are free. Ultimately, it is more important that they be free than that they agree" (1, p. 13). Following in Hook's footsteps, Sheldon P. Peterfreund contends "that the phrase 'American philosophy' is itself inaccurate and may tend to give the reader an impression of a typical American creed. It is more precise," he adds, "to speak of 'philosophies *in* America'" (2, p. 2).

The impetus to articulate the essence of American philosophy, nevertheless, remains strong. John E. Smith's *The Spirit of American Philosophy* (3) is, despite shortcomings (4), the most provocative recent interpretation of American thought. Smith writes: "By the spirit of a philosophical development is meant something which is at once more and less than a set of doctrines" (3, p. 187). It is more in that it means "a style, a stance toward life in the world," and less in that, standing deeply rooted in the life of a people, it is "a kind of unwritten philosophy" (3, p. 187). As Smith sees it, the spirit of American philosophy is focalized in three basic beliefs: first, "that thinking is primarily an *activity* in response to a concrete situation and that this activity is aimed at solving problems"; second, "that ideas and theories must have a 'cutting edge' or must *make a difference* in the conduct of people who hold them and in the situ-

345

ations in which they live"; and third, "that *the earth can be civilized and obstacles to progress overcome by the application of knowledge*" (3, p. 188). Smith is primarily interested in the five classic thinkers—Peirce, James, Royce, Dewey, and Whitehead—to each of whom he devotes a separate chapter, but the twelve new American philosophers participate in this conception of the spirit of American philosophy as well. Secondarily, Smith is bent on attacking analytic philosophy. Here he descries a foreign invasion! He deplores the alleged British domination of contemporary American philosophy (3, p. 203), and he names Bertrand Russell and G. E. Moore as the advance scouts of the invasion (3, p. 198). Yet Smith anticipates a revival of philosophy in America, a revival which he pins to the resurrection of two convictions about reason and experience: "One is the belief that experience—*in its comprehensive and not in its narrow sense*—is a genuine disclosure of reality and that it can be trusted; the other is the conviction that reason is an actual power in the world, that it has its own constitution, and that it is not to be reduced to a mere conjunction of facts" (3, p. 206). And in his concluding paragraphs Smith mentions as leaders in the alleged revival of philosophy Northrop, Randall, Weiss, Wild, Hartshorne, and Quine.

Smith's antagonism to analytic philosophy is due in some measure to its present ascendancy in Great Britain and the United States and to its seeming intolerance of other philosophical positions. Certainly since World War II growing numbers of American philosophers have been analytically inclined. Of course it should be recognized that the term "analytic philosophy" covers a wide variety of philosophical conceptions and procedures, some of which have been illustrated by the thinkers studied in this volume—e.g., C. I. Lewis, Ernest Nagel, and Brand Blanshard. Some analytic philosophers are interested in the construction of formal systems of symbolic logic, others in delineating the conceptual models operative in the sciences, others in examining abstruse issues in ontology and epistemology, others in scrutinizing value judgments in ethics and aesthetics, others in commenting on and criticizing the theories of historically significant thinkers or of influential contemporaries, and still others in tracing the usages of words in ordinary language. In the 1940's most analytic philosophers were inspired by the formalistic work of Russell and of Carnap; the leading younger analytic philosophers today find their directions in the varieties of linguistic analysis fostered by Wittgenstein, by Ryle, and by Austin. As Smith interprets the present situation in American philosophy, the ascendancy of analysis can be harmful.

When the latest fashions in analysis induce young philosophers to neglect the entire Western philosophical tradition—including the impressive contributions of their compatriots to this cultural heritage—the result is too often an academic brow-wrinkling that exhausts itself in captious comments and reviews, in closely reasoned trifling pieces without provision for a broader rationale. When the analytic philosopher becomes so preoccupied with language that he loses sight of the realities to which language refers, the result is an arid enterprise isolated from experience, nature, art, religion, science, and society, a technique divorced from substance. The major hazard of analytic philosophy is its satisfaction with a philosophy without wisdom.

But the contemporary presence of analytic philosophers can be salutary. Human ignorance is so widespread that attacking it on any front and by any rational means should be encouraged. Further, in insisting that the thinker be clear about his meanings and logically sound in his arguments, analytic philosophers render the entire philosophical community an incalculable service. Charles Hartshorne's employment of recent developments in modal logic to strengthen the ontological argument for God's existence is a case in point.

Meanwhile, in recent years many American philosophers have turned to existentialism and phenomenology, countering somewhat the influence of analytic philosophy. Kierkegaard, Nietzsche, Husserl, Heidegger, Jaspers, Sartre, Camus, Marcel are familiar names among American philosophers, and acquaintance with their works is expected to spread and deepen in future years. John Wild, as we have seen, is one American thinker who has already joined the ranks of the existentialists. The *Journal of Existentialism* now takes its place beside *Philosophy and Phenomenological Research,* and in the past few years a national society for existentialism has been formed.

Thus American philosophy today is very much in flux. Within the stream of thought of the past generation twelve thinkers have emerged as advocates of comprehensive systems of philosophy with profound practical applications. No judgment of American culture can be fair unless it takes account of the new American philosophers. In spite of the neglect they have suffered by comparison with the attention given to other fields, the new American philosophers have persevered, and their contributions are all the more remarkable. They are the perpetuators of the golden age of American thought, of that rich philosophical activity in which Peirce, James, Royce, Santayana, Dewey, and Whitehead participated at the highest levels of achievement, and to which Ralph Barton Perry, William Ernest Hocking, George Herbert Mead, John Elof Boodin, DeWitt H. Parker, Wilbur Marshall Urban, Roy Wood Sellars, Arthur O. Lovejoy, Elijah Jordan, and Edgar Sheffield Brightman have added immeasurably. In the works of C. I. Lewis, Stephen Pepper, Brand Blanshard, Ernest Nagel, John Herman Randall, Jr., Justus Buchler, Sidney Hook, F. S. C. Northrop, James Feibleman, John Wild, Charles Hartshorne, and Paul Weiss, twelve men whose theories range over all philosophical fields and human interests, are to be found the fundamental elements of significant philosophy—vision, scope, depth, and pertinence to practice.

It would be tempting to conclude with a summary of the teachings of the twelve American thinkers as the quintessence of contemporary American thought, as indeed the genuine ideology of the American people. But the temptation must be resisted; no such summary can be made. As our exploration of American thought since World War II has shown, American philosophy is in truth a plurality of philosophies. The views of the new American philosophers are as diverse as the forces and factors in American culture.

The pluralism of American philosophy is a most valuable asset, not only because it affords the American thinker the freedom to develop and express his ideas, but also because it endows him with an intellectual flexibility and a catholicity increasingly desirable and even indispensable as the world in which America is implicated expands. Ideally, philosophy is confined to no specific time or place. As the founder of the first philosophical journal in America affirmed a century ago: "For after all it is not American 'thought' so much as American 'thinkers' that we want. To *think*, in the highest sense, is to transcend all *natural limits*—such, for example, as national peculiarities, defects in culture, distinctions in race, habits, and modes of living—to be *universal*, so that one can dissolve away the external hull and seize the substance itself" (5).

NOTES TO EPILOGUE

1 Sidney Hook, *American Philosophers at Work* (New York: Criterion Books, 1956).
2 Sheldon P. Peterfreund, *An Introduction to American Philosophy* (New York: Odyssey, 1959).
3 John E. Smith, *The Spirit of American Philosophy* (New York: Oxford University Press, 1963).
4 For a critical discussion of Smith's book and of other recent interpretations of American thought, see Andrew J. Reck, "Recent Interpretations of American Philosophy," *Review of Metaphysics* XVIII (1964), 334–55.
5 William Torrey Harris, "Preface," *Journal of Speculative Philosophy*, I (1867).

INDEX

Act, Action, Activity, Doing: as factor in logic and knowledge, 17, 168; as free, 325; as grounded in Actuality, 324; as guided by knowledge, 23, 29–30; as judgment, 156; as method, 158; as moral, 266, 268; as root metaphor, 53; as social, 164; as tendency, 264; goals of, 37. *See also* Ethics; Practical philosophy; Purposive act

Actuality, 227, 228, 229, 239, 243, 311, 312, 337; as mode of being (Weiss, 317, 318, 319–24, 327–35 *passim*, 340, 341, 342

Adams, George P., 46

Adler, Mortimer, 143, 257

Aesthetic continuum, 207, 215

Aesthetics, Esthetics, 121, 346; in Feibleman's system, 246; in Lewis' theory of value, 35, 37; Pepper's theory of, 42, 55–64 *passim*. *See also* Art

Affective continuum, Hartshorne's concept of, 293, 294, 312; as alternative to materialism, 295–96; elucidation of, 296–98

Alexander, Samuel, 293, 306

Allers, Rudolf, 163

America, xiii, xv, xx, 7, 120, 121, 126, 165, 166, 167, 194, 208, 211, 278, 256, 318; European philosophies in, 160, 347; naturalism in, 121, 122, 149; philosophies in, 159, 345; religion in, 149; as urban, 138. *See also* United States

American Philosophical Association, xix, 7, 47, 84, 85, 127, 137, 147, 166, 281, 292, 316

American philosophy: between World War I and World War II, p. xv; Blanshard and Nagel controversy in, 117; golden age of, xv–xvi, 3, 348; interpretations of, 345–49; pragmatism in, 126; since World War II, pp. xvi–xx; study of, xiii–xiv

American Psychological Association, 85

Amherst College, 120

Analytic knowledge, Lewis' theory of, 7, 8–18

Analytic philosophy, 82, 85, 127, 223, 346–47. *See also* Linguistic analysis; Logical empiricism; Logical positivism

Anatropism, Wild's concept of, 267, 268–69

Anderson, Sherwood, 221

Anselm, 294, 305, 310–11

Anthropology, 203, 213, 218, 246, 278, 279, 285, 317, 325, 327. *See also* Man

Aristotle, Aristotelianism, 51, 60, 103, 104, 123, 128, 129, 141, 142, 274, 305, 322, 323, 327, 328; Randall's interpretation of, 143–44, 145; Wild's interpretation of, 256–66 *passim*

Aristotle, *Physics*, 262

Art, xix, 45, 46, 55, 56, 57, 59, 138, 139, 140, 145, 156, 158, 200, 247; as cultural institution (Feibleman), 250–51; as object (Pepper), 61–63; as practical (Wild), 268–72 *passim*; Weiss's philosophy of, 317, 338–39. *See also* Aesthetics

Association for Realistic Philosophy, 256–61 *passim*

Atomic theory, 199, 200

Augustine, 206, 284, 305
Austin, John, 211, 213
Austin, John L., xiv, 85, 347
Axiological realism, 221, 223, 246;
Feibleman's progress toward, 223–31;
Feibleman's system of, 231–46
Ayer, A. J., xiv, 21, 28, 65, 96, 99

Bacon, Francis, 132, 201
Bakewell, Charles Montague, 198
Banner, William A., 257
Bauer, Bruno, 183
Baylis, Charles A., 8
Beauty, 56, 57, 181, 239
Becoming, Change, Flux, Process, 53, 56,
242, 291; according to Buchler, 153–
55 passim; according to Hartshorne,
294, 301, 303, 306, 307; according to
Randall, 144–47 passim; according to
Weiss, 322–24; according to Wild,
261–64. See also Process philosophy
Behaviorism, 63, 90, 152, 223, 295
Being, 171; Feibleman's universes of,
237–46 passim; Weiss's modes of,
317–36 passim; Wild on, 259–73 pas-
sim, 286. See also Metaphysics; Ontol-
ogy
Belief: Lewis' concept of objective, 20,
22, 31–32. See also Faith; Judgment
Beloit College, 198
Bentham, Jeremy, 212
Berdyaev, Nicolas, 288, 304, 312
Bergson, Henri, 53, 56, 293, 321, 322,
326
Berkeley, George, 52, 80, 119, 256, 286,
297
———, The Principles of Human Knowledge, 256; Siris, 256
Bernstein, Richard J., 316
Black, Max, 147
——— (ed.), Philosophy in America,
xiv
Blanshard, Brand, xvi, xvii, xviii, xix, 65,
129, 165, 346, 348; life and works of,
81–87; on ethics, 96–104; on metaphysics, 104–18; on theory of knowledge, 87–96; writings by and on, 118–
19
———, The Nature of Thought, 83, 85,
105, 111; Reason and Analysis, 84, 85,
111, 117; Reason and Belief, 84; Reason and Goodness, 84, 96

Blanshard, Paul, 82
Blau, Joseph L., xiii, 122
Boas, George, 121, 144
Boodin, John Elof, xv, 293, 348
Bosanquet, Bernard, 52, 60, 83, 86, 91,
96, 103, 105, 114
Boutroux, Emile, 293
Bradford, Roark, 221
Bradley, F. H., 52, 83, 86, 91, 105, 110,
114, 116, 320, 321
Brehier, Emile, 284
Bridgman, P. W., 21
Brightman, Edgar Sheffield, xv, 306, 348
Brooklyn College, 151
Broudy, Harry S., 257
Bryn Mawr College, 316
Buchler, Justus, xvi, xvii, xviii, xix, 120,
123, 137, 145, 160, 161, 164, 348;
humanistic naturalism of, 149–59; writ-
ings by and on, 163
———, Charles Pierce's Empiricism,
151; Concept of Method, 151, 158;
Metaphysics of Natural Complexes,
151; Nature and Judgment, 151;
Toward a General Theory of Judg-
ment, 151
Buddhism, 206, 217
Business, 221, 222, 224

Cambridge University, 126, 147, 198
Camus, Albert, 347
Capitalism, 185, 190
Carnap, Rudolf, 9, 15, 19, 21, 28, 126,
137, 147
Carnegie Corporation, 85
Carritt, E. F., 98
Carus Lectures, 7, 47, 84, 117, 127
Category, 50, 78, 125, 145, 146, 147,
234, 237, 317, 319, 324, 335
Chakste, Mintauts, 216
Change. See Becoming
Chapman, Harmon M., 257
Chisholm, Roderick M. and others, Phi-
losophy, xvi–xvii
Chomsky, Noam, 147
Christianity, Christian philosophy, and
religion, 96, 140, 228, 229, 230, 270,
312; according to Wild, 284–89
Cicero, 142, 218
City College of New York, 120, 121, 122,
123, 151, 164, 315
Civilization, 41, 138, 139, 140, 141, 205

passim, 294, 297, 298, 304, 318, 328, 330, 347; Hartshorne on, 305–12; Weiss's concept of, 331–36, 341, 342
Goldwater, Barry, 219
Good, Goodness, Summum Bonum, 81, 98, 99, 214, 271, 275, 276; Blanshard on, 101–104; Feibleman on, 239–40; Lewis on, 37, 38; Stevenson on, 27–28; Weiss on, 324–33 *passim*, 338
Grace, 287
Grau, Shirley Ann, 222
Great Britain, xiv, 64, 198, 211, 217, 224; philosophies in, 15, 82, 85, 97–98, 112, 147, 346
Greek philosophy, 96, 224, 270; tragic drama, 244–45
Green, T. H., 44, 52, 103, 104
Growth, 168, 178

Hand, Learned, 211
Hare, R. M., 65, 100
Hart, H. L. A., xiv
Hartshorne, Charles, xvi, xvii, xviii, xix, 77, 80, 226, 316, 346, 347, 348; life and works of, 291–94; on the affective continuum, 294–98; on panentheism, 304–12; on panpsychism and social realism, 298–304; writings by, 312–14
———, *Anselm's Discovery*, 294; *Beyond Humanism*, 293; *The Divine Relativity*, 293; *The Logic of Perfection*, 293–94, 310; *Man's Vision of God*, 293; *The Philosophy and Psychology of Sensation*, 293, 294; *Reality as Social Process*, 293, 294; and William Reese, *Philosophers Speak of God*, 293, 305
Harvard University, xviii, xix, 3, 4, 44, 45, 46, 83, 198, 211, 213, 226, 255, 291, 316
Hegel, Hegelianism, 52, 60, 82, 83, 105, 112, 114, 181, 206, 232, 237, 243, 315
Heidegger, Martin, 171, 278, 279, 280, 347
Heisenberg principle, 116
Henderson, L. J., 198
Hierarchy, Order, 41, 238, 242; Wild on, 267–72 *passim*
Hinduism, 206, 217
History, 138, 144, 187, 201, 209, 317; Weiss on, 339–40
Hitler, Adolf, 188, 214
Hobbes, Thomas, 52, 211

Hocking, William Ernest, xv, 198, 293, 348
Holmes, Justice, 191
Hook, Sidney, xvi, xvii, xviii, xix, xx, 42, 120, 162, 197, 203, 222, 345, 348; intellectual and professional milieu of, 164–67; Marxism of, 181–95; pragmatism of, 167–81; writings by and on, 195–96
———, *Common Sense and the Fifth Amendment*, 192; *Education for Modern Man*, 178; *From Hegel to Marx*, 181, 183, 184; *Heresy, Yes!—Conspiracy, No!*, 191; *The Hero in History*, 186; *The Metaphysics of Pragmatism*, 169; *Political Power and Personal Freedom*, 169, 195; *The Quest for Being*, 171, 172; *Towards the Understanding of Karl Marx*, 181, 183; and H. M. Kallen, eds., *American Philosophy Today and Tomorrow*, 129, 138
Hooker, Richard, 205, 217
Hopkins, Gerard Manley, 61
Howison Lectures, 5, 104
Hull, Clark, 213, 223
Humanism, 90, 149, 150, 168, 170, 173–74, 190, 272
Humanities, 200
Hume, David, 22, 52, 97, 206, 212
Husserl, Edmund, 160, 281, 347
Hutcheson, Francis, 97
Hutchins, Robert, 143
Huxley, Julian, 150

Idea. *See* Concept
Idealism, Idealists, xvi, xvii, 44, 112, 118, 169, 205, 206, 233, 272, 302, 319; defined as organicism by Pepper, 52–53; of Blanshard, 81–85 *passim*
Ideality, Weiss's concept of, 317, 318, 324, 329–42 *passim*
Ideology, 27, 189, 194, 197, 198, 203–208 *passim*, 213, 216–18 *passim*, 348
If-then connection, Implication, 5, 10, 22–23, 114–15, 131
Indiana University, 8, 46, 62, 337
Individualism, 205
Inquiry, 168, 173, 201. *See also* Query
Institute for Philosophical Research, 257
Institutions, xix, 73; Feibleman on, 247–50 *passim*. *See also* Culture; Social order

Pitts, Walter, 204

Plato, Platonism, 51, 60, 91, 105, 114, 141, 142, 143, 206, 223, 226, 231, 237, 238, 239, 241, 251, 256, 257, 258, 259, 263, 273, 274, 304, 327; Wild on, 267–72, 281–82

——, *Meno*, 91; *The Republic*, 269, 270; *The Sophist*, 238

Plotinus, 244, 306

Pluralism, 201, 205, 214, 219, 238, 322, 348

Polarity, 307

Political philosophy, Politics, xix, 145, 179, 208, 215, 246, 256, 317, 318; Hook on, 174–76; Weiss on, 337–38. *See also* Communism; Ideology; Democracy; Law

Positivism, 49, 205, 207, 316. *See also* Legal positivism; Logical positivism

Possibility, 5, 229, 238, 243, 309, 327, 328

Pound, Roscoe, 213

Practical philosophy, Wild on, 256–59 *passim*, 266–77 *passim*

Pragmatism, Pragmatists, xv, xvi, xvii, 44, 45, 46, 51, 83, 90, 126, 127, 137, 142, 152, 159, 160, 164, 166, 167, 197; Lewis on, 3–9 *passim*, 16–18; Hook on, 167–88 *passim*. *See also* Instrumentalism

Prall, David, 46, 60

Pratt, C. C., 21

Prescriptivism. *See* Emotivism

Price, H. H., 49

Prichard, H. A., 98

Princeton University, xvi, xvii, 199

Proception, Buchler's concept of, 152–55

Process. *See* Becoming

Process cosmology, Process philosophy, xvii, 152, 291, 319–23 *passim*, 330

Protestantism, 205, 217

Protocols, 19, 261

Psychology, 44, 68, 72, 85, 105, 106, 213, 247, 265, 295, 302

Purposive act, Pepper's concept of, 47, 65–68, 73, 77–79 *passim*

Quality, 53–58 *passim*, 78, 106, 108, 165, 296, 297, 300, 301. *See also* Feeling; Value

Query, Buchler's concept of, 157–59

Quine, Willard Van Orman, xiv, 9, 42, 147, 346

Randall, John Herman and John Herman Randall, Jr., *Religion and the Modern World*, 149

Randall, John Herman, Jr., xvi, xvii, xviii, xix, 120, 121, 122, 123, 150, 151, 159, 160, 188, 346, 248; historical naturalism of, 137–49; writings by, 163

——, Aristotle, 143–44; *The Career of Philosophy*, 141, 143; *The Making of the Modern Mind*, 138; *Nature and Historical Experience*, 138, 144, 147; *Our Changing Civilization*, 138

Rationalism, 81, 85, 117, 200, 206, 256

Realism, Realists, xiv, xvi, xvii, 21, 51, 83, 90, 120, 123, 127, 128, 129, 136, 144, 147, 154, 170, 218, 255, 319; Hartshorne on, 294, 297, 303; Wild on, 256–66 *passim*, 278, 279, 288, 289. *See also* Axiological realism

Reason, 84, 97, 113, 114, 123, 149, 159, 266, 271, 273, 285, 286, 346

Reck, Andrew J., *Recent American Philosophy*, xv

Reese, William, 293

Reichenbach, Hans, 9, 21, 28, 125

Relations, Blanshard on, 115–16

Relativity, 9, 199, 291, 306, 307

Religion, xix, 120, 138–40 *passim*, 145, 173, 200, 247, 251, 252, 317; philosophy of, xix, 138, 158, 179; Randall on, 147–49 *passim*; Weiss on, 340–41. *See also* Panentheism; Theology

Renaissance, 141, 142

Review of Metaphysics, xix, 316

Revolution, 166, 182–84 *passim*, 271, 273

Richardson, Robert Kimball, 198

Right, 38, 39, 98, 101

Riley, Woodbridge, xiii

Rockefeller University, 123

Roman Catholic Church, Roman Catholicism, 205, 217, 257

Rome, 209, 212, 213, 217

Rome, Sydney and Beatrice, *Philosophical Interrogations*, 117

Root metaphor, Pepper's concept of, 47, 50–53 *passim*, 59

Ross, W. D., 98